The Managerial Presidency

NUMBER FOUR:
Joseph V. Hughes, Jr., and Holly O. Hughes Series in the Presidency and Leadership Studies
James P. Pfiffner, General Editor

The
Managerial Presidency

SECOND EDITION

EDITED BY
James P. Pfiffner

Texas A&M University Press
COLLEGE STATION

First Texas A&M Press edition; previous edition
published by Brooks/Cole Publishing Company.

The paper used in this book meets the minimum requirements
of the American National Standard for Permanence
of Paper for Printed Library Materials, z39.48-1984.
Binding materials have been chosen for durability.

Texas A&M University Press expresses its appreciation for
support in publishing works on the presidency and leadership to

The Center for Presidential Studies
George Bush School of Government and Public Service
Texas A&M University

For a complete list of books in print in this series,
see the back of the book.

Library of Congress Cataloging-in-Publication Data

The managerial presidency / edited by James P. Pfiffner. — 2nd ed.
        p.   cm. — (Joseph V. Hughes Jr. and Holly O. Hughes series in
the presidency and leadership studies ; no. 4)
     ISBN 0-89096-858-6 (cloth). — ISBN 0-89096-860-8 (pbk.)
     1. Presidents—United States.   2. Presidents—United States—
Staff.   3. Executive power—United States.   4. Executive
departments—United States.   5. Bureaucracy—United States.
I. Pfiffner, James P.   II. Series.
JK518.M36   1999
352.23'0973—dc21   98-30490
                                                            CIP

FOR MY MOTHER
Alice Price Pfiffner
(April 12, 1913–September 29, 1996)

AND MY FATHER
James Sturtevant Pfiffner
(January 12, 1917–May 11, 1973)

Contents

Preface

This book is based on the premise that management matters in the presidency. While it has always been recognized that the president is head of the executive branch, in the mid–twentieth century the scope and size of the government has expanded so much that managerial concerns are crucial to overall presidential performance. The Brownlow Committee, whose 1937 report led to the creation of the Executive Office of the President, worked under the presumption that the president was responsible for managing the executive branch. Their recommendations were designed to give the president the necessary administrative tools to fulfill that responsibility.

Modern presidents have all had managerial problems. Franklin Roosevelt's White House was characterized by feuding staffers. Harry Truman was plagued by ethical lapses by his White House staff. Dwight Eisenhower introduced important managerial innovations in the White House, but his chief of staff, Sherman Adams, was forced to resign under an ethical cloud. John Kennedy jettisoned Eisenhower's managerial approach, but soon felt that his organizations had let him down in the Bay of Pigs disaster. Richard Nixon prided himself on his organizational abilities, yet soon after taking office he began to centralize control in his White House staff, which later became embroiled in Watergate.

Presidents Ford and Carter each embraced "cabinet government" and refused to designate a chief of staff. But each soon realized that a chief of staff was necessary and that "cabinet government" was impossible. Ronald Reagan's first term was a model of White House effectiveness, yet his second term brought the Iran-Contra affair and the firing of his chief of staff. The impressive coordination of President Bush's national security team contrasted with a divided domestic policy team that ended with the resignation of Chief of Staff John Sununu. Bill Clinton began his term with a new and untested White House staff and suffered a number of scandals, some of which were rooted in and exacerbated by management lapses.

All of these presidents had varying degrees of success and each suffered minor or major setbacks. While good management practices cannot guarantee political or policy success, there is no doubt that poor management can undermine good policy and political efforts. As President Eisenhower said, "Organization cannot make a genius out of an incompetent. On the other hand, disorganization can scarcely fail to result in inefficiency."

The purpose of this book is to bring together some of the best analyses of managerial issues that affect the presidency. This second edition has kept many of the selections from the first edition, but about half the essays are new to this volume. As in the first edition, some of the selections are classic analyses that have stood the test of time, and others are more recent treatments of issues from the late 1990s. Several of the new chapters were written specifically for this edition (those by Peri Arnold, Steven Kelman, Ronald Moe, and Roger Porter). Some of the authors have direct experience with White House organization; Richard Neustadt, Roger Porter, Steven Kelman, and Hugh Heclo have each worked in the Executive Office of the President. But each of the authors has also made important scholarly contributions to our understanding of the presidency. The central concern of all of the essays in the book is the extent to which presidents can and ought to exert control over the executive branch and control policy.

The first section deals with the first question confronting a new president: how to organize the White House. This question is crucial, especially with a White House Office of more than four hundred and an Executive Office of the President approaching two thousand. If this original organizational problem is not solved, none of the broader problems of organization and policy can be easily solved. Hugh Heclo in "The Changing Presidential Office" sets the tone by arguing that the presidential office has deep structures that each president must confront, and if presidents do not consciously manage their own office, they run the risk of being at the mercy of others' priorities. This chapter is followed by Sam Kernell's analysis of "The Evolution of the White House Staff." Kernell traces the mid-twentieth-century developments that led to the much enlarged White House staffs of contemporary presidents. He warns that if the presidential bureaucracies are not carefully managed, they may take on a life of their own. Kernell concludes that "organizations need policing."

Richard Neustadt worked in the Truman White House, and in 1960 published one of the most influential books on the presidency, *Presidential Power*. The first selection by Neustadt is the memo that he prepared in October, 1960, for John Kennedy's transition into office. He urged Kennedy to break with Eisenhower's formally structured White House and to be his own chief of staff. The memo is an important document in the development of the modern presidency, and it is significant because Kennedy took Neustadt's advice. This memo is juxtaposed with Neustadt's 1987 article in which he rejects his previous advice and concludes that because of the growth of the presidency, a chief of staff is now a virtual necessity.

In the next chapter Pfiffner begins with the premise that a chief of staff is necessary, but warns that if that chief takes too domineering an approach to the job, trouble is sure to follow. He takes up each of the four domineering chiefs of staff and analyzes their downfalls while contrasting them with more successful chiefs. In the final essay in the section Matthew Holden takes a look at the generic nature—across cultures and political systems—of chief executives and their entourages. He argues that presidents, like all chief executives, need certain types of servants/advisers, and that presidential power is best understood as falling on a continuum from command to bargaining.

Section two is concerned with how the White House staff and the president's emissaries to the rest of the executive branch (i.e. political appointees) relate to the career civil servants who make up the vast majority of the government. The first essay by Hugh Heclo, "OMB and Neutral Competence," is a classic statement of the ideal role of civil servants in the institutional presidency (and by implication, the rest of the executive branch). Civil servants must serve the current president responsibly, while at the same time keeping enough distance and objectivity to preserve their institutional capacity to serve faithfully the next president, regardless of political party. This is a difficult balancing act but crucial to the capacity of the government to govern.

Terry Moe's chapter, "The Politicized Presidency," is one of the best analyses of how and why modern presidents have sought personal control over all aspects of the government. He argues that this reach for control is inevitable because the causes are systemic: the imbalance between the need of presidents to fulfill campaign promises and their imperfect control of the governmental means to achieve their goals. Seeking to right the balance, presidents inevitably seek tighter control of administration and personnel. Joel Aberbach and Bert Rockman in "Mandates or Mandarins?" take on Moe's argument directly and argue that extreme politicization is only apparently in presidents' best interests. They argue that in the U.S. system presidents must share power, and that the cooperation of the career services will enhance the achievement of presidential policy goals.

The next piece, by Richardson and Pfiffner, is the report to the National Commission on the Public Service (the Volcker Commission) on the relationship between career civil servants and political appointees. Arguing that the increasing numbers and layers of political appointees are counterproductive to effective presidential control, the Volcker Commission recommended that the number of political appointees in the executive branch be cut from about three thousand to about two thousand. Patricia Ingraham (also a staffer for the Volcker Commission) in "Political Direction and Policy Change" next argues that White House direction of political appointees is often absent. The lack of policy guidance combined with rapid turnover of political leadership in departments and agencies often creates a "political management void," and that effective policy management necessarily entails working closely with career civil servants.

The third section takes a broader approach to presidential management and takes up presidential managerial reform efforts and the congressional role in managing policy agendas and the government. Peri Arnold begins the section with an overview of presidential management efforts in the twentieth century. After tracing the development of organizational efforts, he takes up in some detail the Clinton Administration's National Performance Review, the broadest presidential effort at management reform. Next, Steven Kelman, who participated in the NPR as director of OMB's Office of Federal Procurement Policy, describes his efforts to change the culture and practice of the executive branch toward contracting for goods and services. Kelman examines his efforts in the first term of the Clinton Administration to improve procurement practices and change the bureaucratic culture toward a more efficient and effective approach to federal contracting.

Ronald Moe is critical of recent presidents' approach to management, arguing that they have neglected managerial duties in their emphasis on policy and programmatic goals. But presidents too often do not realize that their legacies depend on the effective management of the government. He concludes that an Office of Federal Management should be established separately from OMB to look after presidential managerial interests. George Edwards in "Director or Facilitator?" emphasizes the limitations on presidential control of policy, specifically with respect to Congress. He argues that presidential success with Congress is much more closely associated with partisan balance in Congress than with presidential skills in convincing Congress to pass presidential policy priorities. Rather than controlling or directing Congress, presidential leadership operates "at the margins."

Louis Fisher takes up the common claim by presidents and their executive-branch appointees that Congress meddles too much in administrative matters. Fisher argues that this charge of "micromanagement" by Congress is often misplaced. Congressional intervention is often the result of real or perceived abuse of power on the part of presidents. But in addition, it is often legitimate and in any case inevitable. Roger Porter, former aide to Presidents Ford, Reagan, and Bush, takes a different perspective on presidential agendas. He argues that presidents can pursue their policy agendas in many other ways than by trying to get legislation through Congress. He examines the sources of presidential agendas and the methods that presidents use to fight for their implementation. He concludes that presidents have multiple ways to approach their policy priorities.

Finally, Charles O. Jones takes a broad perspective on presidential leadership in a government of shared powers. He argues that, despite the approach of many political scientists, the United States is not a presidential system but rather a separated system, with Congress playing an equally important role in setting the national policy agenda. The implications of this argument are that if we want to understand the U.S. system, we must pay attention to the dynamics between the two branches rather than to presidents alone.

As should be clear from the above discussion, the authors of these essays do not all agree with one another in their analyses of how the presidency should best be managed. But unanimity is not the purpose of the volume, nor would it be useful in the pursuit of an understanding of the dynamics of the U.S. presidency at the turn of the century. What one does find from a reading of these essays, however, is a surprising consensus on which questions ought to be asked.

The Managerial Presidency

Chapter 1

Can the President Manage the Government?

JAMES P. PFIFFNER

The twentieth century has been marked by increasing activism on the part of presidents and by the rising importance of the institutional staff of presidents in controlling the government. The formal landmarks of institutional power have been the 1921 Budgeting and Accounting Act, which established the Bureau of the Budget, and the Brownlow Committee Report of 1937, which led to the creation of the Executive Office of the President in 1939. The steady growth of the presidential apparatus since then has been a response not only to the expansion of the size and scope of the federal government, but also to the feeling by presidents that they need more control of the government to fulfill their promises and control their political fortunes. This essay will take up the question of presidential management and the degree to which presidents ought to become involved in managing the White House and the cabinet departments.

Presidents have felt the need to gain personal control over the government because of the relative decline of political parties over the past several decades. Working in tandem with the decline of parties have been changes in the selection processes for president. A series of reforms of the presidential nominating system since 1968 have led to presidential candidates who are more dependent on their personal appeal to voters than on political parties or other centers of power in Washington.[1]

In addition to the breakdown of traditional political institutions and practices, rising public expectations of presidents have led to the centralization of power and the "politicization" of the federal government. Terry Moe argues: "The expectations surrounding presidential performance far outstrip the institutional capacity of presidents to perform." And thus "the president will find politicization irresistible."[2]

As a result, presidents now try to do for themselves things that were previously done by others. Cabinet secretaries used to dominate high-level political appointments, but control has shifted decisively to the White House. Harry Truman assigned one aide to deal with political personnel. By the 1980s President Reagan's personnel assistant had one hundred people working for him in the early months of the administration, and all levels of political appointments were dominated by the White House.[3] The Clinton White House had even more people working on personnel recruitment. Franklin Roosevelt was able to handle his press relations by holding an informal briefing for a handful of reporters. In the 1980s the White House Communications Office had a sizable number of aides supervising five separate subunits.[4] The deals and accommodations that the president used to make by talking with a few "whales" in the congressional leadership now have to be "retailed" to many members in a more fragmented Congress. The Office of Congressional Liaison now has a sizable staff dedicated to the care and feeding of members of both Houses of Congress.[5]

Presidents used to depend on the secretaries of state and defense to be their principal spokesmen and advisers for national security matters. Over the past several decades the president's assistant for national security affairs and the National Security Council staff have come to dominate national security policy making.[6] The Office of Management and Budget in the Executive Office of the President has centralized control of executive branch budgets and personnel as well as central clearance powers over regulatory matters.[7] This dynamic of centralization has greatly increased the importance of organizing, managing, and controlling the apparatus of the presidency.

The Presidency as a Managerial Problem

Conventional wisdom holds that the structure of the White House and organization of the presidency is entirely dependent on the personality and style of the incumbent. Scholars and practitioners have analyzed the variety of presidential styles and structures in the modern presidency from the informally organized approaches of Roosevelt and Kennedy to the much more formal structures of Eisenhower and Nixon, and concluded that there is no one best way to organize the presidency.

On the face of it, this is self evident. There is no one style of organization that characterizes "successful" presidencies. Each president has stamped his administration with his own personality. There are, nevertheless, deep structural continuities in the modern presidency. "At first blush," argues Hugh Heclo, "it would seem that the internal arrangements of his own office are simply a matter of presidential taste. And so they are in most unimportant respects. . . . In terms of its *deep structure,* however, the office is largely a given that a president can change slowly if at all. This structure is a web of other people's expectations and needs."[8] These expectations and needs have been met by the increasing size and complexity of the White House. The White House staff grew from 250 aides in the 1950s to 550 aides two decades later; from one level and eleven subunits in the Eisenhower administration to four levels and twenty-nine subunits in the Reagan administration.[9] The number of staffers with the title "assistant" to the president (including deputy or special assistant) in 1960 was 29; by 1992 it was 81.[10] Presidents can ignore the managerial implications of this structural complexity only at their own peril. There may be no one best way to organize a presidency, but there are predictable organizational issues that must be faced anew by each president.

Some scholars, however, feel that presidents should not be involved in managerial issues. Stephen Hess, for instance, argues that "Presidents have made a serious mistake, starting with Roosevelt, in asserting that they are the chief managers of the federal government. . . . Rather than chief manager, the President is chief political officer of the United States."[11] Hess makes the point that Congress gives department heads the authority to run programs, not the president.

While Hess is right that the president should not become enmeshed in the details of managing departments and programs, managerial issues are crucial to the political leadership of the government. The constitutional basis for presidential intervention is the provision that the president "take care that the laws be faithfully executed." Thus the president has the constitutional right to delve into administrative matters at any level of the executive branch. Whether it is wise or administratively advisable to do this depends on the circumstances but should not be dismissed out of hand.

Recent presidents have learned through hard lessons that managerial matters are important. The Bay of Pigs blunder, Watergate, President Carter's initial problems with Congress, and the Iran-Contra affairs all involved the White House directly. Their negative effects might have been avoided or mitigated with more attention to management. President Eisenhower's dictum is to the point: "Organization cannot make a genius out of an incompetent. . . . On the other hand, disorganization can scarcely fail to result in inefficiency and can easily lead to disaster."[12]

In the aftermath of the Iran-Contra affair Brent Scowcroft, assistant to the president for national security affairs in the Ford and Bush administrations, argued that it is not the president's responsibility to accommodate himself to some abstract ideal of organization, but rather the staff's responsibility to accommodate itself to the president's personality and style. While Scowcroft is certainly right about the appropriate responsibilities, a president cannot afford to assume that his staff will adapt itself to his strengths and weaknesses. The president has to set up a staff structure that will guard against error and get him the information he needs when he needs it. The president must set up, or have set up, a managerial structure that will ensure that he is not at the mercy of others' priorities. That is, he needs to "manage" the White House. "To manage," writes Hugh Heclo, "is something that falls between administering in detail and merely presiding in general."[13] The National Academy of Public Administration, in its 1988 report, *The Executive Presidency,* calls for "management by design," rather than by inadvertence.[14]

But merely saying that the president should pay attention to management does not solve the problem. What level of managerial detail is appropriate for each level of the president's responsibility? Obviously, different levels of presidential attention are required for the White House, the cabinet, personnel appointments, and the career bureaucracy. This essay argues that the president should not try to manage much *directly,* but he must be concerned with managerial *issues* and have deputies pay attention to the details.

So management and administration are crucial to the modern presidency. But what does this mean to presidents? Peri Arnold argues that managerial issues are essential to the president's "ability to transform ideas and commitments into policies."[15] Although management is an essential component of presidential leadership, presidents should not necessarily try to control everything nor make management the central focus of their administrations. The right balance must be struck between management and political leadership.

The answer to Hess's argument that the president ought to be concerned not with management of the government but with political leadership is Arnold's point that the first is essential to the second: good management is essential to political leadership. "Thus the president ought to be concerned with administration, not because he is a manager but because administration is part of the system through which his choices become policy. . . . The president's political and policy concerns come first and lead him to administration. . . . In this view the president is not so much a manager of administration; he is a tactician using it."[16]

The above points bring us to the question of what is the appropriate stance of the president with respect to management in the main areas of presidential authority. There are four central paradoxes of the managerial presidency.

With respect to the White House: The greatest threats to the reputation and political interests of recent presidents have come from overenthusiastic loyalists rather than from political "enemies."

With respect to the cabinet: The best way for a president to "control" the executive branch is to delegate most issues that are not clearly presidential to department and agency heads. Presidential involvement should be very selective.

With respect to political personnel: The president should play a positive role in setting the tone for recruiting political appointees, but should delegate the selection of most subcabinet appointees to department and agency heads. Personal or ideological loyalty to the president does not guarantee the effective implementation of presidential priorities.

With respect to the permanent bureaucracy: The career bureaucracy is often seen by new presidents as an obstacle to the achievement of presidential priorities. But a positive relationship with the career services is essential to accomplishing presidential goals, and enlisting the bureaucracy's enthusiastic support can enhance the probability of presidential success.

Managing the White House

It is notable that many of the embarrassing blunders that have done the most damage to recent presidencies were not the result of external "enemies" sabotaging the president but resulted from the actions of loyal subordinates in the White House. Thus presidents must pay attention to management of the White House, and this management should fall somewhere between detailed administration and presiding in general. For instance, presidents do not need to be involved in the fine points of policy proposals at early stages in the policy development process, nor do they need to decide who will play on the White House tennis courts (as President Carter is said to have done). On the other hand, they should be aware of the major elements of administration proposals, they should make major staffing decisions, and they should be aware of what their immediate staff aides are doing in their names.

Modern presidents have demonstrated a range of styles of White House management. Franklin Roosevelt used a competitive approach to keep his small White House staff in line and responding to his needs. He gave overlapping jurisdictions and incomplete grants of authority to his staff and enjoyed watching the conflict that inevitably developed. Dwight Eisenhower was at the other end of the spectrum of management style. His was a much more formal and structured approach, derived in part from his experience with staff systems in the military.

John Kennedy consciously rejected the Eisenhower approach to managing his presidency and took the advice of Clark Clifford and Richard Neustadt in deciding to be his own chief of staff. Neustadt urged that Kennedy should be closer to Roosevelt's pattern than to Eisenhower's: "You would be your own 'chief of staff.' Your chief assistants would have to work collegially, in constant touch with one another and with you. . . . There is room here for a *primus inter pares* to emerge, but no room for a staff *director* or arbiter, short of you. Neither is there room for sheer, unguided struggle. . . . *you* would oversee, coordinate, and interfere with virtually everything your staff was doing."[17]

Richard Nixon decided to return to a more structured White House and designated H. R. Haldeman to be his chief of staff. Haldeman set up a system that protected the president's time and ensured that all presidential decisions were "staffed out" before being presented to the president.

In trying to distance himself from the legacy of the Nixon administration, President Ford decided to act as his own chief of staff in a "spokes-of-the-wheel" or "knights of the Round Table" fashion. It soon became clear, however, that with 9 people reporting directly to the president and a White House staff of over 500 that someone short of the president had to be in charge. Ford designated Donald Rumsfeld and later Richard Cheney to act as his chiefs of staff. "Someone, I decided, had to be responsible for scheduling appointments, coordinating the paper flow, following up on decisions I had made and giving me status reports on projects and policy development. I didn't like the idea of calling this person chief of staff, but that was the role he would fill."[18]

For the same reasons as Ford, President Carter began his administration without a chief of staff, and for the same reasons, he eventually abandoned the spokes-of-the-wheel approach to managing the White House. Jack Watson concluded that Carter's lack of a chief of staff early in the administration was "a fatal mistake," and Stuart Eizenstat concluded that "It is critical to have one person in charge."[19]

Ronald Reagan's style of managing the White House was at the polar opposite from Roosevelt and Kennedy with respect to presidential engagement. While President Reagan was very active in the promotion of his political and policy agendas, he was perhaps the most passive of modern presidents with respect to White House management. His approach to management was ". . . you surround yourself with the best people you can find, delegate authority, and don't interfere as long as the overall policy that you've decided upon is being carried out."[20]

"The Reagan presidency," concluded Hedrick Smith, "has probably been simultaneously the most centralized and staff-dominated presidency in history. . . . the Reagan presidency could be called a staff presidency because Reagan gave so much authority and latitude to his senior staff aides."[21] This style of staff management of the White House worked reasonably well in Reagan's first term. Many of the administration's initial goals were achieved, and major changes of policy direction were accomplished. Much of the credit for these victories must be given to the political skills of Chief of Staff James Baker and his deputy, Richard Darman. Baker's fine political sense allowed him to not only orchestrate the Reagan administration's dealings with Congress, but also to run the White House in the context of the "troika" of the first term. Even though Baker was chief of staff, Edwin Meese, as counselor to the president, and Michael Deaver, who had worked for Reagan for many years, had direct access to Reagan, and all three had to be involved in any major decision.

During Reagan's second term, Donald Regan took over as chief of staff. He controlled all avenues of access to the president at the same time that other strong aides to the president were leaving the White House. Regan personally approved virtually everything concerning the president: speeches, schedule, paper flow, appointments, and phone calls.[22] But Regan's tight control over the White House and his domineering style of management left him without allies to defend him when the Tower Commission laid the blame for much of the Iran-Contra scandal at his feet. "He must bear responsibility for the chaos that descended on the White House. . . ."[23]

George Bush as vice president had a chief of staff and did not hesitate to take the same approach when he became president in 1989. His choice, John Sununu, had played a key role in Bush's come-from-behind victory in the New Hampshire primary election of 1988. Sununu played the roles of liaison for the president with the conservative wing of the Republican Party and of promoter of their policy values. As chief of staff, he did his best, often in tandem with Richard Darman, to dominate the White House policy process. His style of leadership often irritated members of the cabinet and their subordinates, because he used his position, intelligence, and domineering personality to win his way. He also alienated Republican members of Congress as well as the Washington press corps.

At long last, President Bush felt compelled to fire him after a series of public indiscretions in which Sununu used Air Force and White House transportation for what appeared to be personal trips. Sununu's approach to the chief of staff position was clearly in line with the domineering chiefs of the past: Sherman Adams, H. R. Haldeman, and Donald Regan.

When Bill Clinton became president, he knew intellectually that a chief of staff was necessary in the White House, but his personal style of leadership resisted the delegation of very much authority to anyone. His first chief of staff, Thomas "Mack" McLarty, had been a boyhood friend who combined personal graciousness with a low-key approach to the job that suited Clinton's personality. He spent much of his time acting as a personal emissary for the president and trouble-shooting special problems. In contrast to other chiefs of staff, he spent only about two-thirds of his time actually managing the White House.

The Clinton White House also was a special challenge in that First Lady Hillary Rodham Clinton also played an important role in policy development. While other first ladies had been powerful in selective areas and issues, Mrs. Clinton was active across the policy and management spectrum. The vice president, Al Gore, also played a more active policy role than previous vice presidents. A chief of staff for President Clinton had to negotiate with two power centers in the White House in addition to the president.

Thus the Clinton White House was a special challenge to a chief of staff. In the summer of 1994, President Clinton replaced McLarty with OMB Director Leon Panetta. Panetta tightened up some of the policy-making process by controlling access to the president, clearing staff work before it went to the Oval Office, and limiting the size and scope of White House staff meetings. He could not, however, force Bill Clinton to accept a traditional chief-of-staff system in the White House. In Clinton's second term Erskine Bowles presided as chief of staff as White House management became more regularized.

So in deciding how to organize the White House, presidents must choose along a continuum between a hierarchical organization with a chief of staff and the less structured collegial alternative of multiple advocacy. Each has its strengths and weaknesses. If the intention is to ensure that presidential directives are carried out and that staff work is thorough and coordinated, the hierarchical model is preferable. If the intention is to ensure that creative ideas are brought to the fore and that many sides of issues are argued by their advocates, the collegial model is preferable. If you want information and alternatives presented in a logical, coherent manner, hierarchy is better. If you want to ensure that presidents are not trapped by their channels of information, collegiality is better.[24]

The drawback to the more open system is that it makes heavy demands on the president's time and energy. This approach may bring up issues before they are ready for presidential resolution. It is vulnerable to domination by strong personalities that may overshadow rational argument. If no one short of the president is in charge, more than the usual amount of conflict may result. On the other hand, the chief-of-staff system is subject to the potential information distortions of hierarchies. The process may "overcook" decisions, and the chief of staff may act as too strict a gatekeeper and screen out those whom the president should see.

In recent years a consensus has emerged that a chief of staff is necessary to the management of the modern presidency. The essential elements of the chief-of-staff role are: imposing order on the White House by coordinating paper flow, ensuring that decisions are staffed out, regulating access to the president, acting as arbiter among other White House staffers, and negotiating with cabinet members on issues that are not important enough for the president's personal attention. Chiefs of staff are also stuck with the "dirty work" of delivering bad news to subordinates of the president, for example, firing them. "If there's a dirty deed to be done," says Richard Cheney, "it's the chief of staff who's got to do it."[25] In Jack Watson's words, the chief of staff is the president's "javelin catcher." Finally, one of the chief of staff's most important functions is to be an "honest broker" who will accurately represent the views of other White House staffers and cabinet officers to the president. If the chief of staff is not perceived to be an honest broker, powerful people in the administration will establish backchannels to the president, and order will be undermined.

Even Richard Neustadt, who had urged John Kennedy to be his own chief of staff, has admitted that it is a practical impossibility. "I've given up long opposition to the formal designation of a Chief of Staff, on grounds that in administrative terms it, or something like it, has become a practical necessity. . . . The accumulated experience [since President Truman] is quite enough, I think, to bind future Administrations, as a matter not of law but of convenience and common sense."[26] But Neustadt also argues that the chief of staff should not emulate the strong chiefs: Adams, Haldeman, Regan, and Sununu. They should not control all access to the president and they should not be the only person with direct and regular access to the president. Presidents have often had three or four top aides with whom to consult. Presidents need to have persons with whom they can interact as peers. Someone must say so when the president is wrong. Chiefs of staff in the past have performed this function, but they should not be the only ones that the president can turn to for frank advice.

Just as someone short of the president needs to be in charge of administrative matters and settling lower-level disputes, the president should have the benefit of someone who shares a presidential perspective. That is, someone who has access to the same information and is aware of the same pressures should be available to give an alternative perspective for presidential consideration. For this reason the chief of staff should not be excluded from national security matters. This does not mean that the president's assistant for national security should report to the president through the chief of staff, but that the chief of staff should be apprised of all national security matters so that the president can have the benefit of someone with a comparable scope of perspective.[27]

But the existence of a chief of staff is no substitute for personal presidential monitoring of the White House staff system, as the Iran-Contra affair demonstrated. Even though presidents should not act as their own chiefs of staff, they must take an active role in assuring that an effective staff system is in place. They must monitor it constantly to make sure that it gives them the type of support that they need to do their job. Presidents must make sure they get the bad news as well as the good. They must make sure that there is a devil's advocate. And they must make sure that overzealous subordinates do not do things that presidents do not want done, in the name of accomplishing their goals.

Neustadt frames this question: "How can the President use his circle so that it informs his choices in every dimension relevant to him, political and substantive alike, without relying on his intimates so passively that they, or some of them, make him the instrument of their bad judgement regardless?"[28] Heclo puts it: "The management aim cannot, therefore, simply be to create a unified team; it must be to create the counterpressures that will be useful to him, lest he become victimized by his own helpers."[29]

White House experience over the past several decades has taught us that if the president opts for a chief of staff who plays too domineering a role, there will be trouble. At the very least, other members of the administration will try to set up backchannels of communication with the president. At worst, the domineering chief of staff will—as in the cases of Adams, Haldeman, Regan, and Sununu—run roughshod over potential presidential allies. Each of these domineering chiefs of staff alienated the press, members of Congress, members of the administration, and had the reputation for lack of civility in their jobs. And *each* of them ended up resigning in disgrace after hurting their presidents. On the other hand, those chiefs of staff who acted as neutral brokers—such as Donald Rumsfeld, Richard Cheney, Jack Watson, James Baker, Leon Panetta, and Erskine Bowles—served their presidents firmly and well.

So the president must be involved in the management of the White House to establish a responsive staff system. A chief of staff in the facilitating tradition (as opposed to the strong chiefs) can relieve the president of much "administrivia," but the president must monitor the system to assure that it is not over-protective. This monitoring can never be delegated, but is the responsibility of the president, for the president's legacy and political fortunes depend on it.

Managing the Cabinet

At times in U.S. history the cabinet has been a major source of advice to the president and has played an important role in policy formulation and enunciation. But in the second half of the twentieth century power has slipped from the cabinet to the White House staff. White House staffers wield this power because of their proximity to the president and their control over the president's basic needs. "The White House staff's leverage derives from control of the most rudimentary elements of the president's life: whom he sees, what he reads, what business and what events are worth his time, when he will give speeches and what he will say, what will be said in his name by his press spokesman, and what messages will be conveyed by his staff to his cabinet and congressional allies."[30] The president usually develops trust and support with White House staffers because of long and close association. This relationship is nearly impossible with cabinet officers who are selected because of their independent political standing and must spend most of their time running their departments.

Presidents come to depend on White House aides because of this trust and because of the aides' responsiveness and proven loyalty. Presidential staffers are concerned primarily with their boss's political interests and will respond immediately. White House staffers do not have divided loyalties since they are not encumbered with legal or bureaucratic obligations to departments or agencies. For these reasons presidents are tempted to run everything that is important to them directly out of the White House. But ironically, presidents cannot maximize control of the government without delegating much to their cabinets.

Presidents' use of their cabinets has been declining since 1960. Eisenhower's approach to managing his cabinet was to use it as a deliberative body and to delegate much of what was "not presidential" to his cabinet secretaries. His military background made him sensitive to the distinctions between "staff" positions, which were advisory, and "line" positions, which were the locus of operational authority. White House aides were clearly staff with no authority except that derived from the president; cabinet officers have legal responsibility for their departments. This does not mean that the cabinet made the major administration decisions or that Eisenhower did not actively control policy.[31] It means that he did not choose to centralize control of the government in the White House to the extent that his successors have.

John Kennedy consciously rejected Eisenhower's approach to White House organization and structure. He discarded the position of chief of staff as well as Eisenhower's elaborate NSC machinery. Nor did Kennedy have any use for the cabinet as a consultative mechanism. He felt that more work could get done in small groups or task forces of officials and advisers who were most directly involved with the problem at hand. He also wanted to maximize his personal control over policy options and did not want to be presented with a bureaucratic consensus. The Kennedy and Johnson administrations also marked the beginning of the rise of the president's assistant for national security affairs to a prominence and visibility rivaling and eclipsing the secretary of state.

Richard Nixon began his presidency with intentions of "cabinet government." He intended to delegate most domestic matters to his cabinet appointees. "I've always thought this country could run itself domestically without a President. All you need is a competent cabinet to run the country at home.

You need a President for foreign policy."[32] In foreign affairs Nixon intended to be his own secretary of state.

But disillusionment soon set in for Nixon when he felt that his cabinet appointees were not as concerned with his re-election as they should have been. White House suspicion of cabinet members was reflected by cabinet secretaries who thought they did not have the access to the president that befitted their status as the first officers of the government. In his second term, Nixon replaced a number of his appointees and proposed a major reorganization of the executive branch to give him more control over his appointees and the government.

Jimmy Carter came to office with promises of cabinet government. But as with his initial decision not to designate a chief of staff, Carter soon became disillusioned with cabinet government. He felt that his cabinet secretaries were advancing their own agendas rather than his. The White House staff felt there was no discipline in the administration, and in the summer of 1979, Carter decided to dismiss four of his cabinet secretaries and designate a chief of staff.

The Reagan administration also came to office with promises of cabinet government, but from the beginning it centralized policy making, personnel selection, and budget formulation more tightly in the White House than had any other administration. The White House staff dominated the administration, sometimes to the frustration of cabinet secretaries. Alexander Haig complained that he did not have enough access to the president: "During the transition from the election to the inauguration, I saw the president alone once! . . . That's all. That began to worry me very, very much, early on."[33] Donald Regan also felt that, as secretary of the treasury, he did not get much guidance from the president. "In the four years that I served as Secretary of the Treasury, I never saw President Reagan alone and never discussed economic philosophy or fiscal and monetary policy with him one-on-one. From first day to last at Treasury, I was flying by the seat of my pants. . . . After I accepted the job, he simply hung up and vanished."[34]

While the Reagan administration was one very much centered around the White House staff, this centralization was moderated by the establishment of cabinet councils. The system was intended to bring together those cabinet secretaries who were concerned with a particular area of policy and had overlapping jurisdictions. The councils were staffed in the White House and provided a useful forum to bring together White House staffers and cabinet members to deliberate on policy issues.

While President Reagan established a cabinet-council system that was an innovation in the organization of the presidency, he also presided over one of the major scandals of the modern presidency: the Iran-Contra affair. He had criticized the Carter administration for letting Zbigniew Brzezinski, the president's assistant for national security affairs, dominate foreign policy making. Accordingly, Reagan's first adviser for national security was Richard Allen, who adopted a low-visibility role. The initial intention was to let Secretary of State Alexander Haig run foreign policy. But distrust soon developed between Haig and the White House staff. Haig was seen by the White House staff as self-aggrandizing and power hungry, and Haig felt he was being kept from the president by the White House staff.

Ironically, after Reagan appointed George Shultz in whom he did have confidence, the Iran-Contra initiatives by the National Security Council staff undercut the secretary of state, leaving him out of the loop in major areas of U.S. foreign policy. The administration that began its term with a national security assistant clearly subordinate to the secretary of state and with broad declarations of "cabinet government" ended up with unprecedented operations being run by the NSC staff without the knowledge of (diversion of funds to the Contras) or against the advice of (arms to Iran) the secretaries of state and defense.

It is easy to understand why recent presidents have been tempted to run foreign policy from the White House and give primacy to their national security advisers and the NSC staff. White House aides have the advantage of proximity to the president and can respond immediately to presidential desires. They can operate without the cumbersome interagency task forces, bureaucratic consultation, and red tape associated with the State or Defense Departments. White House aides can assure secrecy, speed, and concentration. They do not have other institutional loyalties or turf interests to distract them from the president's priorities.

In the case of the Iran-Contra affair, the disadvantages of a system overly centralized in the White House became apparent. When the NSC staff is advocate and executor as well as coordinator of policy, its analytical capacity is undermined. The President's Special Review Board (the Tower Commission) concluded: "The NSC staff assumed direct operational control. The initiative fell within the traditional jurisdictions of the Departments of State, Defense, and CIA. Yet these agencies were largely ignored."[35] The NSC staff, which was created to be a coordinating mechanism, had in the 1980s come to dominate and even exclude the official foreign policy–making apparatus. The Iran-Contra affair grew out of a profound distrust of and contempt for the governmental policy-making apparatus in the Departments of State and Defense.

In 1986 the president's national security assistant, Admiral John Poindexter, deliberately misled the secretary of state about U.S. relations with Iran and kept important information from the secretaries of state and defense concerning U.S. aid to the Contras in Nicaragua. Poindexter even declared that he kept crucial information from the president: "On this whole issue, you know, the buck stops here with me."[36] The Tower Commission disagreed: "Setting priorities is not enough when it comes to sensitive and risky initiatives that directly affect U.S. national security. [The president] must assure that the content and tactics of an initiative match his priorities and objectives. He must insist upon account-ability. For it is the president who must take responsibility for the NSC system and deal with the consequences."[37]

President Bush's approach to his cabinet moderated some of the centraliza-tion of the Reagan administration. He appointed cabinet officers he knew per-sonally and trusted to run their departments. He allowed his cabinet secretaries to have more say in the appointment of their political subordinates, and he involved them more regularly in policy development. He also had a much better grasp of policy implementation issues than President Reagan had and was willing to pick up the phone to stay in touch with his cabinet members.

Bush did not, however, return to Eisenhower's approach to the cabinet. His top White House staffers—Chief of Staff Sununu and OMB Director Richard Darman—did their best to keep policy control in the White House. Thus Bush pulled back slightly but did not reverse the long-term centralization of control over policy development in the White House at the expense of the cabinet.

Bill Clinton came to office with no promises of cabinet government to keep. He did spend a considerable amount of time carefully selecting cabinet nomi-nees during his transition into office, but he did not attempt to delegate much policy development authority to his cabinet. The most important policy ini-tiatives of the Clinton administration were run from the White House. The first-year-deficit-reduction package dominated the early agenda and was for-mulated in the White House, as was the NAFTA initiative. The farthest-reach-ing Clinton policy initiative—the health-care reform proposal—was run from the White House by the first lady and a team of 500 detailees and specialists. The Department of Health and Human Services played an important role but clearly did not have the lead.

Thus Clinton continued the trend toward White House staff domination of administration policy development at the expense of cabinet secretaries. The Clinton cabinet met as a body only seven times in 1993. White House staff domination of policy making is partially inevitable and partially desirable, but pulling too much into the White House risks overload and can lead to nega-tive consequences. The president needs to create a balance between the White House staff and the department secretaries so that administration policy mak-ing is coordinated and not unduly conflictual.

With respect to managing the cabinet, the president should expect to estab-lish administration policy and should have a policy development mechanism that ensures White House control but facilitates input from cabinet secretaries who will reflect departmental perspectives. The Iran-Contra affair is an extreme case that demonstrates the need for presidents to insist on a balance between White House and cabinet input.

Ironically, the best way for presidents to control the executive branch is to delegate most of what they want done to their cabinet appointees. There is no way the White House staff has the capacity or the expertise to run the government from the White House. The only way for the White House to be in control is through great selectivity. The president, as elected head of the executive branch, should be able to direct policy and its execution, but he cannot exercise this right too often or the White House will be stretched too thin.

In addition, the more that the White House staff interferes with the execution of policy, the more problems are sucked into the White House. The president must keep a distance from as many problems as possible while retaining the option of intervening when it is important to presidential interests to do so.

A useful illustration is the military doctrine of delegation to the tactical commander. The commander on the scene of the battle is supposed to have the discretion to determine the tactics of the battle without second guessing or control from higher authority far removed from the scene of battle. Thus the complaints from military commanders when their judgments are overruled by headquarters are soundly based in military doctrine. While this makes sense from a tactical point of view, the president is concerned with the strategic implications of military actions.

Thus John Kennedy's insistence that he have direct control over the blockade of Cuba in 1962 was appropriate because there was more at stake in the missile crisis than the tactics of a blockade. President Johnson asserted direct control over bombing targets in North Vietnam. Regardless of the merits of his judgments about bombing targets, the principle that the president should have control is valid because strategic concerns, such as U.S. relations with China, were affected by the choice of bombing targets. Modern communications technology, however, presents presidents with the temptation to take personal control over any situation where the stakes are high. While in principle the president should be able to take control, wisdom dictates that this option of direct presidential control be exercised selectively. The dangers are that the president, far removed from the scene, may make poor decisions and that any problems or failures, even if they are not under his control, will be blamed on the president.

Another reason to delegate as much as possible to departments and agencies is that cabinet officers will be frustrated with frequent White House "interference." Cabinet officers have the legal obligation to implement the law in their areas of jurisdiction. The president can also use cabinet appointees in order to keep White House staff in line. In Hugh Heclo's judgment, "Paradoxically, one of the most effective ways for the president to manage his own office is through the use of his appointees in the departments and agencies. If these department heads are known to have intimate knowledge of the president's thinking, and therefore seem likely to be backed by the president in disputes with White House staffers, White House aides will likely be kept in their proper place as assistants to the president rather than as assistant presidents."[38]

In addition to being better situated to implement presidential policy, cabinet officers are likely to be tied into sources of information that the White House staff cannot possibly monitor. Centralizing too much control in the White House shuts off the president from these valuable sources of information.

Conclusions

This essay has argued that presidential control of the government is legitimate and essential, but that presidents are tempted to define the necessary amount of control too expansively. Construed too broadly, presidential control will overwhelm the president with detail and suck unnecessary problems into the White House.

Viewed with enlightened self-interest, however, presidential control of the government means ensuring that presidential priorities are effectively formulated into policy directions and that policies are carried out with efficiency and dispatch. Effective implementation of policy demands competence as well as loyalty from subordinates.

A president, therefore, should not become involved in any detailed way with staff management, but should designate a chief of staff to worry about the hundreds of staffers in the White House. The president, however, must be involved sufficiently to ensure that his interests are being well served. The president must probe enough to guard against the overzealous subordinate who is willing to bend the laws or the Constitution in what is thought to be the president's interest. No one should be allowed to think that the buck stops short of the president.

With respect to the cabinet, the president should delegate as much as possible to cabinet secretaries. This delegation should include a significant role in policy development through cabinet councils and the primary role in policy implementation. White House control over major policy decisions must be assured, but intervention at lower levels will be most effective if pursued selectively and only when the president's personal interests are at stake. With respect to political appointments, presidents should not abdicate control, but should exercise it sparingly. With respect to the career services, presidents should realize that civil servants are essential to presidential success, and engage them as allies rather than treat them as adversaries.

From a broader perspective, presidential control of the government means realizing that the president leads better by persuasion than by command.[39] Our fragmented separation-of-powers system will not allow the type of tight presidential control over the government that some presidents seem to want. Effective presidential control derives from the realization that real power in the U.S. political system grows out of political consensus forged by true political leadership, not stratagem or management techniques.[40]

NOTES

The author would like to thank Peri Arnold and Michael Genovese for helpful comments on an earlier version of this essay.

1. See Samuel Kernell, *Going Public* (Washington, D.C.: CQ Press, 1986).
2. Terry Moe, "The Politicized Presidency," in this volume.
3. See James P. Pfiffner, *The Strategic Presidency, second edition* (Lawrence: University Press of Kansas, 1996), chapters 3 and 8.
4. See Samuel Kernell, "The Evolution of the White House Staff," in this volume.
5. See James P. Pfiffner, "The President's Legislative Agenda," *The Annals* 499 (Sept., 1988).
6. See Kevin Mulcahy and Cecil V. Crabb, "Presidential Management of National Security Policy Making: 1947–1987," in James P. Pfiffner, ed., *The Managerial Presidency, first edition* (Pacific Grove, Calif.: Brooks/Cole, 1991), p. 142.
7. See James P. Pfiffner, "OMB: Professionalism, Politicization, and the Presidency," in Margaret Wyszomirski and Colin Campbell, eds., *The Executive Establishment and Executive Leadership: A Comparative Perspective* (London: Baisel Blackwell, forthcoming).
8. Hugh Heclo, "The Changing Presidential Office," in this volume.
9. Kernell, "The Evolution of the White House Staff."
10. Paul C. Light, *Thickening Government* (Washington, D.C.: Brookings, 1995), p. 184.
11. Stephen Hess, *Organizing the Presidency* (Washington, D.C.: Brookings, 1976), p. 10; in the revised edition of 1988, see p. 6.
12. Quoted by Fred I. Greenstein, *Leadership in the Modern Presidency* (Cambridge, Mass.: Harvard University Press, 1988), p. 83. For an insightful analysis of Eisenhower's management approach, see Phillip Henderson, *Managing the Presidency* (Boulder, Colo.: Westview Press, 1988).
13. Heclo, "The Changing Presidential Office."
14. National Academy of Public Administration, *The Executive Presidency: Federal Management for the 1990s* (Washington, D.C.: NAPA, 1988), p. 2.
15. See Peri E. Arnold, *Making the Managerial Presidency* (Princeton, N.J.: Princeton University Press, 1986), p. 363.
16. Ibid.

17. Richard E. Neustadt, Memorandum on "Staffing the President-Elect" (Oct. 30, 1960), in this volume.

18. Gerald R. Ford, *A Time to Heal* (New York: Harper and Row, 1979), p. 147.

19. For Watson quote, see Samuel Kernell and Samuel Popkin, eds., *Chief of Staff* (Berkeley: University of California Press, 1986), p. 71. Stuart Eizenstat, interview with James P. Pfiffner, Washington, D.C., July 14, 1983.

20. Quoted by Ann Dowd, "What Managers Can Learn from Manager Reagan," in *Fortune,* Sept. 15, 1986, p. 36.

21. Hedrick Smith, *The Power Game* (New York: Random House, 1988), p. 300.

22. See Bernard Weinrub, "How Donald Regan Runs the White House," *New York Times Magazine,* Jan. 5, 1986, p. 12.

23. *The Tower Commission Report* (New York: Bantam Books, 1987), p. 81.

24. See Samuel Kernell, "How Can the President Be a National Leader and a Chief Executive at the Same Time?" unpublished paper, Dec., 1987.

25. Kernell and Popkin, eds., *Chief of Staff,* p. 62.

26. Richard E. Neustadt, "Does the White House Need a Strong Chief of Staff?" in this volume.

27. While the vice president might seem like a natural candidate for this function, the political dynamics of selecting the vice presidential candidate are such that we cannot count on there being a close and trusting relationship between the president and vice president. On the appropriate scope of purview of the chief of staff, former President Ford said in response to a question about the Iran-Contra scandal: "I would make my Chief of Staff the controlling official in the operation of the White House staff. There would be no bypassing of that individual by NSC. The Chief of Staff has to be the focal point for management. I would not exclude Cabinet members or the head of the NSC or other top officials from having access, but it has to be through a responsible Chief of Staff who knows what's going on." (quoted in *The Next President,* interviews by David Frost, Washington, D.C.: *U.S. News,* 1988, p. 39).

28. Neustadt, "Does the White House Need a Strong Chief of Staff?"

29. Heclo, "The Changing Presidential Office."

30. Smith, *The Power Game,* p. 303.

31. See Fred L. Greenstein, *The Hidden-Hand Presidency* (New York: Basic Books, 1984).

32. Rowland Evans, Jr., and Robert D. Novak, *Nixon in the White House* (New York: Random House, 1971), p. 11.

33. Quoted by Smith, *The Power Game,* p. 310.

34. Donald Regan, *For the Record* (New York: Harcourt, Brace & Jovanovich, 1988), pp. 142–43.

35. *The Tower Commission Report,* p. 62.

36. *Washington Post,* July 16, 1987, p. 1.

37. *The Tower Commission Report,* p. 80.

38. Heclo, "The Changing Presidential Office."

39. See Fred I. Greenstein, "In Search of a Modern Presidency," in Greenstein, ed., *Leadership in Modern Presidency* (Cambridge, Mass.: Harvard University Press, 1988).

40. See Donald F. Kettl, "Presidential Management of the Economy," in James P. Pfiffner, ed., *The Managerial Presidency* (Pacific Grove, Calif.: Brooks/Cole, 1991), pp. 238–49.

Part 1

Organizing
the Presidency

Chapter 2

The Changing Presidential Office

HUGH HECLO

The office of the president has become so complex, so propelled by its own internal bureaucratic dynamics, that it now presents every new president with a major problem of internal management. Without a conscious effort to the contrary, he may not even perceive the prison that his helpers erect around him.

To tackle this problem successfully, a president must be aware of how "his" office can constrain him and must use "his" staff at least as effectively as they use him. He must be aware of the management impact of everything he does. He must choose his priorities carefully and pursue them tenaciously lest he become dependent on the priorities of everyone else around him. He must have a good sense of how his staff act and interact. He must maintain a delicate balance between the Executive Office and his appointees in the departments and agencies. Above all, he must set himself at the center of a web of pressures and counterpressures that ultimately serves his purposes.

The Internal Management Problem of the Presidency

Our most familiar image of the presidency finds a man, sitting alone, in the dimly lit Oval Office. Against this shadowy background the familiar face ponders that ultimate expression of power, a presidential decision.

It is a compelling and profoundly misleading picture. Presidential decisions are obviously important. But a more accurate image would show a presidency composed of at least a thousand people—a jumble of personal loyalists, professional technocrats, and bureaucratic staff with one man struggling, often vainly, to stay abreast of it all. What that familiar face ponders in the Oval Office is likely to be a series of conversations with advisers or a few pages of paper containing several options. These represent the last distillates produced from immense rivers of information flowing from sources—and condensed in ways—

about which the president probably knows little. The great irony is that, as more and more forces combine to program the president, he sees only people who are trying to help him do what he wants.

In 1980 the Executive Office of the President (EOP) is composed of ten disparate major units, including a White House Office with its own two dozen or so basic subdivisions. The number of people involved is subject to a variety of inventive accounting methods, but a reasonable approximation would be 500 or so people attached to the White House and another roughly 1,500 people in the rest of the EOP.[1] There seems little doubt that a trimmer, more rational, staffing arrangement would help a president meet national needs as well as substantially simplify any president's job of managing his own office.

Yet, however the presidency is equipped with staffs and processes, the president's personal management problem remains. His choice is to run or to be run by his office. No conceivable staffing arrangement will meet all his needs, and yet every arrangement carries the potential of submerging his interests into those of his help and their machinery. All the trends suggest that the grip of this well-intentioned machinery on the president is likely to grow, just as it has grown in the past two decades. The president's great danger lies in thinking that by making decisions he is actually managing. His internal management problem—the underside of the presidency—is to use those who serve him without becoming dependent on them. He must avoid being victimized by their loyalty to him or by his loyalty to them. To put it most directly, I do not see how, given contemporary demands on the office, a president can exercise leadership without being quietly manipulative within that office.

Constraints on Internal Management

At first blush, it would seem that the internal arrangements of his own office are simply a matter of presidential taste. And so they are in most unimportant respects. Apart from matters of style, the president's main area of discretion is the choice as to what personalities he will deal with directly in the everyday running of his office. Even this choice is likely to be constrained by personal commitments to familiar aides, particularly since no modern candidate can hope to negotiate the long-drawn-out campaign process without a bevy of loyal aides. Those who manage the campaign bureaucracy inevitably have a claim on the White House bureaucracy.

In terms of its *deep structure,* however, the office is largely a given that a president can change slowly if at all. This structure is a web of other people's expectations and needs. On the surface, the new president seems to inherit an empty house. In fact, he enters an office already shaped and crowded by other people's desires. What the would-be presidents seem to be reaching for on the nightly news is simply the top prize in our ultimate contest as a competitive society. What the winner grasps is an office that is the raw, exposed ganglion of government where immense lines of force come together in ways that no single person can control. The total effect is to program the modern president.

Legal and Political Pressures

One set of constraints arises from a growing number of statutory requirements placed on the office. Core advisory units of the presidency (Council of Economic Advisers, National Security Council, Domestic Council) were established by laws passed by Congress and can be altered only by persuading Congress to change these laws. A president can, of course, use or bypass this formal machinery, but the fact is that over the years these units have generally been accepted as important parts of the presidency and have generated expectations that presidents will not simply ride roughshod over their operations. For example, as President-elect Reagan prepared to take office, a key issue discussed was who would bring to him the work of staffs from the national security and domestic councils, not whether to have and to use these units in the first place.

Legal constraints also arise from statutory requirements which tell a president what he must do. At last count there were forty-three separate requirements for annually recurring presidential reports (environmental impacts, foreign arms sales, and so on). None of these reports are things about which a president bothers himself personally except in the rarest of circumstances. What they require are more staff work, more specialists, and more routines within the presidency. Each process gives someone a proprietary interest in that process—in other words, someone other than the president with a claim on what must get done in the presidency.

A second part of the web preventing a president from designing his own office is the political interest of outsiders. Many people, it turns out, have a stake in the internal arrangements of the presidency. Even a hint of major increases in presidential staff arouses immediate and intense congressional criticism. Thus President Carter in his first few months in office, for example, in order to avoid future trouble with his reorganization plans, had to informally promise a leading congressional committee chairman that he would not increase the size of the EOP even though important, non-political parts of the presidency were seriously undermanned.

Congressional committees hold the purse strings for every major unit in the EOP; they can and have made life miserable for the head of a unit such as the president's Office of Management and Budget (OMB), requiring exhaustive and exhausting testimony, cutting funds for unfavored projects, and adding staff for functions bearing no relation to a president's interests. Since the Nixon administration, moreover, Congress has been far more reluctant to grant funds in special emergency or "management improvement" accounts which presidents could formerly use largely at their discretion. Even a president's papers are no longer his. Under a recent congressional enactment, President Reagan will be the first chief executive in our history who will not be able to take his papers away with him when he leaves office.

Congress is only the most obvious of the political constituencies constraining presidential management of the presidency. Various specialized communities have an interest in staking out claims to particular pieces of the Executive Office. This applies, for example, to the Office of Science and Technology Policy (disbanded in 1973 and reinstated in 1976 at the demand of the scientific community), environmentalists (Council on Environmental Quality), and many others in the recent past. More subtly, the Council of Economic Advisers serves as the voice of the economics profession and the National Security Council does likewise for professional students of foreign and military affairs. Even though each of these communities contains different viewpoints from which a president can pick and choose, he is not free to deny someone from these professional groups a major advisory role in the highest councils of his administration.[2]

Legal constraints and political constituencies in the presidency have grown in the past two decades, but a president can try to "manage around" them by observing the formalities. Whatever the statutory requirements, a president's real management system consists of whom he consults, where he bestows trust, and how he polices those in his trust. There are two remaining sets of constraints that have grown in recent years and that strike at the very heart of this real-life management system. Because they spring from deep-seated social and political trends, these two forces are not elements that can be managed around. Indeed, presidents under the necessity of responding to these twin pressures become the agents for programming their own office. The more that recent presidents have thought they were putting their personal stamp on the office and events, the more they have affirmed a larger design that they cannot control and can rarely comprehend.

The Requisites of a Presidential Party

As far as one can tell from the historical record, the five presidents since Eisenhower did not consciously plan to create their own political parties. Yet that, in embryo, is what has come to exist in the White House. Consider for a moment some of the specialized subdivisions that existed in the Carter White House *before* the active start of the 1980 presidential campaign:

- Assistant to the President (Women's Affairs)
- Assistant to the President (Organizational Liaison)
- Special Assistant for Hispanic Affairs
- Special Assistant for Ethnic Affairs
- Special Assistant for Civil Rights
- Counselor to the President on Aging [ours, not his]
- Special Assistant for Consumer Affairs
- Assistant for Intergovernmental Affairs
- Assistant for Congressional Liaison
- Special Assistant to the President (Press and Public Relations)

Taken as a whole, the list indicates something more important than the desire of particular groups to have their representatives at the president's elbow. What these and similar political operatives for other presidents suggest is an attempt to reach out from the White House and to build at least some lines of reliable political support for presidents. If one were inventing a political party, these are exactly the types of offices at branch headquarters that one would want to create. What is lacking is only the local cells that would give such an organization feet and hands. As President Carter discovered, fireside chats, town meetings, and convocations with local publishers and editors are no substitute for *that*.

The fact is that each president during the last twenty years has felt increasingly compelled to mobilize the White House to build the equivalent of a presidential party for governing. To some presidents (such as Johnson or Nixon) the inclination comes naturally but, whatever the vagaries of personality, every contemporary president has been under pressure to move in the same direction. The reason is clear: a more politically volatile public, a less manageable Congress, a disappearing party hierarchy, proliferating groups of single-minded activists which merge with the networks of policy experts discussed later. All these add up to a shifting political base of support for presidents. This is not atomization—a breaking down of our political life into tiny elemental particles. It is rampant pluralism, with groups crosscutting the political landscape into incoherent patterns. Atomization would produce anomie and anarchy. Rampant pluralism produces what we in fact have: unnegotiable demands, political stagnation, and stalemate.

People in the White House have had little choice but to try and cope with this trend by shoring up the president's own base of support. Given the succession of one-term presidents since the Kennedy assassination, no one would want to claim great success for these efforts, but that is not the point. What modern president could reasonably be expected to give up the attempt at using the White House to build a presidential party?

Once that fact is admitted, we can begin to see how even the most loyal aides and the presidents themselves cooperate in the programming of the modern presidency. When mayors or governors have problems, it is not enough to refer their calls to some departmental appointee or bureaucrat. Doing that will not build the strong relations which a president needs. Hence, someone in the White House is tasked to keep an eye on "intergovernmental relations." A small staff develops. The mayors' and governors' telephone calls are returned from the White House, their entrée to the bureaucracy smoothed a little. By helping them, the president helps himself. In the longer run, however, the president acquires a staff with a vested interest in continuing to process such problems, and he confirms the larger expectation that he is somehow responsible for seeing to it that a fiendishly complex federal system works to the satisfaction of all concerned.

There is no need to belabor the point. The same dynamic applies in one area of presidential activity after another. Will the president work exclusively through top congressional leaders, none of whom can control the actions of the legislature? Or will the president try to string together the many pieces of Congress that are in business for themselves? All the pressures of the moment dictate the latter course. Accordingly, the president acquires an extensive congressional liaison staff, doing favors and attracting demands for more. President Carter in his first year showed little willingness to be programmed as a builder of his own party in Congress, and he paid dearly for following his preferences. Can a president rest content in channeling relations he needs with all the interest groups in our mobilized society through his party's national committee or a federal department? The answer began to come clear as early as 1940 when Franklin Delano Roosevelt, in seeking a third term, had one aide working part-time on relations with ethnics and unions and another preparing materials on what the New Deal had done "for the benefit of Negroes."[3] Since then a veritable political technocracy of such people has developed, entangling the presidential office in extensive networks of activists interested in this and that issue.

There is—or seems to be—a way out of all these entanglements produced by the need of presidents to create a quasi-party for themselves. Richard Neustadt described it in late 1979: "While national party organizations fall away, while congressional party discipline relaxes, while interest groups proliferate and issue networks rise, a President who wishes to compete for leadership in framing policy and shaping coalitions has to make the most he can out of his popular connection. Anticipating home reactions, Washingtonians . . . are vulnerable to any breeze from home that presidential words and sights can stir.

. . . The President with television talent will be likely to put his very talent at the center of his hopes when he takes office."

As viewers of the past four presidents can attest, even chief executives with a definite untalent for television are likely to seize on the tube to deploy their leadership. Unfortunately, by trying to do a little programming of their own on TV, presidents do not escape their personal management problem and may (especially if talented) only add to it by mistaking a successful screen image for the substance of leadership.

The tube is a blunt instrument. It allows a president to explain himself, catch a mood, create a persona. These are important, but they are not things through which a president escapes the programming that crowds in on his leadership. On the contrary. The generalized utility of television for the president has a counterpart in the media's need for its own kind of presidency. The increasingly powerful news media needs stories, preferably with a White House backdrop. They need presidential statements to help create the story, favored access and background information from the White House staff to give them an edge in the competition for stories. When all else fails, the media need care and feeding by the White House press office with a steady stream of handouts to those who cannot find a story. This communications industry complex of the presidency is a far cry from the early off-the-record chats that presidents used in order to give the "boys in the press" an idea of their thinking and activities. The media's expectations run against the grain of the president's managerial needs for private deliberations, for discretion as to when to get into or out of the news, and for an administration that appears united. Television language accurately captures the disutility of the medium for presidential management purposes. The tube *follows* stories, but the president must first manage a process for choosing where *he* wants to go. TV *covers* events in general, but the president's office needs to give sustained attention to specific, often technical, matters where there is never a clear story line.

The requisites for a presidential party, including television, are probably with the White House to stay. The members of his political technocracy will be a constraint or an opportunity—usually some weighting of both—for a president, depending on how he maneuvers among them. But if they are not to be pure constraint, the watchword must be active presidential maneuvering, not lying in repose or trusting in his aides' undoubtedly sincere professions of loyalty. Yet this section has referred only to the political base of the president's office. Another trend strikes even deeper into the presidency than has our growing political fragmentation and volatility. This is a massive social diffusion of policy-making powers.

The Hemorrhage of Presidential Power

The classic question to ask about the presidential office is what has happened to its power. It is a question that invites a thumbs up or thumbs down vote: increasing or decreasing? More imperial or more post-Watergate? The developments of the last twenty years call for a more complicated answer. Presidential power has increased by becoming more extended, scattered, and shared; it has decreased by becoming less of a prerogative, less unilateral, and less closely held by the man himself. The right word for what has happened to the power of the office is diffusion, not dissipation. This condition exists, not basically because Congress or other groups have made successful grabs at the president's power, but because of the very nature of modern policy-making and the growth of federal activity.

Consider for a moment the antibureaucracy Reagan transition bureaucracy. This effort, writ small, is a good snapshot of what has happened to presidential power. The president-elect begins before inauguration with a $2 million, taxpayer-funded budget, a building, a motor pool, a minimum of seven dozen advisory committees, a communications system, and official stationery for the "Office of the President-Elect."

What, a person may well ask, is going on here? Certainly some of this is intended only for public consumption, some as a political liaison job for building the relations necessary to a presidential party. But there is more than that, and it shows up in the substantive work of the various policy groups and "issue clusters." The president-elect may have a few general themes in mind, but to have any impact on complex modern policies he needs to have specific, usually highly technical, proposals. Moreover, whatever he might want to do to increase *or* to decrease federal government activity, he is automatically entangled in a web of relations with other people who can have a decisive impact on the same issue—not just congressmen, but a bureaucracy of congressional staffs numbering well over 13,000 professionals; not just mayors and governors, but analysts and lobbyists to represent these elected officials in Washington; not just grasping interest groups, but a mini-industry in the nation's capital employing 15,000 or more full-time professionals.

The exact numbers are less important than the fact that the federal government has acquired responsibilities requiring successful linkages between all manner of public, semi-public, and private groups. This applies not only to functions acquired in the last two decades—consumer protection, medical and school financing, mass transportation, and so on—but also to older tasks enhanced with more demanding goals: occupational safety, natural resource use and protection, economic management and industrial revitalization, and so on. Can the president, with a few themes and a handful of aides, negotiate his ideas through these linkages and past the many other knowledgeable participants with a stake in what he is doing? Not likely. And so the helpers, offices, and briefing books pile up on the president-elect no less than on the presidency.

The United States does not have a high-level, government-wide civil service that could (as in European countries) help a new chief executive and his top team turn their ideas into administrative realities; there is scarcely even a low-level civil service in the White House to help with the paperwork. The increasing resort to transition bureaucracies is one accommodation to this fact, thereby loading onto the presidency more of the responsibility for turning themes into playable scores than would otherwise be the case. But with or without a competent civil service, the very nature of federal activity impels the presidency to become a predictable bureaucracy so that other participants can play their parts.

Imagine, for example, a president committed to replacing government regulation with market competition and incentives in various policy areas. Having grown accustomed to the old regulations and possessing the power to make or break any proposed "market solution" that affects them, people in Congress, the departments, interest groups, and subnational governments need to know what, in detail, the president proposes to do. To create a market where none has been implies some forethought about how far it will extend, what transitional arrangements with the affected groups will be made, how this will affect programs in related areas, what rules of competition will be enforced, and who will enforce them. Since markets typically impose some costs and spillovers that many people consider unfair, thought must also be given to compensations, subsidies, and other kinds of protections (more regulations!). All of this implies presidential helpers who can work knowledgeably with planners, analysts, economists, administrators, inspectors, lawyers, not to mention all the political legwork involved. To survive in this kind of world, the president needs to be surrounded by policy technocrats no less than by the political technocrats of his quasi-party. But how can the president know that all these bright, committed, and (like the rest of us) self-interested people are doing what *he* would want?

The President as Manager

Whoever the president and whatever his style, the political and policy bureaucracies crowd in on him. They are there in his office to help, but their needs are not necessarily his needs. Delegation is unavoidable; yet no one aide or combination of aides has his responsibilities or takes his oath of office. However much the president trusts personal friends, political loyalists, or technocrats, he is the person that the average citizen and history will hold account-able.

If this diagnosis of the presidential office is close to the truth, then there is one big prescription. The president must take responsibility for deprogramming himself. Since the deep structure of the office is shaped by trends well outside his control, the president must try to preserve his maneuverability within this structure—a maneuverability not just in the images of personal style, but in the substance of work that gets done around him. Trusting a chief of staff or a few senior aides is not enough. Behind the scenes, the president must manage and manipulate if he is not to be suffocated by the political and policy techno-crats of Washington.

To manage is something that falls between administering in detail and merely presiding in general. At most, the president himself can directly administer one or two major issues and half a dozen or so senior aides. And to preside is a dan-gerous abdication to the momentum of forces around him. It is difficult to put the president's management chore into words without seeming to be cynical or sinister. To speak of the president's manipulation of the people in his office should not summon up Nixonian memories, for if ever there was a president cut off from (though criminally responsible for) what was going on in his own office, it was Richard Nixon. The appropriate mentor is still the first inhabitant of the modern presidency, Franklin Roosevelt. For a paraplegic president, his appre-ciation for the primary task of internal management came almost instinctively: to use those who waited on him without becoming dependent on them.

Roosevelt had his tactics; other presidents will have theirs. But the basic necessity for personal management remains and grows as modern presidents become increasingly penned in. Programmed more than paralyzed, today's president needs many different eyes and ears for the things he should know, legs to take him where he should be, and protective devices to avoid situations that leave him vulnerable.

How to do all this? The exact structure and personalities are less important than sometimes thought. Given the record of recent administrations, there are some useful guidelines to be drawn from experience, usually of the painful variety.

1. Self-awareness is the place to begin. The president, by his own actions and even more by the anticipations of his actions that he creates in other people, generates a kind of de facto management system. The more he is willing to do, the more he will be asked to do. The more questions he will take rather than passing them to others, the more he will be asked. The more unconditional his support of his staff seems, the less the incentive for good performance. The

more widely spread his trust, the less its value. These are obvious points familiar to any executive, but under the crush of daily emergencies and decisions in the presidency they become more important and easier to overlook.

2. Selectivity needs to be a part of self-awareness. Since the president can personally administer only a few issues and can manage only a handful of aides, he needs to know the one or two things that matter to him most, subject to changing circumstances. Without this selectivity, there are no goals to work toward and disorientation quickly spreads throughout his office and administration. Most of the rest of his presidency, to put it bluntly, will consist of managing for damage control in the history books.

3. Self-awareness and selectivity have to be linked to a consciousness of the bureaucratic terrain in his own office through which the president is moving. A presidential bureaucracy—rather, a collection of bureaucracies—seems to be with us to stay, and its workings pose special hazards for the president. The following are perhaps the most common hazards:

• Presidential staffs tend to bring into the presidency conflicts and controversies raging among departments, congressional committees, and interest groups. This means that the president, unless he makes a conscious effort to the contrary, is likely to be closely identified with the inevitable ebb and flow of debate that occurs on complex policy matters—a tentative finding this way, an interim decision that way. Even the most firm-minded president is bound to appear indecisive in this situation. Perhaps the best safeguard is for the president to allow a great deal of "precooking" of policies some distance away from him, with low-visibility participation by presidential staff members to protect his interests. This approach seems most appropriate for the bulk of issues that are not among his few priority concerns.

• Each presidential staff, in order to carry weight inside the office and with outsiders, seeks to invent ways that allow it to claim that its members are acting "at the direction of the president." And each such invention ties the president more closely to the work of unfamiliar helpers. Because all these people have a stake in generating presidential decisions, his influence and public standing are likely to be on the line in more places than he might wish. A president can help himself by making sure that issues coming to him really are matters on which he, rather than someone else, has to make a formal decision. The exact machinery is less important than the need for the president to choose some particular system—an administrative secretary, a chief of staff, a secretariat, a formal procedure of decision memoranda—for disciplining the way he gets into decisions and for keeping tabs on what he, rather than anyone else, wants done. It is only the president who, by his own actions, can enforce and sustain any such system.

• The presidential bureaucracy has a natural desire for self-preservation. Internal conflicts which would convey more information to the president by being openly fought out tend to be submerged in sub rosa court politics inside the White House and the rest of the EOP. Rather than a free-for-all among presidential staffs, what typically exists is a kind of truce by which each staff settles for a piece of the president's attention and decision making. This hardly helps the president to know what is going on. To overcome this tendency the president, again by his own behavior, needs to make it clear that he expects in-house disagreements, that suppression of contrary views is punished, and that all can live to fight another day—as long as the battle does not continue once the president has made up his own mind. The same staff procedures used to keep the president out of unnecessary decisions can probably be used to create a fair hearing and due process for such internal conflicts.

• Because of the trends identified earlier, the presidential office tends to be divided into two large hemispheres: a political technocracy and a policy technocracy. On almost every conceivable issue the president needs to hear, unvarnished, the facts from both sides. In general, the competition between the two hemispheres for presidential attention has tended to become unequal as media attention has increased and political fragmentation grown. Political staff work tends to drive out longer-term, institutional interests in policy and administration. This tendency is amplified if the president makes it clear that he gives serious attention only to his short-term personal stakes in the issues coming before him.

4. Paradoxically, one of the most effective ways for the president to manage his own office is through the use of his appointees in the departments and agencies. If these department heads are known to have intimate knowledge of the president's thinking, and therefore seem likely to be backed by the president in disputes with White House staffers, White House aides will likely be kept in their proper place as assistants to the president rather than as assistant presidents.

Unfortunately, every new administration seems to raise false expectations by proclaiming that the president intends to manage through his cabinet officers, or words to that effect. In fact, their individual frames of reference are too narrow to give the president all the perspective he needs, and their collective interests are a fiction without active presidential support and guidance. Hence the president must manage through both his own office's bureaucracies *and* his department and agency heads. In general, the cabinet is a communication—not a decision-making device. It carries information to and from the president. At their best, cabinet officers help the president by telling him things he would not otherwise hear, by conveying his sense of a unified administration, by keeping presidential staff in line. It is the president's management job to see that when department and agency heads fight among themselves—as they inevitably will—it is done in front of him and tells him something worth knowing.

5. In addition to his political staffs, policy offices, and cabinet officers, the president typically has access to his closest personal friends: the Kitchen Cabinet. Experience suggests that it is safest to keep these advisers outside his office staffs or official departmental family. The reason is simple and practical. If the president is to protect himself as he manages, any other person must be dispensable. Because not everyone wishes the president well, putting a close personal friend in an official position leaves both that person, and through him, the president, vulnerable. Informal advisers attract less attention, are changed more easily, and perform their greatest services precisely because they are not caught up in the daily grind of government machinery. Exceptions can, of course, be found; President Eisenhower and President Kennedy made effective use of their brothers in official positions, as did President Truman of his friend John Snyder. But for every Snyder there is a Bert Lance, and it is just as well to recognize the risks at the outset. Only the president can decide whether it is worth having someone so close that his presidency will be gravely wounded through that person's loss to scandal, the appearance of scandal, or larger policy ends.

Cautions about these five hazards add up to an approach to presidential management that tries to use the various tensions and counterpressures inherent in the job. The counterpressures within his own office staffs, between them and cabinet officers, and between all these and the president's closest personal loyalists are opportunities as well as constraints. A president with some self-awareness can use this cat's cradle of tensions to help see to it that he is at the center of things when he wants to be and "out of it" when he needs to be. The management aim cannot, therefore, simply be to create a unified team; it must be to create the counterpressures that will be useful to him, lest he become victimized by his own helpers.

Others, no doubt, will see things differently, but this much seems clear: a modern president who cannot govern his own office is unlikely to be able to govern anything else.

NOTES

Source: Reprinted by permission from ICS Press, San Francisco, Calif.

1. A brief description is contained in National Academy of Public Administration, *A Presidency for the 1980s* (Washington, D.C.: NAPA, 1980), chapter 2.
2. The current advisory mechanisms available to the president are surveyed in Richard Pious, *The American Presidency* (New York: Basic Books, 1979), chapters 7–10.
3. From the Wayne Coy Paper, "Memorandum of October 26, 1940," in the Franklin D. Roosevelt Presidential Library, Hyde Park.

Chapter 3

The Evolution of the White House Staff

SAMUEL KERNELL

The successes and failures of presidents have been increasingly attributed to the performances of their staffs. After the Iran-Contra scandal broke, a special commission headed by former Senator John G. Tower examined the staffing system that yielded such ill-advised schemes as the exchange of missiles for hostages and the diversion of funds to the Nicaraguan Contras. The commission faulted many on the White House staff, as well as the president, but the first political casualty was Chief of Staff Donald Regan, whose replacement was announced before he had a chance to resign. According to the Tower Commission, Regan did not adequately inquire about the actions of others once news of irregularities began to appear in the press. These charges rang true to many Washingtonians. When he took over the staff early in the president's second term, Regan sharply cut the number of senior staff and installed a pyramidal White House organization with himself at the apex. As a result, President Reagan came to depend on his chief more than he had on any individual during his first term, and when his chief failed to perform, the president was left uninformed in the midst of a crisis.

The Iran-Contra scandal has begged for explanation because it contrasted so starkly with the president's first-term successes. Students of the presidency, including Garry Trudeau, the cartoonist of "Doonesbury," had noted Reagan's lackadaisical work habits, and heavy reliance on staff. But the president's remarkable legislative successes in forcing a Democratic House to accept sharp reductions in social programs, equally sharp hikes in defense spending, and a major tax cut had transformed this potential weakness into a strength. (One liberal Democratic congressman confided in 1982 that the president's example had persuaded him to delegate more responsibility to his office staff.) Kudos were heaped on James Baker for organizing Reagan's legislative strategies and Michael Deaver for keeping his public image well burnished. Independent of the individual staff members, the triumvirate that governed the early Reagan White House—Baker, Deaver, and Edwin Meese—was widely complimented as an ideal form of organization.

If awareness of the importance of presidential staffing peaked under Reagan, it certainly did not begin with him. Carter's micromanagement style overloaded the president and prevented him from developing priorities, Nixon's oversized staff of loyalists headed by H. R. Haldeman and John Ehrlichman was widely judged to have contributed to the misdeeds of Watergate. Every president's organization, in fact, has received a measure of credit or blame for the president's performance. But with the president's performance so dependent on the workings of his staff, and the staff's performance apparently dependent on its organization, what accounts for the structure of the modern White House Office?

The conventional scholarly answer is that the organization of the White House staff reflects the style and work habits of the incumbent president.[1] Staffing arrangements have been as individual and as variable as the men who occupied the office. Thus former General Dwight D. Eisenhower rejected Harry Truman's informal staff system and installed an orderly chain of command headed by a chief of staff. John Kennedy, self-assured and charismatic, replaced Ike's structure with an entourage of close advisors who, with himself as team leader, managed the White House informally. Similar personalized arrangements can be observed for each successor. The history of the modern White House can be recounted in terms of highly individualistic, four-to-eight-year bundles of organizational reformulations.

Not only does the conventional wisdom hold that presidents distinctively mold their staffs, it also strongly endorses this influence. Writing in the 1960s, one leading presidential scholar concluded that the president requires "the utmost flexibility in the choice, number, characteristics, and deployment of his staff."[2] This highly personalized view of staff structure appears to leave little to be explained. But appearances are deceptive. Any number of organizational arrangements might satisfy a given president's needs. From all accounts, President Reagan found Donald Regan's strong-chief approach to White House management as congenial as the more open and less hierarchical staff administration of the first-term troika. And when Regan left, his successor, Howard Baker, set up a completely different operation, again without apparent discomfort to the president.

Also, critics have complained, the White House staff has become a separate entity, frequently working at cross purposes with the intent and needs of the president. Increasingly, presidential lapses in judgment and policy appear to reflect failed staff work. The White House Office is clearly far different from what it once was. No longer just the president's entourage of cronies and campaign staff, it appears to have been shaped by more significant and more stable forces than can be found in the comings and goings of presidents.

Development of the Modern White House

Unlike the other presidential agencies created in the Reorganization Act of 1939, or those introduced subsequently, the White House Office was not intended to participate in administration. Instead, its attentions were to be devoted exclusively to the incidental needs of the president, to be, as Roosevelt said, his legs. Consequently, it was no slight to the office or the presidency that the staff was initially kept small and free of statutory responsibilities. These men and women were expected to be factotums.

Shortly after entering office in 1933, Franklin Roosevelt assembled a dozen or so assistants to help plan his assault on the Great Depression. He had also inherited roughly fifty clerks and secretaries from the outgoing Hoover administration.[3] As with his predecessors, many of these were on loan from various agencies, which presumably saw some advantage in having their people stationed close to the president. Precise figures on the total staff are unavailable, since the White House Office was not created until the Reorganization Act allowed a modest professional staff of six newly created assistants to the president.

When James Rowe, the first of these assistants, returned from World War II, he called a friend in the Truman White House to ask how things had changed. He recalled later that they had "nine people doing what I used to do," and guessed that "nowadays they must have 300 or 400 doing what I used to do."[4] Until the aftermath of Watergate reversed the trend, the president's staff grew about five percent a year.[5] Although there seem to have been few constraints on growth, the aggregate numbers imply that presidents have avoided formal increases in staff. Until 1979 they were not required to report to Congress the number of aides loaned to the White House from the agencies, and they clearly preferred this inconspicuous, informal way of expanding. Gradually the number of detailees grew in relation to budgeted staff, until a new president would clean up the bookkeeping by including the positions in the White House Office budget.

Watergate and the subsequent criminal convictions of Richard Nixon's aides drew attention to the president's staff as no event had before or has since. An obvious way for Nixon's successors to dissociate themselves from the stigma of the imperial presidency was to trim personnel. In 1976 Jimmy Carter assured the American people that pruning the staff would be one of the first items of business in his new administration. The trend continued with Ronald

Reagan, although some members of Congress charged that he misrepresented the number of detailees working in the White House.[6] While such borrowing makes firm estimates elusive, the White House Office seems to have leveled off at about 400 people.

Although organizational manuals for each White House do not exist, the increase in size seems to have been paralleled by an increase in complexity. As the number and variety of tasks multiplied, duties were divided and eventually parceled among subunits. The formal designation of roles became more common and so did organization charts.

The development of specialization and chains of command has proceeded with seeming inevitability. Reviewing an early draft of his administrative reform plan, Roosevelt told its author, Louis Brownlow, that he did not want his assistants consigned to "little boxes." Nonetheless, he did make two formal assignments. Aggravated with the tardiness of legal advice from the Justice Department, he created the White House Special Counsel's Office. The counsel, Samuel I. Rosenman, however, spent more time writing speeches than advising on legal matters. Roosevelt also designated the first press secretary, Stephen Early, although previous presidents had informally assigned aides to tend to Washington correspondents.

Even in hindsight, Roosevelt's staff arrangements resist classification. Thomas Corcoran and Harry Hopkins, arguably the most valued aides, were never members of the White House Office. And those who were rarely interacted: the president's personal and appointments secretaries were located in the west wing of the White House, and his new assistants across the street. "Not much of a presence," William Hopkins, veteran executive clerk of the White House Office, summed up this first official staff.[7]

Early in Truman's first term, when long-time personal friend Ed McKim tried to assert management control and began drafting an organization chart, the president promoted him to another job away from the White House. Other efforts to assign fellow staffers to organizational niches were no more successful.[8] Reflecting his military experience, Dwight Eisenhower introduced fixed assignments and a chain of command for the White House staff. But he did so without formal titles, organization charts, or other appurtenances of bureaucracy.

Presidents Kennedy and Johnson restored more informal relations and more fluid assignments, but the staffs greater size and responsibilities meant that they could not return to Roosevelt's desultory management style. Periodically, Lyndon Johnson would become frustrated with his loose staff structure and, in the words of Bill Moyers, get in one of his "organizational moods."[9] Over the years at least five senior aides were assigned, on arriving at the White House, the job of charting a formal staff structure. Since there was little formal division of labor among Johnson's staff, the attempt was doomed. Johnson would look at each effort, wad it up and throw it away, and instruct the now wary aide to try again. Eventually, the president would let the matter drop until some energetic recruit would rekindle his enthusiasm.[10]

No subsequent president has had to suffer Johnson's frustrations. All worked within the confines of formal organizational designations for each staff member. Richard Nixon's White House staff underwent two major reorganizations, and the finishing touches were being given to a third when Watergate struck. Organizational charts identified the implications of proposed changes.[11] Similarly, Presidents Ford and Carter employed charts and formal titles as a way of understanding and at times reorganizing the staff.

According to one account, when Edwin Meese, the head of Reagan's transition team, asked to see what the White House Office looked like, the Carter people produced an elaborate chart that located more than 400 budgeted staff among the twenty or so subunits of the White House. Meese accepted it matter-of-factly. Some changes were made, of course. James Baker had agreed to assume day-to-day management responsibilities as chief of staff, while Meese would take charge of policy planning in his position as counselor, and offices were shuffled accordingly. Some offices, such as Communications under David Gergen, became more important; others, including that of the national security advisor, less. But no major functions or organizational divisions were deleted or added by the new administration.

Both the number of formal subunits and levels of hierarchy have steadily increased, from one level and eleven subunits under Eisenhower to four levels and twenty-nine subunits under Reagan.[12] These increases in size and complexity have transformed a small group closely attentive and responsive to the president into a larger, more formal organization governed by rules and procedures, and have given it the appearance of a steadily institutionalizing organization rather than one remade in each new president's image. The continuity in the organization of Carter's and Reagan's staff further undermines the idea that staff organization merely reflects each president's style.

The decisions of presidents and senior aides provide more direct evidence. In many instances, they appear to have been engaged in a rearguard action to prevent bureaucratization, rather than an expansionist venture. During the transition in 1968, President Nixon's chief, H. R. Haldeman, summoned the new White House aides and read to them Brownlow's principles for assistants, emphasizing the passage instructing aides to cultivate a "passion for anonymity."[13] At some moment in each of their terms, presidents from Johnson to Carter inveighed against large staffs and occasionally ordered cutbacks.[14] One of the ironies of Watergate is that by late 1972 President Nixon had decided that his staff had "grown like Topsy" and directed a disbelieving aide to come up with a plan to cut it by half early in the second term.[15] If neither presidents nor their aides have wanted larger, more complex staffs, why has the White House developed the way it has?

Toward an Explanation of White House Development

One answer is that while the upper reaches of the staff system may have been distinctively shaped by each president, its overall size and complexity have been dictated by the growth of the national government, particularly the president's increased responsibilities since World War II.[16] Or as Donald Rumsfeld, Gerald Ford's chief of staff, commented, "You have all these threads, and the White House staff's function is to see that those threads get through the needle's eye in a reasonably coherent way."[17] In this regard the president's staff is unexceptional; the senior civil service and congressional staffs may have grown and professionalized even faster.[18] According to this argument, work load drives development more than presidential proclivities do.

A variant of this argument claims that the growth of responsibilities has induced a profound transformation, "Whatever his particular policy objectives, whatever his personality and style, the modern president is driven by . . . formidable expectations to seek control over the structures and processes of government . . . [to create] an institutional system responsive to his needs as a political leader."[19] This desire for responsiveness has prompted presidents to centralize decision making in the White House and to politicize the bureaucracy.[20] The size and complexity of the modern office are the products of this centralization.

Clearly, this explanation elucidates one motivating force of presidential behavior. To gain the cooperation he felt he deserved from others, every president has tried to extend his control into the jurisdiction of others. But insufficient responsiveness has less to do with the increasing volume of demands than with the structure of American politics. Suspicious of the conservative sympathies of the old line departments, Franklin Roosevelt located many of the New Deal agencies under his direct supervision. Each subsequent president has followed his lead because, although some may have been more disposed to assert unilateral authority than others, the search for greater responsiveness inheres in the predicament of the office, in the clash of expectations of presidential leadership with a system of separated powers. The search is neither more nor less than the pursuit of power in a system all presidents come to feel has dealt them too little.[21] When Truman remarked of Eisenhower, "He'll sit here and he'll say, 'Do this! Do that!' *And nothing will happen*," he was talking as much about the office as about his successor.[22] Since every president, most of the time, has wished for greater responsiveness, its ever-present pursuit cannot alone explain the modern evolution of the office.

The argument does, however, identify vital features of presidential leadership. Presidents are constantly probing the boundaries of their control, and where they meet little resistance, new authority can be established. Each successive decision becomes marginally less costly as accommodation becomes unnecessary and the president's options less confined by other Washingtonians' prerogatives. The growing size and complexity of the White House Office offers indirect evidence of the steady successes of postwar presidents in poaching in the domains of others.

The interests of presidents and their fellow Washingtonians have been diverging for a long time, and in ways that could not always be reconciled through negotiations and reciprocity. The president, unlike other politicians, has the nation as his constituency. He may at times find a tactical advantage in cultivating support among particular segments of the population, but such concerns are clearly secondary. By contrast, members of Congress represent local constituencies. However interested a congressman or senator may be in a national policy, his or her job requires servicing the district or state first. Similarly, when party leaders were still consequential political figures, they considered their responsibilities to be little more than collecting the claims of state party organizations and presenting them to the White House for action. In both instances, insatiable particularism frequently conflicted with the president's notion of the national interest. It still does.

The conventional view is that these differing perspectives provided the basis of reciprocity, and generally they did. Presidents swapped specific jobs and projects for support for their programs so routinely that expectations sometimes became institutionalized in such informal rules as senatorial courtesy. But in many instances, such exchanges compromised the president's goals. Evidence in the historical record shows that on these occasions, presidents sought to skirt traditional rules. Even Franklin Roosevelt—considered a paragon of the bargaining president—at times chose strategies that undermined the political order founded on reciprocity. He did so when he allowed the Internal Revenue Service to expose corruption among Democratic machines and send the leaders to prison. He did so when he directed Harry Hopkins to create a federal administration for delivering relief programs instead of turning them over to expectant Democratic organizations skilled in the efficient distribution of patronage. And he did so when he resisted the patronage claims of senators who wanted their nominees rather than New Deal professionals to run federal relief and public works programs in their states.[23] These actions reaped political ill will, but they preserved the president's national policy objectives. Well before presidents became habituated to centralization, their preoccupation with the needs of the national constituency sometimes led them to resist arrangements among community members predicated on the axiom that a collective good was the simple sum of highly divisible parts.

Presidents' concern with providing collective goods may explain their preoccupation with other politicians' insufficient responsiveness and their efforts to extend presidential authority. To explain their success, however, one must investigate the weakening of the forces that once contained them and kept political relations in a state of mutual dependency. The evolution of the White House staff is as much a result of the transformation of American politics beyond the Oval Office as of the efforts of presidents searching for responsiveness.

Today's Washington is not the one that greeted President Roosevelt in 1933. Gone are the national party committees that represented state and local party organizations, whose interests had to be attended to by elected politicians. The national apparatus was especially important to the president because it ran his campaign and, after the victory, served as a clearinghouse for the distribution of federal patronage. Gone too is the power of the national party chairman. Although the chairman was always subordinate to the president, that did not keep James Farley from openly courting Democratic delegates for the 1940 nomination or deter him and his successor Ed Flynn from openly feuding with the White House staff.[24] National party chairmen could be disregarded only at the risk of alienating state party organizations.

The stature of congressional leaders has also diminished. When Roosevelt took office, they spoke with such authority that they could cut a deal with the president and return to their committees in the full expectation of being able to implement it. Had the president created an in-house congressional liaison office, as was occasionally recommended, he would have been tacitly challenging the position of the Big Four legislative leaders with whom he lunched each week to plan legislative strategy. Such a tactic would have inevitably redounded to his disadvantage, which, of course, is why Roosevelt spurned such advice. But today the president can no longer rely on the floor leaders, and the congressional liaison office is a necessity.

The limiting power of the press has also changed.[25] In 1933 a comparatively small, homogeneous band of Washington newspaper correspondents controlled the president's access to the citizenry, and to court their favor he obligingly conducted "family gatherings" with them twice a week. For Roosevelt to have avoided the press conference would have been tantamount to surrendering the national stage to his adversaries. He did contemplate more frequent fireside radio chats, but until the war he resisted having more than an average of two a year because he did not want to dilute their effect. Such dedicated presidential courtship of White House correspondents became more desultory, however, as television deprived them of their near monopoly. Before long, broadcast journalists had reduced them to second-class citizenship, and recent presidents have decided that the fewer press conferences the better.

All these evolving political relations are rooted in forces well beyond the control of politicians. Ultimately, the arrival of broadcast technology, especially television, ended the grip of print journalists on political communication from Washington and thereby weakened their leverage at the White House. This does not mean that presidents, the political system's most resourceful participants, merely acquiesced to the new limits and opportunities presented by political evolution; when it served their purposes, they became agents of change. President Kennedy, concerned that the press would turn against him sooner or later, confided to a friend that he adopted televised press conferences to communicate directly to the American people.[26]

To summarize, the modern White House staff is the cumulative product of presidents' strategic adaptations to an evolving political community. Presidents seeking responsiveness probe for new power. Other participants in the political process, because of their own deteriorating power, have found themselves at times unable to resist. The cumulative result of presidential encroachment has been the steady centralization of policy making within the White House. Internally, it has taken the form of increased work, which in turn has stimulated the growth of staff and the subdivision of work into more specialized tasks. This sequence by which presidential strategy has begotten staff structure can be confirmed in the history of the White House Office as an organization. One finds it in the character of new staff work and the timing of its introduction, in its subsequent routinization as resistance from outsiders weakens, and ultimately, in the efforts required of modern presidents and their senior staff aides to harness their staffs disparate activities to achieve coherent leadership.

The Emergence of White House Managers

The modern White House staff is a two-tiered organization. The lower tier consists of such line units responsible for conducting the president's external relations as the press secretary, the congressional liaison staff, the secretary to the cabinet, and the speechwriters. The upper tier comprises staff who are primarily responsible for planning and internal maintenance of the organization. While such a distinction is not applicable to the early staffs, it is essential for understanding the evolution of the modern White House. Even President

Truman, who was his own office manager, had aides such as John Steelman, Clark Clifford, and Charles Murphy to help supervise the activities of others. More recently, formal offices such as the chief of staff have been created for this purpose. Whether or not such offices are present, however, a half dozen or so senior aides who work directly with the president will assume some management control.

These two domains of activity place their members in different settings. As the number and variety of routine external tasks increase, layers of specialized subunits proliferate to handle them. On-the-job training and selective recruitment results in a cadre of experts. How well an aide works the Hill, monitors public opinion, analyzes diplomatic messages, or performs other specialized tasks determines his worth to the organization and relationship to the president. Only as the president requires a particular expertise will an aide be asked to write a memo or be summoned to the Oval Office. The rest of the aide's time, which is most of the time, will be spent on routine relations.

Those charged with planning and coordinating the affairs of the line staff, by contrast, remain generalists, working closely with the president on a wide range of issues. They confront the work outside the White House the same way the president does, not as matters requiring routine relations but as exigencies that demand presidential action. Because their job is to help the president do his job, they must be responsive to his personal style and work habits.

And yet the imperatives of size and complexity are no different for the president's senior staff than for the managers of any other organization. Beneath the surface idiosyncrasy of personalities, predictable organizational trends toward rationalization prevail here as well. Presidents, ill disposed to work within formal structures, may resist such bureaucratization, but they do so at the risk of leaving line staff insufficiently supervised, resulting in such pathologies as presidential overload, aides interpreting for themselves what actions are in the best interest of the president, and fights among subunits for influence over policy.

The White House is the president's workplace. Some presidents work well with many assistants; others prefer to work intimately with only two or three. Some prefer formal and highly structured staffs; others like to mix up assignments and have no fixed schedule for staff meetings. These work habits largely determine the organization and responsibilities of the senior staff, the White House managers.

Yet the special demands on coordination made by the growing size and complexity of the White House staff suggest that the president's choices in these matters will not be totally free.[27] What are the implications for the senior staff of the presidential strategy of centralization and the structure it begets? Coping with a large, complex organization involves more than fine tuning for maximum efficiency. In the absence of coordination, not only will some tasks fail to be performed while others will be unnecessarily duplicated, but also the organization will be rife with personal disputes and battles over jurisdiction.

Organizations need policing. The more complex the organization, the greater the problem posed by the cover of anonymity. And staffs with huge turnover, such as the president's, will have the most serious problems, since its members have little stake in the integrity of procedures but may have a great stake in policy decisions, Hence they find themselves exploiting or even sacrificing procedural integrity to advocate certain policies. This divergence of interests is one reason the White House Office has become so notorious for the leaks and infighting that frustrate the best efforts of every president.

Much of the work senior managers do is to relieve the president from coordination qua policing. President Ford's first chief of staff, Donald Rumsfeld, commented that the chief of staff was always "heaving his body" between White House groups to make sure that the process worked.[28] Similarly, Michael Deaver, one of Ronald Reagan's first-term senior managers, described his role as the "protector" of the president, "Everybody who runs a department within the White House has a constituency," he explained, "And they . . . want to get those people off their backs, so they dump them on us in the scheduling office in hopes that the president will take care of it."[29]

Such stratagems have a purpose. It is not writer's block that makes the speechwriters chronically tardy in turning in drafts for review. They simply do not want the text changed. Lower-level employees leak embarrassing information about their colleagues to gain an advantage as the moment of decision approaches. They push decisions onto the president to avoid blame if things go badly and to show their influence if they go well. Size and complexity imply more than the need for managers to make sure the organizational parts mesh. They must also contain the competition for influence and channel it in constructive ways.[30] As the White House becomes more complex, so too do these management problems. Presidents who manage their own offices will increasingly risk being overwhelmed with police work.

In the early days, senior aides were a president's trusted advisors, and chief executives could mold staffs to their liking without creating a crisis. The experience of Roosevelt, Truman, and Eisenhower suggested that the White House staff could and should be organized however the president wanted. Yet even during these presidencies, elements of organizational imperative were emerging, so that now the question of how to organize the staff has become a paramount concern of those who study and advise presidents. . . .

Governability and the Modern White House

A partial list of the responsibilities of the modern White House Office includes managing the executive branch, tending to the political needs of Washington politicians, planning the president's program, and generating support for him in Congress and across the nation. Such services are now routinely performed by a staff that was originally mandated to do little more than coordinate the flow of people and messages to and from the White House. Expanded work has produced a bureaucracy comprising hundreds of specialists. Presidential aides who deal on an equal footing with other government leaders hold positions created fifty years earlier for half a dozen self-effacing, circumambient White House assistants. Discussions of the nation's governability now invariably turn to the emergence of these aides who have great power and little legitimacy.

Critics complain that the White House staff meddles in affairs best left to others, and the performances of recent aides offer them outstanding justification. Failing to obtain cooperation from the FBI in investigating Daniel Ellsberg, Egil Krogh, a second-tier staffer in the Nixon White House, organized the "White House plumbers" to break into the office of Ellsberg's doctor in hope of discovering incriminating evidence. A decade later, Oliver North, from his NSC office, diverted funds from the sale of missiles to Iran to aid the Contras in Nicaragua. Both men had seen their president frustrated in trying to accomplish his goals through legitimate channels. Zealous loyalty inspired each to undertake illegal actions that ultimately undermined the president they were so eager to serve. Such responsiveness presidents do not need.

Critics also charge that large staffs insulate presidents, preventing them from acquiring political information essential for building a governing coalition in a fragmented governmental system.[31] The vantage of White House aides is, or soon becomes, too parochial for its exclusive counsel to be sufficient. Only by understanding other politicians who view policy choices from different perspectives can a president assess the likely responses of those whose cooperation he ultimately needs. Despite protests from his secretaries of state and defense, President Reagan remained convinced that politicians and the American public would view his dealings with the ayatollah as something other than trading arms for hostages. Had he brought key senators into his confidence, he probably would not have continued to harbor such a naive view. Moreover, less self-reliance at the outset would have subsequently allowed him to avoid bearing the full brunt of responsibility for failed policies.

If somehow the growth and activities of the White House staff had been arrested at a more modest level, these critics charge, presidents and the nation would be a lot better off. For them, the staff is the problem, and pruning it is the solution. "Rigorous efforts should be made to keep this staff small," was the first guideline offered Reagan's transition team by the National Academy of Public Administration in 1980.[32] Presumably, if there were fewer Egil Kroghs or Oliver Norths in the White House, there would be fewer opportunities for staff to run wild. Yet causality runs primarily in the other direction. The modern White House Office is the cumulative result of the ways presidents have engaged an evolving political community. Had the web of mutual dependency that obliged presidents to work closely with fellow Washingtonians not weakened, the size of their staffs would have remained inconsequential to leadership, and therefore would not have grown so. As presidents grew self-reliant and they centralized their leadership, however, they began to outfit themselves with the necessary resources. Consequently, each president, liberal Democrat and conservative Republican alike, has broadened the mandate of his staff as he sought to take on certain activities that his predecessors had relied on others to do. To assume that the governability of the modern presidency simply required reducing the staff and returning it to its original size and importance would be to ignore the pervasive environmental forces that have transformed presidential leadership. To try to remove surgically the problems that attend large organization would only succeed in leaving the president an invalid, as self-reliant as ever, yet incapacitated.

Half a century ago, Louis Brownlow proclaimed, "The President needs help." The president still does, but now it is ironically in figuring out how best to use Brownlow's unintended progeny, the White House staff. Instead of trying to wish it away, the presence of a large, complex staff must be accepted as a given and its problems addressed forthrightly. The president's aides must be recognized for what they are—his agents, routinely representing his interest in their dealings with Capitol Hill and the permanent government. Their value derives from taking those actions the president would if he were undertaking the task himself. The White House staff offers the president economy, but it is not a free ride. The president must give the staff clear direction and vigilantly oversee its performance. Presidents who did so, such as Truman and Johnson, rarely had problems resulting from overly aggressive aides. In the absence of presidential guidance, aides can compromise the presidency and the country. Oliver North, who was identified early as someone who needed to be kept on a "very short leash" but was not, devised and executed his own version of America's foreign policy and very nearly brought down the president.[33] One of the major challenges to the president in staffing and organizing his office is to keep his agents on course, neither shirking their duty nor arrogating to themselves presidential decisions.

The other principal problem of modern presidential staffing is that layers of organization overly filter the president's contact with the outside community, preventing him from receiving advice from other political leaders. Much of the criticism of this problem should be directed toward the strategy of centralization that has removed presidents from the daily transactions of other politicians.

The president will be no more captive to staff than he allows. Yet the concern with suffocation by staff is a legitimate one. Beyond his daily reciting a mantra to remind himself of this, a president can do much to mold the White House staff into a creative force rather than allow it to become a retinue of sycophants.

The raw material for such shaping can be found in the pluralistic character of the modern White House staff. Its division of labor and recruitment of experts with varying backgrounds will create differing opinions about the president's priorities and interests. Moreover, outside pressures for representation on the White House staff are great. Presidents tacitly acknowledge this when they appoint aides from competing wings of their political party. And special groups and constituencies are diligent in trying to infiltrate the staff with one of their number and in cultivating contacts with presidential assistants.

None of these dynamics is peculiar to the modern White House. Each was present in the organization and politics of Truman's staff. But as decisions have steadily shifted to the White House, the forces promoting pluralism have intensified, making staffs more difficult to manage. Uncontrolled, the president's staff becomes a cacophony of voices, leaving outsiders wondering if anyone is in charge at the White House. And yet the political diversity of the modern White House offers an invaluable source of second opinions and new ideas.

The challenge facing modern presidents is to create staff structures that supervise without stultifying. Platitudes are easy; practice promises to be more difficult, for the task involves nothing less than balancing order and creativity. Procedures designed to keep the president's agents well tethered are apt to be enlisted by senior aides to suppress dissent from below. Also, the competition of political interests rarely conforms to the requirements of orderly administration. Protracted disputes among staff members may lead one faction to decide it can do better by disrupting established procedures it sees favoring its adversary. Senior aides bent on order and maintaining the integrity of their administrative apparatus may be quick to enlist hierarchical controls. But these methods easily become oversubscribed. Suppressing dissent only guarantees that competition will be vented in a more virulent form through leaks and personal attacks in the press. The hammered-out consensus of Reagan's first-term staff may have been taxing on its participants, but it unquestionably served him better than the pyramidal management system that replaced it.

Future presidents must better appreciate that the modern White House Office has evolved into more than their personal entourage of legislative or campaign aides. They may be present as the inner circle, but the legacy of centralization is a larger, more inclusive staff whose routine activities are increasingly important to, and to a degree responsive to, the outside political community. And while the president can fairly insist on and expect staff loyalty, he must recognize that as his agents, this staff will daily make choices that affect his welfare. The moral of recent presidential failures—Watergate, the Iran-Contra scandal, and the many pratfalls—reinforces the implication of the evolution of presidential staff. Managing the White House has become an essential feature of presidential leadership.

NOTES

From "The Evolution of the White House Staff," by Samuel Kernell. In J. E. Chubb and P. E. Peterson, eds., *Can Government Govern?* pp. 185–237. Copyright © 1989 by The Brookings Institution. Reprinted by permission.

1. James D. Barber, *The Presidential Character: Predicting Performance in the White House* (Englewood Cliffs, N.J.: Prentice-Hall, 1972).
2. Aaron Wildavsky, "Salvation by Staff: Reform and the Presidential Office," in Wildavsky, ed., *The Presidency* (Boston: Little, Brown, 1969), p. 700.
3. Transcript, William Hopkins oral history interview, pp. 2–4, Harry S. Truman Library.
4. Katie Louchheim, ed., *The Making of the New Deal: The Insiders Speak* (Cambridge, Mass.: Harvard University Press, 1983), p. 285.
5. For more information on the difficulties of measuring the size of the staff, see John Hart, *The Presidential Branch* (New York: Pergamon Press, 1987). pp. 97–109.
6. Personnel detailed to the White House for less than six months are exempted from reporting to the department that pays them. The Reagan administration interpreted this rule as allowing persons to be detailed indefinitely as long as they change positions in the departments within a six-month period. Judith Havemann, "How White House Beefed Up Staff," *Washington Post,* July 22, 1987, p. A17.
7. William Hopkins, interview with Samuel Kernell, Silver Spring, Md., Apr. 1, 1988. In searching through the Roosevelt archives, I turned up only one staff memo, to assistants telling them not to bother the president before 11:30. By the Nixon administration, such notes would become a standard way of coordinating staff activities.
8. George J. Schoeneman to Raymond R. Zimmerman, Jan. 4, 1946, Truman Library.
9. Bill Moyers to Bob Kintner, May 5, 1966, Lyndon B. Johnson Library.
10. By the time Robert Kintner joined the staff in 1966 and was promptly given this assignment, the other aides had become jaded and perhaps in a few instances opposed to the prospect of organizing Johnson. As Kintner made his rounds researching the different duties of staff members, they would pointedly explain to

him the futility of trying to organize the Johnson White House Office. See ibid. The tenor of comments to and about Kintner's efforts suggest that by that late date some aides may have feared reorganization would have removed them from direct access to the president.

11. For example, see John Dean, "Methods for Reorganizing the Executive Branch," Jan. 2, 1973, Richard M. Nixon collection, National Archives.

12. Eisenhower figures are from "Staff Work for the President and the Executive Branch," Legislative Background Collection, Johnson Library, n.d. For Reagan's White House structure, see Samuel Kernell and Samuel L. Popkin, eds., *Chief of Staff: Twenty-five years of Managing the Presidency* (Berkeley: University of California Press, 1986), p. 202.

13. See William Safire, *Before the Fall: An Inside View of the Pre-Watergate White House* (New York: Doubleday, 1975), p. 116.

14. *A Discussion with Gerald R. Ford: The American Presidency* (Washington, D.C.: American Enterprise Institute for Public Policy Research, 1977); and Jimmy Carter, *Keeping Faith: Memoirs of a President* (New York: Bantam, 1982).

15. Richard P. Nathan, *The Plot That Failed: Nixon and the Administrative Presidency* (New York: John Wiley, 1975), p. 53.

16. Hart, *Presidential Branch*, p. 114.

17. Kernell and Popkin, eds., *Chief of Staff*, p. 112.

18. Congressional staffs increased from 3,556 in 1957 to 11,432 in 1981; the number of committee staffers rose from 715 in 1955 to 2,865 in 1981. Norman J. Ornstein and others, *Vital Statistics on Congress, 1984–1985* (Washington, D.C.: American Enterprise Institute for Public Policy Research, 1984), pp. 121, 124.

19. Terry M. Moe, "The Politicized Presidency," in this volume.

20. Hugh Heclo, *A Government of Strangers: Executive Politics in Washington* (Washington, D.C.: Brookings, 1977), pp. 71–75; and Margaret J. Wyszomirski, "The De-Institutionalization of Presidential Staff Agencies," *Public Administration Review* 42 (Sept.–Oct., 1982): 448–58.

21. Thirty-five years ago, Robert A. Dahl and Charles E. Lindblom made precisely this point: "If presidential politicians could be given 'sufficient' *power* over the bureaucracies, the bureaucracies would be *responsive* to presidential politicians—a neat tautology." (Emphasis added.) *Politics, Economics, and Welfare: Planning and Politico-Economic Systems Resolved into Basic Social Processes* (New York: Harper and Row, 1953), p. 351.

22. Quoted in Richard E. Neustadt, *Presidential Power: The Politics of Leadership from FDR to Carter* (New York: John Wiley, 1980), p. 9.

23. Perhaps the most famous and well-documented instance of exposing a Democratic machine under FDR is the dismantling of Tom Pendergast's Kansas City organization. See Lyle W. Dorsett, *The Pendergast Machine* (New York: Oxford University Press, 1968). Roosevelt did not rebuke all machine claims for control of federal relief programs. Hopkins turned over most of the Chicago operations of the WPA to Ed Kelly's organization. Lyle Dorsett describes this exceptional arrangement and more typical patterns in *Franklin D. Roosevelt and the City Bosses* (Port Washington, N.Y.: Kennikat Press, 1977). An example of conflict between senatorial claims of patronage and the president's program can be found in Senator Ellender's insistent appeals for appointments for federal administrative posts in Louisiana. See James Rowe, "Memorandum for the President," May 19, 1939, Rowe papers, Franklin D. Roosevelt Library.

24. The relationship between president and national party apparatus since Roosevelt is discussed by Lester G. Seligman, "The Presidential Office and the President as Party Leader (with a Postscript on the Kennedy-Nixon Era)," in Jeff Fishel, ed., *Parties and Elections in an Anti-Party Age: American Politics and the Crisis of Confidence* (Bloomington: Indiana University Press, 1978), pp. 295–302.

25. For a fuller account of this transformation, see Samuel Kernell, *Going Public: New Strategies of Presidential Leadership* (Washington, D.C.: CQ Press, 1986), pp. 51–81.

26. Blaire Atherton French, *The Presidential Press Conference* (Washington, D.C.: University Press of America, 1982), p. 13.

27. Herbert A. Simon, *Administrative Behavior: A Study of Decision-making Processes in Administrative Organizations,* 2d. ed. (New York: Macmillan, 1957), pp. 26–28.

28. Kernell and Popkin, eds., *Chief of Staff,* pp. 172–73.

29. Colin Campbell, personal interview with Mike Deaver, May 3, 1983, Washington, D.C.

30. Lou Cannon provides a typical example in "Writing Reagan's Final Scenes," *Washington Post,* July 27, 1987, p. A1.

31. "Suffocation" is the way Richard E. Neustadt, writing long before the White House staff reached its current size, characterized the ill effects of large staffs; see "Presidency and Legislation: Planning the President's Program," *American Political Science Review* 49 (Dec., 1955): 102–21.

32. National Academy of Public Administration, *A Presidency for the 1980s* (Washington, D.C.: NAPA, 1980), p. 17.

33. Mayer and McManus, *Landslide,* p. 81.

Chapter 4

Memorandum [to JFK] on Staffing the President-Elect Prepared by Richard E. Neustadt October 30, 1960

Summary

This memorandum makes proposals for initial staffing of the work *you* have to do *in the first weeks after election*. These proposals deal, specifically, with staff to meet your *daily needs*, to get started on your January *program*, to get moving on your *personnel* selections, and to help you plan *next steps*. Proposals are grouped by categories: *continuing* jobs (six), *temporary* jobs (ten or more), jobs for *incumbents* (five), jobs to *defer* (many). One job is in a special category: the Budget directorship. This is not a scheme for White House and Executive Office organization. It is a start which can evolve into a scheme with the least risk of premature commitment on your part.

A president's needs for staff are bound to be different in many ways from a senator's, or even from a candidate's. But *your* needs in the presidency will also differ from Eisenhower's. Many of the needs and many of the differences cannot be fully understood, or met, until they have been experienced. They cannot be experienced until after January 20. The period before inauguration day is thus a time for caution.

In the next two weeks, however, you will have to staff yourself as president-elect, and the way you do so will affect what can be done thereafter. The staff you put together now, in the days after election, must be regarded as the core of your official staff, at least during your early months in office. It is trouble enough to build a staff group for the president-elect out of a campaign organization. It would be a waste of time—and you won't have the time—to shake your organization up again as you cease being president-elect and become president.

Some Things to Keep in Mind

In building a staff for the transition period, four rules of thumb are indicated:

First, define in your own mind the staff jobs for which *you* feel a concrete, immediate need in the weeks ahead. I have indicated below what I think these are. I have tried to be conservative. You may see more than I do. On the other hand, you may be unconvinced about the need for some of them. If so, do not let me or anyone talk you into anything. Wait until your own feel for your own situation validates or falsifies the needs we claim you have.

Presidential staffs have evolved in the last twenty years to meet two kinds of needs: on the one hand, needs of presidents themselves, for help in managing their daily chores, in gaining information, and in keeping control of key government decisions; on the other hand, needs of *other* government officials for backing, support, judgment, or decision, or a borrowing of prestige from the president. *At this stage, I urge you to consider only needs of the first sort—your own.* There will be plenty of people thinking about how you should be staffed in order to help them. You are the only person you can count on to be thinking about what helps *you.*

Second, as among the jobs you see you need, decide provisionally which ones are clearly continuing, bound to persist into your Presidency because foreseeable needs after January 20 are so much like the needs you face right now. Announce prospective government positions only for the men you put into *these* jobs. If you are uncertain about continuation (or about the man), or if a job is clearly temporary, treat it as a "consultantship," without long-term commitment and without a government title.

Third, think through the titles you intend for your continuing staff jobs, with reference to the work you have in mind and for the bureaucratic or public connotation of titles used by Eisenhower. The men whom you appoint now and intend to keep with you when you take office will be very much advantaged in their work during the interim if they are publicly identified quite early as prospective members of your *presidential* staff. But the titles you announce for them should suggest what you expect of them and, more importantly, should *not* suggest what you do *not* expect. Any title now in use by Eisenhower may attract a lot of "customary" business that you actually want handled somewhere else, or not at all, or on which you prefer experimentation. Such a title also may connote a ranking in your staff that you do not intend, or do not want to freeze; Adams's title "the assistant to the president" is a notable example.

Regarding choice of titles, I can spell out the connotations of those in present use and of alternatives, if and when you want me to.

In this connection, you will also find it useful to consider salary differentials among present titles. This information can be readily obtained from the White House executive clerk, William Hopkins, *after* election. Meanwhile, it suffices to say that the White House now includes fourteen statutory positions with salary maximums ranging from $22,500 to $17,500. There are numbers of other nonstatutory jobs in Eisenhower's set-up.

Fourth, before you appoint anyone to anything, give some thought to the kinds of relationships you want, initially, among the jobs you need, and hence among the men who fill them, with regard to one another *and* to you. The interim staff that I suggest below is closer to Roosevelt's pattern than to Eisenhower's: You would be your own "chief of staff." Your chief assistants would have to work collegially, in constant touch with one another and with you. Their respective jobs are demarcated by distinctly separable main assignments, so that they need not flounder, or dash off in all directions or fall over one another. But these are *activity* assignments, in terms of what *you* have to do from day to day, not programmatic assignments to marked-off policy areas. Since your activities overlap, these jobs will overlap; no one's jurisdiction is exclusive; competition is built in. There is room here for a *primus inter pares* to emerge, but no room for a staff *director* or arbiter, short of you. Neither is there room for sheer, unguided struggle. Jurisdictions *are* distinguished as well as overlapped.

Is that what you want when you become president? If so, your interim appointments and assignments must contribute toward it; if not, they must contribute to preventing it.

This is a crucial choice. For if you follow my advice you will commit yourself not to each detail of Rooseveltian practice—some details are out of date, others were unfortunate—but to the *spirit* of his presidential operation; whereby *you* would oversee, coordinate, and interfere with virtually everything your staff was doing. A collegial staff has to be managed; competition has to be audited. To run a staff in Roosevelt's style imposes heavy burdens. He himself dropped some of them during the war. Eisenhower, clearly, could not have endured them for a moment. Truman, though his practice somewhat followed FDR's, never fully understood what half his staff was doing; thus he escaped part of the load.

But if the burdens are heavy the rewards are great. No one has yet improved on Roosevelt's relative success at getting information in his mind and key decisions in his hands reliably enough and soon enough to give him room for maneuver. That, after all, is (or ought to be) the aim of presidential staff work.

Continuing Jobs to Be Filled at Once

I recommend that immediately after election you proceed to define and fill the following jobs, with the understanding that the men selected will take office with you as the core of your continuing staff.

1. An assistant for program. In terms of your ability to make a fast start and a firm impression on the country and on Congress after January 20, here is the key staff appointment before you. This is the "program side," or "message bird-dog" mentioned in my memorandum of September 15.

Before Inauguration, his task would be threefold:

a. To help you organize the consultations, working groups, drafting teams, etc., that you may find you need in order to fill gaps, to reconsider, to refine, and to prepare your initial *legislative* program *and a complementary program of executive action.*

b. To help prepare your Inaugural address, in light of and in coordination with these program preparations.

c. To ride herd, in your name and as your agent, on the work thus set in motion, in order to define and sharpen issues for decision and in order to assure the readiness of necessary action documents—messages, bill drafts, statements, executive orders—by the due date you intend for your first program presentation.

This assumes that you will want to go to Congress very early with priority requests, a rationale for your priorities, and a showing of executive activity to boot.

Inauguration day would find this aide at work completing preparations for that early presentation. Thereafter, he could readily become your principal assistant in preparing or reviewing the endless stream of public documents—messages, speeches, statements, orders, bill drafts, budget amendments—through which you will continue to define and to defend your personal program. With this continuing assignment he would tend to be, and should have scope to be, a focal point for general-purpose staff work in the White House on policy development in every sphere, legislative and administrative, foreign *and* domestic.

The continuing program job, as thus described, bears a close family resemblance to the job that Rosenman did for Roosevelt as his "special counsel" or that Clifford and then Murphy did for Truman, under the same title. (The title suited the man, not *vice versa;* all three happened to be lawyers.) If the job is to be done with maximum effectiveness, it should encompass *all* the public documents which bear upon your program. At the same time, it should be quite clear that dealing with documents means coming to grips with substance, and dealing with public documents requires knowledge of the private ones. This is not *per se* a writer's job, and it is not *per se* an attorney's job. Nor is it a job to be walled off from *any* area of program-making or of policy concern, not even from the area of highest security classification. The man on whom you will rely to help you state your program must have a feel for every part of it, including what cannot be stated.

In Truman's time, the special counsel's job was thought to be primarily "domestic" in orientation. Clifford and Murphy got deep into the substance of domestic policy; they rarely ventured far into the substance of foreign or military policy, though Murphy sometimes did so during the Korean War. But this weighting on the domestic side was a hangover from the days when national security affairs were outside the mainstream of government concerns except in "emergencies." Nowadays these affairs *are* the mainstream and "emergencies" are commonplace. In your administration such a program aide cannot be thought of as primarily "domestic." *His policy concerns should match your own.* His qualifications should be judged accordingly.

This does not mean that he can be a second secretary of state (any more than he can be a second secretary of interior). The program aide has got to shift from problem to problem and policy to policy depending on the speech you next have to deliver or the Executive order you next must sign. His priorities are set by your priorities. He shifts a step before you do. He has to be as much a generalist as you, no less concerned with substance but no more able to dwell for long on any given subject.

Above all else this aide should have a mind and working habits that fit yours. You cannot get good service of this sort at arm's length, either intellectually or personally.

Once you choose your program aide, there will be a need to organize some temporary staffing and consultative arrangements needed for initial program preparation before January 20. The most urgent of these are sketched below under the heading *Temporary Jobs.* The whole subject of producing your first program will be treated in a later memorandum.

2. A personal assistant to the commander-in-chief-elect. This job relates to relatively new activities incumbent on a president by virtue of the weapons revolution in a cold war context. Immediately after the election you should have a man on your own staff, constantly in touch with you, always within reach, to do four things:

a. To brief you and your closest personal assistants on the responsibility that will be yours, as commander-in-chief, on and after January 20, for special categories of reversible and irreversible decisions. Should Eisenhower be confronted with certain of these decisions before inauguration day, he might feel impelled to consult you. You might feel impelled to respond. You cannot wait until then to be briefed.

b. To brief you and your close aides, in detail, on present arrangements for arriving at and implementing such decisions, and to give you a *complete* appraisal of the strengths and weaknesses built into these arrangements including intelligence aspects.

c. To brief you and your close aides on the facts, the inferences, and the discrepancies which are built into Eisenhower's program (and budget) assumptions, and on data pertinent to judgment of appropriate assumptions for developing *your* program.

d. To be your personal eyes and ears in the intelligence agencies of government, drawing your attention to raw data that you ought to see and to especially able specialists, at whatever levels, whom you ought to meet. This is *not* a "liaison" task in the sense of passive channel, but a personal assistantship in the sense of active auditing for *you*.

These things roughly correspond to (and expand upon) the work now done for Eisenhower by General Goodpaster, on a special assignment over and above his publicized job as White House staff secretary. Your man should be in touch with Goodpaster before inauguration and should carry on with you thereafter. Even at the outset he should be more than a Goodpaster; more an assistant than a channel and alert to every facet of your interest and your work. *He needs to be curious, sensitive, independent, and as knowledgeable about policy as about intelligence.*

The quickest way to get your hands on such a man is to request that someone now cleared, qualified, and in the government be detailed to you for temporary assignment. This has the additional advantage of committing you to nothing in the way of permanent arrangements. Senator Jackson has some ideas, here, and will give you the particulars when you want them. I suggest that you also consult Richard Bissell, among others.

To clarify your stakes here—as far as one can do so in unclassified terms—a separate memorandum on this subject is being prepared at my request by Brewster Denny, an intelligence specialist on Jackson's subcommittee staff. His memorandum will be put into your hands.

3. An assistant for press relations. From the moment you are president-elect you acquire many of the public relations risks *and opportunities* inherent in the presidency. Everything you say or do will be watched and weighed, at home *and abroad;* not by the press alone, or by the public, *but by officialdom.*

Therefore, you have immediate need for both types of assistance traditionally expected from a president's press secretary.

First, the "outside" job of acting as your spokesman to the press and as housemother or hand-holder for White House correspondents. *Second,* the "inside" job of counseling on public relations aspects of your actions and statements day by day; a job which brings him into everybody's business, especially the program aide's.

These two types of assistance are *not* easily combined in one man. They tend to pull in opposite directions; they call for rather different skills and temperaments; the man who tries to do them both is under constant strain. No one is likely to do both equally well.

To meet your needs for both becomes a tricky proposition. Before you choose a man as your continuing chief press aide, you will want to decide which of these jobs you expect him to stress and how you mean to buttress his performance of the other.

If you do not want to cross this bridge at once, you could meet momentary needs by carrying your present press relations organization into the transition period. But if your designations are *pro tem,* the men involved must know it; so must the working press. For obvious reasons, such a holding operation grows less satisfactory with each passing week; it probably becomes intolerable by early January.

4. Two assistants for operations. Immediately after election you will need at least two men dividing up assorted daily chores:

a. Arranging your schedule, marshaling visitors, guarding your door. For a time, your personal secretary could keep up with this. But after you are settled down and vulnerable in Washington it almost certainly will become too much for her.

b. Managing your temporary office operation; superintending physical arrangements (and financing), keeping tabs on clerical assistance and on correspondence, handling preliminaries to the takeover of White House facilities and funds. (This sounds like "office-management," but such work at your level has plenty of political and policy content.)

c. Superintending preparations for your trip abroad (if any): physical arrangements, briefings, communications services, etc.

d. Arranging for FBI clearance of your appointees and Secret Service clearances of designees for White House passes.

e. Keeping tabs on and facilitating contacts by your other aides with outgoing officials at the White House and elsewhere.

f. Following up commitments you have made to visitors, and keeping track of their performance on commitments made to you. This includes tactful follow-up of *ad hoc* jobs you have assigned to temporary aides (see below).

g. Watching for noncompliance with the orders you have given (in the few spheres where a president-elect gives orders), identifying blockages and intervening at *your* option.

h. Watching for and helping to unravel snarls in the evolving personal relations among those who are prospectively in your official family.

i. Standing in at meetings you prefer to duck and "studying" proposals you want sat on.

These are the chores of daily operations, not as they will manifest themselves when you take office, but as they will start to look by mid-November. Even at this early stage one can identify, in embryo, the separate jobs of an "appointments secretary," of a "staff secretary," or a possible "assistant to the president" and of several "administrative assistants" on *ad hoc* assignments.

But for the moment two men should suffice, with help from your personal secretary and (as needed) from such temporary aides or volunteers as you find wise. *You can suspend judgment, for the time being, on the numbers (and the titles) ultimately needed* when you shift from being president-elect to being president. You may want to treat this bundle of assignments not as two jobs (and later more) for different men, but as one job for one man with a growing number of assistants: the "Number-One Boy for general operations" projected in my memorandum of September 15. However, on reflection, I would urge you to *go slow.* My "number-one" boy can begin as two and become three or four; depending on the personalities involved, he may emerge through "natural selection" *if* you let him. But you may decide to operate without him. January would be time enough for a decision. By then you will know more about the White House as now organized and more about your own future requirements.

5. A personal secretary. For the time being you can proceed with the secretarial arrangements you found suitable as a senator. By sometime in December, however (depending on your travel plans), your personal work load is likely to confront you with a choice which you will have to face in any event when you take office: do you want your present personal secretary to be just that (an Ann Whitman or a Missy Le Hand) or do you want her involved permanently with "operations" chores, such as your daily schedule? If you find that you have something of the latter sort in mind you will want to save an appropriate title for her and will want to cast about for someone else to handle your dictation and your private files.

Temporary Jobs to Fill Soon

I recommend that before Thanksgiving you begin to fill the following jobs, with the understanding that these are *transition assignments,* involving no long-run commitment to job content or to men.

1. A consultant on personnel. Selection of political appointees at *sub*-cabinet level and in Schedule C could be an area in which you and your whole staff get bogged down at no profit to yourselves. Therefore, as soon as possible after election, you will have use for an interim consultant working quietly *for you* on these appointments. His work would include:

> a. Identifying very able men, in private life *and* government, whom you should know but do not, and arranging that you have an early look at them, for future reference.
>
> b. Seeking talent for specific jobs in which you have an interest and checking talents of those urged on you by others.
>
> c. Checking the proposals of cabinet designees for such of their assistants as are subject to your appointment, with an eye to your interest and your protection.
>
> d. Mastering the schedule of expiring *term* appointments, both Republican and Democrat, in the regulatory commissions and working with a special study group (see below) on standards for replacements. (The list of expiration dates is in the hands of the White House executive clerk.)
>
> e. Mastering the policy jobs in Schedule C, government-wide, and keeping a watchful eye on what your cabinet designees intend—again, in your interest and for your protection. The chairman of the Civil Service Commission can provide assistance here (see below).
>
> f. Serving as a clearinghouse and checkpoint for the talent searchers (in and out of government) that cabinet designees themselves get under way.
>
> g. Serving as your personal advisor on relations with and policies regarding the career services.

The man who does this should be "high-level," sophisticated in government, alert and sensitive to policy, well versed in the "who is where" of business and the professions, knowledgeable about personnel techniques but not a "personnel man," knowledgeable about politics but not a politician (though certainly a Democrat). The Foundations are the likeliest source of such a man. The first prospect I think of is James Perkins. Another possibility might be Dean Rusk.

2. A liaison with the National Committee. Your personnel consultant cannot be your man "out front" on political appointments. For his protection and survival—and for your own purposes—you need somebody else to take the heat, pass the word, fend off the importunate, and soothe the disappointed. I am not concerned now with middle- and low-level patronage jobs—that heat can be contained in the committee for a while—but with high-prestige appointments, where the heat will be immediate, intense and on you.

3. A consultant on organization. Soon after election you will need to start identifying and appraising "next steps" for the later stages of transition in December, January, and February. Much of this work will be done, in the normal course, by your permanent assistants from the moment you appoint them. But you and they together could use at least one interim consultant on the mysteries and choices you all face in organizing and operating the White House Office and the Executive Office. Depending on your current intentions, you may have use for him, as well, in working out immediate reorganization plans for other areas of government (e.g., a Department of Urban Affairs).

By sometime in December you could also use a small group of advisors in the organization field to serve as a respectable repository for reorganization schemes urged on you from outside, until you have the time and resources to deal with them. For this purpose you might want to name three men as prospective members of the President's Advisory Committee on Government Organization. Your interim consultant might (or might not) serve as one of these advisors, but his short-run task is not the same as theirs. He deals with *your* immediate needs; they deal with large-scale questions for the future.

4. A liaison with the Budget Bureau. At the earliest opportunity, you should put a man inside the Budget Bureau as a close observer (not participant) of budget preparation, legislative clearances, and staff performance. Until you name a prospective Budget director (see below) this liaison man should be in close touch with your program aide; afterwards, he should assist them both. His job is not the same as the prospective director's sitting in on Eisenhower's budget making is the job for a reliable assistant with high capability as a reporter.

5. Assistants for ad hoc assignments. As you feel the need, you will want to take on temporary aides for *ad hoc* troubleshooting and fact-finding jobs, both on your own behalf and in connection with the rapidly evolving work of your program aide. But as a general rule: do not add to your own staff more of these odd-job men than you can use and supervise. And do not let your program aide have more men answering to *him* than he can keep under his thumb from day to day.

6. Working groups on programs. There will be some problem areas where you and your program assistant find it necessary or expedient to use a group instead of single aides in the preliminary work of screening ideas, sharpening issues, posing choices, and then actually turning out draft action documents.

For example, in the national security area, a working-level version of the present Nitze group is probably essential both to substitute for departmental staffs and to consult with them on your behalf, and on behalf of your department heads (who will have no departments).

Another example is the economic-fiscal area, where no one man could cope with sorting out and bringing down to earth the cloudy mass of conflicting advice you will receive from every part of the economy, to say nothing of academia. Unless I miss my guess, you and your program aide will need a select, "back-room" group of practical, adroit, low-ego lawyers and economists—or maybe several groups in different areas—to deal with this.

7. Contact men with advisory groups. I hate to think that you might have to set up and then live with formal, consultative groups of prominent persons in private life. However, in at least one area—fiscal-monetary policy—it is conceivable that this could become necessary for symbolic purposes, if better symbols (like a treasury appointment) had to be deferred or seemed unwise.

Should any such groups be created, it will be imperative to keep them from swamping your evolving organization for program preparation. To protect your program aide and his associates from continual interruption and diversion, you will need special, temporary aides as buffers, arrangers, hand-holders, and spies upon whatever formal, outside groups you may bring into being.

8. A study group on regulatory appointments. The regulatory commissions are in such a bad way (by and large) and appointments have been so mishandled under *two* administrations, that it would be well to set these posts aside, while a sophisticated study group (not necessarily publicized) considers standards for recruitment and selection of commissioners. The group might be built around a man like Landis; at any rate he ought to have a watching brief. Your attorney general should be drawn in when appointed. Your personnel consultant should be kept in touch. You may want advice from still other sources. But before you let a single commissionership into your appointments process, you should bear in mind precisely how you plan to treat them all.

Jobs to Be Done by Incumbents

I recommend that in whatever sequence suits the cause of good publicity you announce your intention to reappoint the following incumbent officials. This is not an exhaustive list; it is an immediate one.

Your long-run plans for any of these men (and their positions) are not cramped by such announcements. Commitments of this sort need not bind you to them for very long. In the short-run, your intention gives you claims upon their services, even while they are Eisenhower's subordinates. This would be *useful* to you *and* them.

These announcements also serve some useful purposes in terms of public and personnel relations.

1. Director of CIA (Dulles). The usefulness of short-run stability and service here is obvious, particularly since you would not be dependent on the agency for *personal* assistance. Your C-in-C assistant gives you that (see above).

2. Executive Secretary of NSC (Lay). Lay regards himself as a careerist, having held the job since 1949. It is useful to confirm him in this view (for the time being, anyway). Your programmers may want historical details and data he could readily provide. You will want to take a careful look at NSC machinery and avoid a premature commitment to procedures; he can run it on a basis which protects you from commitments (if you tell him to). He also can be useful as a temporary channel to and from all sorts of persons in the bowels of the bureaucracy.

3. "Science Advisor" to the President (Kistiakowsky). His title, technically, is Special Assistant for Science and Technology; he also serves as Chairman of the President's Science Advisory Committee. You will want easy access to the men who have been dealing from inside with current government concerns and controversies. This is a way to assure it; it also assures you against premature commitments to particular advisors or machinery. Kistiakowsky, as I understand it, wants to leave next spring in any case. You would not be bound, of course, to consult *only* these advisors.

4. Chairman of the Civil Service Commission (Jones). This man is a distinguished careerist (nominally Republican) who served Roosevelt and Truman before Eisenhower. Since there will be a Democratic vacancy in the Commission in March, you could replace him as chairman rather shortly if you chose. But in the interim, to give him status as your chairman is to free him for a wide variety of useful work in servicing and backstopping your personnel consultant. With respect to the whole realm of Schedule C, Jones's technical assistance, contacts, savvy, would be very valuable. But they could not be readily available if he were confined to the role of "Eisenhower's man."

5. Director of the FBI (Hoover). His reappointment seems a matter of course; you might as well make the most of it by an early announcement, particularly since you may well find some things you would like him to do for you, quite confidentially, before Inauguration.

A Prospective Budget Director

As a presidential staff facility, at one remove from personal aides, the Budget Bureau is not what it used to be (and rarely was what it ought to be). But it is still the nearest thing to institutional eyes-and-ears *and memory,* encompassing all parts of the executive branch, which you will have available to you when you take office.

You are almost sure to find (as Roosevelt, Truman, Eisenhower did before you) that when you look down from on high, the Budget Bureau seems a better and more valuable institution than it appears in the eyes of departmental staffs, or congressmen, or even its own critics—from within. It looks better to presidents because they find they cannot do without it; others can.

If you are to make the most of this facility—both in the short-run terms of your initial budgeting and in the longer terms of general staff work—your Budget director needs to be a different sort of man than Eisenhower's appointees, or for that matter, Truman's. Eisenhower had a penchant for certified public accountants. You need a man who is soaked in substance, a broad-gauged policy advisor, not an accountant.

At the same time your man should have real sensitivity to the requirements and limits of staff work in an "institutional" staff role. You do not want him dominated by your cabinet officers, but neither do you want him thinking he is one of them, or above them. *You* are above them; *he* is merely staff to you. Yet this does not mean that you should give him, or that he should seek, the status of a purely *personal* advisor. You want your White House aides to think in terms of *you.* You want this man to think more nearly of the presidency. You then preserve some freedom to select between the two or interweave them. Your Budget director needs the sensitivity to see this from the start.

He also needs toughness (preferably under a bland exterior). The core jobs of his agency are budget preparation and legislative clearance. By their nature he becomes a chief "no" man *for you.* Far more than congressmen or bureaucrats believe, past *presidents* have instigated and supported bureau negatives.

But the reason why your man ought to be program-minded, not a cost accountant, is that national or presidential needs may call on him to urge *you* to say "yes."

In their very different ways, Paul Nitze and Joe Fowler are suggestive of the sorts of men who might make the most of the Budget directorship as a source of help for you. For a younger age-group, David Bell is similarly suggestive. If you incline toward such a man, and find the one you want, then designate him quickly. Even as early as December he could be extremely useful:

a. Working in tandem with your program aide on the substance of issues, and preparing for follow-up on budgetary or administrative aspects of the concrete program choices you will make.

b. Serving as a critic of those choices, bringing independent views to bear for your consideration.

c. Serving also as a source of counsel and critique on the work of your personnel and organization consultants.

d. Arranging for and superintending temporary liaison with departmental staffs where you have deferred top appointments, or where your appointees delay liaison on their own.

e. Serving, temporarily, as liaison with second-level, special-purpose staffs now in or near the White House, which you probably will want to liquidate, but meanwhile need to freeze.

Jobs on Which to Defer Decision

If you follow the proposals in this memorandum, you will not even try to staff yourself with counterparts for many of the senior staff positions in Eisenhower's White House and Executive Office. By January 20, you *may* have found a need to cross *some* of these bridges. You would not cross them now. Instead, your organization consultant and your personal assistants would examine them with care, while you assessed your own evolving needs.

The positions thus left in abeyance include some on which you will be pressed to act. Chief among these are:

1. Special assistant for National Security Affairs. This post should be avoided by all means until you have sized up your needs *and* got a feel for your new secretaries of state and defense. Meanwhile, your programmers and your C-in-C assistant give you help enough.

2. Chairman of the Council of Economic Advisors. The kind of man you put into this post will have so much to do with the kind of use you get from CEA, that you should decide what you want from it before you pick the man. This will take time; and you have time. You can equip yourself with all the counsel you require in the short-run, through your temporary program organization (to say nothing of volunteers).

3. Director of Civilian and Defense Mobilization. OCDM now combines ill-assorted, incompatible, poorly performed functions. No one should be put into this post, lest his presence keep alive what you may want to reorganize out of existence.

Concluding Note

My recommendations are highly academic in the sense that they take no account of given personalities, or mental sets, or skills, or work habits including yours. Even if you see the need for jobs suggested here, and even if you like my general scheme, the moment you begin to put *men* into jobs there will be a need for review, perhaps for readjustment, of the duties and relationships I now propose. The review should be by you, and but the first of many in the months ahead. This brings me back to my starting point: once you are "Mr. President," nobody else can fully gauge your own, personal interests. In the last analysis, that is the "staff job" for *you*.

Chapter 5

Does the White House Need a Strong Chief of Staff?

RICHARD E. NEUSTADT

Practical Need for Chief of Staff

I've given up long opposition to the formal designation of a chief of staff, on grounds that in administrative terms it, or something like it, has become a practical necessity. But the title does not conjure up for me a Sherman Adams during President Eisenhower's illnesses, or a Bob Haldeman at his most assertive, or a Don Regan at his most pretentious. My trouble with the title always was that it did conjure up such visions in the minds of others, not least such as they!

In Harry Truman's time, disputes over allocation of office space and such things, in what then was called the Old State Building—disputes not only among White House aides as such, but between them and the building's other occupants, mainly what we now call OMB—could be settled short of the president himself only by the appointments secretary, who had an informal mandate, when, as (and if) he cared to get between his colleagues. Often he didn't, leaving issues of the sort unresolved for months or even years. Occasionally the president did intervene. The stories of how FDR got OMB into Old State and how Truman ultimately got State out are classic.

With a White House staff of present size and with the rest of the Executive Office shorn, in Jimmy Carter's time, of separate administrative services, there is a need for somebody to have authority in such administrative spheres, not as an adjunct of another role, but as a formal, understood, accepted part of his own role (or of a deputy's acting for him). For eight years now in two administrations, an acknowledged "chief of staff" has served the purpose—as also for sixteen of the twenty-six years before that, back to Truman. The accumulated experience is quite enough, I think, to bind future administrations, as a matter not of law but of convenience and common sense.

An alternative, of course, would be to shrink staff back to Truman's size, as Kennedy did. But no one since has seriously tried, on a sustained basis, except Gerald Ford, who found it couldn't be done. Jimmy Carter evidently wasn't serious. Ronald Reagan didn't try. So bigness wins.

Chief of Staff as Part of a Circle

These impressions are strengthened for me by another change in White House staff arrangements during those same years. What was originally conceived as an intimate personal staff—helping the president do what he personally had to do from day to day and nothing else—became the upper several layers of a massive hierarchy. White House staff, per se, had three levels in Truman's time (above the clerical) and now has at least six. Yet while the chief of staff is nominally at the hierarchy's apex, short of the president, he usually has served in fact as only one of three or four key, virtually coequal top advisers. They ordinarily maintain among themselves and with the president much of the intimacy and collegiality once envisioned for the "White House Office" by the FDR Reorganization Plan of 1939.

What looks like a triangle isn't—quite. The hierarchy capped by White House layers now encompasses the Executive Office of the President in its entirety. The distinction between White House staff and others in that Office has been fuzzed up beyond anybody's power to undo, not only in the media but also in the usages of government. This staff agglomeration performs most of the functions for the president and presidency combined, most of the staff work, personal *and* institutional, that sixty years ago was either done by cabinet officers or not at all. On the other hand, the topmost circle of advisers, the true intimates, the three or four, may just as well include a cabinet member as a holder of a title in the EOP, and often has: Messrs. Dean Acheson, Foster Dulles, Robert Kennedy, and Edwin Meese come to mind. And so long as there is a circle, with the chief of staff but one, and nobody the *primus inter pares* save the president, I conceive that the original intention behind having something separate called a White House staff—Louis Brownlow's intention, with every word approved by FDR, so Brownlow told me—is not lost, despite the numbers and the layering, and distance from the boss, on down the line. (Something certainly is lost in public and governmental relations, but I won't pause to argue the point.)

The Reagan Administration's First Term "Circle"

Indeed, in its first term, the Reagan administration succeeded rather brilliantly, I thought, not only in creating and maintaining such a circle (with vicissitudes and adaptations, naturally, from month to month), but also in removing it a distinct step from the rest of the White House and Executive Office.

Procedurally, as I understand it, there came to be in effect two White House staffs, an "inner" and an "outer." The former was about as small as Truman's or Kennedy's. It included the chief of staff, James Baker, and his deputy, Richard Darman, who superintended most of the rest of the place. But it also included, on at least equal terms, Messrs. Michael Deaver and Meese and (after 1981) the national security assistant. They and their immediate associates—a group of perhaps twenty—constituted what I mean by "inner." Between it and virtually everybody else stood Meese's deputy, Craig Fuller, as gatekeeper along with Darman, deciding what agenda items, when (or whether), cabinet committees could discuss and subordinate staffs raise.

(Incidentally, the term "national security adviser," invented by the press and embraced by incumbents, does not appear on the commissions from successive presidents to successive assistants for National Security Affairs. The term appears to give *them,* among others, an exaggerated view of their place in the world. I never use it!)

How Best to Use the Circle of Advisers

The consequence is that for any president there still remains a problem manifest to everyone before the chief of staff's time but now perhaps disguised by the apparent comprehensiveness and rank of that position: How can the president in person use his circle so that it informs his choices in every dimension relevant to him, political and substantive alike, without relying on his intimates so passively that they, or some of them, make him the instrument of their bad judgment regardless?

Reliance on the judgment of the chief of staff is no solution. Not, at least, on the historical record. The record shows that, aside from Baker, holders of that title up to now have frequently displayed less political judgment than their principals (less reliable, less broad-gauged, less strategic). Compare Sherman Adams with Dwight Eisenhower, H. R. Haldeman or Alexander Haig with Richard Nixon, Jack Watson with Jimmy Carter, Donald Regan with Ronald Reagan. Gerald Ford's "staff coordinators," Donald Rumsfeld and Richard Cheney, might be said to break the trend, along with Baker. They, at least, displayed no notably flawed political judgments. Even so, three out of eight isn't good enough.

And as the interesting case of Admiral Poindexter suggests (assuming he has told the truth), the problem for the president goes beyond any single person's judgment to the need for judgments from around the circle, from all members of the circle, assuming they comprise—or can be stretched to cover— all the points of view it might be wise for him to ponder. But suppose one member feels he has authority, in presidential interest as he sees it, to keep all other members of the inner circle ignorant? Who guards the guardians? In such cases no one can, short of the president himself. If nothing warns him to po- lice, to monitor, the quality of inner staff performance on *some* issues, not of course on all, or if he makes the wrong distinctions between what to monitor and not—if he cannot distinguish between his crown jewels and other objects— then God help him (mortals can't).

The William Casey instance is more interesting still. Here, for the first time, so far as I recall, one member of the inner circle from outside the White House was at once a former campaign manager and old friend to the president, an admired businessman, a veteran covert operator, *and* the director of Central Intelligence. Where secretaries of state and attorneys general had once served, the DCI now stood! Seemingly, throughout the Iran-Contra matter, it was Casey's advice, both political and substantive, that tipped the balance against Reagan's secretaries of state and defense. And Casey's enthusiasm for the "neat idea," the "ultimate irony" of overcharging Teheran to subsidize the contras, together with his mastery of compartmentation (assuming he too kept it from Regan and Reagan), must have encouraged Poindexter, at least inferentially, and surely turned on their boy wonder Colonel North!

I have heard and read much about Reagan's "management style." Plainly it involves habitual delegation more routine and comprehensive than ever be- fore in modern times. But it is delegation at the service of commitments to distinct if general causes in his own mind. He seems to be the intellectually least curious president since Calvin Coolidge (though I'm not clear on Coolidge), which makes dispensing with detail entirely natural. But Reagan also seems to be, ideologically, the most committed president since Herbert Hoover (is this fair to Hoover?). Commitments cluster around a few fixed, firmly held ideas that Reagan brought with him and holds dear. These, along with undeniable political shrewdness, seem to serve as lodestars when specifics come before him.

Mastery of detail is not necessary to decisive choices guided by those lode- stars. They shine the brighter in a wishful sky. What Reagan seems to want from his close circle of advisers is a timely, focused presentation of each issue for decision. And he evidently tends to take for granted that divergences and details he has need to know will trickle up just when he needs to know them.

There's the rub. By design or happy accident for Reagan, the circle in his first term served him relatively well. In the second term a changing group served him abominably ill, in my opinion. But his passivity as monitor and his apparent acquiescence in the changes urged by others for their purposes, not his, undoubtedly contributed more than a little.

Something else, I think, contributed as well—the personality, public relations, operating style and judgments, all combined, of Reagan's second chief of staff, Don Regan. For Regan claimed to be and fought to be the *primus inter pares* that nobody but the president had been, within the circle, up to 1984. Yet simultaneously, for certain purposes, Regan's monitoring, *his* policing, was so slack that Poindexter and Casey were entirely free of him, as well as of the president they all supposedly served—or so it now appears. How come? Conceivably, Regan believed his own propaganda about his role. Conceivably, Reagan believed it too, and with advancing years or wishfulness, was lulled by it. But let us not believe it, for there's more to this than that!

A president who delegates as much as Reagan does runs at least two risks: first, that everybody—even an Admiral Poindexter—will come to think he understands the president's own interests as well as the president does, or much better; and second, that nobody will do the monitoring he himself in prudence ought to do. Why not the chief of staff? Because, no matter that he makes the noises of a Regan, his colleagues can and will evade him or elude him or will play him off against the boss's human weaknesses. What Regan didn't do, Haldeman couldn't do fifteen years earlier, with reference to Chuck Colson. What Haldeman couldn't do, no chief of staff can ever be expected to bring off!

Besides, no chief of staff has ever even claimed the lead on substance in National Security Affairs—not Adams with respect to Foster Dulles, not Haldeman, Rumsfeld or Cheney with respect to Henry Kissinger, not Watson with respect to Zbigniew Brzezinski nor Baker with respect to William Clark, and not Regan with respect to Poindexter (not, anyway, since the Iran-Contra revelations; before then Regan frequently implied it for press consumption).

Let me add that I don't *like* the tendency, however longstanding, to put defense and diplomacy into one staff compartment, with congressional, press, public and political relations—and domestic policies—in another. Taken to extremes, as occasionally has been the case, it leaves the president bereft of *any* staff whose reach is remotely like his own, a poor outcome. (No wonder presidents turn to buddies, brothers, wives.) The tendency is matched, of course, by separations in political science, and three professors of government have contributed: Messrs. Bundy, Kissinger, and Brzezinski. But that doesn't make me like it any better. Perhaps, along with vice admirals and colonels, specialists in international relations should be barred from future presidential staffs until they prove an empathetic understanding of domestic politics?

These comments will, I hope, point up what seems to me self-evident, that the position of a White House chief of staff is neither a solution to nor guarantor of anything, except a needed modicum of administrative tidiness in what remains, to adapt Edward Corwin's phrase, an incurably personalized presidency. Former chiefs are prone to paint the position in vivid colors, larger than life. That I don't mind, but outside observers can try to do better.

Note: This piece was originally published in *Presidency Research* 10, no. 1 (Fall, 1987).

Chapter 6

The President's Chief of Staff: Lessons Learned

JAMES P. PFIFFNER

At the superficial level a new president has a free hand in choosing how to organize the White House based on personal preference or management style. After all, the presidency is a very personal office. There are, however, two firm lessons of White House organization that can be ignored by presidents only at their own peril.

Lesson Number One: A chief of staff is essential in the modern White House.

Lesson Number Two: A domineering chief of staff will almost certainly lead to trouble.

The bulk of this paper will be devoted to arguing for the second principle: a domineering or "strong" chief of staff will likely lead to disaster.[1] But first, the argument that a White House chief of staff is necessary will be outlined in order to put the second lesson into perspective.

Dwight Eisenhower was the first president to establish the office of chief of staff, and he designated Sherman Adams as the person to run his White House. But after Eisenhower, John Kennedy decided to be his own chief of staff and had no one staffer whose scope of duties was comparable to the sweeping authority Adams had in the 1950s. Lyndon Johnson sporadically tried to organize his White House and designate a chief of staff, but he was unwilling to delegate sufficient authority and remained in charge of everything himself.

President Nixon increased the size of the White House staff and continued to centralize control because he distrusted the executive branch bureaucracy and even his own political appointees. H. R. Haldeman was his chief of staff and ran the White House with an iron hand. With Eisenhower and Nixon choosing to name a chief of staff and the two intervening Democrats choosing to act as their own, it still seemed in 1976 that the issue of whether a chief of staff is necessary was an open one. But two trends had converged to preclude the option of operating the White House without a chief of staff. The White House office had grown to over 500 staffers, and control of domestic and foreign policy had been increasingly centralized in the White House.

When Gerald Ford took over, he reacted against Watergate by refusing to name a chief of staff and intended to run an open presidency. Ford first asked Donald Rumsfeld to join his White House staff, but he refused because Ford was unwilling to designate a chief of staff. But after a year of trying to run the White House by himself Ford concluded that his broader duties as president were suffering from the lack of a chief of staff. Ford called Rumsfeld again to ask him to join the administration, and Ford agreed to make him chief of staff in fact, though officially the "staff coordinator."[2] When Rumsfeld was appointed secretary of defense, Richard Cheney became Ford's chief of staff.

Jimmy Carter, also running against the specter of H. R. Haldeman and Watergate, wanted to be his own chief of staff and ignored the lessons that Ford had learned. But after two years of trying to manage the White House himself, Carter also admitted that his "spokes-of-the-wheel" approach of being his own chief of staff was not working and designated Hamilton Jordan to be his chief of staff. When Jordan left the White House to run the reelection campaign, Jack Watson took over as chief of staff. Presidents Reagan, Bush, and Clinton each named a chief of staff shortly after their elections.

Thus Lesson Number One is that the president does not have a realistic option not to have some sort of chief of staff; the role is necessary in the modern White House.[3] The chief of staff is necessary to perform a number of functions. Among them are included:[4]

1. Impose order on the policy process. The White House office is now so large that a president who tries to run it alone will soon be overwhelmed with managerial details to the neglect of broader responsibilities. A broad range of functions in domestic and foreign policy that used to be delegated to cabinet secretaries is now centralized in the White House.

2. Arbitrate among cabinet secretaries. Contemporary public policy issues are complex and usually cut across several departments. Cabinet secretaries are rivals over policy turf and will not cede coordination of policy to a peer. A chief of staff is needed to impose the president's perspective on policy disputes among the departments and agencies.

3. Control access and play the heavy. Someone has to take on distasteful tasks for the president, such as controlling access, saying no to requests, and firing people. The chief of staff is the right person to be the "abominable no man" and also to act as a lightning rod by absorbing attacks meant for the president.

In sum, someone short of the president must be in charge of coordinating the White House. No president has successfully run the White House without a chief of staff since 1968, and since 1979 no president has tried.

But Lesson Number Two of White House organization is that a chief of staff who takes too domineering an approach to the position will cause major problems. There have been four domineering chiefs of staff in the modern presidency: Sherman Adams for Eisenhower, H. R. Haldeman for Nixon, Donald Regan for Reagan, and John Sununu for Bush. *Each* of these domineering chiefs of staff has resigned under pressure; in effect, they were fired. The rest of this chapter will examine the service of these strong chiefs of staff and come to the conclusion that the preferred role for a chief of staff is that of a facilitator, coordinator, and neutral broker. The best model for this role was James Baker in Ronald Reagan's first term, although Donald Rumsfeld, Richard Cheney, and Jack Watson took the facilitating approach to the chief of staff office before Baker.

Eisenhower Institutionalizes the White House

While FDR began the modern staffing system in the White House and Truman organized it more explicitly, it was under Eisenhower that the White House staff became institutionalized. Before he became President Dwight Eisenhower had the advantage of having been an executive for many years, directing U.S. forces during World War II, and having coordinated the allied effort to victory in the War. During his career he had given considerable thought to leadership in organizations and came to the presidency with firm ideas about how the White House should be organized. He was of the strong opinion that White House organization needed improving. "For years I had been in frequent contact with the executive office of the White House, and I had certain ideas about the system, or lack of system under which it operated. With my training in problems involving organization it was inconceivable to me that the work of the White House could not be better systemized than had been the case in the years I observed it."[5] Eisenhower stressed the importance of organization: "Organization cannot make a genius out of an incompetent. . . . On the other hand, disorganization can scarcely fail to result in inefficiency and can easily lead to disaster."[6] Thus Eisenhower organized his White House much more formally than either Truman or Roosevelt.

Eisenhower introduced a number of organizational innovations to the White House, among them were the offices of cabinet secretary and staff secretary and the upgrading of the staff director of the National Security Council to special assistant to the president for National Security Affairs.

But perhaps the most important and lasting contribution of Eisenhower to the organization of the presidency was the Office of Chief of Staff whose function was to oversee and coordinate the much enlarged and more complex staff for the president. The combination of the powers of the office and the personality of its first occupant, Sherman Adams, made it the most powerful position short of the president in the government. Adams's official title was assistant to the president, but his function was chief of staff. "I think of Adams as my Chief of Staff, but I don't call him that because the politicians think it sounds too military," admitted Eisenhower.[7] Though Eisenhower never laid out in detail what Adams's duties were to be it was clear that Adams was to be in charge of the White House. He told Adams that "The organization plan must make it plain to everybody that I am looking to you to coordinate this office."[8]

Adams saw his job as making sure that staff work was complete and that any issues brought to the president were ripe for presidential involvement. According to Eisenhower: "A man like that is valuable because of the unnecessary detail he keeps away from the president. A president who doesn't know how to decentralize will be weighed down with details and won't have time to deal with the big issues."[9] Adams spent a considerable amount of time forcing reluctant cabinet secretaries to settle their disputes and turf battles short of the president. "Either you make up your minds or else tell me and I will do it. We must not bother the President with this. He is trying to keep the world from war."[10] As Adams explained his role, "Eisenhower simply expected me to manage a staff that would boil down, simplify, and expedite the urgent business . . . and keep as much work of secondary importance off his desk as possible."[11] Adams had within his jurisdiction most domestic matters that came to the president and he spent a good portion of his time on political appointments. He did not have distinct policy preferences of his own and did not act as a policy advocate within the White House system, though Republican conservatives regarded him as suspiciously moderate.

Much of Adams's power stemmed from his control of access to the president. Given Eisenhower's preference to be spared details, his absence from the White House much of the time, and his conscious decision to stay behind the scenes, Adams's position became that much more powerful. Despite organization charts and official policy that gave direct access to the president to all cabinet officers and a number of White House staffers, the reality was that Adams usually had final say as to who would see the president and what papers would reach him. Adams once said in response to a question about cabinet access to the president: "What you say about shielding people from the President [sic] is essentially correct. Anybody who had legitimate business of sufficient importance to occupy the attention of the President got in; those that didn't didn't. *I knew the difference.*"[12] Cabinet members were correct in blaming Adams for enforcing tight control of access to the president. This was the source of much of the resentment of Adams.

The tightness of Adams's control can be contrasted with Adams's successor as chief of staff, General Jerry Persons, who reported that he allowed more people to see Eisenhower than Adams had and gave him more details than had Adams.[13] But controlling access was only one of the important roles that Adams played for the president as chief of staff. He took the heat for the president for tough political decisions, such as firing people and negotiating political patronage. He acted as a buffer for the president and organized the White House and cabinet with an iron hand. After Eisenhower's first heart attack in 1955 Adams ran the executive branch virtually by himself for several months.

These are all legitimate and often necessary roles for the chief of staff but the way they are handled can make a large difference. They can be done in a heavy handed manner or they can be accomplished with a firm hand, but without overt hostility. Cabinet members and staff may chafe under the decision in either case, but hostility and ill feeling will result if the bearer of the bad news is gratuitously rude also. Although Adams ran the White House the way Eisenhower wanted, his tight control and personal style contributed to his eventual undoing.

Adams's downfall began when it became public in June of 1958 that a textile manufacturer and old friend of Adams, Bernard Goldfine, had on several occasions requested that Adams determine the status of charges against him with a federal regulatory agency. Adams made the calls for Goldfine from the White House to find out the status of the case but did not suggest any change in agency actions. While the calls in themselves may have been free of improper intent, the very fact that an official of Adams's status, power, and proximity to the president was making the call cannot help but to be taken seriously by any agency in the government. Adams did not seem to be sensitive to the implications or appearance of his calls.

Adams became doubly vulnerable when it was disclosed in congressional hearings that he had accepted gifts from Goldfine who had paid for hotel rooms for Adams and had given his wife a vicuña coat and an oriental rug.[14] Despite Adams's protestations that he had also given gifts to Goldfine in the context of their friendship, the combination of gifts to Adams with the inquiries from the White House appeared too much like official actions in exchange for gifts.

The charges were given added weight because in the 1952 elections the Republicans had severely criticized the Democrats for instances of corruption in the Truman administration. Several of Truman's aides had been fired for accepting financial and other goods while in office. Republicans had promised the electorate that they would "clean up the mess in Washington" and that their administration would be "clean as a hound's tooth." Adams proudly wore the badge of righteousness and had swiftly moved to censure and fire members of the administration who had been tainted by any hint of impropriety. The irony of Adams's being hoist on his own petard was too much for his political enemies to resist.

The publication of these actions, while serious in themselves, might not have led to disaster, but in combination with other aspects of Adams's personality ultimately led to his resignation. The first of these factors has already been mentioned: Adams's tight control of access to the president. People resented it even though the president wanted it that way. The public image of Adams was that he was virtually running the presidency by himself. This was an exaggerated perception and was part of Eisenhower's conscious decision to exercise his power behind the scenes, but the popular image rang true to many Americans.[15] One current joke had it that it would be unfortunate if Eisenhower died and Nixon became president but a disaster if Adams died and Eisenhower was forced to be president.

An additional important cause of Adams's downfall was his personal rudeness to colleagues and others he dealt with on an official basis. To Eisenhower, Adams's curtness was merely his way of communicating in the most efficient manner, ". . . he never added a word to his 'yes' or 'no' if such an answer sufficed. It never occurred to him to say 'Hello'. . . . For Sherman Adams this was neither bad manners nor pretense; he was busy. Absorbed in his work, he had no time to waste."[16] But to others the lack of the usual elements of common courtesy and civility were perceived as his disdain for them as fellow workers and human beings. He seldom said "hello" or "goodbye" on the phone and would not say "good morning" when he came to the office. Adams once explained: "Why should I say hello? They know I'm here."[17]

While Adams's brusqueness did not bother his boss, it often did bother his subordinates and others he dealt with. Adams's habitual harshness frequently reduced his secretaries to tears, and at one time he allegedly had five of them crying at the same time.[18] Adams treated members of the cabinet and Congress the same way, feeling no need for the usual amenities of human communication. This did not endear him to many, and when he was in trouble and needed friends to defend him, few were willing to come forth. Many in Congress and the executive branch felt that he was an arrogant, power-hungry tyrant who was getting his just desserts.

Particularly damaging to Adams's ability to weather the storm about his supposed corruption was his alienation of the Republican leadership in Congress who were put off by his arrogance. But GOP conservatives also saw him as biased against their policies and sympathetic to the liberal wing of the party.

Congressional Republicans were afraid that in the upcoming congressional elections that the Democrats would use the Adams issue to make gains at the polls and defeat Republican candidates. The coup de grace came when Republican leaders informed Eisenhower that campaign contributors would not open up their purses until Adams was gone.[19]

Even a personal plea and vote of confidence from Eisenhower could not save Adams. After Adams's congressional testimony in which he argued that he had done nothing wrong, Eisenhower said, "I believe that the presentation made by Governor Adams to the Congressional Committee yesterday truthfully represents the pertinent facts. I personally like Governor Adams. I admire his abilities. I respect him because of his personal and official integrity. I need him."[20] But the plea was seen more as a weakness on the part of Eisenhower than an effective defense of Adams. Finally Adams was persuaded to resign.

A further irony concerning Adams's moral stature was made public by *The New York Times* columnist William Safire in 1986 upon Adams's death. Safire, who had worked with Adams in the 1952 New Hampshire primary, reported that IRS investigators had found that Adams had not reported over $300,000 in income. At the request of former President Eisenhower, President Johnson told the IRS not to prosecute Adams, and the taxes were eventually paid by a fund set up by Adams's friends.[21]

Nixon's Tight Hierarchy

When Richard Nixon returned to the White House after serving as Eisenhower's vice president and observing the Kennedy/Johnson years, he resolved that his administration would be more formally organized than the Democrats had been and closer in tone to Eisenhower's. Nixon began his term with intentions of delegating authority to his cabinet secretaries to select their own subordinates and to accomplish the goals of his administration. He would spend much of his time on international affairs; in domestic policy he would take only the big plays. In May, 1968, Nixon declared:

For one thing, I would disperse power, spread it among able people. Men operate best only if they are given the chance to operate at full capacity.

I would operate differently from President Johnson. Instead of taking all power to myself, I'd select cabinet members who could do their jobs, and each of them would have the stature and the power to function effectively. Publicity would not center at the White House alone. Every key official would have the opportunity to be a big man in his field. On the other hand, when a President takes all the real power to himself, those around him become puppets. They shrivel up and become less and less creative. . . . your most creative people can't develop in a monolithic, centralized power set-up.[22]

Nixon's initial intentions were echoed by H. R. Haldeman: "Our job is not to do the work of government, but to get the work out to where it belongs—out to the Departments."[23] Nixon's intentions were reflected in his selection of cabinet secretaries of stature and independent political standing and a White House staff that included the disparate viewpoints of liberal Patrick Moynihan and conservative Arthur Burns.

But disillusionment soon set in. Nixon found that the Democratically controlled Congress was not about to give him what he wanted, and he shifted to an administrative strategy to accomplish his goals. He would use all of his tools in the executive branch at his disposal. Nixon became convinced that a wide array of forces were intent upon frustrating his aims. The Congress would not pass his proposals, the media were critically hostile, and the career bureaucracy would drag their collective feet and sabotage his policies. He even came to the conclusion that his own appointees in the executive departments had "gone native" and become more concerned with their own power and standing in their policy areas than in carrying out his priorities.

He decided to rein in the departments and agencies and created several mechanisms to facilitate White House control. Thus instead of getting the work of the administration out to the departments and agencies, Nixon decided to bring the work of the departments and agencies into the White House where he could carefully control policy development and oversee implementation.

Nixon's concept of the presidency was that the executive branch ought to be at his disposal. As John Ehrlichman put it: "There shouldn't be a lot of leeway in following the President's policies. It should be like a corporation, where the executive vice presidents (the Cabinet officers) are tied closely to the chief executive, or to put it in extreme terms, when he says jump, they only ask how high."[24]

As Nixon became disillusioned with the executive branch he gave correspondingly greater power to his White House staff. The role of the staff came to be to buffer the president and to protect his time so that he could read, write, and ponder the big picture. In Nixon's words, "My disposition is to see that the President's time is not frittered away. I've found a way to do it. I'm a reader, not a buller."[25] Nixon's preference for time alone reinforced the tendency of the White House staff to guard access to him. The line between protecting the president's time and isolating the president became a fine one. According to Henry Kissinger, Nixon usually made decisions "in solitude on the basis of memoranda or with a few very intimate aides. He abhorred confronting colleagues with whom he disagreed . . . and he shunned persuading or inspiring his subordinates. He would decide from inside his self-imposed cocoon. . . . All this led to a vicious circle in which the President withdrew ever more into his isolation and pulled the central decisions increasingly into the White House."[26]

From the beginning Nixon had wanted a chief of staff to run his White House, and the role came naturally to H. R. Haldeman, a brilliant and hard nosed organizer who had been with Nixon since his 1960 campaign for the presidency. To the rest of the executive branch and the outside world Nixon seemed isolated behind his "Berlin Wall" of Haldeman, Ehrlichman, and Kissinger. "The White House became an echo chamber that magnified the voice of the president but sacrificed true pitch."[27]

Haldeman was the linchpin in the White House staff system. He became the most powerful White House aide since Sherman Adams and ran the system with an iron hand. He clearly took precedence over the other staffers. "We all knew where we fit. There were five of us that were equal, but as [Bryce] Harlow said: there was a first among equals, and it was clearly me. Nobody questioned it. I never asserted it; I never argued it. I never had to."[28] According to Haldeman, "If I told someone to do something, he knew it wasn't me—he knew exactly what it was; it was an order from the President. They knew an appeal wouldn't get anywhere."[29]

His role, as he saw it, was to institute a "zero defects system" in the staffing operation. He would ensure that all issues and options for the president were fully "staffed out" and that all bases had been touched. Access to the president by anyone except Kissinger was carefully controlled by Haldeman, and cabinet members frequently resented his gatekeeping. When cabinet secretaries actually did get in to see the president, Haldeman would be present to take notes, and the agenda for the meeting would often be presented to the president in such a way as to determine the outcome to the staff's satisfaction but not the visitor's.[30]

He controlled the paper flow and White House staffing. There was a follow-up system that would impose deadlines for staff projects. As the deadline approached the staffer or his secretary would be reminded, and if the work was not ready or of unacceptable quality, increasingly heavy handed reminders would hound the person until the work was completed to Haldeman's satisfaction.

The ostensible purpose of the tightly run system was to save the president from non-presidential details so that he could concentrate on the big picture. The irony was that despite the time that Nixon reserved for thinking great thoughts, he was obsessed with details of the White House operation, both of substance and style. He was concerned with White House furniture, who had what photographs of former presidents in the Executive Office Building, and he wanted extensive memos to him on what wines would be served at White House functions. He had White House staffers log the comments visitors made on the paintings displayed in the west lobby and he kept careful inventory of small gifts (cuff links, ash trays, and copies of *Six Crises*) that were given out to visitors about the White House. There were many memoranda about the White House tennis courts.[31]

Although the Watergate scandals were not caused by the staffing system, both Watergate and the staff organization were reflections of Nixon's psychology and character. Despite the fact that Haldeman was close enough to the president to occasionally delay implementation of questionable off-the-cuff orders and demands by an irritated Nixon there was never any question or doubt in the White House about covering up the initial Watergate break-in. The tone was set by Nixon, and the staff unquestioningly carried out his wishes. The problem was that Haldeman and the staff system he set up faithfully reflected and reinforced Nixon's dark side and need for isolation. Thus the zero-defects system allowed the Watergate "horrors" and led to the resignations and convictions of top White House staffers and the unprecedented resignation of a U.S. president.

Reagan's Contrasting Chiefs

As it is with all presidents, the shape and role of the White House staff was a reflection of Ronald Reagan's personality. By all accounts, both friendly and critical, Reagan was extremely passive in his approach to the White House staff. He was not passive with respect to the major direction of his presidency or public policy; his was an active presidency. But once the direction was set by Reagan, his aides formulated the policies and carried them out; Reagan was interested only in outcomes and did not want to be bothered with details.

Part of his passiveness was his lack of intellectual curiosity, but part of it was due to his uncritical trust in whatever people told him or what he read.[32] This passiveness made him dependent on his staff who had to make sure he was not unduly influenced by the most recent person he saw.[33] Donald Regan recalled, "I cannot remember a single case in which he changed a time or canceled an appointment or ever complained about an item on his schedule."[34]

Reagan's hands-off approach to his staff was based on a management philosophy that relied on delegation of authority. In his words: "Surround yourself with the best people you can find, delegate authority, and don't interfere as long as the policy you've decided upon is being carried out."[35] This approach occasionally frustrated administration officials because of Reagan's unwillingness to give them policy guidance. Donald Regan complained: "In the four years that I served as Secretary of the Treasury I never saw President Reagan alone and never discussed economic philosophy. . . . I had to figure these things out like any other American, by studying his speeches and reading the newspapers. . . . After I accepted the job, he simply hung up and vanished." Reagan "laid down no rules and articulated no missions" and thus conferred great "latitude on his subordinates."[36] To David Stockman, Reagan "seemed so serene and passive," "He gave no orders, no commands; asked for no information; expressed no urgency. . . . Since I *did* know what to do, I took his quiet message of confidence to be a mandate."[37] Stockman observed that whenever there was an argument Reagan would smile and say: "Okay, you fellas work it out."[38]

Reagan's passivity and penchant for delegation made his staff crucial to his presidency in a way that was not true of Franklin Roosevelt, John Kennedy, or George Bush. The unique division of labor in his first term worked in a particularly felicitous way for Reagan. The definition of staff roles began before the inauguration, immediately after the election when the decisions were made about the structure and organization of the top staff. The outcome was driven by the widespread expectation that Edwin Meese, who had run the campaign, headed the transition, and had run Reagan's governor's office in California, would naturally be named Reagan's White House chief of staff. But others around Reagan judged that Meese, though unquestionably loyal and ideologically dedicated, did not have the organizational talent or discipline to perform well as chief of staff. James Baker was their choice.

Reagan must be given credit for accepting their advice that he needed a Washington insider for his chief of staff and for saying no to the loyal Meese, despite Baker's work for George Bush in 1976 and 1980. In order to get Meese to go along with the plan, he had to be convinced that he would still play a major role in the administration. This task was accomplished by a memo initialed by both Baker and Meese that divided up the responsibilities of the two advisers. On the surface, the division was heavily slanted toward Meese, giving him jurisdiction over administration policy, both foreign and domestic. Meese was to have the title of "counselor to the president for policy" along with cabinet rank and was to participate in all meetings of the full cabinet. He was in charge of "coordination and supervision" of the domestic policy staff and the National Security Council.[39] Thus Meese was given a very wide range of responsibilities indeed. What was left for Baker?

Baker was to get the formal title of chief of staff and the traditional process and staffing powers of that position. He was given control over "Coordination and supervision of White House Staff functions," "Hiring and firing authority over all elements of White House Staff," "Coordination and control of all in and out paper flow to the President and of presidential schedule and appointments," and he was to "Preside over meetings of White House Staff." Baker also claimed the traditional chief of staff office in the west wing. An addition, written in longhand, assured that both Meese and Baker had the right to "attend any meeting which Pres. attends—w/ his consent."[40]

On the surface Meese had a huge advantage, with cabinet participation and control of foreign and domestic policy. The memo was written so that Baker received no substance and all process.[41] But in the White House process often determines policy outcomes, especially with as detached a president as Ronald Reagan, and thus Baker had the advantage over Meese in the administration's policy deliberations.

As chief of staff Baker hired skilled Washington insiders to help him, and he orchestrated the administration's policy agenda for the first term. He did not seek complete control over access to the president, sharing it with Meese and Deaver and he exercised his power in a subtle rather than a heavy handed way. With his reputation for pragmatism that invoked the suspicion of the ideological Reaganites, he was careful to keep open his lines of communication to the right wing of the Republican party, and he assiduously maintained his ties to members of Congress. He was accessible to and trusted by the press and often received favorable news coverage which he used to the administration's advantage. He thus was attentive to the major constituencies that Reagan would need in order to accomplish his agenda. Richard Darman became staff secretary and controlled paper flow to the Oval Office.

Michael Deaver, the third member of the troika, had been with Reagan for many years in California and had an almost filial relationship with both Nancy and Ronald Reagan. Deaver became deputy chief of staff, but he was not concerned as much with the substance of policy as with the staging of the president and his presentation to the public.[42] He concerned himself with everything that affected Ronald Reagan as a person: his comfort, his schedule, the backdrops for his political actions, etc. Perhaps most importantly, Deaver was the primary link to the east wing, that is, Nancy Reagan. He would convey her wishes, either explicitly or as his own ideas, to the west wing staffers. Baker appreciated the importance of Mrs. Reagan and was careful to accommodate her wishes.

Nancy Reagan was not active in policy across the board, but she selectively inserted her views very effectively when she felt that the president's person or reputation was at stake. Several times this affected foreign policy and quite often staffing decisions; she played a role in the resignations of cabinet secretaries

James Watt, Raymond Donavan, Edwin Meese, and a number of White House staffers, including Donald Regan.[43]

The White House was to change drastically in Reagan's second term with large scale changes of personnel at the top. Despite the 1986 tax reform, there were no sweeping victories comparable to the economic agenda of 1981, and the administration slid into the disaster of the Iran-Contra scandal. The second term troubles were due, in no small part, to the change in chiefs of staff. Treasury Secretary Donald Regan and Chief of Staff James Baker decided to exchange jobs, and characteristically, Regan, Baker, Deaver, and Nancy Reagan had agreed upon the switch before it was presented to Reagan. Characteristically, Reagan agreed to the staff decision with no questions.

When Regan came in to run the White House he had several personal priorities. He wanted to do away with the collegial staffing arrangement of the first term which he felt led to staff conflict and leaks, which it did. He also wanted to make some personnel changes, but most importantly he wanted to "let Reagan be Reagan."

Regan's personal style and career suggested that he would take a different approach to running the White House than had James Baker. Regan had been an officer in the Marines and was used to being CEO of Merrill Lynch. "When I was chief executive and I said, 'Jump,' people asked, 'How high?' As Secretary of the Treasury, when I said, 'Jump,' people said, 'What do you mean by jump? What do you mean by high'?"[44] According to one of Regan's aides, "He considers the Executive Branch to be like a corporation. Cabinet members are vice presidents, the President is the chairman of the board, the chief of staff is the chief operating officer."[45] Regan was used to being a principal and did not easily slide into a staff role.

Whereas Baker had brought strong subordinates to work with him, Regan would brook no rivals for influence. The staffers he brought from his days at the treasury department were known around the White House as "the Mice" because of their meek approach to their boss. According to White House staffers Regan's personal staff aides were "almost obsequious and scared stiff of him."[46] A former colleague of Regan said: "His weakness is that his ego was so strong he did not pick good subordinates. Or if they were, he broke them. He couldn't stand the competition."[47]

At the same time that Regan was establishing himself as chief of staff other strong advisers to the president were leaving the White House. Baker and Meese were taking cabinet positions; Deaver was leaving the White House to be a lobbyist; Darman left with Baker; David Stockman was on his way to Wall Street. Max Friedersdorf and Ed Rollins stayed for a while in the second term, but soon left.

Regan's determination to "let Reagan be Reagan," led him to think that his own lack of strong policy preferences was a guarantee that he was serving the president's goals and no one else's. But to best serve the president the White House staff must compensate for his weaknesses. In this case the president's weakness was his passivity and not being willing to search out alternatives on his own. This placed the responsibility on the staff to assure that contrasting views were brought to the president's attention. In the first term this was assured, despite the staff's intentions to protect the president from conflict, because the rivalries among the staff and the struggle between conservatives and moderates could not be entirely suppressed.

Reinforcing the president's conviction that many policy problems were simple was another consequence of "letting Reagan be Reagan," but this was not a favor to the president. In criticizing Regan, David Stockman called this "the echo principle" and argued that it shielded Reagan from hard economic realities.[48] According to Richard Darman, one of the advantages of the first term conflictual triumvirate was that the president was forced to face up to some complex realities. "Seeing the interplay between us, a lot of things happened. First of all, Ronald Reagan learned much more about reality."[49]

But Don Regan did his best to stifle this safety valve of White House conflict. He dominated the White House, controlling access to the president, scheduling, paper flow, public appearances, appointments, and phone calls. He also, unlike other strong chiefs of staff, attempted to assert control over national security policy. But Regan's heavy handed attempt to control everything became too much. Long time Reagan intimate Stuart Spencer observed that Regan "became a prime minister, he became a guy that was in every photo op, he wasn't watching the shop. And he surrounded himself with yes people. Those were all signs of weakness to me."[50] Regan's control of the White House was so tight and his demands of subservience so great that a joke circulating around the White House held that Regan was going to resign to become a Catholic Cardinal. The White House staffers' response was: that's good, now we'll only have to kiss his ring.[51]

Contrary to the Brownlowian admonition to have a passion for anonymity, Regan sought the limelight, and was constantly trying to get into photographs with the president that would appear in the newspapers. The most egregious example of this was the official photograph of Presidents Reagan and Gorbachev at the Geneva Summit. The White House photo showed the two leaders sitting on a couch with Don Regan behind them leaning forward as if he were the orchestrator of their agreement. Regan, who as chief of staff made the final decision, insisted that this be the only photo of the summit agreement released by the White House.[52]

In "letting Reagan be Reagan" Regan acted as if the president were his only constituent. He did not seem to realize that in order to serve the president effectively a chief of staff needs to cultivate other constituencies, especially Congress and the press. Regan soon alienated members of Congress with his disdain for Congress as an institution and his distaste for politics. He antagonized the press because of his heavy handed attempts to control leaks and his hostility over unfavorable coverage of the administration. Unlike Baker, he acted as if he did not realize that the press "serves as a bulletin board" upon which Washington insiders post notices, and use it to his (and his president's) advantage.[53]

Regan had other drawbacks as chief of staff. According to David Stockman he had an "insatiable ego" that led him to want to take public credit for the administration's victories and to be jealous when others got favorable press coverage. "I had always wished Regan would stop blaming me for being inadvertently more conspicuous than he."[54] According to Nancy Reagan, Regan liked the sound of "chief" but not the sound of "staff."[55] Nor did Regan care much for Nancy. "Mrs. Reagan regarded herself as the President's alter ego . . . as if the office that had been bestowed upon her husband by the people somehow fell into the category of worldly goods covered by the marriage vows."[56] He also resented the influence of Nancy's astrologer on the management of the presidency. "Virtually every major move and decision the Reagans made during my time as White House Chief of Staff was cleared in advance with a woman in San Francisco who drew up horoscopes to make certain that the planets were in a favorable alignment for the enterprise."[57] At times the president's schedule would have to be changed at the last minute or set for precise timing at the behest of Joan Quigley, the Reagans' astrologer.[58]

Regan, like other strong chiefs of staff, seemed to think that all criticisms of him were attestations to his role as buffer for the president. "If someone gets a cold in this town, I get blamed," he complained.[59] "One of the reasons I've gained so much prominence is because of the blame coming my way. It's kind of nice for the President to be able to lay the blame off and say: 'I didn't do it, it was somebody down the line.' There's nothing wrong with that as long as it goes two ways. Remember when things go right that maybe Regan had something to do with it, however little."[60]

But Regan wasn't always willing to take the heat for administration failures. After the disclosure of the administration's dealings with Iran, and the failed Reykjavik Summit, Regan tried to distance himself from the embarrassment. "Some of us are like a shovel brigade that follow [sic] a parade down Main Street cleaning up. We took Reykjavik and turned what was really a sour situation into something that turned out pretty well."[61] What is troublesome about this statement is that Regan is shifting blame for administration embarrassments away from himself and toward the person who was in charge of U.S. performance at the Reykjavik Summit: President Reagan. The strong implication here is that Regan presented himself as cleaning up after the president made a mess of things. This public shifting of blame to the president is unacceptable for a White House staffer.

The final straw in Regan's term as chief of staff was the report of the Tower Commission. Despite the fact that Regan denied that he had any control over foreign policy, the Tower Commission held him responsible for part of the Iran-Contra disaster. According to Brent Scowcroft, Regan claimed to have jurisdiction over foreign policy advice to the president. "He kept saying he did. One of the reasons [Robert C.] McFarlane quit was because Regan wanted McFarlane to report through him."[62]

The Tower Board that investigated the Iran-Contra scandal did not accept Regan's denials. Although it did not conclude that Regan participated in the scandal or the cover-up, it did hold him responsible for allowing it to happen on his watch. In citing the "failure of responsibility" the board pointed out that ultimate responsibility for the White House staff system belongs to the president, but that Regan was partially responsible for the disaster. "More than almost any Chief of Staff of recent memory, he asserted personal control over the White House staff and sought to extend this control to the National Security Adviser. He was personally active in national security affairs and attended almost all of the relevant meetings regarding the Iran initiative. . . . He must bear primary responsibility for the chaos that descended upon the White House when such disclosure did occur."[63]

After resisting as long as he could and after much prodding from his wife and other intimates, the president asked for Regan's resignation, but agreed to wait until several days after the release of the Tower report as a face-saving gesture. But the coup de grace was administered by Nancy Reagan immediately after release of the report when it was leaked to the press from her office that Howard Baker would be Reagan's new chief of staff. As soon as he heard of the press announcement, Regan immediately resigned.[64]

After the resignation on February 27, 1987, Regan's problems were summed up by a former Reagan White House staffer: "Don never realized that while Wall Street runs one way; Pennsylvania Avenue is a two-way street. He never realized there is a difference between being an elected and an appointed official. He never realized the distinction between being a staff person and the chief executive officer. He never realized that the White House demands talent throughout, rather than talent derived. He never realized his job was to compensate for the perceived strengths and weaknesses of others, rather than to dominate those weaknesses."[65]

Bush's Pit Bull

George Bush recruited a competent White House staff marked by professionalism and a low visibility approach to White House service. The best in White House staff service was exemplified by Brent Scowcroft, assistant to the president for National Security Affairs, who had filled the same role in the Ford administration. Scowcroft was tireless in his service to Bush, and often provided a personal sounding board to Bush's thoughts about foreign affairs. Another model White House staffer was Roger Porter who had served in the Ford and Reagan administrations and was given responsibility for domestic and economic policy staff coordination in the Bush White House. He provided experience, expertise, and sound policy analysis without engaging in public disputes over policy or status or trying to strong arm members of the cabinet.

Bush's White House staff did not tend to interpose themselves between the president and cabinet secretaries or have major fights with the cabinet departments because Bush knew his cabinet well, and unlike Reagan, made it a habit to keep in touch with them. So Bush's White House had no major ego problems or conflicts with the cabinet, with one major exception: his chief of staff, John Sununu.

In order to understand why John Sununu was chosen by Bush to be chief of staff, it is helpful to recall the desperation of Bush's political situation after the Iowa caucuses in the Republican primaries of 1988. Bush had just come in third behind Senator Robert Dole and evangelist Pat Robertson. New Hampshire had always been a rock-ribbed conservative state and a key to the Republican nomination, and Bush's conservative credentials were somewhat suspect.

But John Sununu had a plan. When an aide began to commiserate with him about the disaster of Bush's third-place finish in Iowa, Sununu explained how the situation was in fact an opportunity. "Don't you see how much good I'm going to be able to do for the next President of the United States?"[66] Sununu then took the offensive in calling in every favor he had earned while he was governor of New Hampshire and designed a media blitz that helped Bush win. The strategy centered around having the vice president "take the pledge" of "no new taxes" while television spots bashed Senator Dole as "senator straddle" by charging that he might consider a tax increase as one element of an attempt to shrink the deficit.[67] The strategy worked, and Bush went on to win New Hampshire and the nomination without any serious difficulties.

Hints of future problems arose after the election in the maneuvering over how the Bush White House would be organized. After reportedly turning down two cabinet positions and insisting on the chief of staff slot, Sununu began to define his future role in press interviews. In an interview with *The Boston Globe*

Sununu gave the impression that he would play the role of a strong chief of staff by being a "strong doorkeeper," a "tough critic" of OMB's budget before the president saw it, and the setter of the daily White House agenda. Sununu was also fighting publicly over the possible role of Robert M. Teeter, who was offered the position of deputy chief of staff, but whose relationship with Bush would have guaranteed him a strong voice in the White House. The problem for Teeter, and probably why he decided to decline a job in the administration, was that Sununu insisted that Teeter not be allowed into the Oval Office to see the president alone.[68]

This jockeying for position in public and fighting over access to the president before he even took office or made his own decisions about White House organization was unseemly and provided early warnings about how Sununu would conduct the office of chief of staff. Of course maneuvering for position always occurs during presidential transitions. The problem is letting the disputes become public; the Meese-Baker negotiations were less acrimonious and were not fought out in public.

President Bush, who as vice president had a chief of staff (Craig Fuller), clearly wanted a chief to organize the White House and coordinate policy development. And Sununu performed well many of the traditional chief of staff roles. He made the trains run on time. He was the enforcer with respect to White House staffers, the cabinet, and Congress. He fired people. He took the heat for unpopular decisions.

Sununu presided over the senior staff meeting every day at 7:30 A.M. in the Roosevelt Room in White House. Typically he spent from 8 to 9:30 A.M. in the Oval Office with the president for the national security briefing and setting priorities for the day and ended the day with the president from 4:30 to 5 P.M. During the day he would see the president about ten times and would spend a total of thirty-five to forty-five percent of the day with the president.[69]

One common mistake of chiefs of staff that Sununu did not make was to reinforce a presidential weakness as had Haldeman and Regan before him. He provided a sharp contrast in personal style to the president. He was the president's "pit bull" dog who would act mean and allow the president to take the "kinder and gentler" stance. Sununu, unlike the three previous strong chiefs of staff, had firm ideological convictions and advocated his own policy preferences. But what would ordinarily be a major drawback in a chief of staff worked to the president's advantage in this case. Sununu was more conservative politically than the president and was willing to play a highly visible role as keeper of the conservative flame and representative of the conservative wing of the Republican Party in the White House. This was useful for Bush when Sununu would stake out a very conservative position, for instance on environmental policy, and let the president take a more moderate stance, thus reassuring conservatives their interests were being represented in the White House while letting the president still claim to be "the environmental president."

The danger of a chief of staff who is also a policy advocate is that advice to the president might be skewed to favor the chief of staff's favored outcome. The other common danger of a strong chief of staff is that access to the president will be constricted to a trickle. But neither of these potential pitfalls was a danger to George Bush. He knew enough about the policy issues himself to be able to discount the bias of his staff. And his personal style assured that he would not become isolated, even though Sununu did control access to the Oval Office. The danger of becoming isolated was averted because the president knew his cabinet members well and kept in touch with them. They had the personal relationship with Bush that would assure they could talk with him if they needed to. The president was constantly on the phone touching base with anyone who was involved with current policy issues.

But the president's penchant for keeping in touch, while avoiding the danger of isolation, did not entirely eliminate Sununu's attempts to control communication to the president. Sununu's personal policy agenda made it at times difficult for those in the cabinet or staff who wanted to speak with the president about a different approach to get through Sununu's gauntlet. This problem became public when both *Time* and *Newsweek* ran stories that senior Bush aides were so upset at being cut off by Sununu that the president was forced to open a post office box at his summer home in Kennebunkport, Maine, as a backchannel so that his top advisers could contact him directly without Sununu's censorship.[70]

The existence of this avenue of communication was publicly confirmed by HHS Secretary Louis Sullivan who admitted on television that he used the channel to communicate advice to the president.[71] After the admission Sullivan quickly covered himself by saying that he had no trouble meeting with the president when he needed to on public policy issues but that he had used the post office box for "political advice." The point is not what Sullivan had to say to the president, the point is the very fact that President Bush felt compelled to set up a private post office box physically and organizationally outside the White House was an admission of organizational failure. John Sununu was not acting as a "neutral broker" of ideas for the president so that others would have confidence their ideas would get to the president intact if they submitted them to the White House staff. Instead, Sununu was seen as a biased filter screening out ideas he personally did not like.

Despite his rapport with the president and his ability to perform very valuable chief of staff functions, Sununu made four strategic errors as chief of staff:

1. He let his ego cloud his judgment and affect his behavior.

2. He succumbed to the "John Tower syndrome," thinking that he did not have to be nice to people.

3. He fell victim to the "Gary Hart syndrome," feeling that he was so important that he did not have to pay attention to the conventions of public morality.

4. He developed the "Don Regan syndrome": stay in the limelight, and if things go wrong, blame the president.

Professional colleagues in and out of the White House criticized Sununu for his large ego. When he came to the Republican convention in Houston it was reported that Sununu had vice presidential aspirations.[72] When he was chief of staff he had his staff do research to find out if the fact that he was born in Cuba disqualified him from being president.[73] One of his soft spots was his stratospheric IQ, which reportedly was 180. But it struck many with whom he worked that he seemed to have to put others down in order to demonstrate how smart he was. White House staffers and assistant secretaries did not appreciate being denigrated in front of their peers when their staff work did not seem to measure up to Sununu standards. He told one reporter who asked about his interpersonal skills that it "Depends how badly the other guy's screwing up."[74]

An administration joke had it that the White House was run by "John Sununu and a thousand interns," because he was unwilling to hire high quality subordinates as his own aides for fear that they would challenge his authority.[75] Another aspect of the ego problem was Sununu's extreme sensitivity to criticisms in the press. When critical articles appeared he would have one of his aides highlight the negative comments, deduce their source in the White House, and then upbraid the presumed offender.[76] To one journalist he said, "Small minds ask small questions."[77]

Sununu really seemed to believe his oft-stated maxim that he had a constituency of only one, the president. This led to Sununu's strategic error number two: the John Tower syndrome. Senator Tower was President Bush's first nomination to be secretary of defense. After many years in the Senate on the Armed Services Committee and several years as a Reagan-appointed negotiator there was no doubt that Tower was qualified. But after he had been nominated, people came forward with allegations about his private life, including excessive drinking, sexual misconduct, and possible conflicts of interest. Normally a senator will be given an easy time by former colleagues in confirmation hearings, but Tower had been so rude and arrogant as a senator that few of his former colleagues were willing to come to his defense when the charges of misconduct were raised. Thus Tower was the first initial nomination by a president to a cabinet position to be defeated in history. A similar fate would befall John Sununu when he got into hot water.

Far from being responsible to a constituency of only one, strong chiefs have learned the hard way that serving the president means being able to cultivate other constituencies for his use. Sununu did not recognize this, and thus felt free to alienate Congress, the cabinet, the press, and interest groups as well as his White House subordinates. It is as if his attitude were: "I am so powerful that I do not have to be nice, or even minimally civil, to other people." In this he was ignoring the old Lebanese proverb that holds, "One kisses the hand that one cannot yet bite."[78] When Sununu got into trouble those who previously had to kiss his hand turned to bite it.

Sununu systematically alienated and insulted many members of Congress. He once called Republican Senator Trent Lott "insignificant," a serious insult in Washington, especially to a member of the Senate.[79] His behavior at the 1990 Budget Summit in formal meetings with the leadership of Congress was so obnoxious that he prompted Senator Robert Byrd to chastise him: "I have had thirty years in the U.S. Senate, and I have participated in many such summits, and I have never in my life observed such outrageous conduct as that displayed by the representatives of the president of the United States. Your conduct is arrogant. It is rude. It is intolerable."[80]

Sununu was also willing to alienate cabinet secretaries as well as their subordinates. He often undercut their policy proposals to the president, which may very well have been part of his job as chief of staff policing the policy development function. When he fought HHS Secretary Louis Sullivan on civil rights policy or EPA Administrator William Reilly on environmental issues, it was arguably part of his job and carrying out the president's wishes. But the tone of his communications often left cabinet members feeling that more than policy differences were being conveyed. The gratuitous insulting of others is not a necessary part of the policy coordination function. Treasury Secretary Nicholas Brady, a close friend of the president's, told a friend that he was sick of being denigrated by Sununu.[81] Commerce Secretary Robert Mosbacher complained about being forced by Sununu to accept unwanted political appointees. Sununu also made a tactical error when he refused to let Defense Secretary Cheney use the presidential helicopter to fly to Camp David on official business.[82]

Even though the U.S. Chamber of Commerce is an important Republican constituency, Sununu did not hesitate to brutalize its president, Dick Lesher, when he supported a cut in Social Security payroll taxes. He did so in a series of four-letter expletives.[83] That Lesher was supporting a tax cut that the Bush administration might very well have backed in different circumstances (i.e., it was not a matter of principle) highlights Sununu's extreme response to a relatively minor policy difference.

In defense of his behavior Sununu echoed other chiefs of staff in claiming he was merely doing the president's bidding. "I'm no freelancer. I meet with the president dozens of times during the day. . . . The president knows I'm following his agenda. . . . I know enough about the president to do exactly what he wants done. Exactly what he wants done."[84] In this statement Sununu was both claiming presidential authority for all of his own actions and subtly shifting the blame for any of them to the president.

Sununu's explanation for his lack of civility is that each breach of good taste and manners was carefully calculated: "I guarantee you that contrary to the legend, any strong statements on my part are both controlled, deliberate and designed to achieve an effect. There is no random outburst. It all is designed for purpose. And I think the efficiency of the result is underscored by what we've been able to achieve."[85] This rationalization is consistent with one important role of the chief of staff, playing the heavy for the president, being the enforcer of tough decisions and bringer of bad tidings to others. "I don't care if people hate me, as long as they hate me for the right reasons," said Sununu.[86] But that was the problem. Washington professionals understand that the policy preferences of the president are the responsibility of the chief of staff, and they expect him to be tough for the president. Professionals are willing to accept being beaten in the policy arena, but Sununu's gratuitous *ad hominem* insults and rude behavior generated resentments much greater than mere policy defeats would have. Sununu acted as if he did not understand the import of his own words. People hated Sununu not because he was enforcing the president's wishes but because Sununu was gratuitously insulting and personally obnoxious to them.

Sununu's third strategic error was the Gary Hart syndrome. Senator Gary Hart was married and running for the Democratic nomination for president in 1984. When he was confronted by the press with allegations of adultery, he denied them and challenged the press to follow him around to prove his innocence. Not surprisingly, they did, and reported the next time he spent the night with model Donna Rice. This doomed Hart's bid for the nomination. The point here is not about sexual behavior; it is rather about respect for conventional morality and appearances. Any person running for president must accept constraints on his or her personal behavior in deference to public opinion. If he is not willing to conform his behavior to general standards of public morality, he does not have enough self-restraint to be president. The parallel with John Sununu is that he felt that he did not have to restrain himself in the use of the privileges and perks of his office.

In spring of 1991 *The Washington Post* reported that the chief of staff had taken more than seventy trips around the country aboard military aircraft. Almost all of the trips were designated (by the chief of staff) as official business, even though the purpose of some of them seemed to be to provide skiing trips for Sununu and his family. None of the twenty-seven trips to his home state of New Hampshire were designated as personal. One of flights categorized as personal was to Boston for an appointment with his personal dentist. On such trips he was required to reimburse the government at commercial rates for comparable flights, far less than the cost to the government of operating planes for one person.[87] In addition, Sununu allowed ski-industry organizations to pay for his meals, lodging, lift tickets, and air fare for his wife.

When the disclosures caused a public scandal in May, 1991, the president (whose early priority was to have an administration above ethical reproach) ordered Sununu to clear all future flights with the White House counsel's office. But in June Sununu had a White House limousine take him to New York for a stamp auction he wanted to attend and solicited corporations to provide air travel back to Washington and other trips. The president again was forced to restrict Sununu's travel practices.[88]

In an eerie parallel to another governor of New Hampshire, Sherman Adams, Sununu made several calls to EPA and the U.S. Forest Service to ask the status of applications to double the size of the Loon Mountain ski resort owned by a friend of Sununu, Philip T. Gravink. Gravink was a contributor to Sununu's previous political campaigns and had let him ski for free when Sununu was governor. While Sununu did not demand a favorable outcome for his friend's applications, his actions were described by an official as "a lot of bullying and bluster" that "made it clear what outcome the White House wanted in this case."[89] Ironically Sherman Adams, whose acceptance of favors from a New England businessman forced his resignation, was one of the founders of the Loon Mountain resort.

There is no argument here that Sununu's trips on government planes constituted outrageous or illegal behavior, or that White House staffers should always fly coach. Few would begrudge a few trips on official planes with occasional combinations of business with pleasure. High level officials in Congress and the executive branch have done this for decades, and it is standard practice in corporate America. The point is that Sununu abused his privileges and pushed them to excess. His bending of the rules was routine, pervasive, and systematic. He was unable to restrain himself from taking advantage of his position and amazingly was unwilling to rein himself in even after the president publicly admonished him. As with the Sherman Adams case, the small gratuities he accepted from corporations were not likely to affect his behavior. But the combination of those favors with White House inquiries to regulatory agencies presented the appearance of conflict of interest. By pushing his privileges too far Sununu became an embarrassment to the president who was forced to defend him in public. A chief of staff should never put the president in this position.

Sununu's final strategic error was the Don Regan syndrome: take credit when things go well, and when they turn sour shift blame to the president. At a November, 1991, campaign fund raising speech in New York President Bush remarked that people in the financial community felt that interest rates charged on credit cards were higher than necessary and that it might spur the economy if they came down a bit. The next day Senator Alphonse D'Amato (R-N.Y.) introduced legislation to impose a legal limit on the interest rates credit card companies could charge their customers. The economic wisdom of the proposal was challenged in the financial community and the Dow Jones industrial average fell 120 points. The administration had to back away quickly from the proposed legislation and publicly argue against it.

When asked by reporters about this embarrassing episode, Sununu said that the remark about interest rates was not in the president's prepared text but that the president had "ad-libbed" the remarks on credit card interest rates. This attempt to blame the embarrassing remarks on the president was rebutted by Marlin Fitzwater, the president's spokesman. He told reporters that the lines were in the printed text of the speech and were not ad-libbed. Some administration officials even said that Sununu, himself, was the author of the offending lines.[90]

The issue in this case is not whether the lines were in the speech text or not. The issue is who publicly takes the blame for an embarrassing incident. In this case Sununu publicly tried to shift blame to the president. If Sununu were lying about the speech text, his behavior was outrageous. But even if he were telling the truth, it is not the role of the chief of staff to blame the president for an administration blunder. The appropriate behavior for the chief of staff is to take the heat in order to protect the president.

Sununu's actions in this case can be contrasted with a contemporaneous flap over civil rights. Counsel to the president C. Boyden Gray circulated a draft memo that instructed the end of using affirmative action racial preferences in federal government hiring. When the uproar from the civil rights community threatened to embarrass the president, Gray said that he acted without the knowledge of the president. It is highly unlikely that such an important and controversial policy change was not discussed with the president. But Gray took the blame in order to save the president from embarrassment, thus demonstrating an important role for White House staffers and acting as Sununu should have.[91]

Sununu's general attitude toward the press was reflected in his public reaction to a *Washington Post* reporter who covered the story of the credit card flap.

After a bill-signing ceremony on the White House lawn, he told Ann Devroy loudly and in front of others: "You're a liar. Your stories are all lies. Everything you write is a lie."[92]

The final downfall and firing of Sununu took place soon after the credit card incident, which was merely the final straw. The striking thing about Sununu's term as chief of staff is how long he was allowed to stay. It speaks strongly of President Bush's gratitude for Sununu's support in the New Hampshire primary and of the president's personal loyalty to his subordinate, but it also demonstrates that he was performing highly valued functions for the president.

The firing came at a low point in the Bush administration; the economy was doing poorly, the president was sliding in public opinion polls from his huge popularity after the Gulf War, and the administration seemed to be in disarray. Sununu personally could only be blamed for the last of the three, but the scapegoat factor is a real one in Washington. Nevertheless, without Sununu's strategic miscalculations, he could probably have weathered the storm of problems for which he was not responsible.

When the ax finally fell, and the president asked for Sununu's resignation, he still would not admit to being at fault. He blamed the press, the White House staff, and pro-Israeli groups (supposedly because he was of Lebanese origin and had been active in Arab-American groups).[93] Even in his letter of resignation Sununu implied that all of his actions were at the behest of the president. "I assure you that in pit bull mode or pussy cat mode (*your choice, as always*) I am ready to help."[94]

In searching for enemies who would have liked to do in John Sununu if they had the chance, one is reminded of the Agatha Christie novel, *Murder on the Orient Express,* a murder mystery in which many suspects on the train had sufficient motive to have killed the victim. The mystery is solved when it is disclosed that *each* of the suspects was guilty because each had separately plunged the same knife into the victim. Although the primary cause of John Sununu's demise as chief of staff was his own behavior, he had made so many enemies that there were abundant motives for many people to do the deed.

Conclusion

The experience with White House organization in the modern presidency has highlighted several important lessons. White House staff and organization will faithfully reflect the president, but should strive to counter presidential weaknesses. If the president is reclusive (as Nixon was), the staff should try to bring ideas and people to him (as Persons did for Eisenhower). If the president is too open, the staff should impose some order on access to the president (as

Cheney did for Ford). If the president is too focused on details (as was Carter), the staff should encourage him to look at the big picture. If the president is too detached, the staff should raise issues, even unpleasant ones, to the president's attention (as the Baker system did for Reagan, but Regan did not).

Beyond this we have learned that, regardless of personal style or preference, the contemporary White House needs a chief of staff to impose order on policy development, guard access to the president, and settle administration disputes that are not of presidential importance. As the Ford and Carter presidencies demonstrated, someone short of the president must be in charge, or the president will be overwhelmed.

But if that necessary chief of staff takes a domineering approach to the job, it is a likely prescription for disaster. *Each* of the strong chiefs of staff (Adams for Ike, Haldeman for Nixon, Regan for Reagan, and Sununu for Bush) have:

- alienated members of Congress,
- alienated members of their own administration,
- had reputations for the lack of common civility,
- had hostile relations with the press.

And *each* of them has resigned under varying degrees of pressure, having done harm to his own president and the presidency.

A number of lessons about the role of chief of staff can be gleaned from the experience over the past four decades of the presidency. These lessons which were too often ignored by the domineering chiefs of staff, include:

1. Carrying out the president's wishes will often make some people angry, but gratuitous harshness will not help the president or the chief of staff.

2. It is appropriate to guard access as tightly as the president wishes, but a heavy-handed assertion of personal power will unnecessarily anger members of the cabinet.

3. The chief of staff has a constituency of more than one. It includes:

a. Congress: The president (or chief of staff) will sooner or later need support in Congress, so fences should be mended carefully after congressional feelings have been hurt.

b. The Press: The president needs favorable press coverage. Having a cordial, professional working relationship with the press may not ensure favorable coverage, but it can help to mitigate bad coverage.

4. The president should not be put in the position of having to defend publicly a White House staffer.

5. A chief of staff cannot do the job in complete anonymity, but people will notice if the chief of staff squeezes into every photo-opportunity.

6. As Jack Watson says, the chief of staff is the president's "javelin catcher." The chief of staff should take the heat for the president, and in no circumstances publicly shift blame to the president.

This list may seem a bit preachy and obvious. But the lessons bear repeating because they have so often been ignored by the four domineering chiefs of staff in the modern presidency.

The ideal approach to the job is exemplified by James Baker, Jack Watson, and Richard Cheney. Each served his president well by performing as an honest broker and coordinator of administration policy. These people were in no way soft or ineffectual. They controlled access to their presidents with firm hands and enforced a discipline on the policy development process. They performed the other chief of staff functions such as giving credit for success to the president and taking blame for failures without letting their own egos get in the way. Each demonstrated that the chief of staff job can be done without absolute control by one person. There is, of course, no guarantee that a good chief of staff will lead to a successful presidency, but avoiding the mistakes of the four domineering chiefs of staff can improve chances.

In the end there is no salvation from staff. As presidential scholar Bert Rockman puts it: "No system or organization ultimately can save a president from himself when he is inclined to self-destruct. And no system that a president is uncomfortable with will last."[95] A president cannot manage the White House alone, but he must make sure that someone is managing it to his specifications.[96] Presidents must be ruthless in their judgments of aides who are not serving the presidency. If presidents do not pay attention to these precepts their presidencies will be vulnerable to being run for others' purposes rather than their own.

NOTES

Reprinted from *Presidential Studies Quarterly* 23, no. 1 (Winter, 1993): 77–102, copyright © 1993 by the Center for the Study of the Presidency. Reprinted by permission of Sage Publications, Inc.

1. For a full argument see James P. Pfiffner, *The Strategic Presidency, Second edition* (Lawrence: University Press of Kansas, 1996), chapter 1. For an argument that a chief of staff is neither necessary nor desirable, see Bruce Buchanan, "Constrained Diversity: The Organizational Demands of the Presidency," in Pfiffner, *The Managerial Presidency* (Pacific Grove, Calif.: Brooks/Cole, 1991), pp. 78–104.
2. Remarks by Donald Rumsfeld at the American Political Science Association Meetings, Panel on "Presidential Staffing," (Sept. 4, 1992), Chicago. James P. Pfiffner participated on the panel.

3. Presidency scholar Richard Neustadt argued in a memo to John Kennedy in 1960 that he should be his own chief of staff. By 1988, however, Neustadt had concluded that a chief of staff was necessary in the White House, though not a domineering chief. Richard Neustadt, "Memorandum on Staffing the President-elect," and "Does the White House Need a Strong Chief of Staff?" both in this volume.

4. For other analyses of the office of chief of staff see Samuel Kernell and Samuel Popkin, *Chief of Staff* (Berkeley: University of California Press, 1986) and Bradley Patterson, *Ring of Power* (New York: Basic Books, 1988).

5. Dwight D. Eisenhower, *Mandate for Change* (Garden City, New York: Doubleday and Company, 1963), p. 87.

6. Ibid., p. 114.

7. Michael Medved, *The Shadow Presidents* (New York: Times Books, 1979), p. 243.

8. R. T. Johnson, *Managing the White House* (New York: Harper and Row, 1974), p. 82.

9. Patrick Anderson, *The Presidents' Men* (New York: Doubleday, 1969), p. 161.

10. Medved, *The Shadow Presidents*, p. 245.

11. Richard Tanner Johnson, *Managing the White House* (New York: Harper and Row, 1974), p. 93.

12. Anderson, *The Presidents' Men*, p. 184; emphasis added.

13. Fred Greenstein, *The Hidden Hand Presidency* (New York: Basic Books, 1982), p. 148; Stephen Hess, *Organizing the Presidency* (Washington, D.C.: Brookings, 1988), p. 65.

14. See Medved, *The Shadow Presidents*, p. 253.

15. See Greenstein, *The Hidden Hand Presidency*.

16. Quoted in Hess, *Organizing the Presidency*, p. 65.

17. Medved, *The Shadow Presidents*, p. 248.

18. Ibid.

19. Anderson, *The Presidents' Men*, p. 196.

20. Medved, *The Shadow Presidents*, p. 254.

21. William Safire, "Abominable No-Man," *The New York Times*, December 3, 1986, p. A23.

22. Quoted in Hess, *Organizing the Presidency*, pp. 105–106.

23. Quoted in William Safire, *Before the Fall* (New York: Doubleday, 1985), p. 116.

24. Quoted in Frederick C. Mosher, et al., *Watergate: Implications for Responsible Government* (New York: Basic Books, 1974), p. 44.

25. Quoted in Hess, *Organizing the Presidency*, p. 118.

26. Quoted in Genovese, *The Nixon Presidency* (New York: Greenwood Press, 1990), p. 33.

27. Hess, *Organizing the Presidency*, p. 119.

28. H. R. Haldeman, interview with James P. Pfiffner, Los Angeles, Calif., May 25, 1983.

29. Ibid.

30. See Richard T. Johnson, *Managing the White House*, p. 218–21.

31. See the testimony of Alexander Butterfield before the House Impeachment Committee reprinted in Larry Berman, *The New American Presidency*, pp. 264–72.

32. See Lou Cannon, *President Reagan: The Role of a Lifetime* (New York: Simon and Schuster, 1991), chapter 10 and p. 181.

33. Hedrick Smith, *The Power Game*, p. 305.

34. Donald Regan, *For the Record* (New York: Harcourt Brace Jovanovich, 1988), p. 272.

35. Ann Reilly Dowd, "What Managers Can Learn from Manager Reagan," *Fortune,* Sept. 15, 1986, p. 33.

36. Regan, *For the Record,* pp. 142–43, 144.

37. David Stockman, *The Triumph of Politics,* p. 76.

38. Ibid., p. 109.

39. See Smith, *The Power Game,* pp. 314–15. The memo is reproduced in Bob Schieffer and Gary Paul Gates, *The Acting President* (New York: E. P. Dutton, 1989), p. 83.

40. Memo dated 11/13/80, reproduced in Schieffer and Gates, *The Acting President,* p. 83.

41. Elliot L. Richardson, interview with James P. Pfiffner, Washington, D.C., Apr. 1, 1988.

42. Smith, *The Power Game,* p. 299.

43. See the insightful discussion of Nancy Reagan's role in the Reagan administration in Richard Neustadt, *Presidential Power and the Modern Presidents* (New York: Free Press, 1990), pp. 312–16.

44. William R. Doener, "For Rhyme and Reason," *Time,* Jan. 21, 1985, p. 20.

45. Ed Magnuson, "Shake-Up at the White House," *Time,* Jan. 21, 1985, p. 10.

46. Bernard Weinraub, "How Don Regan Runs the White House," *The New York Times,* Jan. 5, 1986, p. 33.

47. Quoted in Cannon, *Role of a Lifetime,* p. 563.

48. Stockman, *The Triumph of Politics,* p. 18–19, photograph No. 42.

49. Quoted by Schieffer and Gates, *The Acting President,* p. 200.

50. Quoted by Cannon, *Role of a Lifetime,* p. 721.

51. Bradley Patterson, *Ring of Power,* p. 306.

52. Maureen Dowd, "Saving Face Means Having It in the Picture," *The New York Times,* June 16, 1991), pp. 1, 18.

53. Smith, *The Power Game,* p. 81.

54. Stockman, *The Triumph of Politics,* p. 243. See also the caption under photograph No. 16., pp. 118–19.

55. Cannon, *Role of a Lifetime,* p. 566.

56. Regan, *For the Record,* p. 288.

57. Ibid., p. 3.

58. See Cannon, *Role of a Lifetime,* pp. 583–88.

59. Weinraub, "How Don Regan Runs the White House," *The New York Times,* p. 38.

60. Quoted in *Business Week,* Sept. 9, 1985, p. 79.

61. Quoted by David Hoffman, "Regan: Chief of Risk" *Washington Post,* Feb. 28, 1987, pp. 1, 16. The rest of Regan's comments were: "Who was it that took this disinformation thing and managed to turn it? Who was it [sic] took on this loss in the Senate and pointed out a few facts and managed to pull that? I don't say we'll be able to do it four times in a row. But here we go again, and we're trying."

62. Quoted by Cannon, *Role of a Lifetime,* p. 720.

63. *Report of the President's Special Review Board* (Washington, D.C., Feb. 26, 1987), pp. IV-10–IV-11.

64. See the account by Cannon, *Role of a Lifetime,* pp. 722–32.

65. Hoffman, "Regan: Chief of Risk," *Washington Post,* pp. 1, 16. Reagan biographer Lou Cannon argued that Regan had four deficiencies as chief of staff: (1) His ego was too large. (2) He held politics in disdain. (3) He did not appreciate Nancy Reagan's role in the administration. (4) He brought the "mice" with him to the White House instead of recruiting a strong staff as Baker had. See Cannon, *Role of a Lifetime,* p. 567.

66. Dan Goodgame, "Big, Bad John Sununu," *Time,* May 21, 1990, p. 24.

67. See David Broder, "What Bush Owes Sununu," *Washington Post,* May 1, 1991, p. A19.

68. See Ann Devroy, "Sununu Swiftly Backpedals on Site of His White House Role," *Washington Post,* Dec. 9, 1988, p. A9; and "Transition Watch," *The New York Times,* Dec. 8, 1988, p. B20.

69. See Burt Solomon, "No-Nonsense Sununu," *National Journal,* Sept. 16, 1989, p. 2251.

70. See *Time,* Sept. 30, 1991, p. 19; and *Newsweek,* Dec. 30, 1991, p. 4.

71. "This Week with David Brinkley," ABC News, Transcript of program of Feb. 2, 1992, p. 13.

72. See Eleanor Randolph, "The Washington Chain-Saw Massacre," *The Washington Post Magazine,* Dec. 2, 1990, p. 37.

73. Sidney Blumenthal, "So Long, Sununu," *Vanity Fair,* Feb., 1992, p. 168.

74. Quoted in "John Sununu: What Color Is Your Parachute?" *Spy* magazine, Mar., 1992, p. 31.

75. See *The New York Times,* Dec. 4, 1991, p. B12.

76. Ibid.

77. Blumenthal, "So Long, Sununu," p. 168.

78. Quoted in *Time,* May 21, 1990, p. 25.

79. Blumenthal, "So Long, Sununu," p. 168.

80. Ibid.

81. Ibid., p. 113.

82. Ibid., p. 168.

83. Ibid., p. 113.

84. Juan Williams, "George Bush's Flying Circus," *Washington Post,* Nov. 24, 1991, pp. C1, C4.

85. Quoted by Devroy, "Citing Year of Triumph, Sununu Defends Actions," *Washington Post,* Dec. 12, 1990, p. A25.

86. Quoted in Maureen Dowd, "Sununu: A Case Study in Flouting the Rules," *The New York Times,* May 5, 1991, p. 34.

87. Charles Babcock and Ann Devroy, "Sununu Deems Only 4 Plane Trips 'Personal,'" *Washington Post,* Apr. 24, 1991, pp. 1, 6.

88. *The New York Times,* Dec. 4, 1991, p. B12.

89. Goodgame, "Fly Free or Die," *Time,* May 13, 1991, p. 18.

90. *The New York Times,* Nov. 23, 1991, pp. 1, 10.

91. Ibid., Nov. 22, 1991, pp. 1, 20.

92. Quoted in Ibid., Nov. 23, 1991, pp. 1, 10.

93. Devroy, "Sununu Sees Vendetta As Source of Troubles," *Washington Post,* June 26, 1991, p. A5; Blumenthal, "So Long, Sununu," *Vanity Fair,* p. 112; Solomon, "Sununu Will Leave Washington With 'Low Opinion' Unchanged," *National Journal,* Jan. 11, 1992, pp. 90–91.

94. Letter of resignation reprinted in *The New York Times,* Dec. 4, 1991, p. B12; emphasis added.

95. Bert Rockman, "The Style and Organization of the Reagan Presidency," in Charles O. Jones, ed., *The Reagan Legacy* (Chatham, N.J.: Chatham House, 1988), p. 27.

96. See James P. Pfiffner, "Can the President Manage the Government?" in this volume.

Chapter 7

Why Entourage Politics Is Volatile

MATTHEW HOLDEN, JR.

A Problem in Discovery

This essay proposes inquiry on a matter where the most demanding criteria for verification clearly cannot yet be met. It is, so to speak, a project in discovery, subject to verification.[1] Political science competes with a variety of other sources of political theory. As far as the presidency is concerned, political journalism, academic history, and law school political theory all set forth explanations of what presidents do; predictions as to what will happen if they do something else; and normative criteria as to what they should do. (Law school political theory, as translated into briefs and judicial decisions, is notably important in fact. In present times, law school political theory evinces a concept of "separation of powers" fundamentally at variance with that expressed in political science by Frank Goodnow at the beginning of the century, and most notably by Richard Neustadt in recent times.)[2]

Journalism, history, and law school political theory constitute the common pool of assumptions that might be regarded as the political theory that most Americans would accept.

Political scientists have both the task, and the opportunity, to introduce some greater clarity into this area of thought and action. The methodological problems are somewhat complex and not further discussed here, especially as social science must be governed by its acceptance of the principle of the "law of large numbers."[3] The trouble is, of course, that the president is always one, that the circumstances in which the one acts are themselves ever changing, and that even some of the most ordinary data about that one (such as the volume of messages sent and received) may often be unobtainable.

There are some other questions that we might consider. If propositions meet the most rigorous tests of verification now, shall we also forecast that they will meet those tests in ten, twenty, or thirty years? If, as I infer from the work of Paul Light, "the President's agenda" consists to a large extent of what the White House entourage processes, and if the White House entourage appeared impervious to interest groups and attuned to school-trained policy analysis, what conditions sustain that form of decision-making? If we were to examine data about the behavior of people long since dead (say George Washington, Alexander Hamilton, and Thomas Jefferson) would we find the relationships that "explain" executive politics relevant to the past? If we were to examine data about the behavior of governors, mayors, city managers, and county executives, what aspects of executive politics would we expect to find the same as in the presidency? What aspects would we find changed? If we extended the approach to executive politics in General Motors, Harvard University, or the Southern Baptist Convention, what would we expect? The first thing to remember about the American presidency is not that it is *American,* nor that the United States is a *constitutional democracy,* nor that the system is *partisan* or highly *institutionalized.* All these things are true, and important. It is also true that the president's personality, moral aspirations, emotional structure, intellectual capacities, or political "skills" are relevant. All these concern how presidents exercise, waste, or merely avoid their basic power options.

The basic resources of power are force, money, and information—and these are ultimately disposed through administration. Administration is the central, recurring political process. By contrast, legislation and adjudication are intermittent processes, of great value but recurrently vulnerable. Thus, the approach to a theory of the presidency that I find preferable depends upon the fundamental conception that administration is the exercise of discretion about the actual use of force, money, and information.[4] The essential question about chief executives is whether, as people "in charge," they give orders to their subordinates or they make bargains with them. Bargaining and command are alternative modes of giving, and reacting to, executive direction from the center outward. The basic administrative structure (pattern) tends to be tripartite: chief executives, their entourages, and the array of operating entities that people in different times and places call "offices," "congregations," "diwans," "departments," "divisions," "ministries," "boards," "commissions," and so forth.[5] The operating entities perform the ultimate work. The core question concerns the making of decisions; the willing transmission of accurate instructions; and the ready performance of called-for acts by those who, down to the Nth person, are involved in policy, program, and operational detail.

Chief Executives: Decisional Content, Idiosyncratic Disposition, and Coercive Capacity

Chief executives have, inherently, more to do than they can master personally. From that fact arises the inevitability of an executive entourage. The entourage has a dual character. It serves both the needs of the person who occupies the executive office at a given moment and provides a set of institutional arrangements. The personal side of the entourage takes its existence from the chief executives' needs for surrounding themselves with comfortable and supportive people.

The personal side of the entourage includes those friends and peers whom the chief executive knows, and whose experience the chief executive intuitively comprehends or respects. It also includes those ambitious young servants who will perform whatever services are required, or imagined to be required, more or less without question. It includes, finally, the migratory, but politically sensitive, technocrats who can provide the professional services required without being part of an institutionalized and permanent bureaucracy. The entourage becomes an arena for the exercise of personal power in its most nearly pure sense. In the executive presidency, as practiced in the United States at any rate, power in the institutionalized service is sustainable only if (1) the function maintains the personal support of the president, or (2) the function is so important, inherently, that it provides evident advantage to the chief executive.

If a political system were coordinated perfectly, operational detail decisions should be perfectly aligned to the program decisions that precede them, and program decisions should be perfectly aligned to the policy decisions. There should be no deviations because of conflicts of will or preference between the highest level decision maker and those subordinates who must execute the subsequent decisions. In principle, the command model says that the chief executive is (or should be) in command and does (or should) get automatic compliance by subordinates once his (or her) decisions are known.

Bargaining and command are polar opposites in logic. They are not so in practice. Chief executives can *choose* to bargain with other institutional actors and accommodate those actors' interests. Or chief executives can *try* to maximize control over policy and its implementation.[6] *The act of choosing is his or her own, based on his or her definition of the situation.* Command models appear to be in the minds of American presidents. It is not surprising that they want people to do as they ask, especially if they have bestowed office and prestige on those people.

Chief executives may be driven to attempt to assert command, or to allow bargaining, partially as a matter of the level or scope of the decision to be made. There are decisions that, it will be said, have an inherent logic. For some decisions, the inherent logic dictates command. Thus, it is widely believed that foreign policy has such an inherent logic. "The nation can speak with only one voice" is a phrase so widely asserted as to be a truism. "There can be only one commander in chief." Chief executives do tend to assert command under high crisis. Theodore Sorensen's and Senator Robert Kennedy's separate accounts of the 1962 Cuban missile crisis show John Kennedy's immediate engagement with the most intimate details. The Cuban missile crisis involved, in the president's own mind, the possibility that he might have to initiate worldwide nuclear war. At successive lower levels of threat, however, it is possible to ascertain a similar engagement.

President Truman took personal charge and responsibility for deciding the United States's immediate commitment of troops when North Korean forces invaded South Korea in June, 1950. President Johnson took on the responsibility for deciding the bombing targets in Vietnam. President Ford made an explicit decision to put himself at the center of control in the *Mayaguez* episode of May, 1975, and the August, 1976, episode in which two American soldiers were killed in the demilitarized zone between South Korea and North Korea. President Carter made himself intimately a part of the Iranian hostage rescue operation.

Tight command may be reinforced temporarily by crisis, but it tends to fail, unless the crisis is soon dispelled by victory. Crises are seldom resolved by victory. They are more likely to linger as chronic social fevers, generating that loss of morale that is the antithesis of command.

The basic restraint, however, is in the power of the chief executive. Yet it is important to recognize the existence of the sheer fact that the chief executive has available some powerful tools of coercion. The ability "to make an offer you can't refuse" exists by itself. The administrative availability of a vast machinery of inquiry, investigation, prosecution, reward by material payment, and punishment by withdrawal of public esteem are fundamental tools. They are not necessarily nice tools.

It defies our experience of human affairs to believe that raw coercion is never applied. Presidents must sometimes seek to move from the gentler to the stronger forms of inducement.[7] Presidents have the opportunity for the most elaborate communication networks in the country. Virtually any information that presidents want will be available to them. There is virtually no person in the United States who will refuse to take a president's call, if he or she believes that it is really the president calling, not some practical jokester. There is somebody, somewhere, who will undertake to achieve a result, if that person really believes the chief executive wants that result. A little coercion goes a long way. It is almost foolish to doubt that more subordinate officials are careful for having seen someone fired than are assertive for having seen someone win a law case against firing. The most realistic belief is that private networks are a necessary part of the control mechanism. There are, of course, constraints on using these networks. Good judgment may inhibit a chief executive. Temperament and moral commitment may also be factors. It may be that some networks would prove psychologically disturbing to the human being who is president. It may be that the source is an old enemy, so that he or she says, "I just won't ask *that* so and so."

Chief executives sometimes act as if the decision-making choices were wholly free of electoral necessity, the desires of friends and allies, or arguments of prudence. If free choice always existed, command would also always exist. Chief executives' choices, however, are not "free" for long. Organizational demand may rise up from many parts of the government, imposing pressure on the president or another chief executive. It imposes de facto bargaining on what the chief executive can command and achieve without a sullen, demoralized, or rebellious bureaucracy—whether military or civil service. Such pressure may constitute facts of life to which a chief executive accommodates. Organizational demand expresses the essentials of "bureaucratic politics," understood as the narrow self-interest of the bureaucracy.

There is also external demand, which is the inference of interest group and democratic politics. External demand seeks, and sometimes achieves, consideration of matters that, *without its presence,* would be ignored. In the United States, the manifestation of external demand may even extend to the composition of the entourage.[8] Members of the entourage sometimes function, and are expected to function, as liaison with particular groups. External demand may become part of the bargaining process by which subordinates' preferred positions are adopted, contrary to the known preferred positions of superiors (even chief executives). If the chief executive is not yet committed, so that the aide is able to avoid overt conflict with the boss, external demand may be assimilated to tacit bargaining. External demand may also be presented overtly by one agency against another, and obviously by operating agencies against the entourage. Matters begin to get notably sticky if the external demand appears to be generated by the entourage, against the overt preferences of the chief executive.

Bargaining concerns how much presidents will tolerate, how much they can tolerate, without some overt reaction. It has been treated as credible, and presumptively correct, that the chief executive would not tolerate efforts by the entourage to mobilize external demand against his or her initial preference.

Yet that is not obviously correct. During the Reagan administration, Evans and Novak columns, with their obvious leakage from the White House Office, could often be interpreted as efforts by one entourage faction to build enough external demand to cause the president to change his position.

One of the prime instruments through which chief executives may assert command or engage in bargaining, and with which at the same time they must bargain or over which they must assert command, is the entourage. The entourage serves the function of advancing or asserting the unique power of the person who is chief executive and is notably difficult to control from outside. Political actors outside the circle of the chief executive will recurrently seek means by which to impose control over the entourage, and the chief executive will recurrently seek means to avoid such control.

The Entourage as Personal Servants: Power and Vulnerability

Chief executives are human beings who operate under more than normal psychic pressure. Nearly any chief executive must spend so much time at politics that even off-hours social life is political. This is why people whom the chief executive knows and trusts, whose experience the chief executive intuitively comprehends or respects, will be welcomed. This is also why the chief executives' spousal, or other personal relationships, are so important. For a very long time, the overt public doctrine was that the First Lady had nothing to do with the government. Such an idea has been in some danger of obsolescence since the time of Eleanor Roosevelt, was most overtly ignored by Rosalynn Carter, and has been treated with some ambiguity by Nancy Reagan. The idea has been most severely challenged at the three points in twentieth century America when presidents' health has been severely at risk: Wilson's stroke in 1919, Eisenhower's heart attacks in 1955, and President Reagan's several medical problems, above all his hospitalization after someone attempted to kill him. What is even less considered is emotional stress on chief executives.

Chief executives will surround themselves with persons whom they find comfortable. This leads us to expect the presence of the first of three repetitive types of participants in the inner circle. The entourage will contain persons of senior status. The more the chief executive must put personal friendships and associations aside, the more he or she will value the few that remain. The seniors have their own standing.[9]

Errand-running falls to the young, who come equipped with enthusiasm, the zealous obedience born of ambition to rise, and school-taught techniques. The younger people will have had a relatively limited political experience. Sometimes their only experience will have been with the person who is now the chief executive. The professed loyalty to the chief is passionate. The tone toward all others, is preemptory. The ambitious youngsters are able to exert influence in the world by gaining a reputation for having access to the center.

The third sort of person is found in the entourage because chief executives need special advice and information that is neither purely technical nor purely political. There has emerged a special variety of migratory technocrats similar to the seventeenth- and eighteenth-century political technocrats who migrated from court to court and country to country as opportunity induced or necessity might dictate. These contemporary technocrats render their skills to whatever chief executive occupies the office. Henry Kissinger and Zbigniew Brzezinski could have worked for any one of several Democrats or Republicans. The migratory, adaptive, politically skillful technocrats are attentive to indicators of power. They are likely to have more schooling than the president's cronies and more status than the ambitious youngsters. Their articulated concept is service to the nation, and they fill a need.

Entourage politics becomes the arena for the exertion of *personal* power, in its most nearly pure sense. The more personal side of the entourage is both the fastest way up and the fastest way down. Sometimes, of course, the people who practice entourage politics are reciprocally supportive. But quite frequently a lot of effort goes into causing other people to fall. Need one do more than observe "leaking" as a process by which people on the inside build up defenses for themselves, or attack their adversaries?

Life within the entourage is framed by the potentiality of a fall from grace. The very powerful are also vulnerable. Personal dependence and the elements of trust that might be presumed impose a demand for loyalty to the incumbent of the office. Doubt about "loyalty," however grounded, is both a severe impediment and an instrument in the war of one adviser against another. Loyalty is judged on many criteria. Verification of one's own loyalty, to the satisfaction of others, is an ever-recurrent necessity. James Baker, we are told, was taken into the White House staff on the recommendation of Mrs. Reagan and of two aides whom the president trusted. They liked his role in the 1980 campaign. What sealed Baker's position, however, was his action after the 1981 assassination attempt on the president. On Baker's recommendation, the senior White House entourage, and the cabinet, agreed that the Twenty-Fifth Amendment should not be invoked. This assured the inner circle that Baker was not trying to advance the interests of Vice President Bush.[10]

We do know that the performance of at least a few individuals has been criticized when they have seemed to place particular importance on the views of their reference constituencies. This better explains Califano's doubts about Costanza. The policy difference could not have been the point. When Eileen

Shanahan, a distinguished economic reporter, became assistant secretary for public affairs, she had made clear to Califano that she could not represent him on the abortion question.[11]

Obviously, her straightforwardness was to her credit. When she told Califano that she was to attend a women's meeting convened by Costanza, Califano had no basis for calling her loyalty into question. But he did question the loyalty of Costanza, who called the meeting.

One of the essential features of entourage politics is the chief executives' belief about the person in question, and chief executives' view that they have adequate knowledge of those people. In this sense, the ambitious young servants and the migratory technocrats are at a disadvantage compared to the friends and peers. The chief executive may say that, "Old Joe isn't smart enough to understand this international finance problem." On the other hand, the chief executive is less likely to distrust either the motives or the good sense of Old Joe. The chief executive may be much less sure of the recently recruited economist or some young lawyer-on-the-make who stays up late nights studying the documents.

The answer is all too easy if the adviser, whether official or private, comes to be disliked or distrusted. The most dramatic case, perhaps, is still that of Woodrow Wilson and Colonel Edward M. House. Colonel House was treated as a virtual alter ego for President Wilson. But when, in due course, Wilson became offended and convinced that House did not serve him well, the relationship terminated.

The politics may become bitter and tough when the struggle is between different members of the entourage and the chief executive has not made, indeed appears unlikely to make, a definitive choice. Those who have some presumptive claim on access never easily tolerate other claimants whose basis is personal. There was some adverse press discussion about the relationship of the private advisers in President Reagan's Kitchen Cabinet to his official public advisers. There is an inherent conflict between private advisers and public advisers. The private advisers (Kitchen Cabinet) knew the president well enough to call him Ronnie without being pretentious. They were too old, or too wealthy, or had too many interests ever to be induced into full-time service, but they still wanted to shape results. Accordingly, tactical logic dictated that the public advisers generate criticism of the private advisers sufficient to make it necessary for the president to loosen his ties to them. The fight could be framed in terms of competence to work within governmental procedures, something the elderly gentlemen from California neither possessed nor wanted. But if one weapon does not work, as it did in this case, another will. The fights may be particularly intense if the new claimant's relationship offends the established public morality. It is only a matter of time, with changing mores in modern culture, that these allegations of moral offenses should also seep into the press, the Congress, and elsewhere—chiefly as a means of disposing of one aide who is in conflict with another.

Claims of ethical failings, especially of financial self-interest, have also been important tools in the fight, and remain so. Governor Sherman Adams, of New Hampshire, was a key figure in Eisenhower's nomination in 1952. Adams became assistant to the president, a job in which he exercised wide powers and made many enemies. He was unassailable as long as Eisenhower could accept both his loyalty and his usefulness. But Adams accepted personal gifts from a businessman. Adams also sent messages to agencies requesting them to give consideration to the businessman's appeals. Perhaps the money value of the gifts was not extraordinary. Perhaps it could not be shown, on the face of the messages, that Governor Adams asked agencies to do manifestly improper things. But public reporting was highly negative, and Adams's adversaries within the entourage were able to speak more freely. It fit the president's purposes to let Adams go. Yet Eisenhower never questioned Adams's loyalty and regretted the need to let him go.

Lyndon Johnson seems not to have hesitated when his associates seemed likely to produce embarrassment. President Carter did hesitate, when Bert Lance was under attack, though ultimately he had to let Lance go. President Reagan seemed even more resistant. He seemed hardly to have flinched in similar circumstances, retaining subordinates well after others would have let them go.

Politics within the entourage must depend largely on face-to-face relationships. People within the entourage must work together, literally as well as symbolically.[12] The White House Mess is a small place. Colleague-adversaries are likely to come and go between order, salad, entree, and dessert. The members of the group must maintain the stance of a common interest and common fate. Yet there is inevitable conflict. No one of them knows what the others have told the press, the interest groups, legislative leaders, or even what was told or implied to the chief executive at some moment. In such politics the signs of honor and station are vital.

Meetings to which one is not invited are also a critical status symbol. They are a measure of outsider status. There may be no obvious criterion by which to assert a claim to be invited without being made to seem a fool. Walter Heller's account of his time as chairman of the Council of Economic Advisors, during the Kennedy administration, shows how this might work. The president had tentatively decided in favor of a tax increase to finance a military buildup because of the Berlin crisis. Heller deemed an increase at that time to fly in the face of modern economics given the difference between the economy's actual and potential performance. The decision was going against him in the National Security Council, a forum that Heller could not attend. He was saved mainly by the fact that the appointments secretary (Kenneth O'Donnell) opened "a narrow corridor of power, the small corridor leading into the oval office of the president . . . and enabled us to set forces in motion that brought a reversal of [the president's] tentative decision.[13]

There are apparently "small" things of which one cannot credibly be deprived without loss of standing. Consider three such "small" things: the car, space, and a secretary. Imagine that you have no car and must take taxis to attend meetings during the rush hour (when taxis are hard to get). Imagine that everyone else who attends has official transportation. It will be self-evident that you count for less in the system. You will be treated accordingly. It was not a trivial matter in the Nixon administration when Mrs. Virginia Knauer (as consumer adviser) lost her ability to command the services of a White House car. Access to space is singularly important. If an agency head can command the space required, particularly when other people cannot, that is a visible demonstration of power.

Staffing an office is the third "small" matter that can be so vital. If one cannot secure the personnel to perform their operations, he or she will be immobilized. No part of this is more important, under current patterns of office organization, than the secretary. The *experienced* secretary is often the person familiar with the existing organizational details, traditions, rules, personalities, animosities, and code words. Even the new secretary is another brain—and another personality—to attend to things that by temperament, skills, or simple lack of time one cannot do well oneself.

No secretary was the disaster E. Frederic Morrow faced in the Eisenhower administration. He was the first black man ever appointed to the professional staff at the White House. He had been active in the presidential campaign and had expected some such appointment. In the still intensely segregated Washington of 1953, his presence was sometimes a disturbing factor, and he was bound to be excluded or omitted—often—from some of the important informal networks that undergird action. No matter what he did personally that would be a fact. Moreover, he had a disappointing series of delays and offers that he thought beneath his dignity.

After he had been there ten days, he still had no secretary. All the women whose supervisors had offered them jobs in his office had refused.[14] Morrow thought none wanted the onus "of working for a colored boss." Morrow's problem was ultimately solved more or less by an act of grace. One woman appeared voluntarily, tearfully he reported, upset because the situation was so much in conflict with her own religious teaching!

Control over or blocking of other people's access to the higher authorities is a well established method of political combat within the entourage. Henry Kissinger, in particular, was severely criticized for using this method to the fullest. If power depends on close access, it may be particularly important to preclude others' having close access, or at any rate to preclude their having access that you cannot counteract. Brzezinski is remarkably forthcoming about his own intention to claim the right to monopolize a certain portion of the president's schedule. His first challenge, so far as his memoirs record, was from the new Director of the Central Intelligence Agency, Admiral Stansfield Turner. Admiral Turner "not too subtly reminded me that he was the principal intelligence officer of the U.S. government and that it was therefore odd that I should be giving the president an intelligence briefing every morning . . . [and] also noted that Allen Dulles used to brief President Kennedy."[15]

There was obviously something of a problem. At the very least it was now hard to explain to others. But Brzezinski did not concede the admission of Turner. Instead, he went—as soon as Turner left his office—to the appointments secretary (Tim Kraft) and changed the designation of the briefing to "national security briefing." The next morning, he phoned Admiral Turner and called his attention to the president's schedule as published in *The Washington Post*. The maneuver was adroit and effective. "The matter was never raised again and I continued to brief the president alone during the entire four years."

The essentials, from the view of an outside observer, come to one point. Turner lacked the clout. Allen Dulles, briefing Kennedy daily, was following practice from the Truman administration.[16] Allen Dulles was someone whose credentials John Kennedy needed in 1961. Dulles, the paragon of CIA virtues, was a crucial figure in the intelligence community, with a history that went back to the Office of Strategic Services (OSS) in World War II. Kennedy was able to dispense with Dulles only after the failure in the effort to invade Cuba (the Bay of Pigs) in April, 1961.

Turner, Carter's Naval Academy classmate, did not even want the CIA job, and knew that it signaled the end of his naval career.[17] There is no indication Turner ever said, "Let us see if the president wants it that way." Turner did not have the power base to allow him to raise, or even threaten, a storm of controversy.

The obverse of blocking and claiming is the assertion of jurisdiction over a presumptively critical subject matter. This is also a tried measure in entourage combat. Sometimes, of course, it is a mistake in that the claimant chooses subject matter that is not productive. But, to the extent that the subject matter is important, the tactic is likely to be one where the ambitious young servants or the migratory technocrats have an advantage over the people who are merely friends and peers.

Mr. X., the president's boyhood baseball buddy, and now a very important banker, may have a lot of effect on how the president thinks about taxes. Moreover, people may learn to pay attention to Mr. X's ideas. But sooner or later he will have to have some authority to give directions. On what ideas shall members of the entourage put time to prepare policy papers? On what matters shall they try their hands to see if legislation can be drafted? Mr. X cannot be effective unless he can control the flow of work and engage in the discussion that has to go on with the operating agencies. Thus, as a friend and peer, he is displaced in the normal course of business by the people who are there all the time.

Shame is one of the most powerful social controls, and the ability to use it over people is a formidable tool. Shame and embarrassment—the obverse of honor and station—are powerful within the political world. The politician frequently must endure personal humiliation until, in good time, he or she should accrue sufficient power as to need to endure humiliation no longer.[18] In entourage politics, actors cannot attribute the pain of defeat to collectivities for which they are representative. The pain and humiliation are so often their personal pains and their personal defeats.

If shame and insult may be used to make people feel uncomfortable about themselves, because of what they have internalized, these tools are easily effective, If shame and humiliation will not cause the individual to desist, these tools may be used to deprive that person of credit before the rest of the world. The tribulations of Dr. Martin Feldstein during November and early December, 1983, are much in point. There appeared to be some controversy about the size of the federal deficit, the reasons for the deficit, and the appropriate taxing and spending policies. Feldstein's views were not winning many plaudits. The secretary of the treasury (at that time Donald Regan) publicly attacked what was assumed to be Feldstein's preferred policies. Feldstein, Regan asserted, did not represent the administration's policy.[19] This might be mysterious on the normal suppositions. The president could merely have announced that Dr. Feldstein no longer held an executive appointment. Nothing of the sort happened. Instead, as noted, others in the government criticized Feldstein's views. The White House press secretary, an official often presumed to be within the range of intimacy, subjected Feldstein to ridicule before the press corps, even to the extent of mispronouncing his name. The resignation of the national security adviser (Robert McFarlane) also appears to have had similar qualities. Unless the reporters who covered the matter were manufacturing issues, the elements of personnel insult were strong, and the relationship to the chief of staff was a key element.

The Conversion of "Personal" into "Institutional" Roles

The personal roles, which begin with the personal needs of some executive, also provide the foundation for institutional roles. Two presently noteworthy offices—counsel to the president and press secretary—show that the personal needs of particular presidents may become the reasons for institutional growth. The concept used to be that the attorney general was the president's lawyer. The attorney general still seems to act on that principle. President Franklin Delano Roosevelt invited his confidant, Judge Samuel Rosenman, to come to Washington. Originally, Rosenman agreed to do so on a part-time basis only. In due course, Roosevelt said to him, "This isn't going to work at all, I want you to join the staff full time."[20] The job of counsel to the president now includes legal advice and the handling of legally relevant issues that seem to affect the president and the executive departments. In both the Carter and Ford administrations, the counsel to the president took an active role in formulating the guidelines on White House staff communications with the independent regulatory agencies. When Lloyd Cutler was counsel to the president in the Carter administration, he took a specific interest in the legislative veto issue. Mr. Cutler also seems to have engaged in some activities that were not strictly relevant to law but to broader policy, notably foreign policy, This is a subject in which he has a strong interest,[21] and he has since written that, until he went to the White House, he had not appreciated the strong effect of television on foreign policy.[22]

Counsel to the president, in that example, demonstrates the importance of the mass communications media. Thus, it also notes the importance of the office of press secretary. That office also evolved through a series of ad hoc decisions. William McKinley, described as the holder of the first "modern" presidency, gave considerable attention to the presentation of his *persona* through the press. Legend has it that Theodore Roosevelt set up a room for the comfort of reporters, and that became the Press Room. Wilson started providing daily press briefings through his secretary, Joseph Tumulty. Hoover created the office of press secretary, Franklin Delano Roosevelt made the presidential press conference a thing of glamour, and Eisenhower—through James Hagerty—made the press secretary a key figure in the government.[23] Both offices demonstrate the tendency for functions to become institutionalized as they offer benefits that chief executives themselves recognize.

The "Institutional" Entourage and the Chief Executive:
Personal Dependance and Power Sharing

Institutionalization means a certain degree of effective power sharing between the chief executive and the functionaries in the institutional units. This is reflected in the fact that a good deal of what is theoretically "institutionalized" only works if it has some personal support, based on benefits that the chief executive personally recognizes. The Council of Economic Advisors (CEA) and the Office of Science and Technology Policy (OSTP) both show this process.

Neither has, however, constituency or function that gives it an automatic claim on the president's attention, regardless of the president's wishes, The CEA has probably been at its height in influence when its economic leadership could momentarily capture the attention of the president (Heller under Kennedy?) or when its leadership felt able to advocate the president's program against economists' conventional wisdom (Stein under Nixon). Each exists on the White House table of organization. If sympathetic allies cannot be found in the president's inner circle, then the CEA's claims will go unheeded.

Heller's account from twenty years ago provides the evidence from which this lesson is inferred. The lesson is also to be inferred from the recent experience of the Reagan administration and Dr. Martin Feldstein. Once Feldstein had departed the government, there was, apparently, serious debate about whether the CEA would continue to have a useful function. The secretary of treasury (Regan), who had been Feldstein's adversary, now became chief of staff at the White House and agreed to continue the CEA's functions once "I put my own man in there." Absent very high-level political support, Joseph Walka noted—I think correctly, if harshly—the CEA does little more than serve as "the highest paid fellowship in the economics profession."

The Office of Science and Technology Policy, established during the Eisenhower administration, has some of the same relationships as the CEA.[24] Today it is a small unit; it has a staff of about twenty-five professionals and also has a small budget of about $1.67 million in fiscal year 1987. Its missions are, apparently, purely advisory. Expressly, it has no authority to make decisions that other agencies must accept. It evidently has the ability to review the research and development budgets of federal agencies, to make comments on the science and engineering activities and programs of the National Science Foundation, and to work with such science-based task forces and committees as may be established from time to time. In early 1985, this included a Working Group on Bio-technology, a National Commission on Space that Congress authorized, and the White House Science Council.

The staff of the office has been involved with matters as diverse as the president's Strategic Defense Initiative (SDI or "Star Wars"); a variety of matters relating to military forces, telecommunications policy, commercial and military aeronautics; and an FAA plan for "upgrading air traffic control." Its particular relationships are with the pertinent examiners in the Office of Management and Budget; with the Office of the Secretary of Defense; with the intelligence community, NASA, DOT (per FAA); and with some aspects of NASA, the national laboratories, the academic community, and the industrial community.

To a considerable degree, the OSTP's impact must depend on the force and skill of its director. The OSTP lacks line authority. Its policy targets are largely constrained by its judgments of external political reality and financial reality. And it lacks the capacity to develop much pertinent analytical data on its own. Therefore, securing the sanction of the president, or a senior staff member, is the vital test. It was, in this light, a model of tactical wisdom for the OSTP director (Dr. George Keyworth) to become a particularly vigorous scientific advocate of the SDI. The indicator of its political weakness, however, is that when Dr. Keyworth left, many months passed with no full-time replacement that would satisfy the formally organized scientific community as represented by the American Association for the Advancement of Science.[25]

Both the CEA and the OSTP illustrate the institutional functions in their weaker phases, when they are politically exposed to the extent that without the personal interest of the incumbent chief executive they cannot amount to much.

There is, however, a degree of institutionalization in which chief executives and some members of their entourage are linked in effective power-sharing arrangements. The present Office of Management and Budget (OMB) is the best known case of such power sharing. The OMB is one of the institutional agencies that can yield personal advantage to the president. At the same time, the president cannot safely ignore the OMB, for without it he or she must exercise a lesser degree of control over the government. The OMB was created in 1970, under Reorganization Plan No. 2, as an adaptation of the former Bureau of the Budget (BOB). The mystique of the OMB is that it exists to assure the implementation of the president's program. The public record contains only a shadowy picture of the agency's decision-making process, the way the agency's decision-making process links with departmental decision making and White House decision making, and so on. It would be impossible, presently, to have the clarity about OMB's decision-making process that one could get about Congressional decision making.

Nonetheless, a close attention to the Washington governmental community, and the scholarly work of Frederick C. Mosher and some others, provide some basis for interpreting what the OMB is and does.[26] Attention to this subject is one of the prime needs in the study of American government. The basic power of the OMB is its budget-making power. No agency can perform its activities without spending money, and no agency can secure money without the inclusion of its proposed expenditures in the budget that the president submits to Congress each year. Thus, agencies are subject to extremely severe discipline, in that they may be bound by the OMB's determinations.

One of the more instructive accounts concerns the defense side of the OMB during the Carter administration. The Carter administration's defense transition team proposed cuts of $8 billion to $9 billion, "chipping funds from almost every key weapon program and killing quite a few."[27] An Air Force major, holding a political science Ph.D. from Massachusetts Institute of Technology, had been serving as a White House Fellow in the National Security Council during the Ford administration. Brzezinski arranged to have the major remain during the transition, and he was asked to review the budget document. In the end, he was made associate director of the OMB for national security matters. In turn, this led to a vigorous effort to save space-oriented Air Force plans (which some OMB people opposed), to limit the defense budget more than the secretary thought was necessary (which the OMB won), and to oppose Navy efforts to get an additional supercarrier, which the administration won on the question of sustaining a veto. It would have been rather remarkable if the people dedicated to Navy interests did not see themselves the victims of an Air Force lobby. After all, the associate director in question—whatever his intellect or analytical ability—was but the equivalent in rank (and therefore in experience) of a lieutenant commander! It would have been astonishing if the admirals did not resent his approach and suspect his motivation.

Some observers report that the power of the OMB is somewhat exaggerated in the lore of the governmental community. Their basis is that the OMB is, in fact, stretched thinly enough that most budget decisions are dictated by agency initiatives that the OMB is more or less powerless to alter. There are too many agencies, and too many programs, with too many complications.

Martha Derthick has shown at least one case in which the OMB simply put aside its expenditure control function. During the Nixon administration, the federal government developed a grants-in-aid matching program, to facilitate state social services for Aid to Families with Dependent Children (AFDC) recipients. The OMB examiners did not seem to understand very well, or be masters of, the details of the program.[28]

There is little doubt that the OMB is a major focus of action. Agencies must deal with it and must make some effort either to influence its decisions or to overcome its decisions in other quarters. The real issue of power in the executive process is presented only in the case of conflict between the OMB and agencies, or in cases where the OMB or agencies—anticipating defeat—adjust action to avoid a conflict.

The second presumptive source of the OMB's power is legislative clearance. This is a procedure, in the federal government, that requires a certification (clearance) that proposed legislation from executive agencies is in accordance with the president's program. Even Rosalynn Carter, who as first lady was a virtual officer of government, found it necessary to work within this function. Mental health issues particularly interested her. Mrs. Carter's subsequent account shows that she played a crucial role in the President's Commission on Mental Health when the commission reported that the legislative process to implement its recommendations was far too slow for her satisfaction. As there was no senior-level advocate on the White House staff, the major responsibility fell to Health and Human Services (HHS) Secretary Joseph Califano.[29] The first lady's rapport with the secretary was obviously not too good. She comments that it was finally necessary for her to go directly to the president and to James McIntyre at the OMB to get things moving.[30]

"Management," notably in regulatory clearance, is the newest source of power, not yet fully affirmed by practice. There has been, at least since the time of Lyndon Johnson, a great deal said about "better management" in the federal government. Most serious people would agree on the need for better management, in some sense. But there is considerable ambiguity, if not virtual fraud, in the careless use of the word. Reorganization Plan No. 2 of 1970, under which the OMB was created, is framed in neutral management terms, as are the representations to the Congress in contemporaneous hearings. "Management," in the more neutral sense, has been much less important than the 1970 language implied. Most directors appear to have had to go to the Hill, for formal testimony, about once a month since 1970. Only about fourteen percent of that testimony had anything to do with management.[31] Congress has had other things on its mind. Therefore, directors would have other things on their minds.

The term "management" is also a softer and less controversial code word for making judgments about the merits and demerits of particular policies. The political opportunities for a reassertion of attempted presidential control have come again in the early 1980s, and the Reagan administration has shown more purposeful interest in controlling the regulatory process than has any administration since that of Franklin Delano Roosevelt.[32]

Early in his first term, President Reagan issued Executive Order 12291, to be administered by the OMB. This order requires agencies to justify major rules on the basis of a "regulatory impact analysis." Any given administrative agency may, of course, issue rules within the framework of the statute(s) it is given to administer. Normally, the agency must go through a process of discussing internally the issue it wants to consider. At some point it issues a "notice of proposed rule-making." A proposed rule so "noticed" (i.e., issued for public notice) in the Federal Register is more or less analogous to a draft piece of legislation up for debate. The interested parties will file comments, some trivial and some very substantial. Even in what is called "informal" rule-making, the agency will usually take account of the comments and decide whether to drop the proposal altogether or to go forward in some form. If it goes forward, it will eventually issue a "notice of final rule-making," after which—at some point—a final rule, having the force of law, will take effect. Such a final rule, in turn, may be the subject of intensive litigation in the federal courts, not to mention other political attacks.

Under the Reagan administration's procedures, OMB secured a power effectively to stop the process before proposed rules are noticed in the Federal Register. The OMB can thus delay rules before they are noticed in the Federal Register. It can again delay rules before they are finally promulgated. The overt power leverage is that the OMB is to police a regulatory impact analysis procedure on major rules—a major rule is one that has an economic impact of $100 million per year. The regulatory impact analysis calls for a rigorous and comprehensive cost-benefit analysis, including a detailed appraisal of the incidence and magnitude of a rule's positive and negative effects. The analysis must quantify projected costs and benefits "where possible." The discretionary judgments as to the adequacy of an analysis lie within the OMB. Under present circumstances, the OMB is intellectually committed to very rigorous cost-benefit analysis and to the reduction of the role of government. This is the procedural context of some rather pejorative assertions about recent OMB actions.

Quite frequently it is illegal, or at least dubious, for an agency to receive communications on a subject or proceeding that other parties do not know about and do not have the chance to rebut formally. Such communications are called *ex parte*. The Environmental Protection Agency (EPA) has been the focus of some severe controversy between environmental interests and industrial manufacturers. Each group has naturally been quite anxious to see its position adopted, and each has wished to see the other have no chance for private lobbying (*ex parte* communication) with EPA. However, the claim has been made that OMB has made itself the conduit by which industrial claims would reach EPA, and by which industrial contestants would have the opportunity to review EPA material privately, even if EPA did not agree with this procedure. The reason is that the material EPA has had, according to such claims, to give to OMB under the regulatory review procedure is made available, by OMB, to the industrial claimants. The OMB appears to have the opportunity, whether it has the right, to choose the side that it prefers. And it can pass on messages representing that side to the disadvantage of others. Does it do so? If it does, can an agency have the freedom to ignore it or to tell it to withdraw? Some federal agency witnesses have claimed that the answer to the former question is "yes," and that the answer to the latter question is "no."

However, to those with governmental experience, the idea of OMB coercion can be credible. It fits with the political culture of the federal bureaucracy. It violates no common sense because most people have some experience of either receiving or giving statements that could be, and were intended to be, interpreted as threats. Officials within agencies do perceive the OMB as particularly important. Indeed, some career officials perceive the OMB as "vindictive," and are reluctant to engage in any dispute with people from that agency. Whether realistic or paranoid, some career officials are reluctant to challenge the OMB lest OMB personnel store up bad memories for the next time around.

The chief-of-staff function is the most important illustration of a modern "household" (personal) function taking on a governmental (institutional) character of its own. What is missing, even more, in current American thought is the recognition of the emergence of an office substantially akin to a "prime minister" of the United States. The analogy is to the functionary of the late eighteenth and early nineteenth centuries. The prime minister was still the king's agent, and the government still the king's government. The contemporary theory of the presidency is something akin to that. But the theory is no longer valid. Rather, this one executive officer now coordinates all the cabinet officers. Chiefs of staff do not yet assert different policies from presidents, nor do they directly contest political strength with presidents. They control much of program decision making and operational decision making. What is called "the president's program" is a ritual venture to which the chief of staff gives as much reality as does the president.

The chief of staff fully controls the access that domestic cabinet officers have to the president, their nominal superior, and largely controls their discharge and reassignment. Political nature, as one should expect of nature, served up two clear pieces of evidence in 1985. The first was the removal of Secretary Heckler from the Department of Health and Human Services against her express will and before there was any clear sign of presidential interest, but with clear signs that it was something the chief of staff desired.[33] The second is the public evidence of a campaign, within the White House staff, to remove Loretta Cornelius, the deputy director of the office of personnel management. Ms. Cornelius's testimony and other actions had contributed to the final rejection of Director Donald Devine, whom the Reagan administration had reappointed, and had achieved apparent demonstrations of strong senatorial support for Cornelius's actions.[34] Even the four cabinet officers—secretaries of state, defense, treasury, the attorney general—who cannot be denied direct access to the president, are not in complete control over policy decisions.

Presidents have had to share the executive role, *to "allow" this key executive dominance, sooner or later, whether they prefer it or not.* Bio-psychological overload is the overriding organizational problem, especially in an era where we can talk of "launch-on-warning." Presidents share power not to be rid of trivial details, but to be rid of major problems that literally give them headaches.

Presidential critics, in the Senate or elsewhere, seek to impose limits on the set or reservoir of persons from whom advice may legitimately be sought or received. Political pressure to subject such roles to the advice and consent of the Senate is almost inevitable and sometimes irresistible. If the director of the OMB must be confirmed, there is no logic to excluding the chief of staff. The reason is that the very fight over the confirmation establishes a process by which the nominee is somewhat controlled. He or she is very likely to have to explain away many things to which the senatorial minority objects. And he or she is very likely to be summoned soon if later behavior is in conflict with the explanations. The president's opponents cannot easily do this with members of the president's staff. There is a doctrine that says that the president should have complete freedom about "his personal staff," almost as if these were modern versions of the warden of the bedchamber.

Summary Discussion

The focus of this discussion is the permanent tension between bargaining and command as modes of direction and control. The entourage as a control mechanism brings its force to bear on the whole executive system of departments and agencies, acutely in the interest of the chief executive. If the entourage's activities should prove notably embarrassing to others in the government, the embarrassment will be treated as essentially "too bad." Departments and other operating agencies are beyond the usual focus of televised glamour. Most matters of consequence do not, and cannot ever, reach the entourage. Most matters decided in the entourage require implementation by further decisions from the departments and agencies. Inevitably, the volume of the business so dictates.

Between the entourage and the agencies, the phenomena of bargaining and command are ever regenerated. People acting in the chief executive's name, purporting to act so, or allowing themselves to be believed to act so, may go well beyond any claim of authority until challenged. It will, as a practical matter, be very unclear what the president meant, but action still may follow. It will even be unclear who sees the president and communicates sufficiently that it makes any difference.

Most of the president's aides—junior or senior—have not much more access to the president than most people outside the White House. But neither they nor the president have much incentive to tell the world the truth about that. Many of the people who have to deal with these members of the entourage may suspect that presidents do not know what is said in their names. But suspecting and knowing are different, and the price of losing a gamble can be very high. Which department head, with any sense, wants the aide through whom most departmental business will pass to be in a permanently nasty frame of mind? If the aide has lied and created a problem, is it wise to challenge the aide and inform the president? Not unless one can convince the president and displace the aide.

Ambiguity is inevitable, but strong from the entourage are likely to produce some action. It is too chancy for other people to simply ignore the entourage. The fact that action follows magnifies the president's reach. This magnification of the president's reach is why a conflict over the roles of the entourage is ever-recurrent. The entourage, however, only partially serves that purpose. Indeed, some members of the entourage add more burdens for the president than can ever be relieved. Thus, there must be assistants to the president, like other "assistants-to," who sometimes "prove" their worth by having another in basket and another set of decisions for the boss to make, even if the boss has a headache.

The entourage may give commands where commands may not have been legitimated, and bargain where bargains may not be admitted. It is the necessary linkage between the central executive and the operating agencies. The entourage, above all, is the element of the executive system that seeks, in principle, to enforce command and to discourage bargaining. Moses could not dispense with Aaron and Miriam, though they collaborated with the people in some very idolatrous behavior. Nor, in fact, can presidents (or other chief executives, for that matter) dispense with all their aides. Indeed, there is an economy of supervision that says the more it is necessary to control some aides, the more freedom some other aide(s) must be permitted. People are permitted, by the unstated necessities of the central executive, considerable latitude for command authority that they would not be given formally and for bargaining that they would not admit undertaking. There are no easily legitimated means by which other participants can exert control over the entourage. That is both its strength and its weakness.

NOTES

1. I will have to reserve discussion of the methodological issues to another time and place, although there is some preliminary comment in Matthew Holden, Jr., "Judgment and 'the Right Questions,'" *American Politics Quarterly* 1:2 (Apr., 1973): 189–214. Charles Merriam, whose role in the creation of contemporary political science needs celebration, is my model here. Among other things, he said, "We do not teach all that we know, and are driven sometimes to teach a great deal that we are not so sure of." See his presidential address to the American Political Science Association (1925), "The Progress of Political Research," *American Political Science Review* 20 (Feb., 1926): 1–13.

2. This is most acutely expressed in the legal approach of Justice Antonin Scalia. See his dissent in *Morrison v. Olson* (decided June 20, 1988).

3. Political scientists sometimes may be unaware of the degree to which they have, in fact, adopted "the law of large numbers" as their methodological criterion, and of the intellectual assumptions and antecedents that go with it. Cf., the stringent demand of Max Born, *Physics and Politics* (New York: Basic Books, 1962), p. 73. On the intellectual history, cf., Theodore Porter, *The Rise of Scientific Thinking* (Princeton, N.J.: Princeton University Press, 1986).

4. Matthew Holden, Jr., *The Mechanisms of Power* (Pittsburgh: University of Pittsburgh Press, in preparation). Also, *The Centrality of Administration to Politics,* Working Papers in Public Administration, No. 1, Charlottesville: University of Virginia, Institute of Government, 1984.

5. E. N. Gladden, *History of Public Administration* (London: Frank Cass, 1972).

6. Joel Aberbach and Bert A. Rockman, "Clashing Beliefs Within the Executive Branch: The Nixon Administration Bureaucracy," *American Political Science Review* 70 (June, 1976): 456–68.

7. Harris Wofford, *Of Kennedys & Kings* (New York: Farrar, Straus, and Giroux, 1980).

8. By sheer chance, the revisions to this draft are being written on the day after the adjournment of the Democratic National Convention of 1988. Within the past two weeks, there has been much reported about the clashes and accommodations between Michael Dukakis, Jesse Jackson, and their entourages and about the integration of the two entourages for general election campaign purposes. In part, this can be interpreted as an attempt, by Jackson forces, to assure that some of their people will be so placed in the campaign that, after the election, they will be placed automatically in the competition for strategic positions inside the White House circle. Indeed, it is quite plausible that if one were well enough informed, one could at this date virtually indicate which people would be competitors for which White House positions. The random factor, of course, is the inability to predict whether, and how far, a President Dukakis would admit any of these campaign personnel to the White House inner circle.

9. When I began to work on this essay, and related material, Governor Michael Dukakis was not widely regarded as a likely presidential candidate, and I had never heard of Mr. Paul Brountas. However, *if* the public material in *The New York Times* and similar sources is accurate—which I have not tested—then he appears as a virtually perfect fit for the characterization.

10. Jack W. Germond and Jules Witcover, "The Rise of Jim Baker: The Classic Washington Story of Shrewdness and Diplomacy," *Washingtonian,* Oct., 1982, p. 145.

11. Joseph A. Califano, *Governing America* (New York: Simon & Schuster, 1981).

12. Howard McCurdy, "Crowding and Behavior in the White House," *Psychology Today* 15 (Apr., 1981): 21–22.

13. Walter W. Heller, *New Dimensions of Political Economy* (Cambridge, Mass.: Harvard University Press, 1966), p. 32.

14. E. Frederic Morrow, *Black Man in the White House* (New York: Coward-McCann, 1963).

15. Zbigniew Brzezinski, *Power and Principle: Memoirs of the National Security Advisor, 1977–1981* (New York: Farrar, Straus, and Giroux, 1984), p. 64.

16. Harry Howe Ransom, *The Intelligence Establishment* (Cambridge, Mass.: Harvard University Press, 1970), p. 46.

17. This is made absolutely clear in Admiral Turner's own book, *Secrecy and Democracy* (Boston: Houghton Mifflin Company, 1985), pp. 17–18.

18. I borrow this idea expressly from Orville Professor Link, a Shakespearean scholar at Wayne State University many years ago. Link sometimes delivered a lecture, "Shakespeare as an Observer of the Political Process," at Wayne State University some time in the 1960s, in which he articulated this idea. He thought it had reference to Charles DeGaulle, though I told him I thought it applied as well to Adlai Stevenson. In retrospect, he was right. DeGaulle had the capacity for endurance, and the will to overcome. It is not clear that Stevenson did.

19. These matters concerning Feldstein came to a head during the week after Nov. 27, 1983, and were widely reported in *The New York Times, The Washington Post,* and various other papers.

20. Theodore Sorensen in Daniel J. Meader, ed., *The President, the Attorney General, and the Department of Justice* (Charlottesville: University of Virginia, White Burkitt Miller Center of Public Affairs, 1980), p. 42.

21. Lloyd Cutler, "To Form a Government," *Foreign Affairs* 59 (Fall, 1980): 126–43.

22. Cutler, "Foreign Policy On Deadline," *Foreign Policy* 56 (Fall, 1984): 113–28.

23. Gwen Williams, "The White House Press Secretary and the Executive Branch," (research paper in Government and Foreign Affairs 823, "The Cabinet Departments in the Political Process," University of Virginia, spring term, 1985, typescript).

24. This discussion has been notably assisted by a lecture by Colonel Maurice Roeser, assistant director of the Office, at the College of Engineering, University of Virginia, Feb. 22, 1985.

25. This point was the subject of strenuous public representations by the American Association for the Advancement of Science during the early part of 1986.

26. Frederick C. Mosher, *A Tale of Two Agencies* (Baton Rouge: Louisiana State University Press, 1984), which compares the Office of Management and Budget and the General Accounting Office in their historical development; and Larry Berman, *The Office of Management and Budget and the Presidency, 1921–1979* (Princeton, N.J.: Princeton University Press, 1979). Torkia W. Nzidee performed excellent service in bibliographical work on this point during the summer of 1986.

27. James Canan, *War in Space* (New York: Harper & Row, 1982).

28. Martha Derthick, *Uncontrollable Spending for Social Services Grants* (Washington, D.C.: Brookings Institution, 1975), chapter 9.

29. Rosalynn Carter, *First Lady from Plains* (Boston: Houghton Mifflin Company, 1984), pp. 277–78.

30. Ibid.

31. Yi Zhang, "The 'M' in OMB: A Decade of Experience," (research paper in government and foreign affairs 823, "The Cabinet Departments and the Political Process," University of Virginia, 1984, typescript).

32. Barry Dean Karl, *Executive Reorganization and Reform in the New Deal* (Cambridge, Mass.: Harvard University Press, 1964), deals intensively with the work of the President's Committee on Administrative Management, which formulated this doctrine as a part of the public philosophy.

   Humphrey's Executor v. United States, 295 U.S. 602 (1935). The political and personal history of the case is discussed in William E. Leuchtenburg, "The Case of the Contentious Commissioner," in Harold Hyman and Leonard W. Levy, eds., *Freedom and Reform* (New York: Harper and Row, 1967).

33. The experience concerned Secretary Margaret Heckler, who had considerable tenure in the House of Representatives before being appointed to President Reagan's cabinet. After Mr. Donald T. Regan became chief of staff she was persuaded, clearly against her will, to resign from the department and become ambassador to Ireland.

34. The experience referred to concerns Ms. Loretta Cornelius, who became acting director of the office of personnel management, in a somewhat complicated situation, after Mr. Donald Devine failed of reappointment.

Part 2

Political Control of Administration

Chapter 8

OMB and Neutral Competence

HUGH HECLO

In 1970 the Bureau of the Budget (BOB) officially died and the Office of Management and Budget (OMB) was born. Subsequent years have not been kind to the organization. Renaming the agency was supposed to signal a new era in which the traditional job of budget making would be augmented by a new emphasis on government management, but the management side of OMB has been in disarray throughout most of the organization's short life. An agency which traditionally valued its heritage of anonymity and quiet diplomacy inside government has found itself slugging it out in nasty public fights on issues such as impoundment. From now on, every OMB director and deputy director will have to be confirmed by the Senate—a blow to the special presidential status which the old Bureau of the Budget enjoyed. Watergate has taken its toll on morale, and as if that weren't enough, President Ford's transition advisers declared last summer that the power of OMB had increased, was increasing, and ought to be diminished. All in all, it has been a tough childhood for the young OMB.

But the agency's rocky transition reflects something more than the travails of reorganization and the acrimony of a near-impeachment. Watergate was a reminder that we must judge public organizations not only by what they do, but by how they do it—and the reminder was particularly timely after some years during which concern for outputs had almost totally eclipsed concern over the standards governing the production of those outputs. A profusion of program analysts, policy studies, management languages, and techniques attested to a widespread opinion that institutions were to be judged as more or less effective machines for producing desired policy results: "By their fruits ye shall know them" was the going criterion. But this is no longer the case. If the so-called post-Watergate morality means anything, it is that the imbalance between output concerns and process concerns is being rectified. Old-fashioned sentiments such as propriety, moderation, and decency are once again heard in the land. A huge, unpopular war in Southeast Asia failed to generate a serious drive for presidential impeachment; yet several petty burglaries and their coverup—actions meager in output terms, though raising immense questions about basic standards of conduct—made impeachment a realistic prospect.

The Idea of Neutral Competence

So the politics of righteousness is getting a good running in American public affairs, and it is appropriate that it should. But there are important performance standards other than those based on moral rectitude and the absence of venality. One of the most crucial of these standards inside government—and one of the most neglected by the moralizing fervor outside government—is "neutral competence."

In the Anglo-American democracies, neutral competence is a relatively recent growth and corresponds roughly with the appearance of a higher civil service about a century ago. It envisions a continuous, uncommitted facility at the disposal of, and for the support of, political leadership. It is not a prescription for sainthood. Neutrality does not mean the possession of a direct-dial line to some overarching, non-partisan sense of the public interest. Rather it consists of giving one's cooperation and best independent judgment of the issues to partisan bosses—and of being sufficiently uncommitted to be able to do so for a succession of partisan leaders. The independence entailed in neutral competence does not exist for its own sake; it exists precisely in order to serve the aims of elected partisan leadership. Nor is neutral competence merely the capacity to deliver good staff work to a political superior, for a major part of this competence lies in its ability to gain compliance from lower-level officials. The competence in question entails not just following orders but having the practical knowledge of government and the broker's skills of the governmental marketplace that makes one's advice worthy of attention. Thus neutral competence is a strange amalgam of loyalty that argues back, partisanship that shifts with the changing partisans, independence that depends on others. Its motto is "Speak out, shut up, carry up, carry out."

As a performance standard, neutral competence is valuable in a number of ways. For one thing, it smoothes communication and thus improves the capacity of elected leadership to get what it wants out of the government machine. Officials with neutral competence can help bring along the more committed specialists elsewhere who are easily antagonized by outsiders ignorant of their ways. When fights become necessary, aid from those with neutral competence can help political leaders chastise others in a way that encourages them to go along rather than fight further. Equally important, neutral competence accumulates informal sources of information within the bureaucracy, sources which can be the key to governing the sprawling executive machinery and which are otherwise unavailable to transient political appointees. Neutral competence, therefore, helps to avoid gratuitous conflicts that would use up resources and relations needed for more important issues, prejudice cooperation the next time around, and risk the ultimate disaster—a complete closedown of information from the offended party.

Another virtue of neutral competence is that it has a vested interest in continuity. Agencies and officials with the attribute have a highly developed institutional memory and a special concern that initiatives be capable of being sustained for the period ahead. They temper boldness with the recognition that they will have to live with the consequences of misplaced boldness. They worry about administrative feasibility because they do not want to have to deal later with problems of administrative breakdown.

Finally, neutral competence contributes a quality of impartiality to be set against other, more sectional appeals in government. Its viewpoint is no more pure or unbiased than anyone else's, but the axes it has to grind are broader than most. Its analysis is less concerned with the short-term political ramifications of who believes what how strongly, and more concerned with the substance of the policy issues themselves. Moreover, because it has an interest in continuity, it is likely to be more concerned with the brokerage process in general than with any particular issue or case. It cares about good form and the use of discretionary authority in a more even-handed way than might be preferred by individual contending parties. Thus its advice and analysis provide a useful counterweight to those more interested in a given subject matter or immediate advantage and less interested in brokerage, continuity, and staying around to pick up the pieces.

If all of this sounds too good to be true, it is. Even when achieved, each blessing of neutral competence imposes its own curse. Communication and bringing people along can promote delays, timidity, and debilitating compromise. Concern with continuity not only can have all these vices but can frustrate any mandate for fundamental change. Officials raised by the norm of impartiality and speaking their mind can generate more trouble, more unanswerable questions, more reasons for not doing something. No one would want a government composed only of neutral competents. Yet their services are invaluable in the play of power and advice. They survive by keeping the government mechanism well-oiled and in working order.

And the existence of this working order is as important as rectitude in making governance legitimate. Rectitude helps make the whole government enterprise believable to outsiders by virtue of the correctness of its leaders' behavior. Neutral competence helps legitimate government among insiders by giving a voice to those with a vested interest in the continuing good faith and credit of the government's own internal operations. . . .

OMB and the Presidency

Just as important as these changes within the organization itself have been the changes in the agency's relationship with its chief client, the president. A number of postwar BOB directors saw more of the president than their recent counterparts can claim, but these earlier directors typically had access in their capacity as heads of a presidential staff agency. By contrast, the last three Nixon directors—George Schultz, Casper Weinberger, and Roy Ash—showed a stronger tendency to position themselves as personal advisers to the president, with a new office in the west wing of the White House to symbolize the fact. The result was to identify OMB more as a member of the president's own political family and less as a broker supplying an independent analytic service to every president. A milestone of sorts was reached in September, 1974, when the director of the supposedly economy-minded OMB testified to Congress in favor of an $850,000 transition expense account for the departed president.

Changes in the budget-making process also contributed to a much closer identification between the organization and the particular inhabitant of the Oval Office. Traditionally, the final step in this process was the president's personal arbitration between the BOB director and the head of a spending agency appealing its budget mark. After 1969, it was made clear that President Nixon definitely did not favor such personal confrontations in his presence. Procedural guidelines circulated to the agencies made no reference to even the possibility of appealing the OMB director's final budget determination, which was now to be returned to the spending agency with the status of a presidential decision. In practice, the Nixon administration, like its predecessors, handled complaints from disgruntled department heads through an informal committee that sought to hammer out an agreed-upon White House view; The difference is that in earlier years this "White House view" had to contend against the agency head's personal appeal to the president. Developments in the Nixon years left much less separation between the OMB's budget judgments and the president's personal position.

It would be unfair and wrongheaded to imagine that these changes have constituted anything like a full-scale raid by political partisans on OMB. For one thing, the PADs appointed to date have not had any special interest or background in party politics. For another, the interposition of this new layer of political appointees was a response to what some in the White House and BOB itself perceived as increasingly clear institutional deficiencies and coordination needs. As early as 1959, a self-evaluation by senior civil servants decided by only a narrow vote against recommending the use of political appointees in line guidance over the various offices and divisions. By 1967 more painful experience had accumulated: OMB staff was heavily involved in presidential task forces to create major new policies; the new Planning, Programming, Budgeting System was causing headaches for the director and everyone else; Great Society programs were proliferating and creating who-knew-what demands on administrative machinery and future economic resources. To a 1967 BOB study group composed of the institution's political and career leadership, it was clear that things needed to be tightened up. This led, among other changes, to the creation of one politically appointed assistant director with line responsibility to ride herd over the sprawling human resources area of government. For various reasons, this first move turned out to have little impact. But the BOB's 1967 self-evaluation did highlight a strongly felt need to coalesce political judgment without having to rely upon a hectic director's office and the *ad hoc* intrusions of the White House staff.

Quite apart from any dissatisfaction that BOB staffers themselves felt with the old situation, there were good policy reasons for increasing political control over the agency and agency identification with the president. Increasingly interventionist policies—with civil servants dealing in questions of birth control, consumerism, medical care, environment, energy, transportation, civil rights, and so on—provide a legitimate justification for a much greater political interest in civil service decisions. Moreover, the Nixon administration, intent on reversing this interventionist trend but frustrated by an opposition Congress, began emphasizing administrative actions that could be taken independently by the executive branch. In the eyes of the White House, administration policy faced not only an opposition Congress but also an opposition executive, a collection of agencies and departments with a vested interest in the ways of the past. Dependence on the normal run of departmental political appointees was unreliable, given their tendency to "go native." Attempts were made at direct intervention by the White House staff but they proved cumbersome, unsustained, and vulnerable to outmaneuvering due to a lack of coordination among the staff itself.

This distrust of many operating agencies was paralleled by the Nixon administration's growing awareness that it could rely on OMB as its chosen agent in the executive branch. Since responsiveness to the president is the one duality which BOB/OMB has always needed in order to survive, a beleaguered White

House often found itself pushing against an open door. Lacking any outside clientele in Congress or interest groups, OMB can resist only through inactivity; its choice is to be of use to the president of the day or to atrophy. OMB preferred to be of use.

A Shifting Role

Although the internal shakeup at OMB aimed at making it more responsive to the White House, it was not intended to allow the organization to provide policy leadership in the Executive Office of the President. For this function, the Domestic Council was created. As the slogan of the time had it, the Domestic Council would concern itself with what to do, the OMB with how to do it and how well it was being done. The Domestic Council would be the antipode of everything the traditional Bureau of the Budget had been. Its virtue would be not institutional routine but policy innovation, not continuity but personnel turnover, not professional detachment but loyalty to "the man."

It was an ill-starred division of tasks. Thinking about what to do turned out to be difficult without having the people around who could tell you how to do it. Since they had a great deal of the necessary experience and expertise, OMB staff were increasingly drafted into Domestic Council operations—and even directed by council leaders not to inform OMB colleagues of their work (a secrecy which, predictably enough, was rarely pledged and even more rarely maintained). With the departure of John Ehrlichman as its head, the short-lived Domestic Council experiment faded, as did White House intervention in departmental line operations; and today it is no exaggeration to say that apart from a few specific issues and political brushfires, the council has developed as a weak sister of OMB. Thus not only by design but also by inadvertence, the political importance of OMB grew along with the demise of the other principal actors.

From the convulsions of the last few years, then, OMB has emerged stronger than ever. The question is: a strong what? Has OMB balanced the demands placed on it for policy advocacy outside and for quiet diplomacy within government? Has it succeeded in being a close member of the president's political family yet maintaining itself as a detached staff for the ongoing presidency? In short, what has happened to the idea of neutral competence as a result of all these changes?

Well, one thing that has happened is that there has been a fundamental shift in OMB's role away from wholesaling advice to the presidency and towards retailing policy to outsiders. The Bureau of the Budget had carefully shunned public visibility and served as an administration spokesman only infrequently and in specialized areas. Similarly, most public comment on BOB was second-hand, via the well-worn ploy by which spending departments found it convenient to blame BOB for frustrating the demands of the departments' clients. Since 1971, however, the director and his associates have sought more prominence, at least in part because of adverse congressional reactions to presidential impoundment. More OMB officials can now be found going to Capitol Hill to negotiate with congressmen. Orders have come down to OMB career staff to do more liaison work with congressional staff and provide more intelligence on what they learn. There is more OMB lobbying with agencies and the press in order to sell administration policy.

However well-intentioned some of these efforts have been, the fact remains that the easiest way for an organization to become politicized and lose neutral competence is to become visibly identified with a given political bargain or piece of public advocacy. As one experienced official put it: "The organization is becoming more vulnerable the more it gets associated with particular public positions. By doing things for this and not that group, selling this and not that deal, we become more politically identified with one administration." Another OMB official observed: "One of the hardest things to do is to disassociate yourself from a stance taken before large audiences and it's becoming harder and harder to avoid doing that. Frankly it tends to make this agency an extension of the party in power. . . . I guess we've always been that, but we're also supposed to be more than that. It's hard to achieve in practice, but there's something of value in the idea of serving the Presidency, as well as each particular President."

As OMB's visibility has grown, it is understandable if others fail to make the distinction between OMB's governmental authority as an institution of the presidency and its political power as the president's personal staff. Spending agencies find it more tempting to justify themselves to their clients by complaining not just about the normal BOB/OMB penny-pinching but about its arbitrary power as a political partisan of a given administration. Decreasing the rate of growth in scientific research spending, for example, becomes less a question of value for money and more a question of one particular political administration's anti-science attitude. Those seeking to maintain independence from a president's personal difficulties naturally think of holding OMB at arm's length as well. When Elliot Richardson became attorney general, OMB staff were shaken to hear that he had instructed his subordinates to have no dealings with White House or OMB staff; it took later clarification of these orders to reestablish the distinction and proscribe only White House personnel.

Even more threatening than problems with outsiders is the fact that members of the Executive Office of the President themselves may become less able to distinguish service to the president from service to the presidency. The aim of lodging the director in the west wing, of creating a powerful layer of line political officers, and of projecting a visible OMB profile of administration advocacy has been to increase responsiveness to the president's policy. But what happens when the authoritative presidential aide, laying down the political overview which is to guide OMB budget-makers, instructs that only capital projects in certain politically rewarding districts are to be approved? Such questions have indeed come forth, and the answer to the question "What happens?" is that in this case nothing happened, besides a collective shiver of disgust throughout all levels of OMB. But there is no escaping the final implication. If OMB is to be the administration's loyal advocate and lead agency, then there are likely to be people in the White House who expect it to follow with a minimum of questioning.

Dilemmas of the Civil Servant

The change from BOB to OMB expressed a legitimate concern for the political responsibility and responsiveness of the people making important decisions. No one should be surprised by the visibility which goes with this avowed political responsibility, nor is it necessarily a bad thing if the organization itself is held more publicly accountable for what it does. But there are also the legitimate claims of neutral competence in government, and if the organization moves toward increased external political identification, the need for understanding and protecting its internal capacities for impartial continuity becomes even greater, particularly in the relations between transient political appointees and more permanent career staff. Here, too, the traditional performance standards have come under strain and may be even more problematic in the future. Political appointees have too often lacked the experience, time, or inclination to care that abstract boundaries for civil service roles be maintained or to be concerned that, once lost, a tradition of neutral competence can be almost impossible to re-establish.

Experienced civil servants worry both when they are too far from political power and when they are too near, when they are suspected by their political bosses and when they are treated so familiarly that the political/civil service distinction disappears. Many senior officials who were once held at arm's length now find that they are being drawn into a closer political embrace at OMB. The PAD is supposed to be the political person, but in the nature of things he cannot go to all the meetings or engage in all the negotiations that come his way. Civil service staff often substitute, partly out of physical necessity and partly as a result of prodding by some political appointees. And as the officials have become more involved politically, they have found it more difficult to maintain that neutral identity which would allow them to be of service to succeeding administrations.

Most career officials are trying hard to avoid political identification, though a few of the less experienced or more politically ambitious among them are not inclined to send for instructions to cover themselves. One senior official contrasted the current situation with the BOB he had joined in the late 1950s: "Of course, you've always had to bargain, but now I run around town and people assume I am acting in [the PAD's] stead. But in fact I'm a career man and I'm not being paid to become an advocate. I don't have the perquisites, the power, or the status to go with that job. I try and do an honest job of analysis, and the danger is you'll lose your standing as objective. But I'm getting stuck and having to take more and more public positions." A much younger man at the examiner level commented on the perils of "getting stuck": "I got sucked in. I guess you could say I was politicized. You get wrapped up in the crisis and pressures of the administration's mission and don't ask the questions or draw the distinctions you might have done in calmer times. . . . The White House wanted to make decisions and you were supposed to give them the reasons." In some cases, such as the heavy-handed use of impoundment or the dismantling of OEO, for example, independent OMB advice was unduly compromised by close and ingratiating ties between White House and OMB staff.

Increased pressure to deal with Congress has proven an additional source of difficulty. As one middle-aged examiner put it: "We like to think of ourselves as a bureaucracy existing over time. Recently word has come down from the head office that we're supposed to find out more about what is going on up on the Hill. I guess we're supposed to be talking about the status of legislation and lobbying for certain things. That should be the political guys' job. When those people can't do it, they ask us to."

Some who do try to keep on the proper side of the political line are then criticized for providing poor service. One supergrade official commented: "When I am told to go to meetings with Congressional staff, I keep my damn mouth shut. A question of fact I supply, but if they ask for opinion or judgment I look to the guy from the White House or send back for instructions. . . . Then when he's sent me with instructions, [a PAD] has the gall to ask why I can't carry the ball." Obviously, a good civil servant should be expected to look out for himself, to know his proper role and keep to it. But circumstances can help or hinder his efforts, and the trend at OMB has been to make the protection of neutral competence much more difficult. When both the agency and careerists are unshielded from politicization, then communication, impartiality, and continuity all suffer.

The Costs of Politicization

Communication has suffered at OMB first in the passage of information downward. As the civil service is used in more political ways, it becomes, paradoxically, more difficult to transmit a sense of political direction down from the top. More people become involved in the act of giving signals, and political appointees are likely to become slack in their own responsibility to feed information back to officials below. For those who do not become actively politicized, the remoteness of top political leadership makes it difficult to get the vital contextual knowledge that would help them do their jobs. As one high official said: "I don't want to run my hands over every little scar from the last battle but we do need to know the general way something was decided. I will be dealing in the same area again, and knowing that something was decided on its merits gives an indication of what policy is meant to be. If it was decided on tactical, or personal, or party grounds, that's OK, but then I know that the next time it's all up for grabs again. Presently, I'm left in the dark."

At the same time, communication upwards also deteriorates as staff become less sure of what actually happens to their analyses slid recommendations. "We found," said one examiner, "that our pols had struck a bargain but here we were still preparing the veto message." An already cautious mental set grows more so. "Why bother telling them; let them find out for themselves," was the way one excluded official put it.

Impartial brokerage, as well as communication, becomes more difficult when neutral competence is compromised by personal staff loyalty to particular political appointees. According to one participant: "The combativeness of associate directors tends to be mirrored by their staffs. When [a PAD] got uptight with [a cabinet officer] it was reflected in unnecessary argument one or two layers down in each organization's staff. Still today, they will send us nothing on legislation." Overidentification with the political leadership can be particularly serious for budget examiners. To operate successfully they must enjoy the reputation of an honest intermediary who balances loyalty to his political superiors with a fair presentation of the agency's case and his own analysis. "It will do me no good," said one, "to become known as some political appointee's fair-haired boy."

Less cooperation and more compartmentalization have also appeared because of the separate, politically headed staffs. "In effect," said one experienced observer, "PADs have a staff which tends to be their staff. Everyone is much more conscious of protecting his own turf, with less flowing from side to side and from one piece of real estate to another." Of course, internal bickering is nothing new to OMB or its predecessor; but the internal divisions are now more clearly and politically staked out. Substantive issues take on an additional political dimension. What is more, senior career staff are less likely to be in positions of institutional leadership where they can mediate internal difficulties. In the past it was the top civil service staff immediately under the director who helped soothe internal problems—encouraging impatient subordinates to ride out current troubles, trying to take the heat and calm political appointees, shielding career people below from political intervention, and generally attempting to keep the place working together. Today, few senior careerists are in positions to oversee the activity of the institution as a whole. Tomorrow, there are liable to be still fewer.

As communication and impartiality decline, so too does continuity. "Formerly," said one recent promotee, "there was a certain institutional quality to your promotion when there was only a career division chief. Now I was appointed by a PAD, and it's not so clear. And what follows from this identification is the worry of being seen by others as tied to a particular political leadership." As one supergrade official summed up the feeling: "You have to worry about maintaining your career status. Here I am having been hand-picked by a Republican PAD to come over and do a job for him. It's not unthinkable that other people will say, 'Hey, this guy's a Republican civil servant.'" When that is said often enough about civil servants, the principle of neutral competence can be safely pronounced dead and buried. . . .

A System Where Everyone Loses?

In present circumstances the most useful course is to begin by returning to first principles. OMB can be valuable to presidents in many ways, but its most appropriate use is as an independent source of analytic advice and governmental coordination in line with expressed presidential desires. In terms of advice, OMB should be the place to look for analysis with a minimum of political body English—that is, a place with a fine disregard for the political bearing of who believes what at a given time. This is not to say that OMB staff should be politically insensitive and fail to make such marginal notes; but assessing political trade-offs should not be the main focus of OMB work.

But if this is to be the case, then OMB is not enough. There is an important truth in the comment of a leading Nixon participant in the 1970 reorganization who said, "BOB we figured was the kind of place that could make a one-term President out of anybody." If the traditional strength of BOB was its independent analytic view of pros and cons, that was also its weakness. By paying less attention to the political trade-offs involved in acting on the results of its work, BOB was in a poor position to give the political man in the Oval Office all the

service he needed. And strengthening the Domestic Council so that it can perform this political function is not in itself a threat to OMB's neutral competence. What is required now is just such a strengthening of the Domestic
Council to bring political and partisan judgments to bear on analysis. The need
is not for bright and incisive analysts calling themselves political appointees,
but for real pols on the White House staff with the wit and understanding to
use analysis. A group of political appointees is needed to politicize the White
House analysis of issues, not to politicize OMB.

The old problems will not disappear if a president chooses this mixed OMB–
Domestic Council option. White House staff will still lack much knowledge
and internal departmental access, which OMB will have to assist in providing.
OMB staff will still be involved in important decision making in a way that
could abrogate political responsibility. The demands on both the careerists'
political sensitivity find the political appointees' ability to moderate their partisanship will, therefore, also be great. But the costs of the strategy pursued so
far, in further inroads into impartial continuity at the government center, are
likely to be larger still.

By choosing this mixed strategy, one avoids the misleading question of
whether OMB is too strong or too involved in policy. For the sake of the president's own influence within the executive, and the commonsense need to link
spending with policy decisions, OMB needs to be involved in policy. For the
president's and its own sake. OMB has gained too much political power and
lost too much of the governmental authority that stems from neutral competence. This is a matter not of *how much* power but of *what kind* of power. The
current danger is that in reaction to the politicization of the Nixon years, OMB
will be diminished in *all* kinds of power, and that an already weak government
center will be further debilitated at a time when coherent presidential leadership is especially important to prevent self-destructive infighting in the executive branch.

What is at stake for any president or OMB director is not the conventional
question of whether White House staff or OMB is too strong or too weak.
The events of recent years suggest that it is possible for them to be both, and
thus to produce the worst of both worlds. OMB can prove so effective a lead
agency in administration advocacy that it prejudices its chance of acceptance
by a successor administration. Civil servants may simultaneously become too
suspect to, and too intimate with, political leadership. Appointees and "their"
careerists may provide more temporary political responsiveness but at the price
of a lessened long-term capacity to respond, as career staff who are not politically identified are kept further from events and rendered less knowledgeable
than they should be to service a new administration. There can be more inter-

mediaries and less mediation. Political power may become more competitive with bureaucratic power at the same time as the net experience and continuity of the government machine as a whole declines. Bureaucracy can become more politicized and more difficult to control. All of which is to say that the way things are going, we can easily create a system in which everyone loses.

Note: Reprinted with permission from the author from: *The Public Interest*, no. 38 (Winter, 1975): 80–99. © 1975 by National Affairs, Inc.

Chapter 9

The Politicized Presidency

TERRY M. MOE

More than any other modern president, Ronald Reagan has moved with dedication and comprehensiveness to take hold of the administrative machinery of government. At the heart of his approach are the politicization of administrative arrangements and the centralization of policy-related concerns in the White House: developments in the institutional presidency with origins in past administrations, but now significantly accelerated and expanded. The Office of Management and Budget has been thoroughly politicized, both through appointments and its active involvement in distinctly political policy making and lobbying processes. Largely via the functioning of the Office of Policy Development, the actors in the executive policy process—the cabinet, the bureaucracy, the OMB—have been integrated and coordinated from the top, and an array of problems and issues potentially dealt with in other administrative arenas has been drawn into the White House for centralized evaluation, reconciliation, and action. With heavy emphasis on ideology and loyalty, the appointment power has been put to systematic use in "infiltrating" the bureaucracy as a means of promoting political responsiveness, changing bureaucratic decision criteria from within, and facilitating the smooth operation of the OPD.

Among those who study the institutional presidency, there is substantial agreement that, policy and ideological considerations aside, the developments described here are undesirable. Reagan is accused of "deinstitutionalizing" the presidency and eroding its long-term capacity for effective leadership. Politicization is deplored for its destructive effects on institutional memory, expertise, professionalism, objectivity, communications, continuity, and other bases of organizational competence. Centralization is disparaged for its circumvention of established institutions and for its ineffective reliance on an already overburdened White House. These developments need to be turned around, it is claimed, through reforms designed to encourage a far greater presidential reliance on the OMB, the cabinet, and the bureaucracy, and a substantially enhanced presidential respect for their integrity, their distinctive areas of expertise and experience, and the value of protecting and cultivating their neutral competence.

The issues involved here are in fact quite general. They concern the determinants of presidential behavior, the requirements of presidential leadership, and the forces driving the development of the institutional presidency. Any effort to understand or criticize the Reagan administrative expertise must ultimately rest on these general sorts of concerns, which are by nature theoretical, having to do with questions of cause and effect whose scope extends well beyond the confines of a single administration.

This essay offers a theoretical argument that places the Reagan experience, as well as the criticisms directed against it, in larger perspective. The foundation of the argument is an abstract framework for understanding the dynamics of institutional development regardless of the type of institution. This framework is applied to the institutional presidency and elaborated more concretely to yield a theoretical basis for explaining its historical development. The argument is then illustrated by a brief analysis of the institutional presidency that focuses on the emergence of politicization and centralization. As a final step, it is put to use in addressing the standard criticisms that have been leveled against these developments.

The Logic of Institutional Development

All institutions share a simple internal logic that guides their maintenance and development. This logic acquires its dynamic from a reciprocal relationship: the distinctive behavioral structures that define an institution derive from the choices of individuals, while the choices of individuals derive from incentives and resources that are shaped by the institutional context itself, as well as its surrounding environment. Individual choices create institutions, but institutions condition individual choices.[1]

This suggests that institutional development is driven by the degree of congruence between existing structures, on the one hand, and existing incentives and resources on the other. When individuals have incentives to alter existing structures and also have the resources to act with some measure of effectiveness, institutional changes are set in motion. These changes then have reciprocal effects that alter individual incentives and resources, which in turn propel the next round of institutional changes. Over time, the system comes to rest (if at all) when prevailing structures prove to be compatible with the underlying incentives and resources. Stable systems are internally compatible systems.

The logic is the same when the environment is more fully considered. Because the environment can influence all three internal components—structures, incentives, resources—its exact configuration shapes the nature of the incongruence among them, and, in so doing, encourages certain paths of institutional development and certain patterns of institutional outcomes rather than others. As the environment changes, the kinds of institutional developments and outcomes it encourages will also tend to change. But whether the environment changes or not, the directions and dynamics of institutional change are geared to the incongruence among structures, incentives, and resources.[2]

The institutional presidency is a term commonly used in reference to the White House, the Office of Management and Budget, and other elements of the Executive Office of the President—for example, the Council of Economic Advisers and the National Security Council. Less commonly (but properly), it also refers to patterned behaviors that link the presidency to other parts of the political system—policy-making routines, for example, that incorporate the cabinet and the permanent bureaucracy. These elements vary in the extent to which they are institutionalized. The Office of Management and Budget is a complex organization whose behavior is governed by a high degree of regularity and continuity, while many of the structures within the White House are quite ephemeral, often with life spans shorter than a single presidential term. Collectively, however, they constitute a variegated institutional system that conforms to the simple logic just outlined.

Thus understood, the development of the institutional presidency over time should be a reflection of its underlying degree of congruence. The precise meaning of congruence in this context is of course complicated, since in principle it involves the balance that is struck among all structures, incentives, and resources within the system. But little is lost if the focus is simply on the president, who provides the institution with orientation and is clearly the driving force behind it. The question of congruence is, above all, a question about the extent to which existing structures making up the institutional presidency are congruent with the incentives and resources of the president. If presidents are dissatisfied with the institutional arrangements they inherit, then they will initiate changes to the extent they have the resources to do so. These changes subsequently have feedback effects on the president and a variety of other participants, which may then prompt further adjustments. The process will not come to rest—that is to say, presidents will continue modifying and reforming the institutional presidency—until congruence is realized. What we need to know in order to understand the dynamics of this process as it unfolds over time, then, has to do with why presidents become dissatisfied with their institutions, what resources they can put to use in seeking change, and what kinds of changes they are likely to initiate in their efforts to create more suitable institutional arrangements.

Historically, presidents have differed widely in personality, style, and agenda. Nonetheless, certain factors have structured the incentives of all modern presidents along the same basic lines. In the American separation-of-powers system, the president is the only politician with a national constituency and thus with an electoral incentive to pursue some broader notion of the public interest, even if restricted to the interests of the coalition that supports him. This is generally a powerful incentive during the first term, less so during the second, although, even then, the demonstrated value of presidential popularity and the tendency for second-term presidents to be centrally concerned with their places in history encourage them to be responsive to broad national interests. These incentives are reinforced by popular, political, and media expectations: the president has always been a convenient governmental focus, and, as government has taken a far more positive role over the years in addressing a wide range of social problems—and as Congress has shown itself quite incapable of institutional coherence and political leadership—the president has increasingly been held responsible for designing, proposing, legislating, administering, and modifying public policy, that is, for governing. His chances for reelection, his standing with opinion leaders and the public, and his historical legacy all depend on his perceived success as the generalized leader of government.[3]

Whatever his particular policy objectives, whatever his personality and style, the modern president is driven by these formidable expectations to seek control over the structures and processes of government. In view of his limited constitutional powers and the sheer complexity of modern government, the president clearly needs the kind of information, expertise, and coordinating capacity that only a large organizational apparatus can provide. Yet the precise kind of institutional presidency he needs is determined by the kinds of expectations that drive him. He is not interested in efficiency or effectiveness or coordination per se, and he does not give preeminence to the "neutral competence" these properties may seem to require.[4] He is a politician fundamentally concerned with the dynamics of political leadership and thus with political support and opposition, political strategy, and political trade-offs. What he wants is an institutional system responsive to his needs as a political leader. He values organizational competence, to be sure, but what he seeks is "responsive competence," not neutral competence.[5]

A president who finds institutional arrangements inadequate to his needs has incentives to pursue reform, but the reforms he actually pursues are determined by the resources he can marshal and his flexibility in putting them to use. In these respects, the president is severely constrained. Many reforms may seem well designed to enhance executive leadership, but few are in fact attainable. Several types of constraints are important.

The president is embedded in a much larger network of political institutions that seriously limit what he can do. Above all the constitutional system guarantees that the president and Congress will be locked in institutional struggle, particularly over issues bearing on their relative powers. While Congress has long recognized the need for presidential leadership and been willing to grant presidents certain statutory powers and organizational resources, the institutional presidency is nonetheless intrinsically threatening to it. Ideas to expand the presidency in any significant way can count on meeting with resistance if proposed, and for that reason alone presidents must normally dispense with grand designs. Only under special circumstances will quantum leaps in the institutional presidency meet with congressional approval.[6]

Even if the focus is only on his room for maneuver within these limits, the impediments to reform are substantial. A pervasive problem is that all organizations have their own routines, their own agendas, their own norms, their own ways of coding and interpreting the world, their own bases of support, and the president cannot expect to control them easily. This is clearly true for the usual government agencies, whose interests and worldviews center around their own programs, and whose support (which they orchestrate) comes from congressional committees and interest groups with political muscle. But it is also true of so-called presidential agencies like the Office of Management and Budget; while they may "exist to serve the president" and have no other constituency, formal organization inevitably creates interests and beliefs that set them apart from him. This is a fact of organizational life that presidents quickly learn if they do not know it already: neutral competence is not enough.[7]

More generally still, all institutionalized behaviors, whether or not they have an organization chart or formal name, generate expectations conducive to their continuation. A structure that regularly collects and disseminates useful information becomes valuable to those on the receiving end; they incorporate the information into their own decisions, they depend on it, they expect it to continue—and, if it suddenly stops, they join a chorus of demands for its renewal. The same sort of thing occurs when political resources are used in a regular fashion over time. Continued use of the president's appointment power to reward partisans and members of Congress, for instance, does more than serve immediate political ends; it also generates expectations about how presidents in general should use their appointment power, as well as penalties if those expectations are violated. A president who comes into office intent on departing from past practices, therefore, including the organizations and routines within the institutional presidency, will find it difficult to do so without upsetting a maze of supporting expectations and relationships, All things considered, there will often be no net advantage to pressing ahead and much to be lost.[8]

In addition to facing these major structural constraints, presidents and their advisers have a serious knowledge problem: even if they had the resources to impose any reforms they liked, they would not know how to design an institutional system optimally suited to presidential needs. This is not simply because they are new to the scene; in fact, largely as a rational response to the knowledge problem, the presidential team will purposely include members with extensive experience and connections. The reason for their problem, rather, is that the social science of organizations is so poorly developed. While organization theorists have been cranking out thousands of studies for decades, the fact is that no systematic body of knowledge is available to presidents—or anyone else for confidently linking alternative institutional designs to alternative sets of consequences. Presidents may know where they want to go, but science cannot tell them how to get there. As a result, presidents rely—often implicitly, without conscious choice—on experience and popular belief systems about organizations. Experience is a vast storehouse of information about existing and past institutional arrangements, information that derives from the institutional memory of the system as a whole and can be "worked" by presidential team members who know where to look and whom to ask. Popular belief systems about organizations have their roots in social science but are really blends of plausible theoretical notions, common sense, and normative beliefs. In their implicit reliance on both sources of ideas, presidents tend to recognize and respect the great uncertainties involved in making nonincremental changes in institutional arrangements, since these entail very real political risks.[9]

Finally, presidents are severely constrained by time. At the outside, they have eight years in which to prove themselves and achieve their policy goals; but even this—a brief period, by congressional and bureaucratic standards—vastly understates the time pressures under which a president must act. The first year of the first term is crucial. The administration must rush to take advantage of this unique opportunity by developing, evaluating, and gathering support for its program—an effort that requires from the very start an institutional system that responds quickly and with political sensitivity to the president's pressing needs for immediate action. Beyond the first year, opposition grows and there are fewer opportunities for presidential success, but events continue to move quickly and unpredictably. Fires must be put out, bargains struck, rare "windows of opportunity" acted upon, and elections—every other year is an election year—reflected in the calculus of governing. The administration must be nimble and constantly on the move or it will be overwhelmed by the increasing odds against its success. These pressures drive out grand designs and long-term plans; they also drive out thoughtful, careful analysis. But the pressures themselves arise from the realities of politics, and the president ignores them at his peril: if he wants to be successful, he usually has no choice but to think in the short term and to demand supporting institutions that respond quickly and appropriately to his political needs. As Harold Seidman notes, "Presidents operate under rigid time constraints, What they want, they want now."[10]

All of this paints a rather bleak picture. The president is burdened by expectations that far exceed his capacity for effective action, and he has strong incentives to right the imbalance by reforming and elaborating the institutional presidency. Yet his drive toward institutional change is slowed and its directions constrained by severe limits—some environmentally imposed, some internal to the presidency—on the resources he can bring to bear. The result is an institutional system that does indeed contain forces that push it toward greater congruence, but whose constraints guarantee that adjustments will be halting, highly imperfect, and nowhere near sufficient (at least for the foreseeable future) to alleviate the massive imbalance between expectations and capacity.

In general, what should this developmental process of adjustment look like? It is best to begin by emphasizing a simple but important point: institutional change is firmly rooted in the past. The president is virtually forced to accept the basic institutional framework he inherits from his predecessors. Congressional opposition, bureaucratic resistance and parochialism, and the institutional generation of self-supporting expectations work to guarantee that most changes of real consequence will be too politically painful to justify their pursuit. Moreover, the combination of knowledge problems and time pressures helps to guarantee that the president will often prefer arrangements not too different from those already in place; he does not have the time to design and fight for fundamentally new support institutions, and his reliance upon institutional memory and popular concepts of organizational design encourages the familiar rather than the experimental.

The legacy of the past discourages comprehensive reform efforts—but, precisely because it does, it magnifies the president's incentives to pour effort into minor but feasible changes by making maximum use of the structures and resources closest to him and least controlled by outsiders. This channeling of presidential effort into areas of greatest flexibility can actually be a source of real volatility, as presidents chafing at the inadequacies and constraints built into the larger system compensate with flurries of incremental reforms—followed by endless adaptations to new circumstances—that aggregate to substantial change without altering the basic institutional framework. Given the knowledge problem and time pressures, these changes may prove rather ad hoc and ill-advised; but they are often correctable, and over the long haul their movement is guided by the drive toward congruence, reflected above all in the president's desire to make the system more responsive to his needs.

This pursuit of responsive competence, as expressed through the channeling of presidential effort, encourages two basic developmental thrusts. The first is the increasing centralization of the institutional presidency in the White House. Because the president can count on unequaled responsiveness from his own people, increases in White House organizational competence—for example, through greater size, division of labor, specialization, hierarchic coordination, formal linkages with outside organizations and constituencies—appear to him to have direct, undiluted payoffs for the pursuit of presidential interests. By contrast, similar increases in competence within the permanent bureaucracy, or even within the OMB, would be discounted (perhaps very heavily) in value by lower levels of responsiveness, not to mention outright resistance. Moreover, the White House affords him far more flexibility in adapting and drawing upon organizational competence as circumstances and political needs change. The actual level of White House competence may be much lower than that of other government organizations, but the combination of responsiveness, flexibility, and strong incentives to circumvent established organizations and vested interests gives the White House a built-in advantage in the development of presidential support institutions.

In the early stages, the president will be limited in the problems and issues that can successfully be pulled into the White House; he will be forced to defer both to the greater competence of external organizations and to surrounding expectations that traditional structures and processes will be relied upon. But over time the built-in advantage of the White House will prevail: presidents will incrementally enhance its competence, problems and issues will be increasingly drawn into it for centralized coordination and control, expectations surrounding previous patterns will slowly break down, new expectations will form around a White House–centered system, and the new expectations will further accelerate the flow of problems and issues to the White House—thus enhancing the need for still greater White House competence.

The second development is the increasing politicization of the institutional system. This approach to responsive competence is particularly attractive because it is anchored in a formal presidential power that, in its implications for political and bureaucratic control, is perhaps more important than any other he possesses: the power of appointment. By appointing individuals on the basis of loyalty, ideology, or programmatic support, he can take direct action to enhance responsiveness throughout the administration, from presidential agencies like the OMB to the most remote independent boards and commissions. And, by emphasizing professionalism, expertise, and administrative experience, he can take action to enhance organizational competence. In the grander scheme of things, of course, he will want to seek out some candidates primarily for their responsiveness, some primarily for their competence, and some for their mix of scores along both dimensions, depending on where in government they are to be located and what they are expected to do. In addition, by manipulating civil service rules, proposing minor reorganizations, and pressing for modifying legislation, he can take steps to increase the number and location of administrative positions that can be occupied by appointees.

There are limits, to be sure. Presidents have traditionally used many appointments as political payoffs and have been expected to do so by other politicians. Similarly, Congress tends to oppose presidential attempts to politicize the bureaucracy. But to the extent he has the freedom to move in this direction, the president will find politicization irresistible. The appointment power is simple, readily available, and enormously flexible. It assumes no sophisticated institutional designs and little ability to predict the future, and it is incremental in the extreme: in principle, each appointment is a separate action. Thus, while knowledge demands are not negligible—somehow, candidates must be recruited, evaluated, and the like—many mistakes can be corrected and adjustments can be made as the inevitably changing short-term pressures of presidential politics seem to require. By taking advantage of these attractive properties, the president is uniquely positioned to try to construct his own foundation for countering bureaucratic resistance, mobilizing bureaucratic competence, and integrating the disparate elements of his administration into a more coherent whole. Given his general lack of resources and options, these are enticing prospects indeed.

None of this suggests that any given president will be successful, whether in terms of policy, popularity, leadership, executive control, or any other dimension of evaluation. Nor does it suggest that politicization and White House centralization will always contribute to presidential success. Indeed, the enormous gap between expectations and capacity may help ensure that most modern presidents will in the end be regarded as "failures" in basic respects.[11] The suggestion here is simply that the institutional presidency is destined to develop in a particular way over time, owing to the nature and degree of the underlying incongruence, serious constraints of presidential resources, and the consequent channeling of presidential effort into areas of greatest flexibility. In an ideal world, presidents might pursue a variety of institutional reforms in righting the imbalance between expectations and capacity. In the real world they readily embrace politicization and centralization because they have no attractive alternatives. The causes are systemic—they are rooted in the way the larger institutional system is put together. . . .

Evaluating Politicization and Centralization

Students of the institutional presidency are virtually unanimous in denouncing these trends, claiming that they undermine and circumvent the competence of established institutions, inhibit the development of new sources of institutional support, and shift decision-making responsibilities to those least capable of handling them. Their recommendations, variously expressed, involve administrative arrangements that would respect and nurture neutral competence and organizational integrity—particularly in the OMB, since it is so obviously threatened, but also throughout the bureaucracy—and encourage more extensive, more systematic reliance on the cabinet and permanent government.[12]

Why are these sorts of beliefs so popular? The obvious answer is that they are overwhelmingly supported by our accumulated knowledge about governmental organization. But this is simply not the case. After more than fifty years of research on public and private organizations—the bulk of which happens to be on private organizations—we still know very little about even the most basic questions motivating the earliest work: the relationship between structure and efficiency, say, or between leadership and productivity. Actually, the uniformity of opinion has less to do with scientific knowledge than with the ideas and perspectives that have shaped the study of public administration. While the critics of politicization and centralization are a heterogeneous lot, and few would regard their own work as anchored in the academic traditions of public administration, its theoretical and normative background is nevertheless readily apparent in their approaches to government organization and their evaluations of it.

The most pervasive, long-term influences on the study of government organization derive from notions associated with classical organization theory and the politics-administration dichotomy. They entail a distinctive point of view about organizations and government that is intricately woven into the fabric of public administration thought. Dwight Waldo's remarks in 1961 were right on target: "Not only is the classical theory still today the formal working theory of large numbers of persons technically concerned with administrative-organizational matters, both in the public and private spheres, but I expect it will be around a long, long time. This is not necessarily because it is 'true' . . . (A) social theory widely held by the actors has a self-confirming tendency and the classical theory is now deeply ingrained in our culture."[13]

The really interesting thing about the continuing influence of these ideas is that public administrationists are the first to denounce them. Since the 1950s, as most any beginning textbook will illustrate, classical organization theory has served as little more than a straw man for more advanced theoretical perspectives, and the politics-administration dichotomy has been firmly rejected as a naive understanding of the inherently political context and nature of the administrative process. Nonetheless, much of the analysis, evaluation, and reform proposals concerning government organization, even in this age of enlightenment, bears the unmistakable imprint of public administration's formative years, in values as well as theoretical beliefs.

Generally speaking, the ethos of public administration has always looked favorably on the bureaucracy. While the various pathologies and unintended consequences associated with formal organization have long been recognized, the overarching emphasis is on the great advantages of organization and the feasibility of reforms for correcting potential problems. The flip side is a jaundiced view of politics. While it is inevitably bound up with administrative behavior and a necessary component of democratic accountability, politics tends to be seen as a corrupting influence on the integrity and competence of formal organization—an influence that, if not kept to a minimum, can be expected to have destructive effects that far outweigh any democratic payoffs.

Since the Roosevelt years, there has been a continuing tension between the competing values of neutral competence and executive leadership, the latter gaining in importance with modern growth in the complexity of social problems, the size and fragmentation of government, and expectations surrounding presidential performance.[14] This tension has never been resolved, but it has maintained a characteristic balance in favor of neutral competence, which is clearly the core value.[15] The problem for the executive is to mobilize the neutral competence of the government but without compromising it through politicizing attempts to ensure responsiveness. The notion is only that politicization is dangerous but that there is no need to carry it very far in pursuit of responsiveness; for the problem, to the extent it really exists, is basically organizational rather than political. What we need for executive leadership is not political mechanisms to ensure responsiveness but rather a presidential version of neutral competence: a managerial capacity. Hence, the requirements of presidential leadership become, through translation, the requirements of good management. Fundamentally political problems emerge with fundamentally non-political solutions.

Some of the best works on the presidency—Neustadt's *Presidential Power,* for example—are grounded in political analyses of incentives, resources, and behavior. They are essentially attempts to explain why governmental actors behave as they do, and their prescriptions derive from such behavioral foundations. This has never really been the analytical thrust of public administration. Its primary concern has been the pursuit of efficient, effective government through discovery and evaluation of appropriate organizational designs, where "appropriate" derives meaning from strongly held values and beliefs that circumscribe the role of politics and distract attention from its effects and behavioral determinants. It is fitting, then, that presidents are now exhorted to respect the neutral competence of bureaucratic agencies, to rely more heavily on the cabinet, to use appointments in pursuit of professionalism and expertise—and, in short, to move in directions that are consistent with long-standing academic beliefs about how presidents ought to behave, but entirely inconsistent with the way presidents have viewed their own incentives, resources, and constraints. Thus, presidents continue to do what they are not supposed to do, and academics continue to complain that, if only presidents would understand and see things their way, these unfortunate developments could be turned around.

There is an important parallel here with the early political science concern for "responsible" parties. About thirty years ago, many political scientists advocated reforms intended to encourage the development of parties resembling those we have come to expect in parliamentary systems—parties whose candidates run on programmatic platforms and, if in the majority, put their platforms into effect through cohesive legislative action. Since then it has come to be recognized that, however admirable the sentiments behind this position, we are not free to choose the kind of party system we want.[16] Parties develop over time within a much larger institutional system, structured in the United States by separation of powers, federalism, and a distinctive electoral system—and, for the most part, the United States has weak, decentralized, fragmented parties because of the way in which the larger institutional system shapes the incentives and resources of social actors, especially politicians. Thus, we cannot reform the party system in any dramatic way by focusing on the parties, because the parties are not really the cause of their own irresponsibility. While positive steps might be taken at the margins, only much more fundamental reforms in the institutional system can render the goal of responsible parties anything more than an impractical dream.

Reforms directed at the presidency tend to suffer from just this sort of impracticality. They often assume that presidents are the problem, that presidents continually misunderstand the great value of neutral competence, cabinet government, and all the rest. In fact, even if we grant that there is a problem, presidents are not the cause of it. Their incentives and resources are largely determined by an institutional system in which they have no choice but to operate—and the historical drive toward politicization and centralization has its roots here, not in the pathological designs of individual presidents and not in their consistent misunderstanding of administrative organization. In this respect—and it is hard to think of one that could be more fundamental-standard evaluations tend to be quite off the mark, and their proposed reforms, as a result, fail to address the basic causes of the problem.

The auxiliary issue, however, is not so easily answered: is there actually a problem? That is, are politicization and centralization undesirable, whether from the standpoint of efficient, effective government or the president's ability to pursue his own objectives? Students of the institutional presidency tend to give enthusiastically affirmative answers to both aspects of the question. And, to the extent that these issues are amenable to resolution through factual analysis—the value components resist this, of course—they could be quite correct. But their answers arise all too easily from traditionally held beliefs and values. That politicization and centralization might actually be highly positive developments is, for the most part, not seriously entertained.

Given the current state of knowledge, there is no way these questions can be evaluated adequately. There is evidence to suggest that politicization and centralization do indeed have some of the disadvantages claimed. There is also good reason to believe that the president's short-term time perspective discourages investment in competence-building institutional arrangements, to his own disadvantage.[17] But this is less than half the story. It ignores the potential contributions of politicization and centralization to responsiveness, innovation, and other components of presidential leadership. It ignores their demonstrated compatibility with presidential incentives—a crucial property that is the Achilles' heel of standard reform proposals. It ignores the role of institutional memory in transmitting "ephemeral, politicized" structures—for example, for appointments and congressional liaison—from one administration to the next.[18] It ignores the necessary trade-offs that presidents are forced to make in seeking a working balance between responsiveness and organizational competence. And it ignores the very real threats to presidential leadership capacity that entrenched interests and established organizational routines represent.

In general, the standard arguments against politicization and centralization have something valid to say, but they do not tell us what we need to know. Over the long haul, we need to have a full-balanced accounting of both the positive and negative effects, we need to be able to compare them with those associated with alternative institutional arrangements, and we need to assess the extent to which these alternatives are in fact compatible with presidential incentives—for if they are not, they will never survive intact, and indeed cannot properly be regarded as serious alternatives. At this point we simply have very little to go on. Certainly we do not know enough to justify the kind of confident criticism that now seems to prevail.[19]

Conclusion

This essay views the presidency as an institution whose development, like that of any other, is driven by incongruence among structures, incentives, and resources. The fundamental basis for the incongruence is deeply rooted in modern American politics: the expectations surrounding presidential performance far outstrip the institutional capacity of presidents to perform. This gives presidents a strong incentive to enhance their capacity by initiating reforms and making adjustments in the administrative apparatus surrounding them—but here too there is a fundamental imbalance: the resources for acting upon this strong incentive are wholly inadequate, constrained by political and bureaucratic opposition, institutional inertia, inadequate knowledge, and time pressures. It is this imbalance that channels presidential effort into areas of greatest flexibility and generates the major institutional developments we observe, politicization and centralization.

The details of presidential organization—the actual administrative arrangements adopted, the rates and types of change—vary considerably from one administration to another in response to differences in the personality, style, political objectives, and partisanship of individual presidents. Essential as these details may be to our understanding of the presidency, they represent fluctuation within a long-term historical process whose general path and underlying logic are the fundamental components of institutional development. For the most part, politicization and centralization have grown over time not because of who presidents are or what they stand for, but because of the nature of our institutions and the role and location of presidents within them. The basic causes are systemic.

This cannot tell us whether politicization and centralization are good or bad. It does tell us something about our criteria of evaluation: that they must take account of the systemic forces on presidential choice. It is not enough to point to absolute standards against which politicization and centralization may seem to fare poorly—"seem" because most of the evidence is not yet in. However we appraise them in absolute terms, the practical issue is inevitably one of feasible alternatives. Do there exist reforms that are preferable (on whatever grounds), that presidents and other decision makers would actually adopt, and that are sufficiently compatible with the structure of presidential incentives and resources to ensure their continuity? These are the alternatives with which politicization and centralization are properly compared—and it is questionable whether many of the usual reform proposals would pass this test.

There is no reason to think that the near future will be much different from the near past. Barring some fundamental and unforeseen change in American institutions, the gap between expectations and capacity will continue to characterize the presidency, as will the serious constraints on presidential resources and the consequent attractiveness of politicization and centralization. There will likely be no turning back from the general path of historical development this far.[20]

The heightening of politicization and centralization during the Reagan years is the most recent expression of this historical process. It is the continuation of a trend, the same basic response to roughly the same set of institutional forces—but a response that, by sequential ordering, had the advantage of being able to learn from and build upon the achievements, failures, and organizational experiences of preceding administrations. Moreover, some portion of the accelerated push in these directions is doubtless due to special features of the Reagan years: a highly ideological president, a clear agenda, a permanent government openly hostile to the president's program. Assuming a more normal confluence of factors during subsequent presidencies, it would seem that a period of institutional pause and consolidation is more likely than continued rapid change. From this vantage point, then, the Reagan years hardly seem to represent a dramatic new direction in American politics.

On the other hand, Reagan did much more than continue a historical trend. In moving ambitiously down the paths of politicization and centralization, he built a set of administrative arrangements that by past standards proved coherent, well integrated, and eminently workable. Given the sobering experiences of recent activist presidents, particularly Johnson and Nixon, in their attempts—against great odds—to fashion a workable administrative framework, the Reagan effort emerges as a striking success. As such, it is a lesson that will not be lost on future presidents—who will have every reason to learn from and build upon the Reagan example in seeking to enhance their own institutional capacities for leadership. This places Reagan in a pivotal historical position, and could well establish him as the most administratively influential president of the modern period.

NOTES

This piece was originally published in *The New Direction in American Politics,* John Chubb and Paul E. Peterson, eds. Copyright © 1985 by The Brookings Institution. Reprinted by permission.

1. At a minimum, institutionalization refers to regularized behavior patterns. This is the essential property stressed in the traditional sociological work on the subject, and this is the definition I adopt here. More elaborate definitions — incorporating complexity, specialization, and other criteria — are not uncommon. See, for example, Nelson W. Polsby, "The Institutionalization of the U.S. House of Representatives," *American Political Science Review* 62 (Mar., 1968): 144–68.

2. The perspective developed here falls under the rubric of what March and Olsen have termed the "new institutionalism" in political science. For their discussion, see James G. March and Johan P. Olsen, "The New Institutionalism: Organizational Factors in Political Life," *American Political Science Review* 78 (Sept., 1984): 734–49. Creative applications of institutional perspectives to the study of presidents and bureaucracies can be found in Stephen Skowronek, *Building a New American State* (New York: Cambridge University Press, 1982), and Skowronek, "Presidential Leadership in Political Time," in Michael Nelson, ed., *The Presidency and the Political System* (Washington, D.C.: CQ Press, 1984).

3. For a discussion of presidential incentives and the expectations surrounding the presidential role, see Theodore J. Lowi, *The Personal Presidency* (Ithaca, N.Y.: Cornell University Press, 1985); Godfrey Hodgson, *All Things to All Men* (Simon and Schuster, 1980); Richard Neustadt, *Presidential Power* (New York: Wiley, 1980); Thomas Cronin, *The State of the Presidency* (Boston: Little, Brown, 1975); and Aaron Wildavsky, "The Past and Future Presidency," *Public Interest* 41 (Fall, 1975): 56–76. Note that the gap between expectations and capacity is far greater for domestic than for foreign policy. See Aaron Wildavsky, "The Two Presidencies," in Aaron Wildavsky, ed., *Perspectives on the Presidency* (Boston: Little, Brown, 1975), pp. 448–61. Not surprisingly, the growth in the institutional presidency has been disproportionate due to new and larger structures for dealing with domestic policy, and trends toward politicization and centralization are properties of this growth. The analysis of this essay will therefore center around domestic concerns.

4. On the historical role of neutral competence in public administration thought, see Herbert Kaufman, "Emerging Conflicts in the Doctrines of Public Administration," *American Political Science Review* 50 (Dec., 1956): 1057–73.

5. More specifically, with neutral competence there is no mechanism to guarantee that what the organization potentially has to offer is willingly made available in an appropriate form and timely fashion to the president. Nor is there a mechanism to guarantee that the types of competence the organization is equipped to provide are well suited to the president's needs — a problem that has less to do with resistance than with willful resistance than with organizational myopia, parochialism, insularity, and other pathologies of a systemic nature. From the president's standpoint, responsive competence calls for improvements along both dimensions. Ideally, it is competence that is developed and adapted in light of his political needs and willingly made available to him.

6. See, for example, Harold Seidman, *Politics, Position, and Power,* 3d ed. (New York: Oxford University Press, 1980).

7. On presidential dissatisfaction with bureaucratic responsiveness, see Arthur M. Schlesinger, Jr., *A Thousand Days: John F. Kennedy in the White House* (Boston: Houghton Mifflin, 1965); and Lyndon B. Johnson, *The Vantage Point: Perspectives of the Presidency, 1963–1969* (New York: Holt, Rinehart, and Winston, 1971). For theoretical treatments of bureaucratic pathologies, see Anthony Downs, *Inside*

Bureaucracy (Boston: Little, Brown, 1967); Graham Allison, *The Essence of Decision: Explaining the Cuban Missile Crisis* (Boston: Little, Brown, 1971); and John D. Steinbruner, *The Cybernetic Theory of Decision: New Dimensions of Political Analysis* (Princeton, N.J.: Princeton University Press, 1974).

8. The relationship between institutions and expectations is a standard point in sociological theory. See, for example, the summary in Samuel N. Eisenstadt, "Social Institutions," in *International Encyclopedia of the Social Sciences,* vol. 14 (New York: Macmillan, 1968), pp. 409–429.

9. For a sober appraisal of organization theory, see Charles Perrow, *Complex Organizations* (Glenview, Ill.: Scott, Foresman, 1979). For a discussion of how presidential ideas for reform emerge, see Seidman, *Politics, Position, and Power.* See also John Kessel, *The Domestic Presidency* (North Scituate, Mass: Duxbury Press, 1975).

10. Seidman, *Politics, Position, and Power,* p. 87.

11. See Lowi, *Personal Presidency;* Hodgson, *All Things to All Men;* and Wildavsky, "Past and Future Presidency."

12. See, for example, Hugh Heclo, "OMB and the Presidency—The Problem of 'Neutral Competence,'" *Public Interest* 38 (Winter, 1975): 80–98; Berman, *Office of Management and Budget and the Presidency;* Seidman, *Politics, Position, and Power;* Hess, *Organizing the Presidency;* and Frederick Mosher and others, *Watergate: Its Implications for Responsible Government* (New York: Basic Books, 1974). As this list suggests, I am largely concerned here with academic studies of the presidency that focus specifically on questions of government organization. The analysis to follow is not intended to apply to the more popular treatises on the subject by various journalists and insiders—George E. Reedy's *The Twilight of the Presidency* (New York: Mentor Books, 1970), for example. Nor does it apply to those works, increasingly common after Vietnam and Watergate, that seek to argue much more generally that presidents have become too powerful. Arthur M. Schlesinger, Jr.'s *The Imperial Presidency* (Boston: Houghton-Mifflin, 1973) is perhaps the best known of these.

13. Dwight Waldo, "Organization Theory: An Elephantine Problem," *Public Administration Review* 21 (Winter, 1961), p. 220.

14. On the competing values of neutral competence and executive leadership, see Kaufman, "Emerging Conflicts in the Doctrines of Public Administration."

15. Although the value of executive leadership has suffered from the backlash to Vietnam and Watergate, it was less fundamental than neutral competence even during the post-Roosevelt infatuation (especially apparent during the Kennedy and early Johnson years) with the strong presidency.

16. See, for example, Leon Epstein, *Political Parties in Western Democracies* (Westport, Conn.: Praeger, 1967).

17. See especially Heclo, "OMB and the Presidency." This is the most thorough and persuasive statement of the negative side of the issue, but there is no real attempt at a balanced examination of both sides.

18. I should take this opportunity to question the tendency among critics to couple politicization with deinstitutionalization. It is true that the introduction of new layers of political appointees into a bureau previously run by careerists may well upset its established routines and memory processes, with destabilizing effects (at least in the short run). Yet these sorts of effects tend to be emphasized to the exclusion of all else. It is important to recognize, in particular, that thoroughly politicized behaviors can also be institutionalized. Indeed, the critics themselves com-

monly point to the extent to which appointments or congressional liaison—or the National Security Council, for that matter—have become institutionalized over time, without dwelling on the fact that all of these are newly reconstituted with every president and are thoroughly politicized as well as institutionalized. Although bureaucratic structures of all types might be "more" institutionalized if staffed by careerists, this in itself says little about the value or consequences of politicization—which may often promote responsiveness and flexibility while still affording sufficient institutionalization. More institutionalization is not valuable in itself anyway.

19. For a useful step toward a more comprehensive appraisal of the issues, see Lester M. Salamon, "Presidency and Domestic Policy Formulation."

20. Obviously, these trends will not continue unabated until "total" politicization and centralization are reached. Presumably well before such an extreme outcome is even remotely approached, diminishing returns—due, for instance, to organizational pathologies inevitably arising within an increasingly large, complex, bureaucratized presidency—will become readily apparent to presidents and nonpresidents alike, even if our scientific knowledge of cause and effect in government organization remains minimal. Also, members of Congress, bureaucrats, and other outsiders can be expected to place greater limits on the president's flexibility for moving in these directions as levels of politicization and centralization increasingly strike them as threatening or excessive. Such eventualities would prompt presidents to seek other means of enhancing their leadership capacity, thus defusing the historical trends we now observe and initiating new ones. But however likely in the long run, and despite the current misgivings of many academics and some political participants, there is no evidence that these kinds of reactive developments will play roles of any real consequence in the near future.

Chapter 10

Mandates or Mandarins?

Control and Discretion
in the Modern Administrative State

JOEL D. ABERBACH
AND BERT A. ROCKMAN

The development of the administrative state and the growth of political democracy constitute two of the most distinctive tendencies of modern government. The development of an advanced administrative apparatus carries with it claims to the values of continuity, professionalism, expertise, and effectiveness. The other development, that of political democracy, encompasses claims to the values of responsiveness, direction, and revitalization. Notwithstanding the desirability of each set of values, the means for meshing them in an optimal mix are hardly obvious. Even though it is widely accepted in democratic settings that the permanent administration must be accountable to constitutionally elected or delegated political overseers, the precise terms of this agreement are much more controversial.

Almost certainly, few of us come to see the struggle between political control and administrative discretion in entirely neutral terms. Typically, depending on our particular inclination, we tend to adopt perspectives that place more weight either on "political" or on "administrative" values, regardless of the importance we attach to the need for an optimal mix.

Partisans of political leadership (and these almost always include the incumbent set of leaders) are doers, not doubters. They want tools, not obstacles. To the extent that doubt exists about the willingness of career administrators to carry out faithfully the policy directions of the political leadership, career administrators are viewed by political actors as impediments rather than implements. Partisans of politics, consequently, typically look to enhance procedures for control and supervision of the permanent administrative apparatus and, when deemed necessary, to politicize it.

Partisans of the career administration, on the other hand, view it as the ballast that maintains the ship of state in unsteady seas. Its resistor-like qualities to the supercharged enthusiasms of new political leaders are seen as a virtue, not a vice—a deterrent, in fact, to longer-run damage inflicted by political leaders on themselves as well as on the organizational fabric of government. Partisans of public administration thus decry efforts to reduce the independence of career officialdom or to restrict severely administrative discretion.

The political leadership view in the modern democratic polity is one that we characterize as the "mandate" perspective. Underlying it is the logic that the elected political authorities have either a right, obligation or a legitimate need to pursue their goals and policy proposals and that it is essential for the operative instruments of government to be in strict compliance with these. The next step in this logic goes farther—indeed, a critical distance. The next step is that discretionary authority within the administrative apparatus can be meted out only to those who meet requisite tests of ardor for the goals and methods of the elected authorities.

The administrative view we shall characterize as the "mandarin" perspective—a term that resonates, for historical reasons, better in Europe than in the United States. The essence of this view is surely applicable to the American setting as well. It is that a professionalized bureaucracy (which came later to the United States, we should note) elevates the effectiveness of government. The "good government" inclinations of the Progressives, for example, predisposed them to what might be called a democratic mandarinate—the synergistic fusion of executive leadership from a democratically inspired elected executive and an efficiency-inspired professional civil service. Historically in the United States, much of the modern administrative apparatus was created largely to advance the goals of proficiency and universalistic standards sought by the Progressives, and later it was used to advance the goals of social and economic reform and the development of the welfare state through the New Deal, later fortified by the Great Society. A high degree of congruence in purpose between the presidency and the career executive was once thought to exist—a truly democratic (but probably also Democratic) mandarinate was seen to be in the service of the national interest (as that largely was defined by the president).

Although no president is ever prepared to leave what he regards as truly central activities to the career executive, the broad premises of what presidents and their administrative apparatus were about appeared to be in general concordance. Well-articulated and clear-cut strategies for controlling the administrative apparatus or cutting it out of the action would await the machinations of the Nixon White House and its successors, most notably, the Reagan administration. What the Nixon White House made clear in its operative premise about the bureaucracy was that it assumed noncompliance rather than concordance. Moreover, it conceived of the Washington bureaucracy as tending toward uncontrollable fission rather than synergistic fusion. Whatever the realities of the situation, the underlying attitudes and perceptions of the relevant actors have determined the atmosphere in which these relationships recently have developed. The self-perceived possessors of the democratic mandate worked to tighten the leash, to diminish the possibilities of noncompliant bureaucratic tactics, and wherever possible, to ensure that implementation be carried out only by trusted agents. The imperative to command has grown increasingly compelling from the perspective of the White House.

The Intellectual Justification of Political Command

In the American case, however, the constitutional basis of hierarchical command is absent or, more properly, it is plural and thus potentially contradictory. In Richard Nathan's words, "it is the wonderfully animated, competitive, and open character of the American political system that distinguishes it among the democracies of the Western world."[1]

It is exactly this competitiveness—a political market system as we shall think of it—that makes the administrative apparatus a resource worth competing for in an effort to influence programmatic control over federal policy. A system of segmented power such as that exhibited in the syndrome of subgovernmental domination over programs (the triad of congressional committee or subcommittee, clientele group, and bureau) produces what economists and, in their own way, presidents see as inefficient equilibria.[2] While economic theorists might define these inefficient equilibria in the form of misallocated resources, presidents tend to define them in the form of subsystemic resistances to policy change.

In recent years, the president's side of this problem—his ability to manage the executive branch and his need to procure resources in the competitive struggle to govern—has been voiced in sophisticated ways. Richard Nathan articulates well the view that presidents not only need to, but properly ought to, "influence administrative processes in a way that enables (them) to move forward on important policy objectives."[3] Clearly, it is within the power of a presidential administration and within, broadly speaking, the norms of American politics and government to make ideological harmony an important criterion for noncareer administrative appointments. The key obviously is how the "reds" interact with the "experts," and whether the "change agents" recognize any legitimate bounds to their strategies for effecting change. Above all, the central issue is how the presidential administration in its efforts to influence administrative processes interacts with other legitimate authorities, especially Congress and the judiciary.

Nathan concludes, however, that because the American political system is dynamic and competitive, "leadership is hard to exercise. . . . Policy changes are not easy to achieve, yet are often needed. . . . [Consequently, because] American national government at high levels is not a subtle business . . . the administrative strategy of the presidency is a valid and valuable instrument of presidential leadership."[4] In other words, it is legitimate for presidents to seek to politicize the bureaucracy on behalf of their goals because presidential leadership is essential to the system. When the wheel turns, other presidents with different goals may also legitimately seek to politicize the bureaucracy to their own ends. The model is, as a former president used to say, perfectly clear. It is collectively rational for the system that presidents should command, and it is individually rational for presidents to seek to command.

In an especially sophisticated analysis, Terry Moe argues correspondingly that a system such as that described by Nathan gives a rational president few options.[5] Whether individual rationality leads to collectively rational solutions is a matter that Moe leaves open to debate. Even though Moe seems strongly to imply that presidential politicization of the bureaucracy, including the institutional presidency, is a good, his argument is couched very much in the language of individual rationality. What is a rational president to do given the logic prevailing between incentives and institutions? The answer seems to be to strive for control over everything that is not nailed down.

Whether presidential command is a good or a bad is not Moe's fundamental point. Presidents seek to assert control over what they can, he asserts, mostly because they must. The maximization of control is viewed as a systemically necessary strategy.

In the final analysis, writers as different as Lowi, Rose, Nathan, and Moe all have bought into the mandate theory. Putting other analytic problems with such a theory to one side, however, only the system of government that Rose discusses (British party government and parliamentary supremacy) has institutions that are consistent with the premises of the mandate theory.[6] In the more structurally complex American system, Lowi has chosen the statutory instrument as the anchor.[7] This implies a kind of congressional supremacy even while it promotes both administrative and political inflexibility. Nathan and Moe, on the other hand, appear to gravitate to the opposite pole, namely that executive command is an appropriate (either desirable or simply necessary) form of politicization. Yet, the theory of organizational command and the theory that constitutionally organizes the American system of government are at odds.[8] The point is that in the United States it is not enough to talk about what politicians have a right to; one must specify *which* politicians. That being said, an even more fundamental point about the American system that follows from it is that in a system of divided authority, to say that politicians have the right to control is not the equivalent of saying that the president has the right to control. Such rights, as Neustadt once noted, are joint property rights.[9] And, as Neustadt, in essence, also saw, for such rights to be exercised, they would have to be jointly authorized.[10] It is possible, perhaps even probable, to suggest that this may be asking too much of a system of divided authority and of a system that frequently also divides this authority along partisan lines. But it also is likely that such a system requires either unusual consensus-building skills and/or exceedingly clear political signals from the electorate to alter existing equilibria. Otherwise, presidents belatedly may come to discover many adverse political effects from their efforts to monopolize a shared resource.

The Presidential Role in the Administrative Process

More and more, however, what the White House wants of civil servants, as ex–White House aide (and not just coincidentally also ex-convict) John Ehrlichman so picturesquely put it, is the following: "When we say jump, the answer should be 'how high?'"

In recent decades, though, presidents and their entourages have come to conclude that when asked "to jump," bureaucrats are not immediately inclined to ask "how high?" but rather "to where?" For administrations bent on redefining the role of the state or just simply jamming through their definition of priorities, questions and conditionals are mere impediments. Accordingly, they conclude that it is best to cut the operating agencies out of the action as much as possible (centralization) and, when that it is not possible, to cut the careerists out of the sphere of potential influence while relying on increased layers of politically faithful appointees (politicization).

The logic, as presidents are inclined to see it, is that popular sovereignty empowers them to command the apparatus of government. Even if one were to conclude that the only concrete expression that could be given to the public interest lies in the momentary will of the authorized political leadership, the fundamental flaw in this conception is that this will is not derivable from a single source. Members of Congress also lay claim to a piece of the mandate. When the political will of Congress and the president are coincident, ironically, the need for exclusivity of control over the administrative apparatus diminishes. When they are in conflict, it is likely that exclusivity of claims for control will be countered. It is certainly likely that when institutional interests clash and presumptive behavior increases, nothing in Washington will stay uncontested for long. That includes control of the administrative process.

Increasingly, it seems, presidents and political theorists find the idea of "neutral competence" impossible to describe. No one plausibly can lack interests; thus, all advice or discretionary possibilities are skewed. The sentiment on behalf of politicization necessarily assumes this. Consequently, it follows that if all "parties" have interests, the concept of "neutral competence" lacks operational meaning. If that is so, then it is clear that the career executives themselves have to meet political criteria or, as a group, be buried sufficiently far from the centers of power to prevent them from exercising meaningful discretion or from being able to influence decision makers. The decline of the neutral competence ideal corresponds to the rise in Washington of the adversarial ideal—the belief that everyone has an interest that they are seeking to optimize and that all expressions of collective or public interest are only façades (even if these are internalized) for the operation of individual interest or preference. Accordingly, without presidential control of the executive, it is believed by many advocates of presidential control that the expression of those interests and will be chaotic overall and unaccountable.

The case for presidential politicization of the executive boils down to these suppositions. The president is the supreme legitimate governor in the American system. And since no one possibly can be neutral, it is necessary to assure that the apparatus works unequivocally on behalf of presidential goals and needs.

Collective Rationality: Control or Synthesis?

At the outset of this paper and in other writings, we have emphasized that politicians and career officials bring unique and uniquely valuable perspectives to bear in governing.[11] In the United States, however, the distinctiveness of the political and bureaucratic roles is lessened mostly as a consequence of the relatively open-ended structure of American politics and government. Despite the greater overlap between political and administrative roles in the United States—a factor that probably leads politicians toward greater, rather than less, suspicion of bureaucrats—each also follows the patterns of their respective callings.

Politics provides energy and revitalization while bureaucracy brings continuity, knowledge, and stability.[12] One can exist without the other but only to the detriment of effective government. The problem for government and, in our view, the public interest is not to have one of these values completely dominate the other, but to provide a creative dialogue or synthesis between the two. In recent times the dialogue has turned into monologue as deinstitution-alization and centristic command have grown apace.

Each president in recent times has begun office with the supposition that the government has no organic past. At each turn, the wheel is to be reinvented anew. At their core, arguments for furthering the process of politicization and centristic command also conclude that leadership is equivalent to the intro-duction of novelty and that institutionalization is an obstacle to both.

Since politicians are constitutionally empowered to direct government, there can be no argument that the administrative apparatus, other things being equal, must be responsive to the political leadership. The question is what that re-sponsiveness may mean and what, therefore, is the responsibility of the senior civil servant. We quote here from our earlier studies the reaction of a German civil servant to this problem:

> We are not here to receive orders, mentally to click our heels, and to say "Jawohl!"—that's not why we are here. On the contrary, if (senior civil ser-vants) have a different conception (of the problem)—and they should al-ways have a political conception—they must under certain circumstances use their conception in conjunction with their expertise and simply say, "But I would propose thus and such for this reason." And if the minister says, "No, politically we can't do that on account of these reasons," then all right, it already will be done as proposed (by the minister). It must be this way, because the minister is the responsible official, who must have the last word. That can't be avoided.[13]

Even though senior career executives in the United States are more likely to be talking to assistant secretaries instead of the ministerial equivalents of their departments, it is not difficult to imagine discussions of the sort exemplified in the quote taking place much of the time.

Although a good many claims have been made about the recalcitrance of career civil servants to follow the policy and program course that a presiden-tial administration is embarking on, little evidence supports these assertions when effective administrative leadership is brought to bear. Good management, as reflected in open channels of communication, willingness to listen to ad-vice, clear articulation of goals, and mutual respect, in fact, may also consti-tute good politics for department secretaries or their assistant secretaries. No evidence shows that good management is incompatible with effective politics unless the imposition of stringent command procedures is regarded as an in-tegral part of a presidential administration's political style. The anti-bureaucratic styles of recent administrations suggest that this symbolic component has become at least as important as achieving results.

Responsive competence from the executive apparatus is a legitimate request of presidents up to the limits we have described. No one seriously would argue that the administrative mandarinate should be unaccountable. So, the issue is what can, and should, presidents try to control. That, it turns out, is a matter that presidential administrations often must settle internally amongst their own appointees. Even more, it is a matter that presidential administrations must define in the context of other institutions that the American system constitutes as authoritative principals. Thus, it turns out that the real issue often is not politics versus neutral competence but clarifying the principals (and their underlying principles) in the principal-agent relationship. Politicization and centralization are appropriate presidential responses in efforts to define the terms of the relationship—to a degree. Beyond that unspecifiable point, however, strategies for achieving presidential responsiveness turn into tactics for exclusive presidential rule. Efforts to achieve that level of aggrandizement are ruinous for governance in the American system; that is, they are collectively irrational. They also are ultimately ruinous for presidents whose political well-being probably is essential for effective governance and are thus likely to be individually irrational as well.

The key issue, therefore, is not whether some degree of politicization is necessary to promote responsiveness, but rather how much. The issue is not whether responsiveness should be promoted, but rather how reflexively and to whom. The model proposed for more presidential aggrandizement, ironically, is a prescription to rob government of its capability for reality testing, and it is without doubt a model for demoralization of the career service.

Individual Rationality: What Is in a President's Interests?

The argument that presidential command of the bureaucracy needs to be furthered is rooted in the value ascribed to presidential leadership and in the view that presidential goals and directions are overriding. In this view, the bureaucracy needs to be mobilized in accordance with these goals and directions. At the basis of the contention that furthering politicization of the bureaucracy is in the collective interest is the belief that presidential leadership is essential and whatever enhances it is a good.

While we believe that Terry Moe's analysis also is sympathetic to this general view, his more fundamental argument is that presidents ineluctably are driven to politicization and centralization because of the relationship between structures and incentives in the American governmental system.

As Moe asserts: "In an ideal world, presidents might pursue a variety of institutional reforms in righting the imbalance between expectations and capacity. In the real world, they readily embrace politicization and centralization because they have no attractive alternatives. The causes are systemic—they are rooted in the way the larger institutionalized system is put together."[14]

Two points are necessary to address because they represent important ambiguities in any analysis of the subject of presidential prerogatives and the use of the executive. The first is what it is that constitutes politicization and centralization. The second is the need to distinguish between the apparent incentives a president has (or more properly is inclined to see) his interests.

The first point is especially difficult. It is impossible, we agree, to deny the need for politics or for political leadership of the administrative apparatus. However, the reverse argument, that which implicitly denies the need for deliberation, skepticism, and continuity, has become more frequent. What makes this issue so complex is not the readily agreed upon notion that the bureaucracy requires political leadership and supervision, but the problem of defining the legitimate thresholds of this. At what point, for example, should an issue be politicized in decision making?

Rather than the broad argument as to whether politicization and centralization are goods or bads, we need to specify the mechanisms and also the political conditions under which these operate. Some mechanisms are legitimate; others are not. Some may be wise; others are not.

With regard to the second point—that of presidential incentives and interests—we distinguish different conceptions of "interest." The discipline of economics tends to define a person's interests by what one is willing to pay for. Interest has an operative meaning. Therefore, by this logic, how presidents behave in a situation expresses their interest. When they behave so as to aggrandize power, that expresses their interest and reflects the structure of incentives around them. But presidents, like consumers, make choices with uncertain information. Put in front of a candy counter, a child is likely to make dietary decisions inconsistent with his interests. When presidents come to office without having been exposed to career officials, but often only to horror stories told about them, they too may make decisions inconsistent with their interests.

The fact is that presidents can get into very deep trouble when they do end runs around the bureaucracy, when command replaces deliberation, and when White House centrism brings forth the illusion of central control. Nixon's fall from power was paved by the Watergate break-in, but it had as much to do with abuses of the executive as anything else. Even had Watergate not occurred, but with Congress remaining in the hands of the Democratic opposition, it is hard to imagine that the congressional hand would have been stayed for long.

The revelations of 1986–87 involving the White House–NSC operation of arms shipments to Iran and laundered funds to the Nicaraguan contras also threatens to erode fatally the political standing and the policy credibility of the Reagan presidency. Operating through the back door and around the institutionalized apparatus of government can lead to decisions and illegalities that are truly presidency-threatening. It is hard to imagine that this is in a president's interests.

One of the major functions, in short, of the permanent apparatus is to serve presidents by helping them avoid stupid mistakes that threaten their political viability. The urge to command and to centralize often fails to recognize that political impulses should be subjected to tests of sobriety. Though there are a good many reasons to argue on behalf of the basic idea of "neutral competence" and against the politicization of all executive organizations, the most fundamental one that a president ought to consider is the avoidance of error and illegality that have wracked recent presidencies.

Conclusion: Monopoly and Competition in American Government

As we read the insightful and provocative analyses of Richard Nathan and Terry Moe about the need for more presidentialism (or, in Moe's case especially, the needs of presidents themselves), we are struck by how similar their and our descriptions of the American system are. We see, as they do, a system of intense competition for resources in the struggles to define public policy and to jockey for political advantage. In broad contours, the system looks to us (two centuries removed) as Madison hoped it would. The competitive struggle leaves no single institutional actor with sufficient resources to fully dominate the system in the absence of extensive and deep consensus.

The analyses of Nathan and Moe, while imbued with some novel twists, fit broadly into a long line of presidentialist literature that urges reform to make the system more compliant with presidential objectives. The difference, as Moe indicates, is that most of that literature is organized around nonexecutive reforms whose prospects are implausible. The only significant tools available, according to this logic, are executive ones—politicizing the bureaucracy and centralizing executive command. In essence, presidents do what they have to do with what they have available. But the spirit of presidentialism is the motivating ideal. In the end, it is the president on whom falls the responsibility of governing.

That being the case, presidents need, in this line of analysis, to maximize their advantages in a system that endows them with too few. Maximizing advantage through the executive, in Moe's view, is a norm that has evolved because presidents increasingly have found it essential as a means of accomplishing their goals. The trouble with this norm, among other things, is that it tends to induce retaliatory behavior. When U.S. Office of Management and Budget (OMB) or presidential emissaries decide to rewrite regulations to fit their, rather than statutory, definitions of policy, Congress will retaliate when it has the political will. Because presidents have the advantage of initiative in these situations, however, they may see little to lose in pressing that advantage. But retaliatory behavior—and with it, a loss of credibility—has a good chance of being provoked.

In the short run, the system, as Moe argues, provides incentives for maximizing advantage, and since the players, especially the presidential ones, are short-term actors, it is understandable that these incentives seem compelling. Norms have evolved in the White House, particularly among Republican presidents, to politicize and centralize the executive apparatus in especially exuberant fashion. But other norms can evolve as well if, *in the long run,* ceaseless politicization and centrism are seen as having disadvantages.

Through his experiments, Robert Axelrod draws some interesting lessons about how norms of cooperation evolve. In Axelrod's model, which he calls TIT for TAT, time and the continuity of relationship are important elements.[15] Negative sanctions must be timely so that they can be linked clearly to a player's move to defect. Thus, we can infer that using the executive in illegal ways should be met more swiftly than not with congressional or judicial retribution. A larger time horizon is necessary, however, to ensure that a benefit to improving a continuous relationship is perceived. When the marginal cost to defect is low, stemming from a failure to retaliate in a timely way, and, above all, from a belief that a relationship is noncontinuous, it is difficult for norms of reciprocity and cooperation to develop.

Of course, the extent to which Congress or the judiciary will react will depend largely on the prevailing political climate, and to the extent that there is reaction, it likely means that senior career officials will be squeezed from all sides. That is not likely to be a condition that enhances either the status or the role of career officials or the quality of governance. And the slowness of reaction under most circumstances means that presidents often learn the necessary lessons late, perhaps too late.

The incentives toward reciprocity need to be strengthened. If presidents are quickly and forcefully reminded about what they cannot as well as about what they can achieve by efforts to monopolize institutional power through command, perhaps, then, they will be more inclined to seek other means for influencing a government that they only partially head and which has an executive apparatus that is not under their exclusive control. Respect for that principle may turn out to afford presidents the best opportunity to achieve their goals without recurrent backlash. In a system such as ours, it is vital to develop norms of cooperative behavior. That, of course, is a different model of how a system structured around competition might work.

It is hard, however, to be optimistic about this. Precisely because the president and presidential appointees in the executive have such short time horizons, the norms of cooperation are difficult to develop, especially once noncooperative norms of behavior have taken hold.

This is the crux of a crucial current dilemma facing the American presidency as an institution. If presidents follow their short-term interests, they are likely to stimulate more and more restrictive congressional bonds on their behavior, thereby giving presidents incentives to engage in the types of behavior exemplified by the Iran-Contra affair. Yet each individual president is likely to put his short-term interests above the institution's interests. As in many other aspects of American politics, Congress is key here. It will ultimately determine the kind of presidency we get. It must act expeditiously when presidents arrogate for their exclusive use constitutionally shared authority. Otherwise, presidents will take as theirs what Congress by its inaction bestows.

NOTES

Reprinted with permission from *Public Administration Review,* Mar./Apr., 1988. Copyright © 1988 by The American Society for Public Administration, 1120 G Street, N.W., Suite 500, Washington, D.C. All rights reserved.

The authors are grateful to Paul Quirk, Terry Moe, Mark Petracca, and Michael Reagan for comments on an earlier, more extended version of this analysis.

1. Richard P. Nathan, "Institutional Change Under Reagan," in John L. Palmer, ed., *Perspectives on the Reagan Years* (Washington, D.C.: The Urban Institute Press, 1986), p. 121.
2. Richard Rose, "Government Against Sub-Governments: A European Perspective on Washington," in Richard Rose and Ezra N. Suleiman, eds., *Presidents and Prime Ministers* (Washington, D.C.: American Enterprise Institute, 1980), pp. 284–347.
3. Nathan, "Institutional Change," p. 128.
4. Ibid., pp. 132, 133.
5. Terry Moe, "The Politicized Presidency," in this volume.
6. Richard Rose, *The Problem of Party Government* (New York: The Free Press, 1974).
7. Theodore J. Lowi, *The End of Liberalism: The Second Republic of the United States,* 2d ed. (New York: W. W. Norton, 1979).
8. Bert A. Rockman, "The Modern Presidency and Theories of Accountability: Old Wine *and* Old Bottles," *Congress and the Presidency* 13 (Autumn, 1986): 138.

9. Richard E. Neustadt, "Politicians and Bureaucrats," in David B. Truman, ed., *The Congress and America's Future* (Englewood Cliffs, N.J.: Prentice-Hall, 1965), pp. 102–20

10. Speaking of both the White House and Capitol Hill, in regard to direction of the bureaucracy, Neustadt comments (from present perspectives, ironically) that "at both ends of the Avenue, to urge awareness of joint stakes and common risks is not perhaps to ask too much of our established system." Neustadt, "Politicians and Bureaucrats," p. 120.

11. Joel D. Aberbach, Robert D. Putnam, and Bert A. Rockman, *Bureaucrats and Politicians in Western Democracies* (Cambridge, Mass.: Harvard University Press, 1981), especially chapter 8.

12. Ibid., esp. chapter 8.

13. Aberbach, et al., p. 249.

14. Moe, "The Politicized Presidency," in this volume.

15. Robert Axelrod, *The Evolution of Cooperation* (New York: Basic Books, 1984).

Chapter 11

Politics and Performance

Strengthening the Executive Leadership System

ELLIOT L. RICHARDSON AND JAMES P. PFIFFNER

A strong executive leadership system is essential to the effective management of the government and to a successful presidency. The two components of that system, political appointees and career executives, must work together in a partnership; neither alone can run the executive branch. The president needs both the energizing force of committed political executives to lead governmental agencies and the competence and experience of career civil servants who carry out the missions of these agencies. Executive branch agencies must be responsive to presidential direction as the president takes care that the laws are faithfully executed.

Each president brings into his administration a substantial number of people committed to him and to his philosophy of government. These political appointees constitute an essential democratic link with the electorate. This link ensures that the permanent bureaucracies that carry out the policies of the U.S. government will be led by people who are committed to the policies and priorities of each new president. This "in-and-outer" system also brings into the government fresh ideas and new blood to try them out. It brings in people who can work at full speed on the president's program for several years and then return to their previous careers when they approach burnout.

But the huge agencies and complex programs of the government cannot be run entirely by these in-and-outers. The permanent processes and ongoing programs of the U.S. government need the continuity and expertise of specialized bureaucracies. These bureaucracies are led by the senior executives of the career services who comprise the management cadre of the permanent programs of the government.

These career executives are critical to the continuing capacity of the government to function and to the success of their political superiors in each presidential administration. They are highly educated, and they know the intricacies of the laws and regulations governing the programs they implement. They are the repositories of organizational memory. They have built up personal intelligence and communications networks over many years through dealing with the same organizations, people, and issues. Perhaps more importantly, career executives are the professional line managers of the programs of the federal government. They are in charge of mission accomplishment and service delivery.

But the system is not now working at peak efficiency or effectiveness. A consensus is growing among informed observers of the public service that the management infrastructure of the federal government is deteriorating. This decline stems from problems involving both the political executives each president appoints and the career members of the Senior Executive Service (SES). More importantly, the problem involves the interactions between these two essential components of the executive leadership system.

To deal with these problems in the executive leadership system, we propose several changes that we believe will improve the system and make it more responsive to presidential direction. The following section describes the deteriorating conditions that led to our proposals. This section is followed by an analysis of the appropriate roles of political appointees and career executives in the U.S. political system. Finally, each of our proposals is explained in detail.

This report is based on the considered judgment that increasing the number of political appointees does not guarantee a more responsive government, and that career executives possess the professionalism, expertise, and motivation to enable the president to accomplish his policy goals. A change of government in the parliamentary democracies of the United Kingdom, France, or West Germany may bring in 100 new appointees, and there is little doubt that these governments are responsive to new political leadership.[1]

Problems in the System

Although the degeneration of the system of executive leadership cannot be precisely measured or quantified, it is clear that there are a number of disturbing developments in the system. These developments include: rising turnover in the political ranks, an increasing number of political appointees, deteriorating relations between political and career executives, the erosion of executive compensation, and the lack of institutional memory in many executive branch agencies.

Increasing Turnover of Political Appointees

The average tenure of Senate-confirmed political appointees is relatively short and has been decreasing. The average tenure of presidential appointees (excluding regulatory commissioners) during the Johnson administration was 2.8 years; during the Nixon administration it was 2.6 years; during the Carter administration it was 2.5 years; and it was 2.0 years up to 1984 in the Reagan administration.[2] From 1964 to 1984, the proportion of political appointees who stayed in position 1.5 years or less was 41.7 percent for cabinet secretaries, 62 percent for deputy secretaries, and 46.3 percent for under secretaries. From 1979 to 1986, noncareer members (political appointees) of the Senior Executive Service remained in office an average of 20 months. Fully 40 percent of political executives throughout the government stayed in their positions less than one year.[3] In contrast, 70 percent of career executives have been with their agencies for 10 years and 50 percent of them for 15 years.[4] Although the average tenure in office of Senate-confirmed presidential appointees (PAS) may have increased slightly because of the two full terms of President Reagan, the tenure of these top executives is still so short as to be disruptive.

This lack of stability in the top political leadership of the federal government poses a problem for several reasons. First, on-the-job training takes time. If a new appointee needs a year to learn enough about the job to be fully effective, then on average, political appointees spend half of the time they are on the job operating at less than full effectiveness. "Appointees on the job two years have enough time to make mistakes but often not enough time to put the resulting lessons to use."[5] The effect of this turnover at the top is worse when the positions that are considered "political" are extended further down into the bureaucracy. Paul Warnke, former chief arms control negotiator, observes: "If you're going to have the kind of rapid appointee turnover, two, three, four years, you've got to have a first-rate career service. . . . I hate to see this creeping appointeeism. I think it means too many people brought in."[6] When political appointees are replaced, there is most often no overlap of tenure during which institutional memory can be passed on, even if it would be welcome.

Increasing Layers of Bureaucracy
and Proliferation of Political Appointees

The increased layering of political appointees on top of the career system and the interposing of Schedule C special assistants between line political officials and career executives diffuses legitimate political authority. It attenuates the link between the responsible political official and the career implementers of policy.

There has been an increase in the number of positions at the higher level executive ranks ("administrative overbrush") as well as at lower levels. In 1976, for example, the State Department had 11 assistant secretaries; in 1986 it had 17.[7] In 1960, the Department of Health, Education, and Welfare had two assistant secretaries and 23 Schedule C appointees. In 1984, its successor, the Department of Health and Human Services, had 6 assistant secretaries and 101 Schedule C appointees; and the Department of Education, formerly a part of HEW, had 6 assistant secretaries and 98 Schedule C appointees.[8] According to Frank C. Carlucci, secretary of defense in the Reagan administration, "The fact is that we have too many organizational entities, many of which are simply a collection of statutes. We do not need more organizations. If anything, we need to consolidate governmental organizations in mission-oriented departments."[9]

This increase results in confusion in the channels of communication between the president and his senior officers and their line managers. The resulting span-of-control problems lead to additional layering. The clear and coherent transmission of the president's policies through his own appointees to the career level becomes progressively more difficult as the number of presidential appointees increases. In addition, the inflation in the number of appointees dilutes their stature and leads to a corresponding inflation in titles.

Frederic Malek, director of the Office of Presidential Personnel in the Nixon administration, makes the argument:

> Layering the civil service with even more political appointees would only serve to widen the gulf between the chiefs and the Indians, robbing the career executives of an opportunity to carry out many of the more demanding jobs in the government, weakening the attraction of civil service, and reducing the incentive of the best career people to remain in government. Instead, agency heads should seek to make better use of the experience that the career executives do have and should recognize that some continuity of performance can be an invaluable tool for effective management.
>
> Surely there is an optimum balance between the number of career and noncareer appointments in every government organization. At the federal level, that balance should be struck in favor of fewer political appointees, not more. In many cases, the effectiveness of an agency would be improved and political appointments would be reduced by roughly 25 percent if line positions beneath the assistant secretary level were reserved for career officials.[10]

These observations are even more relevant in the late 1980s than they were in the late 1970s, when Malek wrote them and when fewer political appointments were available to presidents.

Possibly more important than the increased number of political appointees and their rapid turnover is the deteriorating relations between political appointees and career executives. This development is attributable in part to the initial attitude of suspicion that many appointees of recent administrations have brought to their jobs. They suspect that civil servants are lazy and self-serving, and they believe that the "bureaucrats" will try to undermine the policies of the administration, drag their feet, or even sabotage administration initiatives. They fear that the rules of the system will be used to prevent the administration from implementing its policies.

Initial distrust leads to excluding career executives from policy discussions and to jigsaw-puzzle management, in which political executives bar career executives from the "big picture" so they will not be able to sabotage it. This attitude on the part of political appointees is self-defeating because it ignores experienced people who have potentially valuable information and advice. It also contributes to declining morale in the career ranks, which leads to early retirements and the brain drain.

Political Appointees Increasing

The number of political appointees in the federal government increased steadily from the 1950s to the 1980s. Although part of this increase is attributable to the creation of new agencies, the increase has occurred while overall civilian government employment has decreased relative to the total U.S. population. At the top levels, the number of presidential appointments that require Senate confirmation has increased from 71 in 1933 to 152 in 1965 to 527 in 1985 (not including ambassadors, U.S. attorneys, U.S. marshals, or representatives to international organizations).[11] But PAS positions constitute only the apex of the pyramid. The total number of noncareer SES appointees has increased from 582 in 1980 to 658 in 1986 (a 13.1 percent increase) at the same time that the number of career SES personnel decreased 5.3 percent.[12] The number of Schedule C positions increased from 911 in 1976 to 1,665 in 1986. But even more striking, the number of Schedule C appointments at the GS 13 to 15 range (mid-level management) was 946 in 1986, more than the total number of Schedule C positions under President Ford.[13]

While there may be legitimate disagreements over how best to count the total number of political appointees, there is no dispute about the direction of the trend. At the same time that the number of political appointees has been increasing over the past decade, total executive branch employment has remained relatively stable. Civilian employment increased at about 0.7 percent annually, primarily in the Department of Defense, the U.S. Postal Service, and the Veterans Administration. Both the U.S. population and the total non-federal workforce grew at significantly greater rates than overall federal employ-ment.[14]

This proliferation in the number of political appointees impairs the effective management of the government for several reasons.

The increase in political appointees undermines the capacity of the career services. Civil servants have spent their careers in the public service with the goal of rising to the top of the career ladder where their years of experience will be appreciated and put to use. When political appointees are placed in positions formerly held by career employees, the latter's long-term career opportunities are diminished. This development discourages good people from entering the public service and from staying in it when they have opportunities to leave.

The absolute size of the increase in political appointees understates this problem considerably. The increase in political appointees is not as important as the fact that the ratio is rising. The significant impact on morale is at the margins, in the positions to which career executives aspire. The more of these positions that are converted to political appointments, the more civil servants are forced to recognize that they are in dead-end career tracks. The awareness that opportunities for them are decreasing does the most harm.

The total numbers involved are not as important as the increased numbers in the lower level executive ranks. Most political positions—secretaries, deputy secretaries, most assistant secretaries, administrators, commissioners, etc.—are not in fact part of the career ladder and have never been so regarded by career people or young people contemplating public service. Thus, when jobs below these levels are converted from career to political positions, the impact on the perception of career executives is magnified. The proportion of the remaining jobs—for example, those at the deputy assistant secretary level—that have been politicized is substantially higher than the total numbers would seem to indicate.

This frustrating of hope and ambition explains why the politicization of the lower level executive ranks (noncareer SES and Schedule C), where it has been increasing at the greatest rate, is so destructive. A career executive who can no longer aspire to be a deputy assistant secretary, and who must contemplate reporting to a much younger, less experienced, less knowledgeable boss whose main qualification stems from loyal campaigning for the winning presidential candidate, will be much less likely to stay with the government when offered a chance to leave.

Similarly, civil servants at the GS-9 to 15 levels see their promotion opportunities shrinking. When Schedule C personnel are promoted at much faster rates than career employees, the effect is doubly discouraging. They, too, may find outside opportunities irresistible. And, of course, the most skilled and talented career employees have the most opportunities to leave.

This trend is also evident at higher levels in the Foreign Service. Ronald I. Spiers, under secretary of state for management in the Reagan administration, has expressed his concern about "the often casual use of Foreign Service positions for political patronage." He continues:

> I am deeply concerned about the diminishing percent of career appointments. From a starting point in 1981, when 75 percent of our ambassadors were career Foreign Service officers, now only 60 percent of our nation's ambassadors are career officers. This is a low point for the past four decades. A net reduction of 23 senior positions filled by career personnel since 1981 makes managing the Foreign Service difficult indeed. Seeing the dubious quality of some of those judged worthy or capable of serving as ambassador, it is painful to recognize the lack of respect this implies for our profession. . . . [I]t is wasteful and demoralizing for well-qualified people to climb a 30-year career ladder, only to be preempted at the top rung by someone lacking the necessary qualifications or experience.[15]

The State Department is a special case because it has about 140 ambassadorial or chief of mission appointments that require Senate confirmation in addition to executive level positions involved with managing the department. But just as the need for professionalism in the diplomatic corps is acute, so is it also in the rest of the government.

In addition, the benefits presumed to be gained by a presidential administration from the increasing number of political appointees is overrated. Political appointees, especially at lower levels, may not be the best qualified, and they may be appointed because of support from members of Congress or interest groups. Thus their loyalty may be split between the president and others. A number of presidential appointees have even argued that political appointees, because of their divided loyalties, are less responsive than career civil servants. In a study done in the 1980s, one third of the political executives interviewed offered unsolicited critical comments about their fellow appointees. Their comments included:

> A lot of political people don't know a hill of beans about their area. Those who are confirmed by the Senate are generally good, but at the lower levels, they don't have a lot of background, and have to rely on the career people.
>
> To tell the truth, I have more problems working with political appoin-

tees because they are subject to political pressures. And they think they understand the political process, and most of them don't.[16]

The authors of the study conclude that the increasing number of political appointees has decreased the influence of the senior career staff at the same time that less qualified political executives are turning over so quickly that they cannot master their jobs. "The result is to weaken their ability to carry out the administration's 'mandate' and, often, to wreak havoc in the day-to-day administration of agency programs."[17]

More Political Appointees at Lower Levels

The more positions are opened up to political appointees at lower levels, the harder it is to recruit high-quality people to fill them. Quality at the higher executive levels is not as much of a problem because of the prestige, power, and challenge of the positions. But at the lower levels, it is more difficult to recruit the best candidates, who must give up their jobs, move their families, and accept lower salaries.

This difficulty is aggravated by the increasing control over political appointments exerted by the Office of Presidential Personnel. Sub-cabinet appointees, who were often selected by cabinet secretaries in the 1960s and 1970s, have been tightly controlled by the White House in the 1980s. The positions that are of most concern here are the deputy assistant secretary positions (or deputy administrators or deputy commissioners), which in the past have been primarily filled with career executives with long experience in their agencies. According to Elliot Richardson, who has held eight presidential appointments:

> More and more political appointees are being pushed into jobs traditionally held by career officials. In addition to reducing the number of positions at the top that remain open to a civil servant, the consequence is to place minimally qualified individuals in highly important posts. It's hard enough to get really good people to give up highly paid positions in private life and take on the demanding duties of an under secretary or assistant secretary; it's harder still to persuade an able and experienced person to accept the less prestigious title of deputy assistant secretary. Almost any job at that level, however, is more responsible and has wider impact on the national interest than most senior corporate positions. In the State Department, for example, a deputy assistant secretary is responsible for all of Southeast Asia. A deputy assistant attorney general heads the war against organized crime. Comparable responsibilities belong to every similar position throughout the government.

Ignoring these facts, patronage offices pressed to come up with jobs for the president's loyal supporters drive the politicizing process. A White House personnel assistant sees the position of deputy assistant secretary as a fourth-echelon slot. In his eyes that makes it an ideal reward for a fourth-echelon political type—a campaign advance man, or a regional political organizer. For a senior civil servant, on the other hand, it's irksome to see a position one has spent 20 or 30 years preparing for preempted by an outsider who doesn't know the difference between an audit exception and an authorizing bill. Small wonder, then, that so many members of the SES have sought other occupations.[18]

If part of what attracts the best and brightest of young people into the career services is the chance to be "in on the action," the trend of excluding career executives from policy deliberations and from the chance to become a deputy assistant secretary will discourage the best students from entering the federal service.

Brain Drain in the Career Ranks

From 1979, when the SES was created, to 1983, 2,632 SES members left the government. This exodus amounted to 40 percent of those who entered the service when it was created in 1979. By 1985, the percentage who had left had increased to 52 percent.[19] While some of those who left were at retirement age and some were undoubtedly no longer suited to the federal service, many of them chose to retire or leave government service before they had to. In 1983, 17 percent of those who were eligible to retire did. By 1985, this number had increased to 30 percent. When asked, "Is your agency experiencing a brain drain?" 73 percent of the respondents to a large survey of government executives in 1988 replied "yes."[20]

The increasing number of senior executives who are choosing to leave government service before normal retirement age is disturbing. This nation is losing some of its most experienced and qualified senior civil servants. They are not easy to replace. For instance, from 1983 to 1987, at the National Institutes of Health, forty-two senior scientists (20 percent of the top scientists in the agency) left for careers in nongovernmental institutions at salary increases ranging from 50 to 300 percent.[21]

The talent hemorrhage at the top is matched by problems in recruiting at the entry levels. Surveys have shown that young people's values have changed over the past several decades; they are now much less likely to be interested in public service than in personal profit and business careers. A declining percentage of the graduates of the country's best public administration and public policy programs view the federal government as a desirable place to work. In a survey by *Government Executive* magazine, 59 percent of the respondents said that the quality of new hires at their agencies was marginally or much worse than in the past.[22] This trend has been encouraged by several political campaigns in which presidential candidates have disparaged the career services and blamed U.S. societal and economic problems on the federal government.

Falling Morale in the Career Service

The morale of a workforce is difficult to define, much less to quantify, yet it is real and can have an important influence on the quality and productivity of work. Although the task force could not measure the morale of federal career executives, it found indicators that morale could be better.

In 1985, the General Accounting Office (GAO) asked those leaving the SES the most important reasons for their departure. Those who responded cited the following reasons: dissatisfaction with top management (47.3 percent), dissatisfaction with political appointees (43.1 percent), unfair distribution of bonuses (41.4 percent), dissatisfaction with agency management practices (35.1 percent), and too much political interference (33.5 percent).[23] In a 1985 Federal Executive Institute Alumni Association survey, 51 percent of the respondents felt that career-political working relations were a deterrent to effective management.[24] Perhaps more important, a GAO survey found that two-thirds of those leaving the SES in 1985 would "advise" or "strongly advise" young people to pursue careers in the private rather than the public sector.[25] In the *Government Executive* survey, only 14 percent of career civil servants rated political appointees as "well qualified" while 86 percent rated them as "marginally qualified" or "unqualified."[26] Even discounting the results for the usual amount of complaining, these figures are unsettling.

While one can quibble about some of these data, the cumulative picture is discouraging. A serious morale problem exists in the government's senior career executives, and much of it is related to the perception that less qualified appointees in the lower levels of the political ranks (noncareer SES and Schedule C) are occupying positions that in the past might have crowned the career of an experienced civil servant. This perception is not conducive to the type of teamwork that is necessary for a well-managed government. To the extent that these perceived problems convince career executives to leave government service before they have to, they contribute to decreasing institutional memory and continuity.

Erosion of Executive Compensation

The Quadrennial Commission on Executive, Legislative, and Judicial Salaries has reported that between 1969 and 1985, the purchasing power of Executive

Level II salaries (to which other executive salaries are tied) had decreased by 39 percent. A pay increase of 90 percent would be necessary in 1987 to achieve the same ratio of comparability (not to achieve full comparability) to private sector executive salaries that existed in 1970.[27]

The *Report of the President's Commission on Compensation of Career Federal Executives* in 1988 argued that SES pay levels present serious problems for the effective operation of the government. According to the report, "the history of broken promises and pay caps, reduced bonus provisions, the effects of inflation, the comparative pay gap with the private sector, compression within and on either end of the SES pay range" is an important component of recruitment and retention problems. The commission concluded that, "An SES beset by retention and recruitment problems results in the will of the people, as expressed through national election, being seriously impaired. . . . Without retaining our best public servants and without the ability to recruit equally qualified personnel, our capacity as a nation to successfully respond to the domestic and international challenges we face will be severely impaired."[28]

Few would argue that public sector salaries should be fully comparable with private sector salaries, and no one argues that money should be the primary reason to choose a public sector career. But the deterioration of executive pay in the federal government has come to the point where it may be a disincentive to recruiting the best and brightest at the entry level, or retaining good people for their career. For instance, David Ruder, chairman of the Securities and Exchange Commission in the Reagan administration, wrote to Commission Chairman Paul A. Volcker: "We regulate an industry which has seen starting salaries for junior attorneys exceed the levels of our most experienced and outstanding attorney-managers. . . . [T]he financial sacrifice asked of our most capable attorneys and other professionals is becoming increasingly difficult to bear. Some competitive compensation relief is imperative to help slow this talent drain."[29]

The widening gap between private and federal executive pay is, of course, a problem in recruiting the best and brightest political appointees as well.

Decreasing Institutional Memory

The turnover of all political appointees when control of the White House shifts to the other party presents a problem of institutional continuity. If career civil servant positions extend to high levels and career executives have participated in the development of policy, the problem is not so severe. But this is often not the case.

While agency files contain written records, much of the nuance of policy development and of unwritten understandings with major participants does not show up in the formal records. This dimension can only be supplied by agency officials who have been privy to the policy development. The more frequently that career officials are passed over for higher level agency positions and the more consistently they are excluded from policy deliberations because of distrust, the more future political appointees—and presidential administrations—will suffer from the lack of that input.

Needed Improvement in Career Employee Attitudes

The need for change in political appointees is important because they are in the positions of greatest authority and power. They set the tone for their departments and agencies and for the whole administration. But improvement in the attitudes of career civil servants is also necessary.

Career employees ought not to accept the stereotype that all new political appointees are political hacks. Most career executives have seen political hacks, just as most political appointees have seen their share of deadwood in the career ranks. The cynical attitude that "I can outlast any political appointee and thus do not have to give my full support" is destructive to our democratic system, the civil service, good management, and is unacceptable. Little will be accomplished in such a climate, and career employees displaying this attitude will give credence to the negative stereotypes of the career services.

Career executives ought to keep in mind that new political appointees join the government as the president's surrogates, and are likely to have a positive approach to their stint in the public service. New appointees may suffer from the uncertainties that result from joining a new organization and of being unfamiliar with its personnel, processes, and programs. Just as career employees want their new political bosses to give them the benefit of the doubt, so too they should extend that same good will toward new political appointees and avoid prejudging their political superiors.

Career executives should also examine their own attitudes toward members of Congress and their staffs. The negative stereotypes of members of Congress and congressional staff are no more accurate than negative stereotypes of executive branch civil servants. Hostile or biased attitudes are not conducive to the cooperative efforts that are necessary to the effective management of the government.

Appropriate Roles of Political and Career Executives

Any solutions to these problems will work only if political appointees and career executives accept their mutual responsibilities to make the system work. The legitimate role of political appointees is to represent the president, who was democratically elected to head the nation and to lead the bureaucracy. The role of civil servants is to contribute their experience and expertise in the machinery and programs of government and to help carry out the legitimate priorities of the incumbent administration in its implementation of the laws.

The Functions of the Political Process

The function of the political process in the United States is to elect to government those who, in some general way, represent the will of the electorate. Elected officials have the right and the duty to make choices among competing claims within the society. Techniques of rational analysis can contribute to narrowing the range of choices, but ultimately the tough choices among competing priorities must be made on the basis of political values. At that point (in the executive branch), the president and his appointed officials have the duty to make choices within the legally defined boundaries of their positions.

Career civil servants do not have the legitimate right to make those choices, and they should not attempt to do so. The appropriate role of the career executive is to contribute relevant information, rational analysis, and experienced judgment as input to executive branch decision making. That advice to political appointees can appropriately include judgment about politics as well as the implementation of the policy under consideration. The experience and expertise represented in this advice can be valuable, but the role is clearly advisory. Responsibility for ultimate decisions is legally, constitutionally, and morally that of the president's representatives in the departments and agencies.

If career executives are not able to support legal policy decisions made by the administration in power, their appropriate response is to resign. They should not try to undermine or sabotage policies or programs secretly. It is the corresponding duty of the president and his political appointees to "take care that the laws be faithfully executed."

In addition to their legal duties, political appointees also are responsible for leading the executive branch. The new perspectives and fresh thinking that political appointees bring to government can contribute greatly to motivating the career services. Leadership necessarily involves not only respecting the contributions that career executives make to governing, but also bringing out the best in career officials—by convincing them that their efforts can make a difference and by challenging them to extend themselves to accomplish the goals of the administration and the government.

The Politics-Administration Dichotomy

Some argue that a distinction exists between policy and administration. From this perspective, political leaders decide policy questions and those in the bureaucracy merely follow orders from their political superiors. Some observers have argued that such distinctions are clear and self-evident: there is no Democratic or Republican way to build a road.

But in the modern, industrialized, technocratic state these simple distinctions break down. Just as a legislature cannot specify all of the details of complex programs, neither can political appointees give precise and complete orders about how their policy decisions must be implemented. They lack the time, and, more importantly, the expertise. Career civil servants have devoted their careers to managing the details of programs, and may even have helped to draft the legislation that established those programs. They have the information upon which programmatic decisions must be made. They formulate the regulations that establish rules for applying the law to specific, individual cases. In addition, they are experts at applying the bureaucracies' own rules and regulations to the management of particular programs: they oil the budget, personnel, and paper flow parts of the bureaucratic machine.

Political appointees do legitimately get involved in the details of programs, and career executives are often involved in policy discussions because of their experience and political judgment. In the modern policy arena, where the questions are whether to build the road and where to build it, policy cannot be strictly separated from administration.

In this overlap of function, it is all the more crucial to maintain the normative distinction between the two roles. Despite the fact that career bureaucrats are involved in policy decisions, they ought not to lose sight of the democratic imperative that presidential appointees are the legitimate locus of decision making in the executive branch. The appropriate posture of the civil servant is to carry out faithfully legitimate policy decisions, despite personal preferences. Without this chain of legitimacy, the democratic linkage between the electorate and the government would become unacceptably attenuated.

To argue that career voices ought to be heard at the highest levels in the executive branch is not to argue that those views should prevail. The career executive is likely to present an institutional perspective, mindful of the longer term consequences of decisions. Short-term, political criteria are likely to be taken into account by political appointees. The point is that those political appointees at the higher levels ought to have the benefit of the best judgment of career executives about the policy in question. When political appointees are placed lower in the bureaucracy, they will put their own political spin on advice at an early stage in the process, and those at the top may never hear the straight views of career executives about policies. According to former Comptroller General Elmer Staats, President Truman would say: "Give me your best professional analysis, I'll make the political judgment."[30]

Contrasting Perspectives

In addition to these normative distinctions, differences of background and style distinguish politicians and bureaucrats. Each set of officials contributes differently to the formulation of public policy. Appointees' political skills are needed to identify goals and to mobilize support for them. The strength of civil servants, on the other hand, lies in designing programs to implement those goals. These differences reflect contrasting roles and are rooted in institutional positions. Political appointees are in-and-outers. They are recruited to serve a particular president, and rarely stay longer than that president's term, usually much less. Presidential appointees want to make their marks quickly and to move on, either to a higher position in the government or back to the private sector where salaries are much more attractive. Much of their agenda is driven by the desire to re-elect the president or to leave a good record on which the partisan heir apparent can run.

Career executives, in contrast, have longer term perspectives. They will still be operating programs and administering agencies after this season's political birds of passage have flown. This realization causes them to pay attention to the health of institutions and to the integrity of the processes that ensure nonpartisan implementation of the laws. This longer term perspective makes them less willing to upset long-established practices quickly. Bureaucrats are concerned about the institutions they manage as well as about the current policies of those institutions. Politicians tend to see organizations as convenient tools to achieve their policy objectives.

One basic dilemma that underlies government in the United States is that the permanent bureaucracy must be responsive to the incumbent president, yet it must maintain the professionalism in its career managers necessary to serve the next president equally as well. The conscientious civil servant does not want to make choices among competing political claims; that is the function of the political process and of presidential appointees. The different strengths of political appointees and career bureaucrats must therefore be merged in an appropriate balance if government is to be both responsive and effective. A certain amount of tension, however, will always be present in that balance.

The Cycle of Accommodation

Career executives are critical to the success of their political superiors in many ways. They are highly educated, and they know the intricacies of the laws and regulations that govern programs they implement. They possess institutional memory. They know where to go for help in central management agencies or in Congress. They have built up personal intelligence and communications networks over many years through dealing with the same organizations, people, and issues. They have earned the respect of their fellow professionals through years of service.

Career executives must follow legitimate orders, but they should do more than merely carry them out passively. A "yes, boss" attitude is not merely inadequate, it may be downright dangerous. True neutral competence involves "loyalty that argues back," as Hugh Heclo, author of *A Government of Strangers,* has aptly said. For the boss to have "my own person" in the job is not enough; that person must have the requisite knowledge and skills to make the bureaucratic machine work, and the good judgment to delineate the pros and cons of various options.

Some political appointees make the mistake of using an unsophisticated version of the politics-administration dichotomy to exclude career executives from policy deliberations. This attitude has negative long-term consequences. Heclo puts it this way: "When senior political appointees fail to include higher civil servants in substantive policy discussions, there is little reason for permanent career staff to acquire more than a narrowly technical, routine perspective. When careerists are denied access to an understanding of the political rationales for top-level decisionmaking, they inevitably become divorced from the 'big picture' and incapable of communicating it to subordinates. . . . In short, without good faith efforts at the highest political levels, the upper reaches of the bureaucracy go to seed."[31] Elliot Richardson argues that to be an effective political appointee one must treat career subordinates with respect:

> People in the career services need to be met with respect from a point of view that takes for granted that they would not be there if they did not care about the merits of the public service in which they are engaged, and with a willingness to listen and to ask questions.[32]
>
> People who have devoted a lifetime or a significant part of it to expertise in their field are entitled to be listened to with respect. . . . Many Presidential appointees make the gross mistake of not sufficiently respecting the people they are dealing with . . . and get themselves into trouble as a result."[33]

Despite initial distrust and suspicion toward career executives, political appointees usually develop trust for and confidence in the career executives who report to them. This predictable cycle of accommodation has operated in all recent presidential administrations, if not in all political appointees. Initial suspicion is followed by a period of learning to work together, resulting in a more sophisticated appreciation of the contribution of the career service and in mutual respect and trust.

In comparing the quality of high-level executives in the public and private sectors, Alan K. (Scotty) Campbell, who was the first director of the Office of Personnel Management (OPM) and later executive vice president of ARA Services, Inc. said: "The quality of top managers I knew in the federal government . . . is every bit as high as we have at ARA; and on the whole, the people at ARA are paid from one and one half to three times more than their public sector counterparts."[34] In letters to Chairman Volcker, members of the Reagan administration voiced similar opinions. According to Secretary of State George P. Shultz: "Speaking as one who has also served in the private sector and academia, I [believe] that the Department's workforce is on a par with the best I have known in the private world." Secretary of Energy John S. Herrington wrote: "On the whole, I believe career federal employees are as capable, conscientious and effective as their counterparts in the private sector."[35]

In a survey, the National Academy of Public Administration asked all presidential appointees between 1964 and 1984 to characterize how responsive and competent the career executives in their agencies were. Favorable responses (four or five on a five-point scale) were reported by 77 percent or more in each of the past five administrations. The responses broken down by administration appear in Table 1.[36] The sooner that this cycle of accommodation begins in an administration, the sooner a president can accomplish his goals.

Reagan administration Secretary of Agriculture Richard Lyng offered this advice from his several tours as a presidential appointee: "In every case, I found career people that were absolutely splendid. Their experience was absolutely invaluable. I needed them, it was essential. The career people kept me from shooting myself in the foot. . . . The way you get them with you is to treat them like equals, point out I need you to help me. These people want the job done right. I never cared if a fellow was a Democrat or a Republican, because . . . all of them are nonpartisan. . . . A Presidential appointee who doesn't work with the career people will not make it."[37]

Table1. Appointees' Perception of Career Civil Servants

	Competent	Responsive
ADMINISTRATION		
Johnson	92%	89%
Nixon	88	84
Ford	80	82
Carter	81	86
Reagan	77	78

Recommendations for Improving the System

Even a partial acceptance of the preceding data and arguments would compel the conclusion that the executive leadership system of the federal government has problems that require attention. The combination of rapid turnover of political appointees and their increasing numbers in the lower executive ranks has created a management void in many places. Using more political appointees to achieve political control eventually reaches a point of diminishing returns, and that point has long been passed in the federal government. "Ironically . . . the politicization of government positions has tended to reduce, not increase, political leadership; we need more political leadership, less politicization."[38]

RECOMMENDATION 1: We recommend that the Office of Presidential Personnel establish explicit criteria for the qualifications of people nominated for each position, and that these criteria emphasize managerial experience and substantive expertise as well as loyalty and philosophical compatibility with the president. . . .

RECOMMENDATION 2: The total number of political appointees in the departments and agencies of the executive branch should not exceed 2,000. . . .

RECOMMENDATION 3: The president and department and agency heads should fill more positions in the mid and upper levels of the executive branch with career civil servants rather than political appointees. Particular emphasis should be placed on taking advantage of the continuity and institutional memory that career executives can provide across administrations. . . .

RECOMMENDATION 4: In order to facilitate the recruitment of political appointees, we recommend that presidential nominees establish personnel planning operations immediately after the nominating conventions. . . .

RECOMMENDATION 5: The Office of Presidential Personnel should be used as an active recruitment office and not as a passive screening office. . . .

RECOMMENDATION 6: The president should delegate to department heads the recruitment of noncareer SES and Schedule C appointments within the bounds of general criteria established by the White House. The president should give significant weight to the preferences of cabinet secretaries in the selection of their immediate subordinates who are presidential appointments. . . .

RECOMMENDATION 7: Executive salaries should be significantly increased and financial reporting requirements should be reexamined. . . .

RECOMMENDATION 8: The president should establish orientation programs for all new political appointees in the executive branch. . . .

RECOMMENDATION 9: The president should seek commitments from the appointees in his administration to remain in office for a full term. . . .

We conclude by quoting Secretary Carlucci on the pressing need for improvements in the executive levels of the public service: "There was a Prime Minister in the Fourth Republic who, as best I can tell, was known for nothing other than the following quote: 'Politics is the art of postponing decisions until they are no longer relevant.' Well, that may work on most issues, but it will not on this one. Current trends are making the situation worse, and it just will not go away. Many of us have devoted a lifetime to government service. Others are at the peak of their careers. We served because we believed in the meaning of government and a free society. Nothing has happened to change that."[39]

NOTES

This selection is the report to the National Commission on the Public Service (the Volcker Commission), a group of prominent Americans who were concerned with the state of the public service. In 1989 the commission issued a report, *Leadership for America: Rebuilding the Public Service,* which called for a number of reforms in the recruitment, training, compensation, and performance of the Public Service. The selection reprinted here was the report by the Task Force on the Relations Between Political Appointees and Career Executives. The members of the Task Force were Frederick V. Malek, Robert C. McFarlane, Walter F. Mondale, Benjamin Read, Anne Wexler, and Alan Wolff. The chair and convener of the Task Force was Elliot L. Richardson, and the project director was James P. Pfiffner.

1. See James W. Fesler, "The Higher Civil Service in Europe and the United States," in Bruce L. R. Smith, ed., *The Higher Civil Service in Europe and Canada* (Washington, D.C.: Brookings, 1984), p. 87.

2. See Carl Brauer, "Tenure, Turnover, and Postgovernment Employment Trends of Presidential Appointees," in G. Calvin Mackenzie, ed., *The In-and-Outers* (Baltimore: Johns Hopkins University Press, 1987), p. 175; Carolyn Ban and Patricia Ingraham, "Short-Timers: Political Appointee Mobility and Its Impact on Political-Career Relations in the Reagan Administration," paper presented at the National Convention of the American Society for Public Administration, Anaheim, Calif., 1986. 3. Ban and Ingraham, "Short-Timers."

4. Patricia W. Ingraham, "Building Bridges or Burning Them?: The President, the Appointees, and the Bureaucracy," *Public Administration Review* (Sept./Oct., 1987), p. 429.

5. Hugh Heclo, "The In-and-Outer System: A Critical Assessment," in *The In-and-Outers*, p. 208.

6. Quoted in Paul Light, "When Worlds Collide: The Political-Career Nexus," in *The In-and-Outers*, p. 157.

7. Data supplied by the Office of the Under Secretary of State for Management, Jan., 1988.

8. These data are taken from the *Plum Books* of 1960 and 1984: U.S. Government Policy and Supporting Positions, House Committee on Post Office and Civil Service (86th Cong., 2d sess.) 1960; and U.S. Government Policy and Supporting Positions, Senate Committee on Governmental Affairs (98th Cong., 2d sess.) 1984.

9. Frank Carlucci, "A Private Sector and National Perspective," in *The State of the American Public Service* (Washington, D.C.: National Academy of Public Administration, 1985), p. 7.

10. Frederic V. Malek, *Washington's Hidden Tragedy* (New York: The Free Press, 1978), pp. 102–103.

11. For the first two years cited see David T. Stanley, et al. *Men Who Govern* (Washington, D.C.: Brookings, 1967), p. 4. For the 1985 data see Ingraham, "Building Bridges or Burning Them?" p. 427.

12. General Accounting Office, *Federal Employees: Trends in Career and Noncareer Employee Appointments in the Executive Branch* (July, 1987), GAO/GGD-87-96FS, p. 11.

13. Ingraham, "Building Bridges or Burning Them?" p. 429.

14. Congressional Budget Office, *Federal Civilian Employment,* Special Study (Dec., 1987), p. ix.

15. National Academy of Public Administration, "Perspectives on the Public Management Challenge," remarks by Ronald I. Spiers (Mar., 1987), pp. 30–31.

16. Quoted in Ban and Ingraham, "Short-Timers."

17. Ibid.

18. Elliot L. Richardson, Article for the Ripon Society (Sept. 10, 1987). For another version of these remarks see Elliot L. Richardson, "Civil Servants: Why Not the Best?" *Wall Street Journal,* Nov. 20, 1987.

19. Ingraham, "Building Bridges or Burning Them?" p. 431.

20. Clyde Linsley, "The Brain Drain Continues As Top Government Managers Leave for the Private Sector," *Government Executive,* June, 1988, pp. 10–18.

21. *The New York Times,* Dec. 14, 1987.

22. Timothy Clark and Marjorie Wachtel, "The Quiet Crisis Goes Public," *Government Executive,* June, 1988, p. 28.

23. General Accounting Office, *Senior Executive Service: Reasons Why Career Members Left in Fiscal Year 1985,* GAO/GGD-87-106FS (Aug., 1987), p. 8.

24. Ingraham, "Building Bridges or Burning Them?" p. 431.
25. Charles H. Levine and Rosalyn Kleeman, "The Quiet Crisis of the Civil Service: The Federal Personnel System at the Crossroads," National Academy of Public Administration (1987), p. 6.
26. Clark and Wachtel, "The Quiet Crisis Goes Public," p. 28.
27. U.S. Commission on Executive, Legislative, and Judicial Salaries, "High Quality Leadership—Our Government's Most Precious Asset," report of the commission, Dec. 15, 1986, pp. 19–20.
28. *The Report of the President's Commission on Compensation of Career Federal Executives,* Feb. 26, 1988, pp. 3–6.
29. Letter from David Ruder to Paul Volcker, dated Nov. 3, 1987.
30. Statement at the panel meeting of the Presidency Project of the National Academy of Public Administration, May 17, 1988. Elmer Staats was chair of the panel.
31. Hugh Heclo, "The In-and-Outer System: A Critical Assessment," in *The In-and-Outers,* p. 202.
32. Testimony of Elliot Richardson, Hearings before the Senate Committee on Governmental Affairs on the *Presidential Transition Effectiveness Act* (100th Cong., 1st and 2d sess.) 1988, p. 91.
33. Quoted by James P. Pfiffner, "Political Appointees and Career Executives: The Democracy-Bureaucracy Nexus in the Third Century," *Public Administration Review,* Jan./Feb., 1987, p. 61. The interview was conducted for the Presidential Appointee Project of the National Academy of Public Administration.
34. Quoted in James Fesler, "Politics, Policy, and Bureaucracy at the Top," *The Annals* 466 (Mar., 1983): 33.
35. The letters are in the files of the National Commission on the Public Service.
36. National Academy of Public Administration, *Leadership in Jeopardy: The Fraying of the Presidential Appointments System* (1985). See Paul Light, "When Worlds Collide: The Political-Career Nexus," in *The In-and-Outers,* p. 158.
37. Quoted by Pfiffner, "Political Appointees and Career Executives," p. 61.
38. Elliot L. Richardson, Testimony before the Senate Committee on Governmental Affairs. Printed in Hearings on the *Presidential Transition Effectiveness Act* (100th Cong., 1st and 2d sess.) 1988, p. 89.
39. Carlucci, "A Private Sector and National Perspective," p. 10.

Chapter 12

Political Direction and Policy Change in Three Federal Departments

PATRICIA W. INGRAHAM

Politics within the bureaucracy is a long-standing issue. It has been given new life, however, by recent presidential efforts to more closely monitor and control the activities and output of executive departments and agencies. Most presidents since the time of Franklin Roosevelt have expressed frustration with the workings of the federal bureaucracy, but the efforts of Richard Nixon, Jimmy Carter, and Ronald Reagan are notable in this regard.

Richard Nixon perceived the career bureaucracy to be ideologically hostile to efforts to redirect and/or eliminate federal programs.[1] Through a series of attempted administrative reorganizations, careful political appointee placement, and several legal efforts to "rein in" career activities, he established the basis for what has come to be called the "administrative presidency."[2] Jimmy Carter, though professing a different purpose, followed the same path toward enhanced presidential and political control with some components of the Civil Service Reform Act (CSRA) of 1978.[3] Building on the provisions of CSRA, the Reagan administration created new systems for political management and direction.[4] It also contributed to a now pervasive sense that career assistance will be gained by coercion and cooptation, rather than by cooperation and trust. One outcome of the new political management strategies is that relationships between career civil servants and political managers are one component of what has been termed the "quiet crisis" in the American public service.[5]

Though a great deal has been written about bureaucratic politics in general, and presidential management efforts in particular, a number of issues and assumptions remain unexplored. Some of the questions are remarkably simple, at least on their face. How, for example, do presidents or their appointees "direct" bureaucrats to do their bidding? Even more basic, how do presidents direct appointees to carry out specific tasks and functions? How systematically does either set of activities occur? This analysis begins the examination of these questions. To do so, three case studies of political efforts to redirect bureaucratic activities are analyzed. All three cases were identified by political appointees as examples of "successful" political direction; they demonstrate, however, that both the components of, and the reasons for, success are complex and diverse.

Background

Presidential efforts to increase control of the permanent bureaucracy have relied on four basic strategies: more careful screening of political appointees for policy and ideological compatibility with the president,[6] greater numbers of political appointees,[7] placement of political appointees in nonpolicy positions,[8] and bypassing career civil servants whenever possible.[9] Political efforts to control the bureaucracy have also been enhanced by the performance evaluation and Senior Executive Service components of the CSRA.[10]

Of the four components of the presidential control strategy, greater numbers and expanded placement are the most amenable to external evaluation. Screening for policy compatibility, for example, is essentially closed to those outside of the White House. It is possible, however, to count visible political appointments and to determine where those appointees are placed in the various agencies. For the purposes of a presidential control strategy, the most significant appointees are those who direct or manage policy activities and programs in the executive and central management agencies. Though the precise numbers here may be disputed, there is consensus that the total is larger today than twenty years ago.[11]

Since 1979, there has been an overall increase of about 200 full-time authorized presidential appointment positions. The major portion of this increase is attributable to additional appointments under Schedule C authority, most notably in grades GS-13 through GS-15. There was a total of 2,794 presidential appointments in 1979; 1,438 were Schedule C appointments. In 1985, of a total of 2,906 appointees, 1,665 were Schedule C appointments. In 1976, there were 443 Schedule C appointments at the level of GS-13 or above; in 1986, there were 946 such appointments.[12] Appointments at this level are notable for three reasons: first, for the presidential control model, which essentially assumes hierarchical control to be effective, appointees must have excellent management skills. Lower level appointees are not likely to possess such skills. Most appointees receive little or no training prior to assuming the appointive position, so the absence of management skills at time of appointment is a critical deficiency.[13] Second, increased political control assumes purposive direction to political appointees. This assumes a management capacity in the White House that may not exist.[14]

Third, tenure in position, long a problem with political appointees, is even lower for GS-13 through GS-15 appointments than at other political-appointment levels. One recent analysis of appointees just under the PAS (presidential appointment with consent of the Senate) level indicated that although average tenure in position was about eighteen months, nearly one-third of the appointees remained in one position for a very brief period of time, often less than one year.[15]

The combination of larger numbers of political appointees with limited management capabilities and short tenure raises serious questions about whether more appointees really do lead to increased control. Further, it leads to questions about the nature of political direction within the bureaucracy. As noted earlier, underlying the larger numbers strategy is an assumption of hierarchical control. Is this assumption correct? If so, the solution to better presidential control may simply be to select better appointees and to train them rigorously for the tasks they will assume. If this is not the solution, however, the continued layering of political appointments on already burdened public bureaucracies may well have outcomes quite different from those envisioned by the president and the president's policy advisers.

Methodology and Research Questions

This research is based on case studies conducted in three executive departments: the Department of Health and Human Services (HHS), the Department of Housing and Urban Development (HUD), and the Department of Transportation (DOT). The cases were selected after network interviewing within each organization. Respondents were asked to name one program in the department that had been given high political priority and could be considered a "success story" (that is, in which a specific action desired by political appointees was achieved). The other major criterion for selection was that the program or policy named be containable (that is, defined narrowly enough so that actions relevant to it could be examined in-depth). When the cases were selected, in-depth interviews were conducted in each agency with the political appointees most directly responsible for the change mandate and with the career civil servants who reported directly to those appointees. A limited number of interviews were also conducted with managers in other parts of the organization whose activities were relevant to the case, with staff of the Domestic Council and with staff at the U.S. General Accounting Office. A total of sixty in-depth interviews were conducted in the period from January to June, 1987. All of those interviewed were guaranteed anonymity to ensure candor and to protect against possible retribution. Consequently, all quotations in this analysis, though drawn verbatim from the transcripts of the interviews, are presented anonymously.

The interviews, and this analysis, were guided by the following research questions:

1. How does political direction occur in each organization?
2. What are the organizational characteristics that enhance or impede successful political direction?
3. What characteristics of political executives enhance or impede political direction?
4. What characteristics of career civil servants enhance or impede successful political direction?

The research is exploratory. Although only three case studies are analyzed here, the long-term intent is to determine which characteristics of these successful cases, if any, may be generalizable to the larger question of successful political management.

The Cases

A brief synopsis of each case is useful in understanding both the extent of change necessary to achieve the desired outcome and to understand the policy management demands placed on political appointees and career managers by the change process.

The Department of Housing and Urban Development— The Housing Voucher Program

Early in the first term of the Reagan administration, it was determined that housing vouchers for low-income housing, rather than new construction, would be a priority within HUD. This decision was based in part on the recommendations of the President's Commission on Housing. It was also strongly influenced by Housing Secretary Samuel Pierce's strong agreement with a Rand Corporation study that concluded that the low-income housing problem should be defined in terms of affordability, not availability. Because HUD's housing construction programs were based on an assumption of inadequate supply, the Rand study struck at HUD's very core. Further, there was both an existing program and extensive research and development work upon which a "new" voucher program could be based.

Accordingly, Secretary Pierce did not request funds for the Low Income

Housing Construction Program in the 1982 budget, but he did include a request for a new, limited, Housing Voucher Program. Congress followed the HUD recommendation to kill the existing New Construction Program but initially refused to approve the voucher proposal. For a two-year period, therefore, political executives at HUD concentrated on modifications of the existing Housing Certificate Program, which closely resembled the voucher program they wished to create. This decision automatically involved a nonhousing component of the agency, the Office of Community Planning and Development, which used housing certificates in the rental rehabilitation program it administered. The voucher legislation was resubmitted each year, however, and in 1984, with congressional approval, was initiated as a demonstration project in twenty cities.

The new program was very similar to both the existing Housing Certificate Program and to an earlier program that had been initiated in the second term of the Nixon administration. That program, the Experimental Housing Assistance Program (EHAP), had been tested and evaluated in HUD's Office of Policy Development and Research for several years. This caused three major components of HUD to be involved in the housing-voucher case study: the Housing Office, the Office of Policy Development and Research, and Community Planning and Development. Technical responsibility for development of the voucher program resided with the assistant secretary for housing, but the assistant secretary for policy development and research played a key role. The Housing Voucher Program itself has always been directed by a career manager. The first results of the evaluation of the voucher demonstration were released in July, 1987. Also in 1987, Congress permitted the program to operate independently from other HUD housing programs—most notably the Housing Certificate Program—for the first time.

The Department of Transportation—
Transferring National and Dulles Airports
The DOT case differs from the HUD case in that it describes the transfer of management and operations responsibilities rather than program redesign. In addition, the DOT case reflects consistent high-level political involvement throughout the process. Though "blue ribbon commissions" were involved in both the HUD and the DOT cases, the DOT commission was used differently. At HUD, the Commission on Housing was asked to assist in setting policy objectives. At DOT, the Holton Commission was asked to devise a strategy for reaching a predetermined policy objective. Their charge from Secretary Dole was: "Don't tell me what. Tell me how!"

The change that Secretary Dole wished to achieve was this: since 1941, the

Federal Aviation Commission had operated first National Airport and then Dulles Airport as well. As early as 1948 internal agency reports had advocated removing airport management from the Federal Aviation Administration (FAA). Other secretaries of transportation, too, had recognized the awkwardness of continued federal operation, but no definitive action had been taken. Secretary Dole, finding herself devoting increasing amounts of time to airport management issues, simply declared that it had to stop. The appointment of the commission to "study" the issue was the first step in a very short and very intense process that culminated in the transfer of the airports to a new regional authority in June, 1987. The secretary herself remained involved in critical decision points throughout the process, but also assigned a member of her personal staff (an expert on airport management) to oversee the process on a daily basis. The other key staff person from DOT headquarters was a career civil servant, a lawyer who specialized in environmental law. The secretary and her staff worked very closely with the Holton Commission, but essentially bypassed the FAA, choosing instead to work directly with the staff of the Metropolitan Washington Airport Authority, a unit of the FAA. The working group was very small and very cohesive. From the time the secretary initiated the project until Congress approved the legislation creating the new authority, probably no more than ten staffers (both political and career) were actively involved in the project.

Health and Human Resources— The Regional Health Planning Program

The case study at HHS is of the death of the Regional Health Planning Program, which was created in 1974. The program was administered by a branch of the Public Health Service, the Health Resources and Services Administration. Originally proposed by the Nixon administration, regional health planning was viewed by Nixon and his Secretary of Health and Human Resources, Caspar Weinberger, as a cost-containment measure for rapidly escalating health-care costs. Cost containment was to be achieved through planning and through the rigorous regulatory function of certificates of need. The certificates were to limit the development of new resources and to control the expansion of existing resources. The legislation creating the program was very specific. It described the composition of the planning boards and their responsibilities in minute terms, while excluding some major health-care providers from planning and other program activities. From the beginning, it was clear that the program, both for its regulatory function and for the participatory structures it created, would be very controversial.

From the first days of the Reagan administration, administrators at HHS were told that the government did not belong in health planning. This position found strong support among some members of Congress and their staffs, as well as among some of the career staff who had become associated with the program. Though the program was substantially revised by amendments in 1980 and 1981, there was, among top-level political appointees and some members of Congress, a growing conviction that the program had to be completely abolished. In 1982 and 1983, money for the Regional Health Planning Program was not included in the Public Health Service budget request, but in both years Congress reauthorized the program for one more year.[16] Finally, in 1984, members of Congress who supported the program were unable to muster the votes for another continuing resolution. The HHS was told they could fund Regional Health Planning agencies only through September, 1986. Because an overlooked provision of the original legislation gave the local agencies authority to carry funds over for two years, September 30, 1987, became the closeout date for receipt of federal funding.

Anticipating this closeout, a career manager was directed, by another career manager, to assume the management of the program within HRSA for the specific purpose of eliminating the program. By spring, 1987, there were no staff within HRSA assigned to the program. During this process there were no political executives within HRSA itself, though the process was monitored at HHS headquarters by a deputy assistant secretary for health who had previously been a staffer for one of the members of Congress who wished to abolish the legislation.

Findings

In the introduction, two basic questions were posed: how do presidents tell political appointees what to do, and how do appointees proceed in their efforts to carry out presidential direction? The case studies suggest answers quite different from those advanced by advocates of the "administrative presidency" and increased political control. Additional discussion, while serving to flesh out the disparities, also serves to clarify the extremely loose coupling of the presidential management system as it relates to appointees within the various executive departments.

The Nature of Policy Direction

The basic dilemma facing presidents and their immediate staff in relation to policy direction was aptly summarized by a staff member of the Domestic Council. He noted: "The President and the political leaders know they can't change the whole thing. In any agency, you'll find programs that political leadership doesn't touch and doesn't manage. The President issues broad policy inclinations. The top political executives apply those broad guidelines to their own departments. If possible, we comment on specifics, but that's often not possible."

Respondents within the agencies agreed with this description. In fact, political executives in all three agencies described the program change they had initiated as being an integral part of the president's broad directive to transfer federal authority to a more appropriate level of government. Said one careerist of the housing voucher approach: "This is part of a grand plan to turn everything over to the lowest possible level of authority—the individual citizen." In DOT, one respondent noted: "Airport management just doesn't belong in the federal government. The biggest impediment to both airports was being tied up by Congress and the Executive branch." At HHS, the termination of the Health Planning Program was explained in these terms: "It was part of the effort to de-regulate and to emphasize private sector initiatives." Further, there were strong defenses of an appointee's right to "interpret" presidential directives: "The Secretary has the President's signature on her wall. She was appointed because she agrees with him. She knows what he wants her to do."

In relation to lower-level political appointees, there were similar descriptions of interpreting both presidential and secretarial intent. One respondent described the process as one of "osmosis"; others described the great amount of freedom and flexibility available to assistant secretaries and deputy assistant secretaries as they chose priority policy activities. One deputy assistant secretary noted the many opportunities to be "creative." Another said, "There is a tremendous amount of latitude. I can look at something and say 'that's bad policy!'—we can have policy making from my level up to Assistant Secretary and Under Secretary." The overall sense of appointees at the assistant and deputy assistant–secretary level was aptly summarized by an appointee at HUD: "Does someone tell you this is what the policy is? No. No one says that in so many words. Sometimes it comes by listening, by reading speeches, by using common sense."

Given this remarkable flexibility, one might well ask how, or if, policy clarification and coordination does occur. When respondents did describe a system of policy communication that was somewhat systematic, they cited the budget review activities of the Office of Management and Budget. One person described the process in this way: "To the extent that we get any direction from outside the agency (in terms of executive direction) it comes from OMB and the budget passback activity." Another added: "OMB plays a critical role. It has been extremely activist in this administration. And, after all, most policy ideas are budget related." Aside from the budgetary control, however, the political direction from outside the agency was described in all three cases as intermittent and vague.

It is also important to note that the perceptions of their own authority by top political executives is critical to clarifying this diffuse process or to diffusing it further. The secretary of DOT provides an interesting counterpoint to the secretary of HUD in this regard. Secretary Dole was consistently described as a decisive policy maker who outlined very specific directives to the various parts of the organization and micromanaged them to their conclusion. Secretary Pierce was most often described as a "corporate" manager who delegated very broad directives to employees and rarely intervened further, except at budget time. As a result, respondents often spoke of "policy gaps" at HUD. They also described the difficulties created for career staff when assistant secretaries, acting on essentially individual policy agendas, pursued objectives not clearly—or closely—linked to other program activities.

In addition, as many theorists have noted, the organizational complexity of public bureaucracies is compounded by the politics of the organization's external environment. In this respect, too, political management is critical to further diffusing or to clarifying policy initiatives. Stephenson's analysis of the Urban Development Action Grant Program at HUD suggests, for example, that achieving organizational policy change is at least as much a factor of understanding and managing external politics as it is of directing and managing career civil servants.[17] External politics was critical to both the Regional Health Planning Program and to the transfer of National and Dulles airports, as well as to the Housing Voucher Program. In relation to the Health Planning Program, one career manager noted, "Nobody took an ax and killed it. We just watched it die." He then discussed the extent to which lack of departmental support for the program permitted external political forces to determine how, and when, the program would end. This view of largely external decision making (despite earlier agreement that killing the Regional Health Planning Program was a political management success) is substantiated by Mueller's (1988) analysis of the program's death.[18] At HUD, failure of political executives to convince key members of Congress of the validity of the housing voucher approach resulted in the limited demonstration program rather than the administration proposal. At DOT, on the other hand, the secretary's early decision to deal with the external politics of the proposed change was unanimously cited by respondents as being critical to success. One person commented, for example, "The Secretary understood from the beginning that this was a political problem and that politicians could not get ahead of their constituents on it. That was the first issue we had to resolve."

These complex characteristics of the organizations being studied suggest that serious demands will inevitably be placed on the political executives who view themselves as agents of change. In this regard, it is significant to note that, in a recent study by the National Academy of Public Administration, only half of the political executives surveyed considered themselves skilled in the policy areas their jobs had encompassed. Only 12 percent felt skilled in the ability to deal with external politics.[19] Quite clearly, the organizational complexity just described is a serious factor in the ability of presidents and political appointees to effect policy change with public organizations. The difficulties this complexity and the organizational variation pose for presidents and for those who would assist presidential management efforts, were succinctly stated by a staff member of the Domestic Council: "If we had time, we could figure out agency by agency where careers should go and how far down political appointments should go. We could use political leadership to good advantage. But we don't have time." When these problems are combined with the very diffuse policy directions described earlier, the demands placed on political executives become very serious indeed.

In the environment just described, three characteristics of political management appear to be most significant: (1) the extent to which political management penetrates the organization, (2) the skills of political management, and (3) the extent to which political executives use career staff strategically to obtain political objectives. In addition, of course, the response by career staff is critical. The three case studies reported here represent very diverse experiences in this regard.

POLITICAL PENETRATION AND MANAGEMENT CAPABILITY

Housing voucher program. Since the Nixon administration, when its programs fell out of favor, HUD has had a reputation as a dumping ground for political appointees. Both organizational data and the program-specific data collected for the case study support the contention that there are an unusual number of political appointees at HUD. Most of them do not stay very long. Proportionate to its size, HUD has more Schedule C appointments at grades GS-13 through GS-15 than any other executive department. Furthermore, that number has more than doubled, from forty-two to eighty-six, in the years since 1976.[20] This case study and previous case studies at HUD indicate that many of those appointees serve as special assistants or deputy assistant secretaries, creating a special pool of political management for use by assistant secretaries and higher level appointees.[21]

Theoretically, such large numbers should lead to micromanagement of many programs. In fact, however, this has not been the case, primarily because tenure is very short and program-relevant skills are very limited. Though Secretary Pierce has remained with HUD throughout the Reagan presidency, his delegated management style has placed primary responsibility for program change with lower level political appointees. At that level, turnover has been high and there have been other problems. The assistant secretary for policy development and research, an early and staunch advocate of the Housing Voucher Program, resigned from the agency under threat of indictment. His successor had another agenda, which she vigorously pursued to the detriment of consistent attention to the voucher program. Since the department began its voucher initiative in 1982, there were five assistant secretaries for housing and three assistant secretaries for community planning and development. There have also been long periods in between appointments, when, for all practical purposes, deputy assistant secretaries ran the shops. This level of appointment, however, is notable for its political campaign connection rather than for policy or management expertise. There was also frequent turnover among deputy assistant secretaries. As a direct result, political leadership of the Housing Voucher Program was intermittent, at best, and nonexistent at worst.

The best indication of the weak direction deals with the choice of the voucher as the Reagan administration's priority. As noted earlier, vouchers—or programs very much like them—have a long history in the organization. After asking a blue ribbon commission to assist in identifying program priority areas for HUD, Secretary Pierce seized on existing programs and experiments as a means of attacking the "affordability, not availability" problem. He now had a new problem, however, because those programs not only were not Reagan initiatives, but also had flourished at HUD during the Carter years. One political appointee described the "policy choice" in these terms: "Yes, the Housing Voucher program is a lot like the EHAP program and the certificate program. But we wanted a new program. So we renamed it." Certainly this is not the first time that a new administration's appointees "redesigned" an existing policy for their purposes. Lynn and Whitcomb describe in detail the efforts of Carter appointees at HHS to rework analyses of welfare reform from the Nixon administration.[22] Indeed, Hogwood and Peters suggest that virtually all "new" policy results from policy succession, rather than new policy ideas.[23]

This is not to suggest that political leadership has been totally superfluous to the voucher program. There have been strategic points at which political action, however limited, has kept the program on track. Obviously, the decision to adopt the Housing Voucher Program as a Reagan initiative and to rename it was the first strategic point. The second occurred well into the demonstration, when a new deputy assistant secretary for housing concluded that the program was languishing. Deciding that the careerist in whose office the voucher demonstration was located "didn't believe in the program," the deputy removed the demonstration from the careerist's office. The career manager reassigned responsibility for the voucher demonstration had a separate staff and new hiring authority at a time when the organization as a whole was cutting back. In the deputy's words, "I needed to challenge the status quo. I had to move the director. I had no choice. Then I arranged for a memo from the Secretary to Central Office staff. That memo said you must concentrate on the voucher program. It's a priority. Then we had memos from the five Assistant Secretaries to the Field Office Staff telling them the same thing. In this office, I have assigned political appointees to sit with careers to follow through on implementation. They are supposed to sit with them, work with them, live with them, if necessary."

Transferring National and Dulles airports. Political penetration of the DOT organization is different in a number of ways. The number of political appointees is smaller in total numbers and proportionate to the size of the organization. There are no political appointees in the Metropolitan Washington Airport Authority (MWA) and very few at the FAA. The secretary has a staff of special assistants, however, upon whom Secretary Dole relied for management of specific policy initiatives. During Secretary Dole's tenure, most of the special assistants, and many of the other political appointees in the department, remained in one position for a considerable period of time. There was both political and policy continuity. The DOT respondents were unanimous in crediting the success of the transfer policy to this continuity. One respondent noted: "The Secretary viewed this thing as her baby from the start. Had she gone, or had Shirley [the special assistant for policy] gone, the whole thing would have been gone." Another said: "She [Secretary Dole] used the bureaucracy in a different way. She directed them, but then she managed them on an almost daily basis." Another explained the success this way: "The Secretary ran this outside of normal bureaucratic channels. That would have been the doom of a really good idea. As a result, it was always an anticipatory approach. The Secretary's management team implicitly understood that they couldn't spend their time putting out fires. At all times, they knew the issues before they surfaced."

At DOT, despite the fact that the available pool of political management is much smaller than at HUD, those resources that were available were used strategically and intensively. As a direct result, their impact on the organization and its policies was widely acknowledged. Which is not to say that it was universally loved. As the interviews for this research were being conducted, the administrator for the FAA resigned. His departure was attributed, at least partially, to Secretary Dole's management style and her tendency to exclude the FAA from many policy discussions and decisions. One FAA respondent noted, "You would not find an FAA executive who would not complain about the Dole style and about the inefficiencies this has produced. We spend an enormous amount of time responding to inquiries and to new policy directives set by the Secretary's staff." Asked if the Dole style had contributed to the administrator's resignation, the respondent replied, "Without any question." It is important to note here that this dispute is one between political appointees and not one between political appointees and career civil servants, though careerists at FAA also expressed some dissatisfaction with being excluded in the early stages of the policy activity.

Regional health planning program. The HHS case is different from both HUD and DOT in terms of political penetration. With a limited number of presidential appointments, and fewer top-level Schedule C appointments than HUD (eighty-one at HHS, eighty-six at HUD),[24] the ability to penetrate into this very large organization is extremely limited. Further, in the Reagan administration, there have been three secretarial appointments at HHS. Turnover at lower levels of political appointments has also been higher than for many other executive departments.[25] In addition, the existence of the Commissioned Officer Corps in the Public Health Service, many high-level doctors and scientists in the National Institutes of Health, and a general requirement for rather esoteric technical expertise in many of its programs causes HHS to be an extremely difficult agency for short-term political appointees to master and manage. As a direct result, there is very little choice but to rely heavily on career expertise and management to carry out "political" direction.

It is somewhat difficult to identify specific policies that are characterized by sufficient political attention and direction to qualify as "political mandates." The Regional Health Planning Program analyzed here is one such program; as noted earlier, however, congressional direction was also a very important factor in the policy change. One person who was interviewed suggested, in fact, that this might be a case of "negative" political executive action, adding: "Everybody recognized that change was necessary . . . [the assistant secretary] just happened to be inside the agency. But he just didn't understand the politics of it—the change had to come legislatively." Another, however, had no hesitation to link the policy change to political direction and characterized the opposition of one political appointee to the program as "Adamant, vocal, livid, and irrational." Because there were no political appointees within the HRSA during the program's actual demise, political direction was, of necessity, once removed, emanating from Health and Human Resources headquarters rather than from within HRSA. No matter how vocal the political opposition to the program may have been, it could not—and did not—have the consistency or the intensity of the policy change mandated by Secretary Dole at DOT.

As this brief discussion demonstrates, the nature of political direction in these three cases differed dramatically. In the HUD case, more was not necessarily better. Given the tenure patterns at that agency, more may have been worse. Both HUD and HHS demonstrate that political leadership may well be marginal, even in policy areas that have high political priority within the organization. At DOT, on the other hand, political leadership was decisive and there was a clear political management strategy. The intensity of the strategy mandated, however, that its use be limited. Significantly, all three cases demonstrate the centrality of career personnel to political policy change. It is worthwhile, therefore, to analyze career perceptions of the need for change, as well as perceptions of how the direction and parameters of change were communicated to them by political managers.

USE OF CAREER SKILLS/CAREER PERCEPTION OF POLICY DIRECTION
The overwhelming finding in this regard is that key career participants did not oppose change. No matter how unclearly the mandate for change was expressed, virtually all of the careerists interviewed supported the change in their organization. Even in those cases where the initial response was negative, key career staff were turned around fairly quickly. At HUD, for example, the redesign of the existing programs was based on joint career-political collaboration, which occurred at a three-day retreat. One career official described the process this way: "The certificate program needed to be fixed I shared about five ideas for fixing it with the new political appointees. Then we had a three day brainstorming session with the General Counsel, the Undersecretary, the Assistant Secretaries for Housing and Policy Development and Research, and some careerists. We decided to modify the certificate and basically, we designed the new program."

At DOT, at the same time that the secretary and her staff were devising the plan for the Holton Commission and the new regional authority, career staff at FAA and MWA were pursuing their own ideas for changing the management structure of the airports. One described that process in these terms: "At the time of the Secretary's initiative, we were strategizing about making another run on a government corporation. We were envisioning having a go at it in our '86 budget. When the Secretary's plan came along, we laid that [the government corporation] aside and went with her initiative." He described the need for change in different terms than did the secretary's staff, emphasizing that the deteriorating conditions of National Airport absolutely mandated that something be done to get it out from under federal budget restrictions. This was a case in which the two motivations for change coincided nicely. MWA staff participation and leadership was critical to Secretary Dole's campaign for the legislation on the Hill.

At HHS, there was similar career conviction that change was necessary. Further, there was an acute awareness of the change the program had already gone through in its ten-year lifetime. One respondent described those changes and the career response in these terms: "Over that ten year period political leadership went from saying, 'Make it tough,' to 'Give it more teeth,' to 'Kill it!' If you are a career civil servant, you must have the ability to 'kill your own children' or to abolish your own job or that of your best friend." Another careerist described changing the program this way: "My perception of the health planning program is that it was mismanaged from day one. I asked to be given it years ago, but when I finally got it it was too far gone. Health planning was an excellent example of how not to run federal programs. It was designed to be a failure."

The strength of the above statements should not be interpreted to suggest that all careerists in all three agencies were begging for change. That is certainly not true. In all three cases there were some careerists who resisted the change or who were initially hesitant to participate in the necessary change activities. At DOT, those careerists were, or at least were perceived to be, primarily in the FAA and were bypassed. At HRSA, the career manager who was directed to phase out the Regional Health Planning Program noted that there was opposition among the staff of the program to doing so. She added: "I was placed in health planning against my wishes. I sensed that the program was dying, but I also had some commitment to the program and a lot of respect for the people who worked there. I didn't want to go, but it was a management decision, so I went."

At HUD, as already noted, there was career opposition to the new voucher program within the Housing Office and the Office of Community Planning and Development (CPD). The opposition within the Housing Office was at least partially silenced by moving the program to an independent office and giving it separate staff, but the opposition from CPD played an important part in shaping the early program both within HUD and on the Hill. The absence of any secretarial dictum on the program allowed the intra-agency dispute to become quite intense, and congressional support for what was essentially the CPD position caused the voucher demonstration to be closely linked to the certificate program until 1987.

The overall point, however, is this: in all three agencies, there were top-level career civil servants who believed that change was necessary before political management announced its intent. These careerists were willing, and even eager, to work with political appointees to actively pursue the desired change. In some cases, the change was viewed as a new personal challenge or opportunity; in others, as a messy, but necessary, part of the job. In all cases, there was a pool of career expertise available to political managers who chose, or who were able, to use it. The challenge for political managers was to use that pool effectively enough to divert opposition from other quarters.

Conclusion

As this discussion indicates, the case studies represent very diverse definitions of, and explanations for, political success. The transfer of National and Dulles airports was the result of a clear and very intense political management strategy that carried the policy change through Congress, as well as through the bureaucracy. As noted earlier, however, the very elements of the strategy that made it successful also severely limited its application. The number of programs or policies to which such a strategy can be applied is constrained by both political management resources and time.

At HUD, despite the presence of large numbers of political appointees, the absence of a clear and consistent political management strategy allowed both internal and external politics to shape the program dramatically. Very short tenure in position exacerbated the political management program. Further, despite the distrust of many political executives for career managers, the program was "successful" in the long run because key careerists provided continued momentum when political leadership did not.

Finally, at HHS, limited political penetration of the organization and a general lack of political skills among top political appointees (until fairly late in the program's slow death) meant that congressional action and bureaucratic inaction were significant characteristics of that policy "success." Again, career commitment to the policy change was a key variable in determining that the program would indeed die. It is important to note, however, that there are also commonalties in the findings from the case studies.

The common findings include:

1. The link between the president and/or the Executive Office policy apparatus and the political appointees in the executive departments is frequently unclear and tenuous. This creates a policy environment within those organizations that permits political executives at all levels of the organization great latitude in determining policy priorities.

This finding is somewhat surprising, given the Reagan administration's reputation as a "tough" policy manager. Though it could be argued that "send programs to a more appropriate level of government," is adequate policy direction, quite clearly, such amorphous "direction" will lead to a wide variety of very unpredictable outcomes.

2. In the absence of coherent top-down policy articulation, policy ideas often originate with lower level political appointees and "percolate up" through the organization.

Given the fact that this level of political appointment is often filled by persons with extremely limited managerial or policy expertise, this characteristic adds additional uncertainty to political direction of policy change.

3. Frequent turnover among political appointees responsible for policy direction contributes to a situation in which political direction may be intermittent or seriously conflicting with other political direction. In the one case in this study in which there clearly was aggressive political management, respondents were unanimous in attributing success to the longevity of Secretary Dole and her key advisers, and the concomitant ability to carry through critical aspects of the change process.

4. In all cases, policy "success" was based on a long history of previous changes and alterations, or proposed changes and alterations. At DOT, changes had been proposed for over forty years. At both HUD and HHS change had been considered for over ten years.

5. In all three case studies, key career personnel were convinced of the need for policy change and committed early to working with political executives to effect the change.

6. In all three case studies, policy "success" was attributable to joint action by political executives and high-level career managers.

It has become fashionable, in this country and others, to place policy problems at the feet of the bureaucracy. The "administrative presidency" and similar efforts were stimulated by a conviction that bureaucratic resistance and red tape mandated clear and decisive intervention by political leadership. We have spent great effort extolling the virtues of that leadership; we have praised its private sector values and perspectives, its incisive ability to spot "worthless" or "wasteful" programs, its breath of fresh air in the dead bureaucratic environment. We have spent far less time asking what difference that leadership really makes. The intent of this analysis was to begin the exploration of that question. The findings call assumptions of universal bureaucratic resistance and adherence to the status quo into serious question. These findings also clarify the enormity of the management tasks facing political appointees. In the end, these findings demonstrate again the frequent existence of a "political management void," rather than decisive political leadership.[26]

The findings of this research point to the critical role played by career personnel in providing a durable center of policy expertise. Only in the DOT were key political personnel in place long enough to carry the policy change through its most critical stages. At HUD and HHS, it would be only a slight exaggeration to say that the change occurred in spite of political leadership. In all cases, dimensions of the change, as well as appropriate change strategies, were influenced by career participation.

In sum, the research calls into question the underpinnings of theories such as those supporting the "administrative presidency." The political executives described in this research are often not a coherent management team. They are a dramatically disparate group of individuals who obtain policy direction and guidance from many different sources that may, but most frequently do not, include the president or White House staff. To expect coherent policy to emerge from such a setting is the stuff of exquisite fairy tales. Further, as many have noted, increasing the numbers of political appointees does not enhance or clarify political direction.[27] Indeed, it may exacerbate the problem. If presidents and appointed officials really wish to achieve political policy objectives, these realities must be confronted and addressed by a stronger system of political management. That system must embrace the value of career expertise and ability. The cases presented here do not describe a system of hierarchical political direction and control; they describe a system in which *joint* political-career action is critical to success.

NOTES

1. Joel Aberbach and Bert Rockman, "Clashing Beliefs Within the Executive Branch: The Nixon Administration's Bureaucracy," *The American Political Science Review* 70 (June, 1976), pp. 456–68.
2. Richard Nathan, *The Administrative Presidency* (New York: John Wiley and Sons, 1983).
3. Patricia W. Ingraham and Carolyn Ban, *Legislating Bureaucratic Change: The Civil Service Reform Act of 1978* (Albany: SUNY Press, 1984). See chapter 1.
4. See, for example, Terry M. Moe, "The Politicized Presidency," and James Pfiffner, "Political Appointees and Career Executives: The Democracy-Bureaucracy Nexus in the Third Century," both in this volume.
5. Charles Levine and Rosalyn Kleeman, "The Federal Civil Service at the Crossroads," unpublished paper presented at the Conference on A National Public Service for the Year 2000, Washington, D.C., Sept., 1986.
6. Moe, "The Politicized Presidency," in this volume.
7. Patricia W. Ingraham, "Building Bridges or Burning Them? The President, the Appointees, and the Bureaucracy," *Public Administration Review* 47 (1987): 425–35.
8. Michael Sanera, "Implementing the Mandate," in Stuart Butler, Michael Sanera and Bruce Weinrod, eds., *Mandate for Leadership II: Continuing the Conservative Revolution* (Washington, D.C.: The Heritage Foundation, 1984), pp. 560–99.

9. Frederick Malek (for the White House Personnel Office), "The Malek Manual," in Frank Thompson, ed., *Public Personnel Administration* (Oak Park, Ill.: Moore Publishing, 1979), pp. 160–69.

10. Patricia W. Ingraham and Carolyn Ban, "Models of Public Management: Are They Useful for Federal Managers in the 1980s?" *Public Administration Review* 46 (1986): 152–60.

11. Ingraham, "Building Bridges."

12. Ibid., pp. 427–28.

13. See Calvin Mackenzie, ed., *The In-and-Outers: Presidential Appointees and the Problems of Transient Government in Washington* (Baltimore: Johns Hopkins University Press, 1987).

14. Pfiffner, "Political Appointees."

15. Ingraham, "Building Bridges."

16. Keith J. Mueller, "Federal Programs Do Expire: The Case of Health Planning," *Public Administration Review* 48 (1988): 719–25.

17. Max Stephenson, Jr., "The Policy and Premises and Urban Development Action Grant Program Implementation: A Comparative Analysis of the Carter and Reagan Presidencies," *Journal of Urban Affairs* 9 (1987): 1–14.

18. Mueller, "Federal Programs."

19. Paul Light, "When Worlds Collide—The Political-Career Nexus," in Calvin Mackenzie, ed., *The In and Outers,* pp. 156–73.

20. Ingraham, "Building Bridges."

21. Herman Mellor, "Conservative Policy and the Poor: Enterprise Zones," in Robert Rector and Michael Sanera, eds., *Steering the Elephant: How Washington Really Works* (New York: Universe Books, 1987), pp. 198–215.

22. Laurence E. Lynn, Jr., and David Def. Whitman, *The President as Policymaker* (Philadelphia: Temple University Press, 1987).

23. Brian Hogwood and B. Guy Peters, *Policy Dynamics* (London: Wheatsheaf, 1983).

24. Ingraham, "Building Bridges."

25. Carolyn Ban and Patricia Ingraham, "Political Executives and Career Managers: Adversaries or Allies?" unpublished paper presented at the Annual Meeting, American Society for Public Administration (Anaheim, Calif., Apr., 1986).

26. Ingraham, "Building Bridges."

27. Pfiffner, "Political Appointees"; Ingraham, "Building Bridges."

Part 3

Presidential Management in a Separated System

Chapter 13

The Managerial Presidency's Changing Focus, Theodore Roosevelt to Bill Clinton

PERI E. ARNOLD

The presidency and administrative government merged during the twentieth century. Vis-à-vis the executive branch agencies, the presidency became managerial, meaning that the political incentives of the office merged with the possibilities and responsibilities assumed by the administrative state. As the administrative agencies of government grew, gained new authority and increased resources, presidents discovered they could draw upon the administrative state to achieve new capacities for shaping policy and new influence over policy implementation. However, before the presidency could be conceived as managerial vis-à-vis the administrative state, it had to gain primacy within the American separation-of-powers regime, reversing the pattern of congressional domination of administration that characterized nineteenth century American government.[1]

As presidents sought managerial leverage over the administrative state, administrative reform offered the fulcrum point for that leverage. From the beginning of the twentieth century, administrative reform (or reorganization) has constituted the means through which presidents have addressed the political opportunities and challenges of the administrative state. In the process, presidents became consumers of administrative theory. In the role of administrative reformers, presidents found justifications for their dominance over the executive branch. At the same time, they found in administrative theory tools for reorganizing the administrative state to enhance presidential interests.

However, the political goals of the managerial presidency have been a moving target over the course of the twentieth century. The political purposes of the managerial presidency have changed, as have the possibilities presented to presidents by administration, and as have the political problems entailed in administration. The means through which presidents attempt to construct their managerial role remain alike throughout the twentieth century. While presidents sought reform through ad hoc commissions or task forces, assuring the public that what they sought was more effective government, the underlying problem of governance that presidents addressed through reform changed over time. For half the century, executive reorganization aimed at justifying and articulating presidential administrative authority in the expanding state. A second phase, beginning in the 1960s, focused reform on the analytic means for assessing policy options and performance. In its third phase, to the present, administrative reform has attempted to address the intense public dissatisfaction with the scale, cost, and performance of the administrative state. This chapter will characterize the several different stages in the evolution of the twentieth-century managerial presidency, concluding with a discussion of President Bill Clinton's initiative for the reinvention of government.[2]

The First Era: Managing the Expanding State

From Theodore Roosevelt's succession to the presidency in 1901 into the years after World War II, presidents sought means for effecting direction over the administrative state's sprawling agencies and functions. For the presidents of that era, the managerial presidency meant capacities for direction of administration, be it the executive budget, planning capacities, or control over promotions and assignments in upper levels of the civil service.

Theodore Roosevelt created the first presidentially initiated executive reorganization commission. Commonly called the Keep Commission, it was composed of sub-cabinet officials and chaired by Charles Keep, assistant secretary of the treasury. Conservative Republican congressional leadership hampered Roosevelt's ambitions, and he did not intend to allow Congress to make administrative reform a hostage. Thus he warned the commission that he would take seriously its recommendations "in proportion as they do not call for legislation."[3]

The Keep Commission addressed a highly decentralized executive branch that was almost random in the variation of procedures across agencies. The operational fact of the executive branch was that agencies were subject to congressional, party, and sectional domination. The commission's recommendations aimed at standardizing and centralizing discrete administrative processes such as salary policy, clerical procedures, and purchasing.[4] Not willing to submit the details of administrative changes to Congress for enactment, President Roosevelt asked Congress to grant him "authority to concentrate related lines of work and reduce duplication by executive order. . . ."[5] However Congress refused to delegate that authority to the president.

President Taft extended Roosevelt's effort at reorganization. Assisted by Frederick Cleveland, a leading scholar of administration, Taft formed the President's Commission on Economy and Efficiency. Congressional initiatives at administrative reform had atomized administration, focusing on details, and never seeing a comprehensive whole—a bureaucracy. By contrast, the President's Commission adopted a comprehensive view of the administrative state, observing to the president: "One of the reasons why more notable results have not been obtained from previous investigations is due to the fact that these investigations have not concerned themselves with the problem of Government as a whole."[6]

The President's Commission aimed to achieve a coherent and centrally managed executive branch. Existing agencies were melanges of different activities and purposes. The commission concluded: "Only by grouping services according to their character can substantial progress be made. . . . Until the head of a department is called upon to deal exclusively with matters falling in but one or a very few distinct fields, effective . . . control is impossible."[7] In addition to coherent organization, the commission saw a capable president as a prerequisite for good administration. Thus, the commission recommended an executive budget, giving the president responsibility for managing the executive branch's appropriation requests to Congress.

Amidst the political turmoil of the late New Deal, Franklin Roosevelt turned to administrative reform to achieve increased control over expanded government activity. The Brownlow Committee, which he created in 1936, was quite direct about its aim. The president was responsible for administration, and "the President needs help."[8] It was not the president as political leader who needed help. The president as envisioned by the committee was an administrative manager who required foresight into national problems and sought administrative efficacy to solve them. The Brownlow Committee's key recommendations were for expanded presidential staff—both personal and institutional, centralization of personnel policy in the presidency, and the institutionalization of presidential reorganization authority. The Brownlow recommendations ran into stiff congressional opposition, and because of such opposition, Roosevelt's reorganization bill failed in 1937 and 1938. The successful 1939 Reorganization Act stripped away the most controversial provisions but still retained key new resources for the president.[9]

In 1947 the Republican Eightieth Congress created the first Hoover Commission, aiming to use administrative reform to plan a transition for the Republican president expected to be elected in 1948.[10] Republican congressional leaders secured the commission's conservatism by making Herbert Hoover its chair. The fate of the commission was, in fact, a litmus test for the standing assumption of the presidency's managerial stance over the administrative state. Despite Republican intentions, and Hoover's hostility to the Democrats' expanded government, the commission eventually reported recommendations to strengthen the president's managerial role. The key to that transformation was Harry Truman's victory in 1948. After the election, Truman had no obvious incentive to cooperate with an administrative reform study that had a hostile, partisan agenda.

However, Truman understood that Herbert Hoover was capable of viewing government through the lens of apolitical administration as well as through his political ideology.[11] Indeed, as a cabinet member and as president during the 1920s, Hoover had advocated executive reorganization.[12] In effect, Truman invited Hoover to switch his conceptual lenses to save his commission's chance for success. One of the commission's members observed that after the election Hoover seemed to have decided "no more [criticism of New Deal] policy."[13] Now the commission would focus on apolitical administration, and the recommendations it adopted relevant to the presidency were akin to those of the Brownlow Committee.

The Second Phase: Managing the Policy State

By the 1960s, problems of governmental performance displaced issues of managerial capacity as the concerns of presidents regarding the executive branch. The managerial presidency by this time had convincingly linked the presidents to responsibility for government's performance. Thus, the presidents were necessarily concerned with acquiring means to improve that performance. This shift in the central focus of administrative reform is apparent first within the Johnson administration.

Lyndon Johnson's presidency was an engine of policy innovation.[14] Johnson aimed to fulfill the remaining liberal agenda while redefining that agenda itself.[15] From community empowerment and urban redevelopment to preschool education and job training, the Johnson administration generated policies to address tenacious problems of American society. Many of the programs of Johnson's Great Society were conceived by academic research and stimulated by foundation funding, implying that government itself needed expanded capacities for developing and assessing new policy ideas.

President Johnson's leadership agenda made problems of policy and program assessment even more pressing because he audaciously promised economy in government at the same time that he launched frontal attacks on poverty, education, and urban decay. Shortly after taking office, Johnson ordered all the federal agencies to prepare plans for reducing their overall expenditures, and in his 1964 State of the Union message he promised "an actual reduction in Federal expenditures and Federal employment" while launching new domestic initiatives.[16]

Johnson turned to administrative reform to achieve his dual goals of expanded government and reduced expenditures. He initiated the Task Force on Government Reorganization in the summer of 1964. Chaired by Don K. Price, dean of Harvard's Kennedy School, it had ten members drawn from universities and government. The problem Johnson posed for reorganization may have itself invited a new approach to reform: how could new programs be made effective while also reducing government's expenditures?

During the 1960s, a paradigm shift in academic public administration promised new capacities for analyses of organizational and policy operations.[17] In the Defense Department under Robert McNamara, systems analysis became the prerequisite to serious decision making.[18] Following McNamara's example, in August, 1965, President Johnson ordered the extension of systems analysis techniques to the budget process throughout the national government.[19] The managerial presidency's focus was now on the efficacy of government's "outputs." Organizational issues did not vanish from presidential concerns, but they had decreased weight in the 1960s and were secondary to the quest for analyses of government performance.

The Price Task Force reported to Johnson in November, 1964.[20] The managerial presidency's changing focus was evident in the report's recommendations for the Executive Office of the President. The task force wrote of the need for "improvement in [the Executive Office's] capability for program evaluation and review . . . assessing the comparative costs and comparative benefits of the programs of various departments. . . . Such analysis can now draw on the modern techniques of . . . analysis such as . . . the new system of executive direction and control in the Department of Defense."[21]

In October, 1966, President Johnson's domestic policy staff recommended another study to examine the design and implementation of Great Society programs.[22] Consequently, Johnson established his Task Force on Government Organization, chaired by Chicago businessman Ben Heineman and including twelve high-level government officials as members. Its attention to policy science was ensured by the inclusion of two economists who had directed the Budget Bureau, Kermit Gordon and Charles Schultze, as well as Secretary of Defense Robert McNamara. The task force's main assignment was to determine "an organizational structure to insure coordination and effective implementation of programs in the field."[23]

In June, 1967, the Heineman group reported, suggesting that policy evaluation and organizational control should be linked to achieve optimal presidential managerial capacity.[24] It also recommended a policy coordination staff within the Executive Office and an enhanced capacity for program evaluation in a reorganized Budget Bureau. The task force's reasoning was that effective agency management depended upon assessments of programs that were only available through program evaluation. Following that logic to its conclusion, in September, 1967, the task force submitted to the president "A Recommendation for the Future Organization of the Executive Branch."[25] Herein it proposed that departments be responsible for whole and coherent spheres of policy. It envisioned reducing to seven the existing twelve cabinet departments. The new departments would be Social Services, National Resources, Economic Affairs, Science and Environmental Preservation, Foreign Affairs, National Security, and Justice. Robert McNamara's managerial success in the Defense Department was taken to illustrate the utility of rational techniques for managing a vast bureaucracy. Thus the tools of policy analysis were seen as tools by which presidents and their minions could direct huge departments.

Coming as they did at the end of the Johnson presidency, there was no time to implement the Heineman recommendations. However, they influenced President Richard Nixon's early initiative in executive reform. In April, 1969, Nixon established his Ash Council, chaired by Roy Ash, head of Litton Industries, and composed of business executives. The council's reports came in stages between summer, 1969, and early 1971. As was the case with the Heineman Task Force, the council's initial concern was with the Executive Office's capacities for presidential management within the executive branch. Its earliest recommendations culminated in Reorganization Plan no. 2 of 1970, reorganizing the Bureau of the Budget and establishing the Domestic Council. The Bureau of the Budget was remade into the Office of Management and Budget.[26] The new OMB was to have expanded capacities for assessing policy and managerial performance, coordinating programs, and strengthening agency managerial practice. Also, an expanded number of positions in the OMB subject to presidential appointment insured that the agency would be attuned to administration priorities. The Domestic Council was inspired by the National Security Council. Composed of the heads of the cabinet's domestic departments, the council aimed to enhance cross-agency policy formulation. The council's staff would give the president new resources over policy formulation and assessment.[27]

The Ash Council also proposed reorganizations of cabinet-level departments that were identical in principle to the Heineman Task Force's September, 1969, recommendations for future organization of the executive branch. Like its predecessor, the council assumed that policy coherence was a key to enhancing presidential management over cabinet departments and that sheer size, by itself, was not a barrier to management. Consequently, in March, 1971, President Nixon acted on the council's recommendations, proposing to Congress four reorganized departments into which almost all domestic programs would fit: Natural Resources, Economic Affairs, Human Resources, and Community Development. The president described these proposed departments as a reform that would transform the executive branch into what it "ought to look like in the last third of the twentieth century."[28]

The period of policy-oriented administrative reform planning strengthened presidential policy management. This period also saw the establishment of staffs for policy assessment in many of the cabinet departments in addition to the expanded policy-oriented capacities within the Executive Office of the President. None of Nixon's "super-department" proposals were adopted. However, the period did see the establishment of two new departments during the Johnson administration, Housing and Urban Affairs and Transportation. These new departments were not envisioned within reform planning. Rather, they originated with the president's using administration to incorporate representation of interests within his political coalition. The lesson therein is that the managerial presidency is always constrained by electoral considerations; interests and voters trump the subtleties of policy and organizations. That lesson becomes even clearer in the third, and most recent, phase in the evolution of the managerial presidency. Recent presidents confront a collision between their managerial role and the voters' negative assessments of the federal government and administration. Thus, in the most recent phase of the managerial presidency, incumbents have wrestled with the political entailments of the presidency's identification with the administrative state.

The Third Phase: Managing Big Government in a Time of Populist Anger

In his 1976 campaign for the presidency, Jimmy Carter transformed the president's managerial responsibilities into an electoral issue. He promised, if elected, he would seek comprehensive change in government to make the executive branch more comprehensible and more accessible to Americans.[29] Carter described the characteristics of good administration in moral terms. He said: "Nowhere in the Constitution . . . or the New Testament do you find the words 'economy' or 'efficiency.' . . . But you do discover other words like *honesty, integrity . . . compassion, love.* . . . These are the same words which describe what a government of human beings ought to be." (emphasis in original)[30] Carter's campaign promise for reorganization addressed Americans' skepticism about government. In wake of the experiences of government's conduct of the Vietnam War, the Watergate affair, and inflation that seemed out of control, distrust of government was widespread. In promising comprehensive reform Carter was, in effect, addressing that distrust. He argued that if administrative reforms are comprehensive, and "presented in such a way as to arouse the support of the people, then the special interests . . . back off because most of them don't want to be exposed to a public altercation against the people. . . ."[31] Until Carter, the managerial presidency had used administrative reform to embrace and manage big government. Jimmy Carter's public justification of reorganization ended that tradition as he adopted a critical pose in the president's relationship to the administrative state.

Beginning with Carter, and continuing through the present, administrative reform has responded to populist concerns about government's size, cost, and performance. In the 1992 election Ross Perot demonstrated how alive that impulse remains in American life. He said: "You are the owners of this country. Nobody else can do the job. Our system has been corrupted because we weren't exercising our responsibilities as owners. This is the year to assert your ownership."[32]

Having won the presidency and launched executive reorganization, a paradox emerged in President Carter's conduct of administrative reform. Articulating new, normative goals for reform, he adopted an approach to reform that was wholly conventional and belied his stated purpose. Furthermore, he promoted executive reorganization as a bold stroke toward simplifying government. Yet the administration's reorganization process, and its recommendations, were incomprehensible to all but the most attentive observers. Thus, Carter's Reorganization Project had little obvious connection with the rhetoric that President Carter attached to executive reorganization. Some of its recommendations were non-controversial and were implemented through presidential orders authorized under the Reorganization Act of 1977. However, the project's plans for large-scale departmental reorganization, incorporating most of the existing departments in fewer, comprehensive departments, required legislation and was stillborn.

Jimmy Carter's criticism of the administrative state allied him with the values and rhetoric of his vanquisher in 1980, Ronald Reagan. Winning the presidency in 1980, Ronald Reagan's relationship to administrative reform was more ambiguous that Carter's. His main effort in the managerial presidency was not to change the administration's organization and procedure but to control government by assuring that its upper-level managers, political appointees, and top-level careerists, were political conservatives.[33]

Alongside the effort at the political control of administration, Reagan was also involved in a large-scale administrative reform effort. In February, 1982,

Reagan initiated the President's Private Sector Survey on Cost Control, chaired by businessman J. Peter Grace. The Grace Commission was the largest ever episode of executive reorganization planning, staffed by roughly two thousand commission and task force members. Participants were business people who volunteered their time while remaining employed in the private sector. After two years of work, the commission issued forty-seven public reports containing 2,478 recommendations.[34] The commission promised a savings of $424.4 billion in three years, if all its recommendations were implemented.[35]

As portrayed by the Grace Commission, the federal government was a swamp of wasteful practices and lax administration. Throughout, the reports compared federal agencies and their operations to large, private firms, and the latter were shown to operate far more efficiently than the public agencies. Government was depicted as wasteful and incompetent, precisely as Ronald Reagan had charged in his election campaign. In fact there was little in the Grace Commission report to guide real reform. The overwhelming number of the commission's recommendations were ill-founded and many of its savings estimates were groundless. The commission had a talent for advertising horror stories of government inefficiency, but those tended to rest on misunderstandings of government operations and accounting practices.[36]

For quite different reasons, the major recommendations of President Carter's Reorganization Project and President Reagan's Grace Commission found little support toward adoption. The Reorganization Project failed, in large part, because its overall, public purpose had no relationship to the welter of recommendations it created. The Grace Commission recommendations failed, perhaps, because they were really intended to castigate government and not change it.

President Clinton and "Reinventing Government"

Like Carter and Reagan before him, Bill Clinton won the presidency as an outsider to Washington. Like his immediate predecessors, he used the promise of administrative reform as part of his self-presentation as an outsider against government. However, President Clinton's use of administrative reform has been more ambitious, more extensive, and, so far, more successful than the initiatives under Carter or Reagan. Unlike Carter's initiative, which focused on structural issues and was bogged down in complexity, and unlike Reagan's Grace Commission, which was primarily rhetorical, President Clinton connected a perspective that was critical of big government to a specification of goals that were brilliantly appropriate to citizen dissatisfaction.

On March 3, 1993, President Clinton announced his National Performance

Review (NPR). Saying virtually nothing about the NPR's method, the president spoke volubly about its aims. He said: "Our goal is to make the entire federal government both less expensive and more efficient, and to change the culture of our national bureaucracy away from complacency and entitlement toward initiative and empowerment."[37] The president's language about NPR implied that government ought to be a provider of services whose performance can be improved through techniques and concepts borrowed from the recent experience of corporate reengineering. Consistent with his centrist, "new Democrat" appeal, Clinton said that Americans want to be served by government. They want "better schools and health care and better roads . . . but they want . . . a government that works better on less money and that is more responsive."[38]

Declaring the administrative state as failed, Clinton aligned with the populist attack, saying: "We intend to redesign, to reinvent, to reinvigorate the entire national government."[39] The president's announcement made it sound that Clinton had joined, or coopted, Ross Perot's tirade about government's being broken. However, Clinton's effort to repair government would be anything but Ross Perot's characteristic promise of simple fixes. The NPR launched a broad and multi-layered process of reform.

Clinton's immediate inspiration for the NPR originated in the 1992 book, *Reinventing Government,* by David Osborne and Ted Gaebler. The book urged a new paradigm of service-oriented government and reported a number of cases of customer-oriented, antibureaucratic reforms all across the country and at different levels of the federal system.[40] Osborne and Gaebler argued that government must be reconceived and remade if it is to serve its citizenry. Here was an approach to administration that promised to merge President Clinton's managerial role and his political interests. Presidents Carter and Reagan had excoriated bureaucracy but had not found a mode of managing administration that changed the administrative state. Adopting Osborne and Gaebler's goals of service and customer satisfaction for public administration, Clinton found an approach that seemed designed to address, head on, citizen dissatisfaction with government. Not insignificantly, this approach to government had the attractive quality of justifying government's importance while attacking its conduct. Herein was a formula whereby Democrats might balance their support of government with an approach responsive to public hostility to government. "Reinvention" would become the central theme of Clinton's reinterpretation of the managerial presidency and the NPR's official slogan.

President Clinton made clear the importance he gave the NPR, and heightened its interest to the news media, by making Vice President Al Gore responsible for it. Gore's Senate service gave him a grasp of government organization and its issues. His interests in technology led him to see the roles of new information systems and new means of communication in administration. Finally, Gore's close relationship to the president, and his role as heir apparent in the Democratic Party, made his tie to NPR a signal of the initiative's importance to the president.[41]

As the instrument for his policy of "reinvention," President Clinton created an interagency task force, titled the National Performance Review. An interagency task force had severe limits; it could not have its own personnel or an autonomous budget. Its staff would have to be borrowed from federal agencies, and its budget would have to originate in appropriations for established agencies.[42] However, an interagency task force had a tactical advantage over other kinds of ad hoc planning vehicles, such as a presidential commission. The task force's staff would be career civil servants on loan from agencies and sensitive to existing conditions in the executive branch. Consequently, an interagency task force might plan reforms for President Clinton that would be more likely to find adoption than had the recommendations of Carter's Reorganization Project or Reagan's Grace Commission, which were staffed primarily by outsiders.

When it was fully organized, the NPR staff numbered 250 career government employees loaned to the task force by their agencies.[43] Vice President Gore delegated supervision of the enterprise to his assistant, Elaine Kamarck. Named as the NPR's director was Bob Stone, an experienced, upper-level careerist from the Defense Department. Several associate directors were drawn from other agencies. The staff's collective government experience made it capable of a quick start. This was a crucial capacity because President Clinton announced that the NPR would report its recommendations in September, 1993, giving the task force a mere six months to assemble a report.

The NPR's basic approach to reform drew on several different elements. First, David Osborne was a consultant to the task force and influenced the choice of recommendations and the mode of language used in the NPR's September, 1993, report. Second, the civil servants who became NPR's director and associate directors crafted a framework for the task force's work based on four principles. These principles were: (1) putting customers first; (2) empowering federal employees to put customers first; (3) cutting the "red tape" that keeps employees from putting their customers first; and (4) cutting back to basic missions.[44] Third, through its method of work, the NPR was closely integrated with ongoing thinking about reform within the individual executive branch agencies, each with its own agenda. Fourth, President Clinton's commitment to reducing the number of federal employees, and effecting some budget savings, would shape NPR's recommendations, conflicting with some other interests of the NPR. Fifth, the NPR was deeply influenced by administrative reforms that had restructured government during the 1980s in several other democracies, most notably Britain and New Zealand. Often referred to as the new managerialism, ideas about downsizing government organizations, while making them more responsive to those they serve and more attuned to markets, have guided major restructurings in these countries.[45]

The theoretical underpinnings of new management reforms abroad are public choice theory and the new economics of organization.[46] The NPR incorporated a pastiche of ideas related to the new management about shrinking agencies, reducing overhead management and costs, "unleashing" entrepreneurial managers in line activities, and empowering workers. However, it did not articulate the new managerialism as a conceptual framework for reform. Margaret Thatcher's reforms in Britain and New Zealand's bureaucratic revolution, as examples, boldly articulated antigovernmental and pro-market ideas. In these cases new management theory drove reform, making theoretical claims about the limitations of public administrative agencies.[47] Donald Kettl notes that "British and New Zealand reforms . . . have aggressively followed rational choice economists in privatizing programs and contracting out for programs remaining within the government."[48] By contrast with the British and New Zealand experiences, the NPR's public language is more optimistic about government. The goal of reinvention is an easily communicated and dramatic one whose language can both incorporate, and remove the sharp edge from, new management approaches to reform. The language of "reinvention" is more packaging than it is theory, and it allows the NPR to frame reform of the administrative state in a way that negotiates between criticism of government and President Clinton's commitment to moderately activist government.

The NPR aimed at a quick and very visible impact. As with all comprehensive reform initiatives, NPR's initial challenge entailed a two-front struggle. It had to organize itself for its job, made all the more difficult by its quickly approaching deadline. Then the NPR had to gain credibility and support for reform among several constituencies, government's career professionals, rank and file employees, Congress, and not least, the public. Without achieving credibility, the NPR's recommendations would have little support for adoption. Vice President Gore's role in the NPR was crucial to establishing its importance, and its credibility. He could make the enterprise compelling within government, reach out to former colleagues in Congress, and make its accomplishments visible to the public.

Furthermore, if President Clinton was to gain political benefit from making reinvention the focus of the managerial presidency, the conduct and accomplishments of the NPR would have to be well publicized. Vice President

Gore launched the NPR's campaign for visibility and support, meeting with agency employees to preach the gospel of reinvention and reaching out to business leaders for support. Gore stressed government's possibility for performing tasks differently in an era of developing information and communications technology. Then the vice president led a "Reinventing Government Summit," in Philadelphia, on June 25, 1993. The summit served two functions. It continued the campaign for establishing the NPR's importance and public visibility. However, it was important for its substance as well as its public relations. The meeting brought together executives from the business world who had been "reinventing the corporation," leaders in innovation from every level of government, and management consultants specializing in reform. The summit's message was that reinventing government was part of an ongoing, larger movement of modernizing major American institutions. It associated reinvention with the ideas and management techniques that had revived the competitiveness of American corporations.

The NPR's work was conducted through two forms of study teams, focused either on major agencies or on government-wide activities, such as purchasing and budgeting. The study teams were composed of civil servants from the agencies under study or those who were experienced with the process under study. Furthermore, President Clinton directed the executive branch agencies to establish "reinvention teams" to work with the NPR's teams.[49] Reinvention teams further linked the agencies to the NPR and made the reform planning process a conduit for reform ideas existing within agencies' agendas. In this light, the role of the reform initiative was to move items from agency-level agendas to a government-wide reform agenda rather than to craft new reform recommendations.[50]

Because the NPR's reinvention process was linked to the agencies, the character of the reforms developed varied according to an agency's own character and conditions. Surveying reinvention activities during 1993–94 in five different cabinet departments and the Agency for International Development, Beryl A. Radin discovered: "These six cases indicate the great variation among federal departments and agencies in their response to the NPR activity."[51] The mode of an organization's internal response to the NPR initiative depended, Radin found, on the mix of appointees and careerists within the agency involved in reform, on the manner in which the intra-agency reform planning process was organized, on the balance between policy and management concerns within the reform effort, and not least, the existing agenda of problems facing the agency as NPR began. In effect, Radin found that the NPR process incorporated reinvention planning processes from within agencies. Each agency assembled reinvention teams that established agendas that reflected the agency's own issues. The aim herein was threefold, first, to attach agency expertise to the reinvention process that begins external to the agency; second, to coopt agency concerns as part of the reinvention process; and third, to establish internal to the agency a center for ongoing reform.

While the NPR worked closely with the agencies on devising its recommendations for reform, it had no sustained contact with Congress. Neither the NPR nor the White House had consulted with chairpersons of the salient congressional committees before the public announcement of the NPR's recommendations.[52] Nor did there appear to be a strategy within the White House for gaining congressional action on those recommendations that would require changes in law. *Congressional Quarterly Weekly Report* writer Mike Mills observed: "The administration is reaching beyond Congress to develop a formidable coalition within it. . . . Clinton and Gore hope to create a populist movement that will propel Capitol Hill to accept . . . changes that have been shelved several times before."[53]

On September 7, 1993, President Clinton presented the NPR's initial recommendations in an elaborately staged event on the White House lawn. Titled *From Red Tape to Results: Creating a Government That Works Better and Costs Less,* the report promised a reinvented government that would be lean, serve citizens well, be adaptable to change, and eliminate unnecessary activity.[54] A chapter is devoted to each goal: simplifying administrative processes—"Cutting Red Tape," establishing market-like mechanisms in agencies—"Putting Customers First," decentralizing responsibility and creating employee initiative—"Empowering Employees to Get Results," and eliminating unnecessary activities while increasing productivity—"Cutting Back to Basics." The report's style is readable and breezy.

Each chapter of the report opens with an anecdote dramatizing the chapter's theme. For example, chapter four opens with the story of Bruce Bair, a Federal Aviation Administration (FAA) meteorologist reporting local flying conditions at the Russell, Kansas, airport. That airport was lightly used and automated weather reporting would have sufficed. Even after mechanical reporting was introduced, Bair's employment continued at $11 an hour. In a letter relating his story to Vice President Gore, Bair explained that he finally quit his FAA job and wrote: "I'm no longer stealing from the government."[55]

After anecdotally illustrating the administrative problems to be addressed, each chapter is organized into "steps" toward fulfilling the chapter's thematic goal. In turn, each step is to be implemented through a set of "actions." For example, in the first chapter, titled "Cutting Red Tape," step two is "Decentralizing Personnel Policy." The first action regarding that step is that the Office of Personnel Management will "deregulate personnel policy by phasing out the 10,000 page Federal Personnel Manual and all agency implementing directives."[56]

From Red Tape to Results was a document for public consumption as much as it was a blueprint to guide administrative reform. The report was not a dry compilation of study team reports. It was, rather, a document that had been shaped by an editorial group headed by David Osborne with an eye toward its accessibility and public impact.[57] The document did not offer a theoretically unified vision of government. Its major recommendations (steps) had no necessary relationship, one to another, in terms of specificity, justification, or means of implementation. Rather, the report's thrust was toward conveying the sense that President Clinton, and his NPR, were dedicated to a less expensive government that would be acutely attuned to service. In effect, *From Red Tape to Results* was a document that offered a compelling vision of transforming government into a service supplier and citizens into customers of those services.[58]

After September, 1993, the NPR's work shifted from planning reform to implementing it. Implementation meant two kinds of work. First, there were recommendations that could be implemented from the top, such as the reduction of the federal workforce. Workforce reduction was of particular importance because the Clinton administration sought quick results from reinvention, addressing government's budgetary deficit as well as its trust deficit. *From Red Tape to Results* promised budgetary savings of $108 billion over five years, should its recommendations be implemented. The single largest element of budget savings within the NPR's recommendations was workforce reduction, calling for reducing the federal workforce by 252,000 federal employees (that target number was expanded to 272,900 by Congress). The categories of positions targeted for reduction were middle management and administrative support personnel, in budgeting, procurement, accounting, and personnel. There was dramatic reduction in the federal workforce over the next several years, with a reduction of more than 316,500 executive-branch employees by March, 1996.[59]

The second kind of implementation work faced by the NPR required work from the bottom, for example, training agency personnel to implement reforms regarding service standards and procedural simplification. Equally important, the NPR had a continuing public relations job, maintaining an awareness of the goal of reinvention among federal career personnel, as well as communicating to the public about reinvention's progress. Even the NPR's roles in helping agencies develop new practices in service standards, or in the use of technology, had a public relations element to it. In much that it did the NPR was primarily a facilitator for change. Technical support for change was provided by other agencies, such as the Government Information Technology Services Board and the Office of Management and Budget.[60]

What made the NPR's recommendations successful in its first year was not just the good work of the task force. A good share of the responsibility for that success lies elsewhere. The task force's own means were limited. It sought publicity for the enterprise, but it never conducted an effective liaison with Congress, and even some of its favorable observers do not see the task force's leadership as strategically nimble. The real impetus for implementation came from the president's and Congress's will to pursue and use administrative reform in 1993 and 1994. Vice President Gore's close identification with reinvention involved more than his personal interests in reform. That identification rested on his assessment of the political importance of reinvention and its utility for his own political leadership. In Congress, even among those skeptical about the NPR's rhetoric and operation, many of the recommendations were naturally attractive because they promised to reduce bureaucratic costs and simplify administration in a time of citizen hostility toward government. Additionally, congressional passage of the Government Performance and Results Act in 1993 created requirements of strategic planning for federal agencies that meshed well with some of the NPR's reforms. Thus, there was a political wind behind the implementation of administrative reform.

The Republican capture of Congress in 1994 was politically devastating for President Clinton, and the managerial dimension of his presidency played a central part in his response to that defeat. *From Red Tape to Results* had originally described its interest in "*how* government should work, not on *what* it should do."[61] In 1995 the new Republican majority called for a reduction in *what* government does. As a response, the NPR elevated to high-priority status its concerns with government's substantive policies.

The NPR responded in two ways to this new, post-election role. First, it articulated the reinvention exercise as the correct approach to addressing American's frustration with government. As the NPR's September, 1995, annual progress report stated: "The federal government is ailing and needs a cure. It needs to be treated systematically, not amputated or—less drastic, but no more effective—dabbed with some dubious topical salve. Even if the wholesale elimination of federal agencies and programs was what Americans wanted—and it is not—that approach would do nothing to improve what is left."[62]

Reforming government regulation of business was the second aspect of reinvention that the NPR highlighted. *From Red Tape To Results* had recommended simplifying regulations in occupational safety and environmental protection and fostering partnerships between government regulators and business in place of distrust. In 1995 the White House directed the NPR to further high-light its efforts to improve regulation while reducing its burdens on business. The NPR recommended that agencies review their regulations to eliminate outdated provisions and reduce the number of regulations. It also proposed performance standards for regulation, focusing on ultimate goals rather than enforcement measures. It urged that cooperation between regulators and those affected by regulation replace punitive regulatory enforcement.[63]

Regulatory reform during 1995 offered a window onto the NPR's methods. Substantive work toward reform was undertaken within the regulatory agencies, which themselves reviewed their entries in the *Code of Federal Regulations* and proposed changes in their regulatory procedures. The NPR oversaw the creation of the reform teams and coordinated efforts across government, particularly where issues were crosscutting. It also operated as a public relations vehicle to publish the reform proposals produced by the agencies and to generally trumpet the administration's success at regulatory reform.[64]

In a March 4, 1996, speech Vice President Gore signaled the entry of another politically potent issue onto the NPR's agenda in a presidential election year. Speaking to the National Press Club, Gore addressed the topic of "Governing in a Balanced Budget World." The vice president said: "I think we have witnessed the formation of a durable bipartisan consensus that our nation must and will have a balanced budget."[65] In fact, since its initiation, the NPR had articulated a goal of "doing more with less," but as "governance in a balanced budget world" became the Clinton administration's political concern, the NPR heightened its stress on budget savings through reform.

The NPR published Gore's speech under the title *Reinvention's Next Steps: Governing in a Balanced Budget World,* accompanied by supporting papers that described how the NPR's work contributed to doing more with less.[66] What was contained in the report was culled from the NPR's earlier recommendations, but a new recommendation was proposed as an NPR response to Gore's speech. The NPR proposed transforming some service-providing agencies, such as the Patent Office, into performance-based organizations. Those organizations would be allowed by statute to operate free from civil service rules, procurement regulations, etc., and the heads of these organizations would be chief executives appointed by contracts and held accountable for performance.[67]

The NPR entered another phase at the beginning of 1997, as the president began his second term. Clinton had won the battle of the budget during 1996 against the congressional Republicans, and he went on to win the 1996 presidential election. The question for reinvention was what role would it play in the second administration? President Clinton signaled that the NPR remained a major concern of his in a meeting with the cabinet in January, 1997, where he and Vice President Gore briefed the department heads on reinvention and its priorities.[68]

The NPR's focus since early 1997 has been narrowed to a group of about thirty agencies selected because of their high-profile impact on the public, through either service delivery or regulation. This group includes the U.S. Park Service, the Internal Revenue Service, the Passport Office, the Environmental Protection Agency, and the Occupational Safety and Health Administration. The NPR's directors or associate directors, and then Vice President Gore, met with senior leadership of each agency to plan with them reinvention goals to be implemented during Clinton's second term. This focused planning is entwined with the Government Performance and Results Act requiring all agencies to produce strategic plans during 1997. It was envisioned that in the case of these key agencies, plans for reinvention would be the heart of the agencies' strategic plans.[69]

Conclusion

President Clinton used the managerial role of the presidency to wield administrative reform in response to populist anger about government. He bested his immediate predecessors in shaping a mode of leadership that combined managerial responsibility with a political response to popular dissatisfaction. Carter had promised reform but could not escape his own propensity for mundane administration. Reagan pretended that he was apart from government but had little effect in changing it. Clinton found a formula that allowed him to be a populist and managerial, simultaneously.

In turn, President Clinton's National Performance Review exhibited a kind of flexibility that allowed him the nuance he has used in the managerial presidency. The NPR had a chameleon-like quality. It adapted to the president's changing political needs by asserting new priorities in reform at these different stages: service standards and customer satisfaction in 1993, then government regulation after the 1994 election, budgets in the 1996 election year, and reform of those agencies with the most intense public contacts in 1997. In each new priority, what was presented was assembled from elements already present in the NPR's work. It had a remarkable ability to continue to present new faces to fit President Clinton's managerial needs.

The NPR's plasticity in serving Clinton exemplified the fit between presidential needs and administrative reform that characterizes the history of the managerial presidency. Over the course of this century, administrative reform has adapted to fit a changing presidency within an expanding administrative state. It will likely continue to do so in the next century.

NOTES

1. On the origins of the administrative state, see Stephen Skowronek, *Building the New American State* (Cambridge, U.K.: Cambridge University Press, 1982). On congressional dominance over administration in the nineteenth century, see Leonard D. White, *The Republican Era* (New York: Macmillan, 1958). See also Oscar Kraines, *Congress Against Big Government* (New York: Bookmens' Associates, 1958).

2. For a full exposition and analysis of the changing managerial presidency and the varying uses of administrative reform in twentieth-century national government, see Peri E. Arnold, *Making the Managerial Presidency: Comprehensive Executive Reorganization, 1905–1996* (2d ed., revised; Lawrence: University Press of Kansas, 1998).

3. Oscar Kraines, "The President Versus Congress: The Keep Commission, 1905–1909," *Western Political Quarterly* XXIII:1 (Mar., 1970): 35.

4. Ibid., pp. 5–54.

5. Theodore Roosevelt, Annual Message to Cong., 1907, in James B. Richardson, ed., *Messages and Papers of the Presidents* (New York: Bureau of National Literature, 1918), vol. 17, p. 7485.

6. Frederick Cleveland, "Report on the Organization of the Government," p. 3, President's Commission on Economy and Efficiency, 210.1, RG 51, National Archives, Washington, D.C.

7. Ibid.

8. President's Committee on Administrative Management, *Report* (Washington, D.C.: Government Printing Office, 1937), p. 5.

9. 53 Stat. L. 36.

10. See Ronald C. Moe, *The Hoover Commissions Revisited* (Boulder, Colo.: Westview Publishers, 1982).

11. Key evidence for this understanding on the Truman administration's part is in Memorandum, James Webb to Harry Truman, Nov. 5, 1948, Webb Papers, Truman Presidential Library, Independence, Mo. Webb told Truman, there is "a possibility of getting the last Republican President . . . to accept an implementation of . . . executive responsibility that the Republican party has historically denied to Presidents."

12. See Peri E. Arnold, "Ambivalent Leviathan: Herbert Hoover and the Positive State," in J. David Greenstone, *Public Values and Private Power in American Democracy* (Chicago: University of Chicago Press, 1982), pp. 109–36.

13. James Rowe, Jr., interview with Peri E. Arnold, Washington, D.C., Oct. 23, 1979.

14. Eric Goldman, who worked for a time in the Johnson White House, said of Johnson that he "was determined to enact a sweeping Great Society legislative program after the election. . . . He wanted to carry the nation by so large a majority . . . that he would take his program before a [Congress] which was subdued and ready to follow. . . ." Eric Goldman, *The Tragedy of Lyndon Johnson* (New York: Knopf, 1969), p. 170.

15. For a discussion of Johnson's effort at extending the liberal agenda he received, see Stephen Skowronek, *The Politics Presidents Make* (Cambridge, Mass.: Harvard University Press, 1993), pp. 325–60.

16. On Nov. 30, 1963, the president had issued a "Memorandum on the Management of the Executive Branch" in *Public Papers of the Presidents, Lyndon B. Johnson, 1963–64*, p. 15; Annual Message to the Congress on the State of the Union, Jan. 8, 1964, *Public Papers of the Presidents, Lyndon B. Johnson, 1963–64*, p. 12.

17. The changing foci of public administration can be seen in Fremont J. Lyden, George A. Shipman, and Morton Kroll, eds., *Policies, Decisions, and Organizations* (New York: Appleton-Century-Crofts, 1969). For a critical discussion that places policy evaluation into the historical setting of American reform, see Edward D. Banfield, "Policy Sciences as Metaphysical Madness," in Robert A. Goldwin, ed., *Bureaucrats, Policy Analysts, Statesmen: Who Leads?* (Washington, D.C.: American Enterprise Institute, 1980), pp. 1–19.

18. See Robert Art, *The TFX Decision: McNamara and the Military* (Boston: Little, Brown, 1969).

19. See Allen Schick, "Systems Politics and Systems Budgeting," *Public Administration Review* 29:2 (Mar./Apr., 1969): 137–51.

20. President's Task Force on Government Reorganization, "Report," Nov. 6, 1964, container 1, Task Force Reports, Johnson Library, Austin, Tex.

21. Ibid., pp. 13–14.

22. Memorandum, Califano to President, Sept. 30, 1966, White House Central File, General, container 406, Task Force on Government Reorganization, Johnson Library.

23. "Task Force on Government Organization," n.d., White House Central File, aides, Gaither, container 318, Johnson Library.

24. Task Force on Government Organization, "The Organization and Management of Great Society Programs," June 17, 1967, Task Force Reports, container 4, Johnson Library.

25. Task Force on Government Organization, "A Recommendation for the Future Organization of the Executive Branch," Sept. 15, 1967, Task Force Reports, container 4, Johnson Library.

26. See Larry Berman, *The Office of Management and Budget* (Princeton, N.J.: Princeton University Press, 1979).

27. For a look at what this staff mechanism became in practice, see John Kessel, *The Domestic Council* (North Scituate, Mass.: Duxbury, 1975).

28. *Public Papers of the President, Richard Nixon, 1971*, p. 474.

29. Jimmy Carter, *A Government as Good as Its People* (New York: Simon and Schuster, 1977), p. 54.

30. Jimmy Carter, *Why Not the Best?* (Nashville, Tenn.: Boardman, 1975), p. 116.

31. "Interview with Jimmy Carter," *National Journal*, July 17, 1976, p. 999.

32. Ross Perot, *United We Stand* (New York: Hyperion, 1992), p. 4.

33. Richard Nathan, *The Administrative Presidency* (New York: Wiley, 1983); Terry Moe, "The Politicized Presidency," in this volume; and Peter M. Benda and Charles Levine, "Reagan and the Bureaucracy," in Charles O. Jones, ed., *The Reagan Legacy* (Chatham, N.J.: Chatham House, 1988), pp. 30–59.

34. William R. Kennedy and Robert W. Lee, *A Taxpayers Survey of the Grace Commission Report* (Ottawa, Ill.: Green Hill Publishers, 1984).

35. Charles T. Goodsell, "The Grace Commission: Seeking Efficiency for the Whole People," *Public Administration Review* 44 (May/June, 1984): 169–204.

36. Stephen Kelman, "The Grace Commission: How Much Waste in Government?" *The Public Interest* 78 (Winter, 1985): 62–82; also see Ronald C. Moe, *Reorganizing*

the Executive Branch in the Twentieth Century: Landmark Commissions (Washington, D.C.: Congressional Research Service, Report 92-293 GOV, 1992).

37. William J. Clinton, "Remarks by the President," Mar. 3, 1993.

38. Ibid.

39. Ibid.

40. David E. Osborne and Ted Gaebler, *Reinventing Government: How the Entrepreneurial Spirit Is Transforming Government* (Reading, Mass.: Addison-Wesley, 1992).

41. See Richard Berke, "The Good Son," *The New York Times Magazine*, Feb. 20, 1994, pp. 33–34, and also see Martin Peretz's informed speculation that NPR will be among the things that distinguish Gore's concerns and work within Clinton's administration, "Al Pal," *The New Republic*, Feb. 17, 1997, p. 42.

42. John Kamensky, interview with Peri A. Arnold, Washington, D.C., Mar. 19, 1997.

43. John Kamensky, "A Brief History of the National Performance Review," (National Performance Review Library, http://www.npr.gov), p. 1.

44. Ibid., p. 3.

45. For a comparison of approaches to administrative reform in the 1980s in Britain, Canada, and the United States, see Donald J. Savoie, *Thatcher, Reagan, Mulroney: In Search of a New Bureaucracy* (Pittsburgh: University of Pittsburgh Press, 1994).

46. On the theoretical underpinnings of recent reforms in the Whitehall systems, with an eye particularly on the New Zealand case, see Jonathan Boston, "The Theoretical Underpinnings of Public Sector Restructuring in New Zealand," in Boston, John Martin, et al., eds., *Reshaping the State: New Zealand's Bureaucratic Revolution* (Auckland: Oxford University Press, 1991), pp. 1–27. More generally, on contemporary approaches to reorganization, see B. Guy Peters, "Government Reorganization: A Theoretical Analysis," in Ali Farazmand, ed., *Modern Organizations* (Westport, Conn.: Praeger, 1994), pp. 108–12.

47. Donald F. Kettl, "The Global Revolution in Public Management," *The Journal of Policy Analysis and Management* 16:3 (Summer, 1997): 447–49.

48. Ibid., p. 448.

49. John Kamensky, "The Best Kept Secrets in Government: Implementation of the Recommendations of the National Performance Review," in Patricia W. Ingraham, James R. Thompson, and Ronald P. Sanders, eds., *Transforming Government: Lessons from the Reinvention Laboratories* (San Francisco: Jossey-Bass, 1998).

50. This idea of reform agendas draws on the concept of agenda setting in John Kingdon, *hr Agendas, Alternatives, and Public Policy* (2d ed.; New York: Harper Collins, 1995).

51. Beryl A. Radin, "Varieties of Reinvention: Six NPR 'Success Stories,'" in Donald Kettl and John DiIllio, Jr., *Inside the Reinvention Machine* (Washington, D.C.: Brookings, 1995), p. 125.

52. Mike Mills, "Clinton and Gore Hit the Road To Build a Better Bureaucracy," *Congressional Quarterly Weekly Report*, Sept. 11, 1993, pp. 2381–89.

53. Mike Mills, "Clinton and Gore Hit the Road To Build a Better Bureaucracy," p. 2381.

54. National Performance Review, *From Red Tape to Results: Creating a Government That Works Better and Costs Less* (Washington, D.C.: GPO, 1993).

55. National Performance Review, *From Red Tape to Results*, p. 93. Interestingly what goes unmentioned in the report is that Russell, Kansas, was not just any small town on the Great Plains, but it was the much-publicized home of the then Senate majority leader and 1996 presidential candidate, Bob Dole. That an anecdote about

the federal government's policy implementation in Russell might not be generalizable must not have occurred to the reinventers.

56. National Performance Review, *From Red Tape to Results,* p. 22.
57. John Kamensky, "The U.S. Reform Experience: The National Performance Review," (paper presented to Conference on Civil Service Systems in Comparative Perspectives, Indiana University, Apr. 6, 1997), p. 4.
58. For a vigorous critique of the NPR's focus upon customer service and administrative flexibility, ignoring law and responsibility to Congress, see Ronald C. Moe, "The 'Reinventing Government Exercise.'" *Public Administration Review* 54 (Mar./ Apr., 1994): 111–22.
59. Stephen Barr, "Gore's Team Turns to Making Reinvention Deliver," *Washington Post,* Mar. 3, 1998, p. A15.
60. There has been a reticence at the NPR to establish an analytic component within its staff, with some of those in its leadership thinking that such a capacity would be a kind of academic luxury for a group with as few resources as the NPR possesses. John Kamensky, interview with Peri E. Arnold, Washington D.C., Mar. 19, 1997.
61. National Performance Review, *From Red Tape to Results,* p. ii.
62. National Performance Review, *Common Sense Government* (Washington, D.C.: GPO, 1995), p. 20.
63. Ibid., p. 141.
64. Each regulatory agency's reform plan was published separately by the NPR. The earliest in this series, published in April, 1995, is *Reinventing Drug & Medical Device Regulations* (Washington, D.C.: GPO, 1995).
65. Speech reprinted in National Performance Review, *Reinvention's Next Steps: Governing in a Balanced Budget World* (Washington, D.C.: GPO, 1996), p. 5.
66. Ibid.
67. See Ibid., pp. 17–20.
68. The documents from the cabinet summit briefing were published. National Performance Review, *The Blair House Papers* (Washington, D.C.: GPO, 1997).
69. John Kamensky, interview with Peri E. Arnold; and John Kamensky, "The U.S. Reform Experience," p. 10.

Chapter 14

White House–Initiated Management Change

Implementing Federal Procurement Reform

STEVEN KELMAN

This paper presents an account of significant change in the operations of executive-branch organizations initiated and pursued by the White House during the Clinton administration. The area to be discussed is changes in government procurement—that is, the way the federal government buys goods and services from the private sector for government use.

The success of White House–initiated change efforts here is surprising on a number of accounts. It is surprising first of all because the idea that there might be sustained White House interest in an area of the operational management of the executive branch is hard to imagine. Presidents may manage in the strategic sense of laying out a vision and seeking the political support and broad organizational capacity necessary to realize the vision.[1] They generally seek to manage executive-branch departments to increase their ability to influence the policy performance or the political decisions emerging from those departments. Whether consciously or not, they inevitably manage the organization of the Executive Office of the President. And they periodically show interest in broad legislative or executive-branch organizational reform initiatives, at least for brief, spasmodic periods.[2] But it is almost a truism that presidents spend little or no time and energy, not to speak of sustained interest, in the specifics of what people in Washington call "management," that is the operational performance of executive-branch organizations. Second, government procurement is a traditional area of congressional policy interest, so major reform efforts needed to involve Congress as well as the executive branch.

Government procurement will seem to many an arcane topic. In fact, however, approximately $200 billion a year, fifteen percent of the federal government's budget, consists of goods and services purchased from the private sector. Even more noteworthy, government procurement accounts for about forty percent of the discretionary budget, after excluding entitlements and debt service. Some of what the government buys is goods and services needed to run everyday operations: office supplies, cleaning services for federal buildings, telephone service, package delivery services, or food for soldiers. Some is goods and services essential to the operating missions of government organizations: military equipment for the Department of Defense, computer systems that control air traffic or run the tax collection and Social Security systems, or weather forecasting equipment for the National Weather Service. With the increased attention to contracting out noncore government functions, procurement becomes a more important topic, since contracting out is accomplished through procurement, and the effectiveness of contracting out as a strategy will depend in significant measure on how well the procurement system does its job.

Finally, the procurement system is important because, for many Americans, it became during the 1980s a symbol for what was wrong with the management of the public sector. During the military buildup under the Reagan administration, various "horror stories" suggesting that the government dramatically overpaid for a number of common, easy-to-understand items used by the Department of Defense received extraordinarily wide publicity. It was alleged, for example, that the government paid $91 for a simple screw that would cost 3 cents in a hardware store, or $600 for a $6 hammer. In fact, these stories were erroneous.[3] Nonetheless, they became unusually widely known (because they were easy to understand) and widely believed (because they corresponded with people's intuitions about public management). Improving government procurement might thus serve as a metaphor for *improvements* in the management of the public sector, just as the $600 hammer had served in the 1980s and since as a metaphor for the *problems* of public management.

The discussion of achieving change in government procurement to be presented in this essay will be a first-person account. In July, 1993, I went on leave from a position as professor of public management at Harvard University, John F. Kennedy School of Government, when President Clinton nominated me to the Senate-confirmed position as administrator of the Office of Federal Procurement Policy (OFPP). This is a twenty-person office that is part of the Office of Management and Budget in the Executive Office of the President. OFPP was established by Congress in 1974 to assume overall responsibility for development of executive-branch procurement regulations and for formulation of the views of the administration on procurement legislation. OFPP does not itself buy anything for the government; actual purchasing is done by departments who need the goods and services being bought (as well as by the General Services Administration, which buys items used by many different organizations, such as office supplies, automobiles for government use, or airline tickets).

The effort to reinvent the federal procurement system is widely regarded by outside observers as having made significant progress. In 1988, in its five-year "Report Card" on the National Performance Review, the Brookings Institution gave procurement reform the only full "A."[4] An article in early 1996 in the *Financial Times* regarding the U.S. government's innovative use of credit cards to pay for low-value everyday purchases (where the administrative costs of executing the purchase sometimes are greater than the value of the item being bought), stated that the American government had "pioneered the use of credit cards issued to staff members to . . . dramatically cut the cost of procurement" and referred to the innovation as "a lead that US corporations are rapidly following"—surely one of the few times a business publication had praised government for taking the lead on a new management practice![5] *Purchasing*, a publication for private-sector, nongovernment purchasing professionals, has written that "25 years after creation of the first commission on waste in government buying, there is evidence of some significant change in the way (the U.S. government) buys."[6] A 1997 survey of federal managers about information technology noted the "survey surprise" that "IT procurement is not an issue. . . . For decades, both IT managers and non-IT managers were frustrated by delays and red tape when they needs IT products and services. . . . It's clear that recent IT reforms have had the desired effect, freeing managers to concentrate on the more important aspects of their agency's IT."[7]

During the Clinton first term, Congress passed two pieces of procurement reform legislation, the Federal Acquisition Streamlining Act of 1994 and the Federal Acquisition Reform Act of 1995. The latter passed with administration support by the Republican-controlled Congress that emerged from the 1994 congressional elections, one of the few examples of bipartisan legislation passed during the 1995 session of the Congress. These laws removed rules applying both to government officials and to contractors and moved the government procurement system closer to a commercial model. In 1997 important parts of the *Federal Acquisition Regulation* were rewritten in the same spirit.

Most significantly, there have been a host of changes in management practices that have been attempted in different federal departments, which are yielding a growing number of concrete results. To take a few examples (many more could be cited):

(1) Using new buying procedures authorized through a test program under the Federal Acquisition Streamlining Act, the Federal Aviation Administration bought new voice recorders to record ground-air communications between planes and air traffic control in seven rather than the traditional twelve months. More importantly, the new recorders were installed in six months rather than the one or two years such installation otherwise would have taken, worked as expected, and were supplied without requiring expensive changes to the original contract, because the procedures used to buy the recorders gave the agency greater certainty about exactly what it was purchasing. Furthermore, the agency received a sixty percent discount from the catalog price for the recorders, compared to its original expectation of a twenty-five percent discount.[8]

(2) In a Department of Defense program for developing a "smart" bomb, also designated as a test program under the Federal Acquisition Streamlining Act, a lengthy government specification was replaced by a straightforward performance specification explaining what requirements needed to be met. The final winning price bid for the system in 1995 was $2.5 billion, compared to a final winning bid of $5.5 billion for the system in 1993, before the changes were made.[9]

(3) In 1996 the Department of Defense stopped buying socks for soldiers based on a government specification. The previous socks tended to fall down because they lacked elastic at the top, they felt rough, and they used dyes that tended to bleed. As a result, soldiers often threw the socks out and bought their own. The new socks are ordinary commercial socks with elastic and a normal feel. The previous socks had cost $1.99 a pair; the commercial socks cost $1.49.

(4) Previously, the government seldom considered past performance on earlier contracts in making new contract awards. Well-performing suppliers were not rewarded; poorly performing ones were not punished. A follow-up survey of contracts re-awarded using past performance as a significant criterion in selecting the winner showed an average increase in the satisfaction of the government customer with the contractor's performance of twenty-one percent.[10]

"Reinventing Government"

One issue that was part of the successful presidential campaign of Bill Clinton in 1992 was the commitment to "reinvent government." Clinton got the phrase from the title of a 1992 best-selling book by David Osborne and Ted Gaebler, who in turn had borrowed it from the phrase "reinventing the corporation" that had become common in management consulting during the late 1980s.[11]

The political thrust of "reinventing government" was to assist Clinton's self-identification as a "New Democrat." He neither wanted to eliminate government, like conservative Republicans, nor retain the old reliance on bureaucratic governmental institutions, like traditional Democrats.

Thus, in March, 1993, Clinton created the "National Performance Review" (NPR), a phrase taken from a similar effort in Texas state government, to examine within six months the operations of the federal government and make suggestions for changes, on the principles of the Osborne and Gaebler book. Vice President Al Gore was placed in charge of this effort. With much fanfare, Gore organized a series of "town meetings" with government employees to get their suggestions for change, and career government officials were placed in charge of making suggestions for changes in their own agencies. Gore specifically noted that this approach contrasted with earlier studies of "waste in government" where outsiders came in and, implicitly or explicitly, attacked federal civil servants as the source of the problems in public management. Gore, instead, stated that he believed the problem was that "good people" were trapped in "bad systems"—and that the management system needed to be changed.

In September, 1993, Gore published the report of the National Performance Review, called *From Red Tape to Results: Creating a Government That Works Better and Costs Less* (henceforth the "Gore report").[12] The Gore report was divided into four sections: "cutting red tape," "putting customers first," "empowering employees to get results," and "cutting back to basics." Part of chapter one of the Gore report, on cutting red tape, was devoted to "streamlining procurement," and the report contained twenty specific recommendations under this rubric.

In its approach, the Gore report associated itself with the "discretion" side of the traditional debate within organizational theory about "rules" versus "discretion."[13] The introduction stated:

> Is government inherently incompetent? Absolutely not. Are federal agencies filled with incompetent people? No. The problem is much deeper: Washington is filled with organizations designed for an environment that no longer exists. . . .
>
> From the 1930s through the 1960s, we built large, top-down, centralized bureaucracies . . . patterned after the corporate structures of the age: hierarchical bureaucracies in which tasks were broken into simple parts, . . . each defined by specific rules and regulations. With their rigid preoccupation with standard operating procedure, their vertical chains of command, and their standardized services, these bureaucracies were steady—but slow and cumbersome. And in today's world of rapid change, lightning-quick

information technologies, tough global competition, and demanding customers, large, top-down bureaucracies—public or private—don't work very well. . . .

Effective, entrepreneurial governments cast aside red tape, shifting from systems in which people are accountable for following rules to systems in which they are accountable for achieving results. . . . They strip away unnecessary layers of regulation that stifle innovation.[14]

My mandate was to use OFPP to take responsibility for the administration's reinventing government program as it affected procurement. I was selected for this job based on my interest in the improved management of the public sector and my previous research on government procurement. In 1990 I had published a book called *Procurement and Public Management: The Fear of Discretion and the Quality of Public Performance*, which was highly critical of the existing system of government purchasing.[15]

Although the personal involvement of the vice president gave the Gore report more visibility than studies such as those of the Hoover Commissions or the Reagan-era Grace Commission, there was every reason to believe as of September, 1993, that, as in past instances, White House interest would be fleeting, resistance among executive-branch departments great, and the final results flimsy.

The Pre-Reform System

The pre-reform system was dominated by bureaucratic rules regulating the procurement process. Many of these rules arose from distrust of participants in the system, both the government employees who were buying and the companies who were selling. Left to their own devices, it was believed that government officials would show favoritism (or even corruption) and not treat potential suppliers fairly. It was also believed that, left to their own devices, suppliers would cheat the government.

My own research had focused on the bureaucratic rules dominating the source selection process for major contracts, that is, the process by which the government makes decisions about from whom to buy. The rules established an elaborate set of procedures to assure that no potential contractor was treated unfairly. Typically, these rules were oriented toward emphasizing identical treatment of bidders and minimizing the exercise of judgment in government officials' award decisions. One impact of these procedures was to make the source selection process extremely lengthy and expensive; it was not unusual for a major source selection for an information technology procurement to take several years. A second impact, even more serious, was that it interfered with the government's ability to choose the supplier most appropriate for the job. For example, as I noted in my research, the view within the system was that it was "unfair" to take account of a supplier's past performance on earlier contracts when making new contract awards, because such decisions ran the risk of being too subjective. Such a strange practice produced, of course, poor incentives for good contract performance and often led to selection of an inferior supplier over a better one. The reliance on rote evaluation of lengthy written proposals also frequently led to selection of a supplier based on their abilities at proposal writing rather than at accomplishment.

A second feature of the traditional system that was driven in significant measure by a bureaucratic concept of "fairness" was the government's frequent use of specially designed government product specifications (in the Defense Department environment often called "military specifications" or "milspecs") to establish the features of what the government would buy. The idea was that if firms were simply given a general description of what the government wanted (say, socks for soldiers), that it would give an unfair advantage to producers of brand-name off-the-shelf commercial products, and create a potential for unequal evaluation. Instead, the government developed its own specification for, say, socks, so that everyone was bidding to the same set of demands. However, there usually ended up being something in the specification that ordinary commercial products couldn't meet, so the odd result of this system was that only companies bidding to the government's specification, producing a product not even offered to the commercial marketplace, were able to meet the specification. This produced an enormous price and quality penalty for items bought this way.

The traditional idea was that these rules for selecting suppliers were enforced by government contracting professionals, who were experts on the regulatory requirements and guardians of the system against favoritism. The main source of potential favoritism was seen as the government end-users for the products or services being bought. For this reason, end-users were not allowed to buy anything directly but had to go through their procurement offices so that it could be assured that the rules were followed.

A second broad area of rules, on which my own research had not focused but which had been a significant area of concern among many suppliers to the government, were those designed to assure that firms selling to the government did not cheat. These included requirements in many situations to develop detailed data about a company's production costs, submitted to the government to help it negotiate a good price, and special inspection and quality procedures that differed from those normally used in the commercial marketplace. Often, compliance with these requirements was enforced by civil or even criminal fines. These special government requirements added to companies' costs of supplying the government (and hence to the prices government paid). They also discouraged many commercial companies from even being willing to do business with the U.S. government, leaving a disproportionate amount of government contracting in the hands of firms, or divisions of firms, that specialized in doing government business only. By reducing competition and increasing firms' costs (since government-only firms or government-only divisions of other firms might have uneconomically low production runs), these rules also increased the government's costs.

The Process of Change

When I took the job as administrator of OFPP, I perceived three major, daunting obstacles to achieving change:

(1) *Congress:* There were few members of Congress interested in procurement issues, but they dominated procurement policy making. And most appeared to be firmly committed to the status quo. Members interested in procurement were generally on the Governmental Affairs Committee of the Senate and the Government Operations Committee of the House, the committees with legislative and oversight responsibility for government management. The existing system had been put in place through laws coming out of these committees, such as the Competition in Contracting Act of 1984. Some members appeared to have strong ideological beliefs supporting the existing system of bureaucratized competition and an orientation to basing procurement policy on "horror stories" of corruption or collusion. They also had a distrust of government suppliers (as part of a general ideological distrust of business). All this was particularly the case for the long-time chair of the House Government Operations Committee, Congressman Jack Brooks, who played a crucial role in overseeing procurement policy in the executive branch. Brooks was obsessed by worries that "monopolies" such as IBM would dominate government procurement unless strict rules prevented the government from showing "favoritism" to them. Brooks had left the Government Operations Committee in 1991 to become chair of the Judiciary Committee, but his successor promised Brooks to stay faithful to his tradition, and many of the staffers who had worked for the committee under Brooks remained in place. In addition, the rule-bound structure of the existing procurement system included many laws directing procurement dollars to small and minority-owned businesses, and some Democrats on these committees were strong supporters of such programs as well.

There were also some members of Congress, particularly on the House and Senate Armed Services committees, interested in changes in the traditional system. But these committees did not have primary jurisdiction over procurement, and the prospects for gaining congressional support seemed dim.

(2) *Career Procurement Officials in the Departments:* Each department has career officials whose expertise is procurement. They are trained in knowledge of the procurement regulations, Traditionally, contracting professionals worked in separate procurement organizations. My research had suggested that most career procurement officials saw their role mostly as guardians of the regulations, that they seemed to relish this role, and that they generally viewed end-users with suspicion, as people who needed to be watched over lest they violate the regulations and behave illegally.[16] Furthermore, an enormous body of literature suggests that all organizations typically resist change. I assumed that the career contracting workforce would resist change—and that they would react unfavorably to a nonprocurement outsider, especially an academic, coming in trying to suggest to them how to improve the system they ran.

(3) *Lack of White House Leverage:* The federal procurement system is enormous in scope. There are over 20 million purchasing actions a year in every department of the government. Neither the vice president nor I had responsibility for buying anything ourselves. I would have a staff of about twenty. The challenge of locating leverage points over such a large and decentralized system seemed very daunting. As a management professor, I was of course familiar with the literature, starting with the classic book *Implementation* by Jeffrey Pressman and Aaron Wildavsky, suggesting how common it was for grand programs to be announced at the top and then to turn to dust in the everyday reality of organizational operations.[17] And, although I knew my organization would have some considerable influence over the content of procurement regulations, I was skeptical that regulatory changes by themselves would bring about changes in behavior.

Developing a Strategy for Change

I spent a good deal of time between being told I would be selected for the job (in June, 1993) and when I arrived in Washington (in September, 1993) thinking about a basic strategy and approach. My initial strategy was informed by features of what I had taught or read about as a professor of public management:

(1) *Focus on the procuring organizations more than on Congress:* This was a subversive idea for a political appointee in Washington, where success has traditionally been measured in terms of laws passed, not lower-visibility activities

inside the bureaucracy. But my training in the problematical nature of implementation led me to believe that changes in law would play only a secondary role in determining whether the procurement system actually got any better. In addition, while I felt that organizational change would be very difficult, it would be no more difficult than the brick wall I believed I was likely to face in Congress, and it at least had the virtue of being an area that was personally interesting to me as a management professor.

(2) *Try to achieve some early success in the procuring organizations:* Success builds on success, I believed. If, somehow, a successful change could be accomplished early on within the procuring organizations, it might be possible to use that as an inspiration for other changes. But it had to be something that could gain visibility, within the procurement community at least. One way to gain such visibility was for a change to be pursued simultaneously among a large number of procuring organizations, as a common project of senior career procurement managers across government, hopefully in some way through the efforts of OFPP. Such a joint effort would also focus at least some attention on OFPP as an organizer of improvement efforts, which would in turn augment OFPP's standing to push other innovations. I was not at all confident that such a simultaneous change effort would be possible, however. I thought I would try to convene the agency procurement executives—the senior career officials in charge of procurement in each cabinet department—for a one- or two-day meeting to brainstorm possible ideas for a joint initiative that did not require legislative change, and to conclude the meeting by reaching agreement on one or two that they would commit themselves to pursue jointly. I had a list of possible such ideas—high on the list was increased use of supplier past performance in the source selection process, the major theme of my book on government procurement—that I hoped might gingerly be injected into the list of ideas for consideration. But I thought there was a significant chance that procurement executives simply would show no interest in even showing up for such a meeting, or for the idea that anything needed to be changed, so I concluded that it was more important that the procurement executives agreed on *some* joint improvement initiative than on what the actual content of the initiative might be.

(3) *My rhetorical theme would be "antibureaucracy":* I knew that political debate often turns around efforts by advocates of different viewpoints to emphasize to those they seek to persuade that aspect of their viewpoint (or, to use the phrase of Richard E. Neustadt, the "face of the issue") that is the most broadly attractive.[18] For procurement reform, that face was opposition to bureaucracy. I was determined to employ the adjective "bureaucratic" to descriptions of the current system, as with phrases such as "bureaucratized version of competi-

tion" or "bureaucratic source selection process." The positive rhetorical image I wanted to emphasize was "commercial practice"—the idea that the government's procurement methods should become more like those used by the most successful business enterprises.

The position to which I had been appointed required that I be confirmed by the U.S. Senate. The confirmation process generally takes several months (in my case, it lasted from September through Thanksgiving, 1993. Once the president announced that I would be nominated for my position, I could begin to work (as a "consultant"), but I could not formally assume the job. These several months allowed me to sit in on meetings without the responsibility for making decisions (or even being required to talk, though I was allowed to) and for getting to know people I would be working with, not only inside OFPP but, especially, in the procuring agencies and in Congress.

Successful organizations, and individuals, I had taught in my management classes, don't understand, or have a strategy for dealing with, everything in advance; they work, however, at being attentive to signals from the environment and adapting their behavior, in pursuit of their overall goals, in light of what they learn.[19] My several-month apprenticeship in the fall of 1993 taught me a great deal that turned out to be crucial to the strategy I would follow on my job:

(1) *The vice president's National Performance Review was for real:* One of the first things I became involved with after the president had announced his intention to nominate me, but even before I arrived in Washington, was the procurement material in the Gore report that was still in the process of being written. As it turned out, procurement had been a very frequently mentioned topic in the vice president's town meetings in federal agencies. It got raised mostly by federal employees whose association with the procurement system was incidental to doing their jobs—by people whose offices had everyday needs for office supplies, simple services, or personal computers. They complained that it took too long to get what they needed and that what slowed things down was that they had to make their requests through their agency procurement offices rather than simply being trusted to buy what they needed themselves. The problem with procurement, phrased that way, fit in very well with the general NPR theme that the control of centralized staffs, enforcing bureaucratic rules, needed to be reduced in favor of empowering line managers to make decisions, and holding them responsible for results. Partly as a result of those town meetings, procurement was to be featured both in the overall Gore report and in a separate set of procurement recommendations then being developed, with the participation of OFPP staff. Then, the week in September when the NPR report appeared, Vice President Gore appeared on David

Letterman to make fun of a government procurement specification for an ashtray that required that the glass break into no more than a certain number of pieces when hit with a hammer. (On national television, Gore took out one of the ashtrays and a hammer, put on safety glasses, and proceeded to smash the ashtray.) A few days later, Gore visited a warehouse stocking purchased supplies to make the point that the government should use commercial distribution systems instead of warehouses run by central procuring agencies. On arriving, I immediately began attending marathon meetings in the New Executive Office Building, across from the White House, to craft an administration NPR procurement reform legislative package. And in late October, President Clinton led a procurement reform event in the White House, to inaugurate the administration's NPR procurement legislative agenda. What I now realized was that the NPR was a major effort, which might be an important priority for the vice president, and that procurement reform was going to be part of that effort. I had no way of knowing how long such interest would last, but, perhaps naively, I hoped it would.

(2) *There was reform activity underway in Congress:* In 1990 Congress, at the initiative of the Senate Armed Services Committee, had established a study commission (called the "Section 800 Panel" after the section of the Defense Department authorization bill that had created it) to examine government-unique laws applying to companies selling to the Defense Department. In January, 1993, the Section 800 Panel issued a report recommending elimination of many of these laws. Senate staff then began work on a legislative response to the recommendations, as did the Defense Department. (The Defense Department's effort got folded into a broader administration effort after publication of the Gore report. Some of the recommendations of the 800 Panel had been incorporated as Gore report recommendations, although many of the Gore report procurement recommendations were in other areas.) Before coming to Washington, I had not even known that the Section 800 Panel existed, nor that any legislation was being considered in reaction to it. In a conversation with an old college friend who worked on the Senate Armed Services Committee staff, I mentioned that my inclination on my new job, given what I assumed would be congressional resistance to change, was to concentrate on working with the agencies on reforms that were possible without legislative change, and he responded, "Steve, there's a lot of legislative activity moving in this area because of the 800 Panel report. You're not going to be able to avoid becoming involved in it."

(3) *There was reform activity underway at the Defense Department:* The Defense Department reacted positively to the 800 Panel report. A number of the new senior leaders in the Defense Department had been involved with defense

procurement reform through the efforts of the Defense Science Board. The new secretary of defense, who had previously been chairman of the House Armed Services Committee, established an acquisition reform office headed by a former senior House Armed Services Committee staffer who had worked on procurement issues in Congress, Colleen Preston.

(4) *There were reform-minded procurement executives:* After my procurement book had come out in 1990, I had done some consulting for the procurement operation at the U.S. Postal Service, a government corporation that is not subject to the procurement laws and that was working to make their own system less bureaucratic. One of the calls I made on arriving in Washington was to the person who had brought me in as a consultant, to arrange a lunch. At the lunch he mentioned that a number of friends of his who were procurement executives in some of the major nondefense cabinet departments had formed a group called the Procurement Executives Association. They were a reform-minded bunch, and he thought I ought to try to meet some of them. I called the head of the group, and we got together. I was amazed. He thought the procurement status quo needed significant change. He seemed honored I had called him to get together. I hesitatingly broached my idea of trying to get procurement executives together on a joint project. He was very enthusiastic. Maybe, I said to myself, it might be possible to work with some procurement executives and not simply to be rejected as a foreign body.

(5) *There were front-line procurement professionals eager for change:* A member of the Procurement Executives Association whom I called after having lunch with the head of the group was the procurement executive for the Department of Health and Human Services. In between the two lunches it had occurred to me that it would be an interesting part of my "apprenticeship" to spend some time visiting a number of procurement offices to listen to employees about what (if anything) they didn't like about the status quo and to get their reactions to some of my ideas. The Health and Human Services procurement executive offered to let me visit a number of offices over a one-week period (and indeed accompany me for much of the time). The meetings—often a group of ten or fifteen sitting around a big table with their supervisor and me—made a tremendous impression. To my surprise, I discovered that the dominant view among working-level procurement professionals was that the system involved too many rules and maddening red tape; as a group, they were frustrated with the status quo and hopeful that the NPR might conceivably do something about it. A few images from that week stand out vividly in my mind. One was entering the modestly sized office of one of the supervisors whose buying office I was visiting and seeing that one of the few books he had on his bookshelf was a book on "total quality management." A second was how often during these

meetings the front-line contracting professionals used the word "customer" to describe the program officials for whom they bought goods and services. When I had done my research several years earlier, most of the contracting professionals with whom I spoke regarded the program people as the enemy—as potential criminals anxious to skirt regulatory requirements—and certainly not as their "customers." Something had gone on during the intervening years; the vocabulary of total quality management and of the customer-orientation movement in the business world had entered government. A third incident involved visiting a buying office at the National Institute of Health and talking with a contracting professional who was complaining how some government-unique requirements—such as the requirement that all purchases under $25,000 be made from small businesses—that applied even to the purchase of a few computer disks made it impossible simply to go across the street from her office, where an inexpensive computer superstore was located, to make simple purchases.

As it happened, back at my meetings downtown working on the administration's procurement reform draft legislation, the issue of eliminating legal impediments to quick purchases of small everyday-use items for government offices was one of the items the group was busy working on. But this contracting professional had mentioned some legal impediments that the legislative group working back downtown had not noticed and were not in the administration's draft legislation. I returned that afternoon downtown, went to a meeting of the legislative group, and told them excitedly what I had learned. The contracting professional's suggestions were promptly incorporated into the administration draft. As I was taking the car back downtown, I had said to myself that if the procurement reform bill ever became law, I would try to get the front-line professional, Michelle Craddock, who had made these suggestions, invited to the bill-signing ceremony in the White House, as a way of dramatizing the participation of the front-line workforce in the process of change.

Making Change Happen

What my several-month apprenticeship had taught me was that the prospects for change were greater than I had expected. It might very well be possible to work with the agency procurement executives. Activity was underway in the Department of Defense. There was motion in Congress. And there was at least some support for change among the people on the front lines.

Still oriented more toward management changes within the executive branch than to legislative changes from Congress, I developed toward the end of my apprenticeship period a version of my original idea of trying to persuade a number of procurement executives to agree to work together on some concrete reform action in their agencies. Originally, I had hoped I might bring together a number of procurement executives for a day or two to see if they might be willing to agree to something—almost *anything*—among themselves. Based on my initial experiences, I decided it might be possible for *me* actually to make a suggestion to *them,* without the day or two of meetings. One of the days during my week with the Department of Health and Human Services, I made the suggestion to their procurement executive that perhaps a number of the procurement executives might agree to increasing their use of the government credit card by 100 percent over a one-year period. As I was sitting in the car, I thought out loud to him that perhaps such an agreement could be called a "pledge," a somewhat strange-sounding word reminiscent of the expression "taking the pledge" used by temperance advocates trying to get people to forswear alcohol. He said that sounded like a good idea to him.

Thus was born the first signature activity of the procurement reform efforts under my tenure as OFPP administrator, the "pledges." Before we were done, between October, 1993, and October, 1994, OFPP organized five pledges. The idea behind the pledges was to get a number of agencies voluntarily to agree to undertake some specific action or reform effort, typically involving specific contracts that were going to be awarded. For example, the first big pledge, signed in January, 1994, involved the use of past performance in the source selection process. In that pledge, twenty agencies pledged to take a total of sixty specific contracts and make the past performance of bidders a major factor in selecting the winner. The idea was to make the pledges center around a specific, concrete action—not a study or a report or a recommendation—so as to show that procurement reform could get started. The hope was that the joint activity would be able to generate publicity that would get out a message, at least within the procurement community and hopefully beyond, that procurement reform was underway, without waiting for changes in laws or regulations. The joint activity would also give agencies "cover" in trying something new that they might otherwise be hesitant to do, would allow us to gather lessons that could be useful in spreading the innovations further, and might give us ambassadors (the people working on the pledged contracts) to help spread the word in the agencies. Finally, the organization of pledges suggested one model of the role of a central management staff function such as OFPP in the process of organizational change in government operations, as the node organizing joint activities and megaphone amplifying the voices of change that might otherwise be lost in the enormous cacophony of government.

I suggested a pledge involving the credit card to the Procurement Executives Association, and they organized it, signing an actual document to coincide with the president's procurement event at the end of October, before I was confirmed. For the past performance pledge, I spent weeks on the phone as soon as I was confirmed trying to persuade agencies beyond the seven in the Procurement Executives Association to sign up. If we could get at least eight agencies, we would, I decided, go ahead. I asked the procurement executives in the association for help talking with procurement executives in other agencies. I contacted senior information-technology (nonprocurement) managers I had interviewed for my book in the late 1980s, and my staff used contacts they had, particularly in the Department of Defense. After we got to eight or nine agencies, the number of participants started snowballing, and soon we were able to say to the holdout agencies, "Almost everyone but you is participating." The agencies then had to come up with significant upcoming contracts to pledge; by the week before the public announcement of the pledge, OFPP staffers working on the project started feeling like salespeople receiving orders over the telephone as agencies called in to announce two or three or four more contracts. When we were done, we held a pledge-signing "ceremony" in the ornate Indian Treaty Room of the Old Executive Office Building, with signatories sitting around a large table, and the director of OMB and of the National Performance Review in attendance and making brief remarks. The signing ceremony was covered in both the *Washington Post* and the *Washington Times*. In the wake of the pledge, we formed an interagency team of the pledging agencies to work on implementation of past performance.

Meanwhile, on a separate track, the Department of Defense was also proceeding without legislative or regulatory change and pursuing internal efforts to reduce reliance on milspecs. In early 1994 the secretary of defense issued a memo stating that henceforth milspecs could be used only with higher-level approval, a change in the previous policy that required higher-level approval to *eliminate* existing milspecs.

Legislation

In November, 1993, a coalition of Democratic and Republican senators from the Governmental Affairs and Armed Services committees introduced the procurement reform bill they had been working on since the beginning of the year, the Federal Acquisition Streamlining Act of 1993. The bill itself was something of a hodgepodge. At its center were proposals to adopt many of the recommendations of the Section 800 Panel on making it easier for the government to buy commercial items and to raise the threshold for the use of simplified purchase procedures from $25,000 to $100,000. But the bill also included a considerable number of provisions sought in previous years, prior to the National Performance Review, by particularly the Democratic senators on the Government Affairs Committee, most of which actually added new regulations or requirements to the system. The bill had nothing in it that would increase the discretion of government officials, or simplify the process in awarding large contracts over $100,000, which was the main area in which I traditionally had been interested.

The Senate bill provoked considerable controversy within the executive branch. Staff from the Office of the Vice President were anxious mainly to produce something that could be described as a legislative victory for the NPR. The Senate bill contained nothing in it that grew exclusively out of the Gore report and in fact contained a number of features people in the executive branch would characterize as "antistreamlining." However, the Office of the Vice President supported attempting the amazing task of getting the bill passed, in the Senate at least, within a few weeks, before the end of the legislative session around the beginning of December, to create momentum behind the reinventing government effort. They were not averse to trying to get some improvements in the bill if Senate staffers would agree, but if they wouldn't, they favored simply accepting the bill as introduced. By contrast, the acquisition reform office in the Department of Defense was distressed at the bill for not going far enough. Defense supported getting the bill the administration had been working on introduced.

The Defense Department proceeded with behavior a psychologist might characterize as "passive-aggressive." They did not formally dissent from the view of the Office of the Vice President that no administration bill should be introduced and that the Senate bill should be passed promptly. But, in a series of lengthy, exhaustive meetings to examine the Senate bill line-by-line against the administration bill, Defense advocated an aggressive list of proposed changes to the Senate bill that rewrote, added, and subtracted in a way that made the changes to the Senate bill come to look virtually identical to the administration bill. The Office of the Vice President was in no real position to intervene because they didn't know enough about procurement to understand how extensive the proposed changes really were (the same was true of me at that point, though I was trying to learn as quickly as I could, but as I wasn't yet confirmed was still just watching). So the proposed changes got presented to the Senate, along with the expressed, but unrealistic, hope that differences could be resolved in an intensive series of meetings for perhaps a week and the bill passed before adjournment, as the Office of the Vice President wished. Senate staff reacted to the proposed administration changes with shock and outrage, accused the administration of trying to rewrite the entire bill, and stated that, given the sheer volume of proposed administration changes, there was no chance that a bill could be adopted by adjournment. For good measure, the staff director of the Governmental Affairs Committee made clear that if the administration's attitude of trying to rewrite the entire bill to the wishes of the Defense Department persisted, there was little prospect any bill would get adopted at all.

It was just after the Senate bill blew up that I got confirmed and began my job. Both the Senate and the Office of the Vice President were furious at the Defense Department. I had listened and learned enough to have considerable sympathy with the department's substantive views, and I also felt that the bill had enough weaknesses that it probably shouldn't have simply been passed in a few weeks. However, I respected the desire of the Office of the Vice President to get a bill passed, even if it was imperfect, and I also understood why Senate staffers were enraged by the insouciant administration statement that we wanted a bill passed in weeks, while proposing a list of changes that clearly would have taken months to consider. Finally, I knew that the Office of the Vice President was so angry at the behavior of the administration group working on the procurement reform legislation, formally led by OFPP but dominated by Defense, that they were close to ordering the group off the procurement reform legislation, apologizing to the Senate, and simply telling them that the administration would support their bill unmodified.

So my first legislation-related job, pursued at the same time I was working to organize the past performance pledge, was to try to get the bill back on track, while gaining some improvements and keeping the working group centrally involved in the administration's efforts. The strategy I developed was to get agreement within the executive branch for a concrete, and limited, list of major provisions that needed to be added, subtracted, or changed from the Senate bill. We would present this list to Senate staff. We would state that our other concerns, not on the list, remained and that we would seek to have as many additional improvements as possible incorporated into the bill before it became law, but, crucially, we would commit to Senate staff that if our list of major concerns was dealt with, the administration would support adoption of the bill even if the further changes we supported were not made. I presented this strategy to the Office of the Vice President as an alternative to firing the working group, arguing that those within the administration who felt the bill had serious problems were not incorrect in emphasizing the lack of NPR flavor to the bill. They accepted my approach. I then announced it to the working group, whose chair I had now assumed, and stated that we would have to reduce our concerns to a manageable list of truly important issues, preferably no more than five and definitely fewer than ten. We ended up with seven, involving some changes in bill language to bring it closer to Section 800 Panel recommendations, removal of some of the antistreamlining features that had been holdovers from earlier pre-NPR bills, and addition of some specific NPR recommendations.

The approach got the bill back on track. By September, 1994, after many additional roller-coaster rides, though none as bumpy as the first, the Federal Acquisition Streamlining Act (FASA) had passed both houses of Congress. The bill itself accomplished less than some of the rhetoric suggested; I still remained convinced that many real changes were matters of changes in management practice, not in laws or regulations. But it did make some genuine improvements. And it sent a very important message that change in the procurement system was underway that went *far* beyond specific changes in the legislation. (One soon began hearing about changes agencies were introducing "as a result of FASA" that did not involve legislative changes in FASA at all!) Michelle Craddock, the front-line procurement professional I had met the previous September, was invited to the bill-signing ceremony and acknowledged in the president's remarks. And right after the bill-signing ceremony, the last of the five OFPP pledges was signed.

Continuing the Process of Change

With the signing of the bill, I wanted to begin to devote most of my attention to implementation issues—to getting change actually to take place in buying offices. I announced in an interview in a publication specializing in federal procurement policy that 1995 would be "the year of implementation." And I knew how difficult that still was. My thought was to approach it like an effort to beat a large feather pillow into submission; one would need to hit and hit and hit from every possible direction, hoping that eventually its ability to resist and spring back would diminish.

One initial thought I had was somehow to transfer the "pledge" idea into the activities of local buying offices. I suggested to the Procurement Executives Association the idea of my co-signing with the agency's procurement executive a letter to each front-line contracting professional in their organization, asking each recipient to make a personal, individual pledge to undertake during 1995 some specific action (of their choice) to improve the way the procurement system functioned in their office. However, the procurement executives were not enthusiastic, so I dropped the idea.

A related thought, which I also shared with the Procurement Executives Association, was to make myself available as often as once every two weeks to visit a buying office where I would give a talk and do a "town meeting" (where contracting professionals could share ideas, suggestions, or frustrations with me).

My only condition would be that the buying office, in exchange for my making the visit, would present me an action initiative they were pledging to undertake over the upcoming year. I ended up not establishing a *quid pro quo* condition for visits to buying offices, but I did begin toward the end of 1995 to spend increasing time visiting buying offices for combined speeches and town meetings—and typically the buying office would give me a briefing on local reform initiatives underway. During 1995 and 1996 about ten to fifteen percent of my time was spent this way. And just about whenever I gave speeches, in any context, I centered the speeches around a suggested list of activities that those in the audience could undertake personally, in cooperation with others in their buying office, to improve the system.

Another thought I had was to try to get the National Contract Management Association, the professional association of government and industry contracting people, more involved in the implementation of procurement reform. At their fall, 1995, annual conference, a few months after the Federal Acquisition Streamlining Act was passed, they signed a "pledge" regarding their participation in procurement reform. They pledged to encourage their local chapters to decide on some procurement reform initiative of special interest to the chapter and to work on its implementation in their local area. They also agreed to open a section of their monthly magazine to a regular feature called "Reinventing Acquisition," which would feature articles jointly initiated by OFPP and the Defense Department acquisition reform office. The local chapter pledge initiative petered out; a number of local chapters did decide to work on an area, but I never heard any follow-up about anything the chapters did. However, the "Reinventing Acquisition" feature in the monthly magazine flourished.

In a similar vein, in 1996 I established, together with my colleague Colleen Preston, the head of the Defense Department acquisition reform office, a "Front-Line Procurement Professionals Forum." We solicited from each of the cabinet departments and the Defense Department military services nominations of nonsupervisory contracting professionals. We eventually chose about thirty from among the nominees (about half from outside Washington), and the group started meeting about once every two months, in the White House Conference Center. These meetings allowed us to hear what was on their minds and what was going on in local buying offices. It also allowed us to get reactions to planned initiatives before they were announced. It gave us a chance to present new initiatives to the group, whose members then went back to brief their bosses and colleagues on what they had learned. Finally, it provided a new institutionalized voice for front-line contracting professionals in procurement reform. I worked to get members of the forum invited as panelists in various procurement-related conferences. One member of the forum testified in a hearing before a congressional committee, and in 1996 the forum made favorable public comments (as a group) on proposed, and controversial, changes in the *Federal Acquisition Regulation.*

I was convinced that an important part of my job was to serve as a node to gather, and then to publicize, "success stories" that were individual examples of improvements that buying offices had achieved through procurement reform. Success stories were crucial for a number of reasons. They served as models of what could be accomplished through a willingness to change. They also provided behavioral models that taught and could be imitated by others who learned about them. Giving people recognition for their successes — whether it be through the vice president's recognition program under the National Performance Review or letters from me to the supervisors of those who had created the success stories — encouraged them to keep trying and gave others an incentive to imitate.

Success stories also could serve as an important defensive weapon against critics. The over-bureaucratization and over-regulation of public management have typically arisen in the past in reaction to scandals and abuses that the regulations are then designed to curb. I knew that efforts to de-bureaucratize and deregulate government management might be reversed by future scandals or abuses that could be attributed to earlier deregulation. My view has been that the only way to fight off such counterattacks would be through a rain of success stories. These would allow us to say, "We strongly oppose abuses. Any who have abused a less regulated system should be punished, through existing criminal laws as appropriate. But look at the success stories reinvention has produced. Let's deal with the abuses directly, not by returning the system back to its earlier state." So whenever I gave speeches I would end the speech by giving my fax number and urging people to send me questions, comments, and examples of success stories of which they were proud. Gradually, the initial concentration in the "Reinventing Acquisition" feature in the National Contract Management Association magazine on policy statements written by OFPP or the Defense Department acquisition reform office shifted to articles written by local contracting people about success stories growing out of procurement reform. When I testified before Congress in February, 1995, on the progress of procurement reform, I decided, instead of discussing laws, regulations, and policies — as one would typically do in such testimony — to center the testimony around a half-dozen examples of local improvements in the system. In each case, I mentioned in the testimony the name of the team leader in charge of the improvement, and I sent letters about my testimony to each member of Congress who was their representative, assuming that they would follow up with recognition letters themselves.

Another way to hit the big feather pillow was training. An entire private-sector industry exists to train people in government contracting. We shared a joint interest in getting the word out about new policies and approaches. For us, it helped spread our message. For them, it was a business opportunity. Soon after procurement reform efforts began, I began seeing training advertisements for courses in areas of reform, such as past performance and buying commercial products, that we were promoting. I sent out a number of letters to training vendors, urging them to put certain material in their courses. In addition, OFPP began, for the first time, publishing "best practices guides" that gave nonregulatory suggestions and ideas for implementing new policies. In 1996 the National Performance Review also set up an Internet acquisition reform home page, called "Acquisition Reform Net," which featured training materials as well as an interactive "chat room" capability for procurement professionals to discuss ideas on-line. The Defense Department established an "Acquisition Deskbook" with suggestions, ideas, and best practices on the Internet.

Finally, I sought to get more senior management in their agencies involved in procurement reform. Outside of the Defense Department, procurement issues seldom had much visibility above the level of the procurement executive. The Office of Management and Budget had organized a "President's Management Council," a committee of the deputy secretaries of the cabinet agencies. In 1996 a "procurement committee" of the President's Management Council was established, headed by the deputy secretary of transportation and I. One of the main goals was to increase the communication between deputy secretaries and their senior procurement people, on the principle that deputy secretary interest would make it easier for the senior career procurement people to bring about change.

Reasons for Success for White House–Initiated Change in Department Operational Management

In thinking about the reasons why it was possible to change the procurement system, one should certainly pay attention to the increased fiscal constraints that agencies were facing. These were apparent during this period both at the macro level of the federal budget as a whole and at the micro level of special fiscal constraints on certain individual agencies and activities:

(1) At the macro level, budget cutbacks began with President Clinton's 1993 deficit-reduction plan. The National Performance Review also proposed, and the administration adopted, the goal of a 250,000 employee cut in federal civilian employment (over ten percent of the civilian federal government workforce). The 1994 Republican victory in the congressional elections dra-

matically increased the fiscal constraints on the federal government, as Congress and the president both proposed plans to bring about a balanced federal budget by 2001.

(2) At a micro level, the Defense Department budget started steadily declining in the mid-1980s, after the large Reagan-era defense buildup of the first part of the 1980s. By the mid-1990s the real level of the defense budget was half that of the mid-1980s.

(3) Also at a micro level, during the Clinton administration the central purchasing agencies (that is, those agencies that purchased goods for use by other government agencies) lost both their status as mandatory sources of supply, which they previously had enjoyed for some of the items they bought, as well as their funding through the budget. Instead, they would henceforth need to fund themselves through a small surcharge on the prices of what they sold other agencies. The less they sold, the less money they would get.

Advocates of procurement reform, including me, specifically referred to these fiscal constraints in arguing the need for reform. Secretary of Defense William Perry stated on numerous occasions that savings from acquisition reform were the only way the Defense Department could afford adequately to defend the country, given the tight defense budget situation. I also argued in many of my speeches that only by improving the results the procurement system delivered to taxpayers could the government help turn around the high level of popular cynicism about government performance that would otherwise continually threaten the funding for agency programs. The need to find ways to save money was also one way I achieved more support for my efforts among senior officials at the Office of Management and Budget.

There is evidence that fiscal constraints had an influence on the success of procurement reform:

(1) On the whole, change in the Defense Department, which faced more dramatic fiscal constraints than most civilian agencies, was greater than change in the civilian agencies.

(2) Probably the most dramatic procurement reform changes during this period occurred at the central purchasing agencies (General Services Administration and Defense Logistics Agency) that were fiscally most under threat.

However, there are also limits to an explanation based solely on fiscal constraints:

(1) The changes at the Defense Department lagged budget reductions by several years. Little procurement reform occurred during the second Reagan administration or the Bush administration, though defense spending was decreasing rapidly. The trend of defense spending increases actually slowed during the Clinton administration, but the pace of procurement reform increased rapidly.

(2) Although change at civilian agencies has in general been slower than at the Defense Department, there have been a number of civilian agencies—such as the Internal Revenue Service, the Veterans Administration, and the Department of Transportation—where there has been significant change efforts despite a relatively mild budget climate.

It must also be kept in mind that a simple fiscal constraint explanation provides only a black box that tells us little about how people are able successfully to bring about change in response to growing fiscal constraints. After all, even in the private sector, many companies respond better than others to an economic environment of increased competition; some do well, while others lose market share or go bankrupt.

The White House made a significant difference, I believe, in the success of reform efforts. The White House couldn't produce change itself. In the area of procurement, neither the vice president nor I bought anything. But two features of the vice president's involvement and strategy for reinventing government were crucial:

(1) *Working with rather than against the career workforce:* Initially, the National Performance Review approach of involving the career workforce in making recommendations for change, and stating that the problem was "good people trapped in bad systems" might have appeared—and may conceivably have been—mere efforts at product differentiation (highlighting the contrast with the bureaucrat-bashing Grace Commission) and at mollifying important constituencies (federal employee unions and traditional Democrats who didn't like antigovernment rhetoric). However, whether conscious or not, this approach turned out to be the solution to the classic problem—in management reform in particular and presidential efforts at influencing the executive branch in general—of intermittant presidential or vice presidential attention.

Change would have been impossible without a significant number of career people who already wanted change. I had first realized there were forces for change within the system during my 1993 apprenticeship; during a 1995 procurement reform conference where I was speaking at lunch, I asked the government contracting professionals in the audience how many of them would have said that the system was broken and needed change if I had asked them the question in the late 1980s. To my surprise, most raised their hands. Those in this audience were more change-oriented than the average procurement professional. But I was still surprised. I would have expected that most of them would have regarded themselves as relatively content with the existing system in the late 1980s and would have changed their minds since then. Instead, it appears as if there was a sort of "underground" of those seeking change even at a time when that point of view was hardly noticeable at the surface. It turned out that procurement reform had a core of supporters waiting for a movement. By obtaining allies among the change-oriented elements of the career workforce, the White House got help when it mattered (during times attention inevitably moved to other subjects) and where it mattered (on the ground, where change would need to happen).

The key dynamic was that the White House alliance with change forces within the career workforce strengthened the hand of those within the system who were *already* seeking change. It raised their relative standing within their organizations. It made it easier for them to be willing to try out new ideas.[20] It encouraged and inspired those seeking change, while persuading some of those previously unenthusiastic or sitting on the fence. It provided "cover" (a good excuse if a given change effort failed or created problems) to those seeking change. It helped get rid of external political obstacles (such as bad legislation, or, more broadly, an unfavorable political climate) that inhibited the work of those seeking change And, finally, the White House served as a visible node, gathering and spreading information about "success stories" and innovations.

(2) *Occasional personal attention, while assuring the attention of White House agents:* Gore's interest did not dissolve after the initial release of the 1993 report. Anniversary reports were published each year. Gore gave the issue of reinventing government only intermittant attention—and procurement reform attention that was considerably more intermittant—but he gave it ongoing attention. Ongoing attention, even if intermittant, was very important. No official at remotely near Vice President Gore's level in the political system had ever showed any sustained interest in questions of operational management before. Furthermore, Gore set in place a White House structure to work on reinvention fulltime. These included one of his senior staffers, Elaine Kamarck, who ran the reinvention efforts for the Office of the Vice President, and a National Performance Review staff, career civil servants on detail from their agencies, in the Office of the Vice President. It was that *continued* interest that allowed the White House to play the various encouragement roles discussed above.

The vice president spent only a very modest amount of his personal time on procurement policy. But he made himself available if his help was needed, to resolve a knotty problem in negotiations with Congress or to meet to have his picture taken with members of the Front-Line Forum. I worked as his agent to show fulltime White House interest; a congressional lobbyist from the Office of the Vice President was also assigned to work on procurement reform legislation. And I paid lots of attention to my role as encourager and inspirer (through the Front-Line Forum, use of "heroes" such as Michelle Craddock, or bringing front-line people to testify before Congress), as well as a node to spread success stories, through speeches I gave.

The White House effort was strategic in the best use of the term. Although there was no shortage of slogging and hand-to-hand combat, involving the vice president's agents working fulltime on reform, the big picture is best understood through a jujitsu metaphor, where judicious use of a limited quantity of effort found leverage points that brought the old system to the ground.

NOTES

1. Mark Moore, *Creating Public Value* (Cambridge, Mass.: Harvard University Press, 1995).
2. Paul Light, *The Tides of Reform* (New Haven, Conn.: Yale University Press, 1998).
3. Steven Kelman, *Making Public Policy: A Hopeful View of American Government* (New York: Basic Books, 1987), pp. 274–76.
4. The Brookings Institution, *Reinventing Government: A Fifth-Year Report Card* (Washington, 1998).
5. Tom Foremski, "Plastic Route to Big Savings," *Financial Times,* Feb. 7, 1996, p. 6 (Information Technology Review supplement).
6. "Cutting Uncle's Red Tape," *Purchasing,* Jan. 11, 1996.
7. Nancy Ferris, "Managers Give Technology a Thumbs-Up," *Government Executive,* Mar., 1998, p. 2A.
8. Sue Handy, "FAA Delivers Recorders in Record Time under Pilot Acquisition Program," *Contract Management,* July, 1996.
9. Department of Defense, "Defense Acquisition Pilot Programs Status Briefing," June, 1996.
10. Office of Federal Procurement Policy, "Final Report on the Past-Performance Pledge Program," Jan. 27, 1997.
11. David Osborne and Ted Gaebler, *Reinventing Government: How the Entrepreneurial Spirit Is Transforming the Public Sector* (Reading, Mass.: Addison-Wesley Publishing, 1992).
12. Al Gore, *From Red Tape to Results: Creating a Government that Works Better and Costs Less* (Washington, D.C.: Government Printing Office, 1993).
13. See, for example, Henry Mintzberg, *The Structuring of Organizations* (Englewood Cliffs, N.J.: Prentice Hall, 1979).
14. Gore, *op. cit.,* pp. 3, 6.
15. Steven Kelman, *Procurement and Public Management: The Fear of Discretion and the Quality of Public Performance* (Washington, D.C.: AEI Press, 1990).
16. Kelman, *Procurement, op. cit.,* pp. 24–26.
17. Jeffrey L. Pressman and Aaron B. Wildavsky, *Implementation* (Berkeley: University of California Press, 1973).
18. Graham T. Allison, *The Essence of Decision* (Boston: Little Brown, 1973), p. 168.
19. This is the approach outlined in Henry Mintzberg, "Crafting Strategy," *Harvard Business Review* (July, 1987) and brilliantly illustrated in the classic article, Richard T. Pascale, "Perspective on Strategy: The Real Story Behind Honda's Success," *California Management Review,* May, 1984.
20. This point is made in a somewhat different context in Martha Derthick, *The Influence of Federal Grants* (Cambridge, Mass.: Harvard University Press, 1966).

Chapter 15

At Risk

The President's Role As Chief Manager

RONALD C. MOE

The president of the United States is charged by the Constitution, statutory law and tradition, with performing a number of roles. A recitation of these roles invariably, and properly, starts with the president's role as chief of state, then on to chief politician, chief legislator, and chief diplomat until finally chief manager is reached. The chief manager's role, however, was not always viewed as the least in importance. Presidents earlier in this century from Theodore Roosevelt through Dwight Eisenhower saw their managerial role and responsibilities as critical to their effectiveness as national leaders. Since then, however, most presidents have retreated from their responsibilities, viewing management as a profitless function detracting from their more important political tasks. The trend has been to leave to others responsibility for much of top-level management. In the case of the current administration of President Bill Clinton, the management portfolio is largely assigned to Vice President Al Gore and a nonstatutory body called the National Performance Review (NPR). It is the thesis of this essay that this retreat by presidents from their managerial responsibilities has been costly to the institutional presidency, the executive branch generally, and ultimately to the American people.

Organizational Management Principles

Traditional public administration, from the Federalists through the latter-day Progressives writing in the 1950s, rests on the premise that legal authorities and organizational structure are critical variables in determining an organization's success or failure. There are "principles" or "guidelines" to be followed in organizing governmental activities, and those arguing for deviation from these principles have a heavy burden of proof to overcome. In the American democratic context, the basic objective of organizational structure is to provide legal authority to politically responsible officials.[1] A hierarchical structure was emphasized as it tends to enhance accountability within the political system.

In the last sixty years, three major presidential commissions have issued reports proposing comprehensive executive-branch reorganization schemes. The first was the Brownlow Committee report (1937),[2] next was the first Hoover Commission report (1949),[3] and finally there was the Ash Council report (1970).[4] The reports of these three commissions accepted as their point of departure the essential validity of the traditional principles of organization and management and, while they differed in emphases, each sought to enhance the managerial capacity of the president.

Three themes emerged from these reports; the disparate executive branch should be re-aggregated into fewer, functionally based executive departments; the policy-making processes in the executive branch should be better coordinated and integrated; and the institutional interests of the president should be promoted by properly staffed central managerial agencies.

The thrust of the major commission reports, plus some lesser task force reports during the 1950s and 1960s,[5] was to provide a conceptual and legal basis for the president's exerting centripetal pressure against the natural centrifugal tendencies of the other actors in the political system. This integrative thrust for reorganization efforts, accompanied by accretions to presidential authority, would cease in the mid-1970s.[6]

Along Comes Richard Neustadt

In 1960, Richard Neustadt's *Presidential Power* appeared and launched a broadside against the institutional/legalist view of the presidency. While never fully rejecting the role of law in the armory of presidential powers (no one would be that foolish), Neustadt's thrust was clearly in the opposite direction, toward enhancement of the president's political role. "Laws and customs," Neustadt averred, "tell us little about leadership in fact."[7] The message was for scholars and practitioners to study the techniques of influence and persuasion rather than public law and organizational management if they wanted to understand how decisions were really made. The nub of Neustadt's thesis was to be found in the aphorism: "Presidential power is the power to persuade."[8] Peek behind the decision-making curtain, Neustadt suggested. Political scientists, like almost everyone else, took up the suggestion and found the results stimulating.

Scholars could now forsake the rigorous study of laws and institutions and write of the individuals involved, without feeling scholarly guilt.

In the Neustadt schema, the personalized presidency largely displaced the institutionalized presidency. Neustadt criticized President Eisenhower for relying too much on structured decision-making processes and for lacking the desire for power. Presidents should love power and know how to use it. "Laws and customs now reflect acceptance of him as the Great Initiator, an acceptance quite as widespread at the Capitol as at his end of Pennsylvania Avenue."[9] Presidents who seek to manage the executive branch are performing mere clerkship functions and will miss their opportunity for heroic destiny. In Neustadt's pantheon, Franklin Roosevelt was a great president because he knew what power was, how to get, and how to use it. "His image of the office was himself-in-office."[10] Eisenhower, on the other hand, was pictured by Neustadt as a man who never really understood political power. He was an "amateur," and thus never used it to his personal or policy advantage. "His love was not for power but for duty—and for status."[11] This viewpoint, that increased political power is the proper objective of "great" presidents, fit in with the Kennedys' view of the office, and Neustadt became one of their favorite academicians.

By the early 1960s, the president, principally as an individual and secondarily as an institution, had become the center and dominant force in the American political system as interpreted by the academic establishment of the period. America would be great if the president was great. Great presidents, according to the foremost presidential apologist, James MacGregor Burns, should not feel unduly constrained by the Constitution or laws. In extolling the presidency and the example of Thomas Jefferson, Burns recited his version of Jefferson's virtues: "When the chips were down, when a great decision had to be made and pressed quickly, Jefferson violated congressional rights, by-passed accepted constitutional processes, refused to go through the long process of a constitutional amendment and threw himself and his party on the mercy of the new popular majority that he was building up."[12]

This open shift from the notion of the president as an equal, but limited partner in a constitutional system to one of a president as the dominant actor in the system was accompanied by a frontal attack on Congress. Congress should recognize its inherent institutional weaknesses, the critics averred, and let the president lead without those pesky, obsolete nineteenth century checks and balances. Samuel Huntington, in an influential 1962 essay, summed up the academic view that Congress should simply get out of the legislative business and turn it over to the president: "Legislation has become too complex politically to be effectively handled by a representative assembly. . . . The redefinition of Congress' function away from legislation would involve, in the first instance, a restriction of the power to delay indefinitely presidential legislative requests. Constitutionally, Congress could, as Walter Lippmann and others have suggested, bind itself to approve or disapprove urgent presidential proposals within a time limit of, say, three or six months. If thus compelled to choose openly, Congress, it may be supposed, would almost invariably approve presidential requests."[13]

Underlying these arguments was the view that the president ought to be the supreme political leader, not a manager in any hands-on manner. Principles of organizational management were viewed as politically unsophisticated and the goal should be organizational flexibility, almost for its own sake. Insofar as general principles of organization might have relevance to the president, these issues were properly handled by others, in most cases the Bureau of the Budget.

By the late 1960s, however, the dominant-president argument began to lose its appeal among academicians, many of whom were liberal in their politics. Divided by the Vietnam War and chastened by the consequences of their uncritical promotion of the dominant presidency, these academicians retreated and attempted to rewrite their own theories. Into this politically volatile situation stepped Richard Nixon.

Nixon and the "Administrative Presidency Strategy"

Richard Nixon, upon assuming the presidency in 1969, assembled a management panel chaired by Roy Ash (Ash Council) that provided the president with a reasonably coherent proposal to reorganize most of the domestic side of government into four, later five, departments with restructured lines of accountability leading ultimately to the president. Congress never acted upon these proposals.[14] Nixon, influenced by the defeat of his straightforward, legislatively based executive reorganization strategy, and persuaded by the Neustadtian vision of the aggressive presidency, decided to change strategies. In pursuit of presidential policy and organizational objectives, Nixon determined that the most effective route was to rely on "administrative action—that is," in Richard Nathan's words, "by using the discretion permitted in the implementation of existing laws rather than advancing these policy aims though the enactment of new legislation."[15]

President Nixon attempted to implement as much of the Ash Council recommendations as possible through Reorganization Plans (e.g., the Bureau of the Budget became the Office of Management and Budget in 1970)[16] and administrative orders (e.g., creation of a "super cabinet") bypassing, in the latter instance, the requirement of congressional approval. The "administrative presidency strategy" included such tactics as impounding appropriated funds and the use of the appointment process to thwart the implementation of legislatively mandated programs, tactics calculated to upset Congress. Congress responded, not surprisingly, by following a legislative (public law) strategy of its own. The strategy included passing laws such as the War Powers Joint Resolution of 1973 (87 Stat. 555) and the Congressional Budget and Impoundment Control Act of 1974, (2 U.S.C. 601) inserting numerous legislative veto provisions into new and existing laws,[17] extending Senate confirmation requirement to additional appointees,[18] all actions designed to combat the administrative presidency strategy and to decrease presidential discretion in administrative matters.

The legacy of the Nixon presidency, which had begun as a testament to traditional organizational management doctrine, albeit with some sophisticated political updating, turned out to be a legacy of institutional diminution. With few exceptions, this counterproductive administrative presidency strategy continues today resulting, paradoxically but predictably, in a progressively weakened institutional presidency.

Why Presidents Have Retreated from Their Management Responsibilities

In addition to the larger philosophical issues raised by the Neustadtian vision of a politically centered presidency, recent presidents seem to have been influenced as well by other, less heroic, factors in their decision to remain one step removed from executive-branch management. First, and possibly foremost, presidents and their aides perceive little political advantage accruing from their managerial role. Presidents are not elected for their managerial skills and assume that most of government pretty much moves of its own volition without their active leadership. White House aides are quick to point out that the costs of managerial improvements tend to be immediate while the benefits tend to be in the future, in someone else's administration.

Management is not a field that interests most incumbent presidents as it involves both abstract theory and detailed application. Presidents seek not so much to manage the executive branch through properly conceptualized management laws and trained professional managers as to control government through short-term political appointees, many of whom are only of marginal competence, placed deep within departments. Writing in 1989, the National Commission on the Public Service (Volcker Commission, after its chairman, Paul A. Volcker), concluded that the total number of presidential appointees was excessive and counterproductive to the ability of the president to meet his administrative responsibilities.[19]

The utility of this political management cadre to the institutional presidency and the executive branch generally is problematical at best. Paul Light recently observed that the "thickening" of leadership ranks in the federal government, by which he means the growth in layers of management in departments, ill serves the president and the nation. "Leadership is not measured by the number of people the president brings into office or the number of helpers at the top and middle of government. It is not achieved by further tightening of the command-and-control model that evolved under Eisenhower and his successors. Instead, a president's leadership is most likely to be judged by his clarity of vision, his articulation of cause, and the ultimate value produced by what government does."[20]

Some recent presidents have not only distanced themselves from the executive branch, they have led the political and cultural forces questioning government's legitimacy. The "bureaucracy" they putatively lead is viewed and described as an alien force and the state a candidate for some drastic deconstruction. President Clinton has taken an additional step in the process of presidential disengagement by informally delegating Vice President Al Gore responsibility for management of the executive branch.

The Demise of "M" in OMB

Prior to the 1970 reorganization of the Bureau of the Budget into the Office of Management and Budget (OMB)[21] and into the late 1980s, the consensus had been that management responsibilities were most effectively performed when linked to the budget. It was the budget that gave management the "clout" it needed to achieve results. It is this linkage argument, however, that for many has failed to retain its persuasiveness. Indeed, it is increasingly argued that linking the priorities of the budget process to management priorities serves to weaken the managerial capacity of the executive branch and the institutional interests of the president.

In one of the ironies of administrative history, the decline of management oversight within the executive branch began at the very moment that management received its symbolic equality with the budget responsibilities of the president. Prior to 1970, the top leadership of the Bureau of the Budget had been largely drawn from the career civil service, a cadre that took "neutral competence" seriously as its ideal.[22] The objective of the agency had been to protect the institutional interests of the presidency, not the immediate political interests of the incumbent president. The latter was the responsibility of the White House staff.

Since 1970, however, several trends have influenced the policies and practices of OMB, trends that resulted in a much debilitated OMB and hence a weakened presidency. The first trend was the politicization of OMB;[23] second was the policy of disinvestment in the management infrastructure of the executive branch, a policy that included the management side of OMB;[24] and finally, the contemporary thrust of the NPR report and other "reinventing government" exercises has been to weaken the central management oversight of the executive branch and to favor a devolution of authorities and encouragement of managerial risk-taking.[25]

While staff numbers are necessarily a crude measurement, the loss of personnel on the "management side" of OMB has been impressive. In 1970, 224 employees were on the management side of OMB. This number was considered minimal at the time. By 1980, when President Jimmy Carter left office, the number had fallen to 111. The Reagan administration's concentration on budget cutting and regulatory review further reduced the management staff to only 47,[26] compared at that time to 8,500 at the staff level of agency inspectors general. Finally, the Clinton administration, distrustful of the careerists in OMB and willingly dependent upon a nonstatutory, noninstitutional NPR team dispensing management advice, decided to put the few remaining persons on the management side of OMB out of their misery. Under the guise of an OMB reorganization ("OMB 2000 Review"), they simply eliminated most of the positions and integrated them into the budget side of the agency.[27] Five Resource Management Offices (RMOs) structured along budgetary, functional lines were put in charge of comprehensive management issues. Insofar as designated management functions remain in OMB, they are located in much reduced statutory elements of the agencies, such as the Office of Federal Procurement Policy.

The integration (critics argue a better term would be "subordination")[28] of management functions and personnel within the larger budgetary side of the agency is permanent and represents recognition that a "reinvented government" is one where general management laws are no longer viewed as of primary importance in holding the executive branch accountable to the president and through the president, to Congress. The supporters of the NPR approach to management accept the diminishing role of the president in management as part of their concept of competitive, agency-specific management and the reorganization of many agencies (e.g., Patent and Trademark Office) into semiautonomous "Performance Based Organizations."

There is, however, another view of this trend toward downgrading OMB's capacity to supervise the management of the executive branch. The retreat of the president and the OMB from their management responsibilities has been responsible for many of the problems and scandals that have plagued the executive branch for the past thirty years. Reporting in 1990 on the HUD debacle, a House subcommittee concluded: "Given the mismanagement and abuse of certain HUD programs during the 1980s, it is important to inquire why OMB oversight of HUD management failed to uncover or prevent it. The answer has been evident since OMB's creation in 1970. OMB's management efforts have been largely unable to compete for resources or attention with the high-priority budget process, and have therefore been minimal. Even when certain management oversight strategies have received attention and resources from OMB, their effects have been adversely influenced by the short-term budget mindset and highly politicized nature of that organization."[29]

There is a subtle but powerful element of politics at play when discussing the decline of the institutional presidency, OMB, and government-wide management standards. Management in the executive branch is increasingly viewed as an exercise in exceptionalism where agencies are permitted to "go their own way" in pursuit of an entrepreneurial objective unencumbered by adherence to specified general management laws. In circumstances where exceptional politics prevails, interest groups and agency leadership have the advantage in agency policy making and management.

The loss of central management capacity and accountability is typified by the recent case of the Federal Aviation Administration (FAA). On April 1, 1996, the FAA was exempted by law from provisions of Title 5 which apply to personnel management except for specific provisions of other laws (e.g., Section 2301(b), relating to whistle-blower protection) and is required to create its own personnel and compensation systems. Similarly, most of the provisions of federal acquisition law (e.g., Federal Acquisition Streamlining Act; 108 Stat. 3242) are no longer applicable to the FAA. While this may at first blush be viewed as conferring flexibility on the FAA, it should also be recognized that in the absence of general management law standards, the agency must create its own "general management laws" and defend them in suits. Affected parties are now much more likely to look to friendly congressional committees to legislate redress, on a case-by-case basis, for policies and practices they find unacceptable. It is an invitation for congressional micromanagement. What recent experience suggests is that when management shifts to agreements between departmental and agency heads on the one hand, and congressional committees, and increasingly this means appropriations subcommittees as was the case with the FAA, the president and OMB risk becoming nonplayers.

Congress as Co-Manager

Congressional involvement in the detailed direction of executive management is not aberrational behavior nor is it part of some larger political strategy employed by an "imperialistic" Congress. Because of Congress's immense Constitutional and legislative powers to organize and control the orientation, even the very existence of every aspect of executive branch management, Congress has always had the potential—frequently realized in contemporary practice—to be a veritable co-manager of policy and program administration.

Robert S. Gilmour and Alexis Halley, after reviewing ten case studies of administrative management issues, concluded:

> [T]he relationship between Congress and the executive branch, leading to the overall conclusion that the Congress observed in these cases was not only an active and authoritative overseer but also a thoroughly involved participant—a co-manager—with (or sometimes in spite of) the executive in directing the details of policy implementation and program execution. The cases collectively suggest that the term *congressional co-management* of policy implementation and program execution characterizes the transition from a congressional reliance on post-audit oversight of executive branch performance to pre-audit congressional program controls and direct congressional participation with the executive branch in the full scope of policy and program development and implementation. . . . The cases also suggest that congressional co-management is as much a result of actions in the executive branch as it is a result of actions in the legislative branch.[30]

Recent presidents have tended not to accept or appreciate the legitimate congressional role in executive management and have followed strategies to circumvent Congress, which, for the most part, have resulted in countermeasures by Congress to protect their prerogatives and limit presidential discretion. In the absence of a staff agency to remind presidents of their institutional interests, presidents are prone to listen to political aides and indulge in unwise legal confrontations with Congress.

President Clinton is enamored of the administrative presidency strategy and tweaks the congressional nose whenever possible.[31] For instance, as this is written, the president and the Justice Department have determined to employ an extraordinarily narrow interpretation of the Vacancies Act[32] as a means to avoid requiring one of their officers to be subject to Senate confirmation. The merits of the controversy are not of interest here. What is worth noting from our perspective is that the principle and tactics employed by the White House to obtain its short-term objective are likely to result in further weakening of the institutional presidency. Congress may well feel compelled to react to protect its own institutional interests against what it views as presidential encroachment. The Vacancies Act will likely be studied anew by Congress and there is reasonable probability that further restrictions will be placed in the law to prevent a reoccurrence of the situation currently occupying the leadership.[33] A review of confrontations over the years suggests that the administrative presidency strategy has not strengthened the presidency, rather, on balance, it has served to weaken the institution.

The current "reinventing government" exercise, according to critics, is another misguided attempt by the political presidency to limit congressional involvement in executive management. Don Kettl understands the political objectives of the NPR when he states: "First, 'reinventing government' seeks the transfer of power from the legislative to the executive branch. . . . Almost all of what the NPR recommends, in fact, requires that Congress give up power."[34] The NPR, based as it is on a questionable conceptual understanding of the theory and practice of executive branch management,[35] will produce many unanticipated and undesired consequences including a further contribution to the erosion of the president's management authority and capacity.

Congressional response to presidential confrontations and evidence of executive branch mismanagement has not been to assign more discretion to the president and agency heads to clean up their own houses, quite the reverse. Congress has followed a three-part strategy; more committee investigations of agency management; increased use of the legislative veto, and the passage of more supervisory management laws. This public law strategy of passing general management laws that collectively impose additional requirements upon executive managers thereby decreasing their discretion, are reflective of presidential weakness, not strength. For the most part, presidents have become reactive agents to, rather than initiators of, management laws.

Presidents would be well advised to recognize that their institutional interests are important and have much in common with the institutional interests of Congress. Their shared interests as co-managers of the executive branch are real and continuing. Presidents, in following the confrontational tactics of the administrative presidency strategy, have unintentionally weakened their office and have lost much of their capacity to frame the larger management issues. It may be a truism, but it is one that has been largely forgotten, that the nation's ability to meet the political, economic, and technological challenges of the next century depends in no small measure upon the quality of the government we have, and this challenge is especially the province of the president. Yet, as we have seen, presidents have not developed the institutional capacity to address these challenges, relying instead on ad hoc political solutions. In institutional terms, it is difficult to be a good partner with Congress if there is no single staff agency able to speak for the president and executive agencies on management.

General Management Acts: Key to Accountable Management

The Constitution provides in Article II that "the executive Power shall be vested in a President. . . ." and that "he shall take Care that the Laws be faithfully executed. . . ." It is neither possible nor desirable for the president to be involved in all executive actions taken in his name, but it is possible, through proper delegation, diligent execution of general management laws, and strong central management agencies to ensure that the president's institutional interests in an integrated executive branch are protected.[36]

General management laws are intended to provide appropriate uniformity and standardization for government organizations and processes. Uniformity and standardization by themselves, however, are not the objective of general management laws. Such an objective would stultify government as "one size does not fit all." What these laws do reflect, therefore, are the conceptual and legal agreements between the branches respecting the management of the executive branch. In functional terms, general management laws are statements of presumption guiding governmental behavior; that is, certain doctrinal provisions reflected in legal language stand until and unless an exemption is permitted. Exemptions may be assigned by a general statute to a category of agency or they may be present in provisions of the agency's enabling statute.

General management laws come in various guises and may be dramatic in their coverage and impact, as is the case with the Administrative Procedure Act, Budget and Accounting, Paperwork Reduction, and Freedom of Information Acts, or they may be of relatively low visibility (although visibility is not necessarily equatable with importance), such as the Federal Advisory Committee Act, Federal Tort Claims Act, and the Anti-Deficiency Act. In recent years a number of additional general management laws, (e.g., Federal Managers Financial Integrity Act of 1984 and the Government Performance and Results Act of 1993), have been enacted, each supported and justified on its own definition of a problem, but often with what some observers believe to be little consideration of its probable impact upon other related general management laws.

Presidents must remember, if not discover anew, that their key tool for managing the executive branch, broadly understood, is found in the general management laws and their subordinate regulations and executive orders. Considered collectively, these laws permit a politics of general management with the burden of proof for exceptions resting on the supplicants. The alternative, increasingly the case in practice, is a politics of exceptional management where each agency's management structures and processes are determined in its enabling legislation, as amended, or by agreement with their oversight committee in Congress. Agency-specific politics tends to place the president at a disadvantage in meeting his executive responsibilities. Furthermore, the growth in the number of agencies and programs not within the executive branch or under the authority of the central management agencies has created a burgeoning "quasi government" effectively outside accountability to the president or anyone else.[37]

In the arena of exceptional politics, where the management of each agency tends to be viewed *sui generis* and is the sum of exceptional circumstances, interest groups and agency leadership have been pursuing their own agendas for policy making and administration. The logical end result of an executive branch functioning under a culture of exceptional politics and administration is an executive branch that is disaggregated and largely unaccountable to both the Congress and the president, especially the latter, for its activities. We are closer to this logical end of exceptional politics than is generally appreciated even by otherwise sophisticated observers of the governmental scene.

The presidential retreat from hands-on managerial responsibilities for the executive branch, coupled with neglect for maintaining the currency and integrity of general management laws, and topped off with the wholesale abandonment of the professional corps of government managers are the ingredients of an unintended major shift of political power away from the institutional presidency and toward Congress, departments and agencies, and private organizations.

Proposed Office of Federal Management

The presidency as an institution has and retains its capacity to protect its interests on political matters. This is not the case, however, with respect to matters of executive management. The contemporary presidency has been steadily losing its capacity to lead the executive branch on a day-to-day basis, in large measure because of the absence of an institutional presence to project and protect the president's interests in government operations. It is not enough to rely on the budget process with its short-term deadlines and spending biases. Nor can ad-hoc groups tied to some unit within the Executive Office (e.g., National Performance Review; President's Management Council) substitute for permanent management leadership, properly defined and understood. The challenge is how to equip the president with institutional support for his managerial responsibilities. One proposal receiving serious consideration is that Congress should pass, hopefully with the president's approval, legislation to reorganize the current OMB into two separate and equal agencies, an Office of Federal Budget (OFB) and an Office of Federal Management (OFM).

The intended purpose of the 1970 reorganization resulting in the Office of Management and Budget was to upgrade the management function of the agency to equal status with the budgetary function. After twenty-eight years, it is time to judge this experiment a failure. The problem has not been one of negative intentions or incompetence but rather of two incompatible missions being thrust upon one agency. What we have today is an institutional crisis that requires an institutional response.

The proposal to establish a separate Office of Federal Management in the President's Executive Office has a history. The first time it was proposed and discussed was in a National Academy of Public Administration (NAPA) report in 1983,[38] to be followed by other reports[39] and scholarly writings.[40] Several bills to this effect have been introduced, notably one by Representative Leon Panetta, chairman of the Budget Committee, in 1991. In introducing his bill, Panetta stated: "The truth is that budget priorities will always tend to displace management priorities. For one thing, their timetables are at odds. Budgetary timetables of necessity tend to be rigid, short-term, and almost exclusively bottom-line oriented. Management priorities, on the other hand, tend to be flexible, long-term with success generally measured in non-financial terms. Both budget and management have suffered from this forced marriage."[41]

The Panetta bill, like an earlier Senate bill introduced by Senator William Roth, chairman of the Governmental Affairs Committee, did not have much support. Nonetheless, writing in favor of the proposal continued to appear. Representative Stephen Horn, chairman of the Subcommittee on Government Management, Information, and Technology, concluded after extensive hearings in 1995:

> The capacity of the president as the chief executive officer of the Federal Government and its principal manager has been diminished over several Administrations. The Executive Office of the president has abrogated its responsibilities to oversee and improve the Government's management structure.
>
> The capacity available to the president in the Office of Management and Budget has steadily declined and now barely exists, despite a competent Director of OMB and a Deputy Director for Management, whose talents in this area are underutilized. Federal management organization, oversight authority, and general influence have been consistently overridden by recurring budget crises and budget cycle demands, despite conscientious intentions to give "Budget" and "Management" equal voice within OMB. . . .
>
> Management of the Federal Government should be a presidential priority. . . . To enhance the President's management capability, Congress should

establish in the Executive Office of the President a top-level management and organization oversight office (Office of Management) headed by an administrator who has direct access to the President.[42]

The absence in the Executive Office of an agency with institutional memory is costly, not only in management terms, but political terms as well. After making the case that the president's institutional interests require attention, Paul Light summarized the current debate over the proposed OFM:

> Some, once including this author, believe the answer [to the institutional decline of OMB] is in rebuilding the old Division of Administrative Management, the notion being that the budget is the crucial lever for enforcing whatever management reforms a President might pursue. Far better to leave the M in OMB than to have it ignored entirely. Others, including senior members of the National Academy of Public Administration (NAPA) have argued for the creation of an entirely new Office of Federal Management (OFM), the argument being that budget will always crowd out management. Far better to have the M ignored on its own than completely submerged by budget. After waiting for three decades for OMB to begin the rebuilding, it appears that advocates of a separate office operating elsewhere in the Executive Office of the President have the winning argument.[43]

Organization and staffing of agencies should be reflective and supportive of their mission. In the case of the proposed OFM, a director would be appointed by the president, subject to confirmation by the Senate, with the remaining key officials selected principally from the senior career service. The OFM would have a regular support staff for the director plus a number of operating offices, each headed by career or nonpolitical officers. These offices would be delegated responsibilities by the director for performing functions assigned OFM by law, a listing that is impressive by any standard.[44] These offices, however, would not be established separately by law as is now the case with the Office of Procurement Policy, the Office of Information and Regulatory Affairs, and the Office of Federal Financial Management. The establishment by law of subunits within an agency weakens the authority of the agency head to the degree that authority is assigned directly to a subordinate of the agency head.[45]

It is appropriate for Congress, in agreement with the president, to stipulate the functions of the OFM, the general structure of the agency, and the types of authorities to reside in the agency head. Beyond this point, however, it is probably wise to leave the president discretion to organize the OFM as he deems appropriate for the mission at hand. Although this is not the forum for providing details on an "ideal" OFM structure, several suggestions are worth mentioning.

Among the operating units to be considered for an OFM would be the offices of organizational management and design; legislative clearance; financial management systems; federal procurement policy; regulatory affairs; federal personnel policy; program design and performance evaluation; and management development. The heads of these eight offices (and there could be more or less than this number) would report to the director of OFM. The purpose would be to have a horizontal organizational structure without the layering of political associate directors. A review of current and possible future coordinating groups (e.g., Financial Officers Councils) would be required with the director's being responsible to ensure that their actions are in accord with the president's wishes and programs and that the councils themselves would have institutional support. The approximate number of career civil service personnel necessary to staff the several OFM offices would be 350, many of whom would be transferred from the present OMB.

The emphasis and incentive structure of the OFM would be very different from that present in the current OMB. Management principles and practices would not be viewed as simply an extension of budgetary priorities and procedures. Prospective management seeks to build both the capacity and accountability of agency management to implement the laws. The OFM, representing the president, would speak with one voice to Congress on the broad management issues impacting upon the capabilities of all agencies of government. Thus, if provisions of the Freedom of Information Act are proving to be unreasonably burdensome on agency heads, the latter need not go to Congress seeking exemption from the unwanted provisions but would have to go to OFM where the issue would be reviewed with an executive-branch perspective.

Many of the most vexing governmental management problems today are the result of poor organizational and program design. Thinking in a thoughtful manner about the proper and achievable objectives for agencies is an all too rare activity today. Many hundreds of millions of dollars are spent annually on the offices of inspectors general, internal and external audits, and congressional hearings and investigations to ferret out alleged misdeeds. Yet, very often little or nothing is invested in organizational design and management incentives at the outset of an agency or program. The proposal for an OFM is a reflection of what its supporters believe is the failure of the OMB experience. The problem is not one of intentions or incompetence but one of two incompatible missions being forced upon one agency.

Conclusion

The contemporary president, just as much as George Washington, is chief manager of the executive branch and cannot escape judgment regarding that stewardship. His choice is not whether to manage; but how to manage. Whether by choice or neglect, recent presidents have been ineffective managers, and the negative results have been cumulative. Presidents must recognize anew the distinctive character of their Constitutional responsibilities to insure the laws are faithfully executed.

The foremost tools by which a president can manage and hold accountable the world's most complex social system is through high quality, conceptually sound general management laws and their administration by a properly designed Office of Federal Management (OFM) reporting directly to the president. If the general management laws are permitted to proliferate and become burdensome to agency heads or if those laws are subject to detailed amendments altering their character, the quality of public administration will suffer. The establishment of a separate OFM is a first step toward restoring the president's institutional capacity to manage executive-branch operations. It is a necessary, but not sufficient component of a revitalized institutional presidency.

To build a competent government requires a long-term commitment, one lasting over several presidencies and one transcending partisanship and political philosophy. Such a commitment can be met only with strong institutional support, the kind of support that will be possible with an OFM. There is nothing romantic about the desire for competent government. Competent government is simply a necessity if the United States is to retain its pre-eminent status in the twenty-first century.

NOTES

1. Cornelius M. Kerwin, "Public Law and Public Management: A Conceptual Framework," in Phillip Cooper and Chester A. Newland, eds., *Handbook of Public Law and Administration* (San Francisco: Jossey-Bass, 1997), pp. 26–40.
2. U.S. President's Committee on Administrative Management, *Report with Special Studies* (Washington, D.C.: Government Printing Office, 1937). Richard Polenberg, *Reorganizing Roosevelt's Government: The Controversy Over Executive Reorganization, 1936–1939* (Cambridge, Mass.: Harvard University Press, 1966).
3. U.S. Commission on Organization of the Executive Branch of the Government, *Hoover Commission Report* (New York: Macmillan Co., 1949). Ronald C. Moe, *The Hoover Commissions Revisited* (Boulder, Colo.: Westview Press, 1982).
4. Peri Arnold, *Making the Managerial Presidency, 1905–1980* (Princeton: Princeton University Press, 1986), chapter 9. For an overview of these commissions and other "reform" efforts since World War II, see: Paul Light, *The Tides of Reform: Making*

    Government Work, 1945–1995 (New Haven, Conn.: Yale University Press, 1997); Harold Seidman, *Politics, Position and Power: The Dynamics of Federal Organization,* 5th ed. (New York: Oxford University Press, 1997); James Pfiffner, *The American Tradition of Administrative Reform,* Working Paper No. 97:2 (Fairfax, Va.: George Mason University, 1997).

5. Herbert Emmerich, *Federal Organization and Administrative Management* (University: University of Alabama Press, 1971), pp. 174–76.

6. Since 1977, there have been three additional comprehensive reorganization efforts; President Carter's Reorganization Project, the Grace Commission under President Reagan, and the National Performance Review under President Clinton. These reorganization efforts, while differing in managerial theories and operating styles, shared a common objective in seeking to de-construct the state and generally weaken the president's managerial role. Peri Arnold concludes that executive reorganization is "no longer focused on the long-term project of developing executive governance, reform gains a populist accent and becomes a means through which 'outsider' Presidents manage hostility to government." "Reform's Changing Role," *Public Administration Review* 55 (Sept./Oct., 1995): 407.

7. Richard Neustadt, *Presidential Power: The Politics of Leadership* (New York: John Wiley and Sons, 1960), p. 6.

8. Ibid., p. 10.

9. Ibid., p. 6.

10. Ibid., p. 126.

11. Ibid., p. 165. There has been in recent years the emergence of a "revisionist" literature on the presidency of Dwight Eisenhower which disputes the Neustadtian view of the "political amateur." The general theme that emerges from this revisionist literature is that Eisenhower was much more involved in making political decisions than was perceived at the time by the press at the time or by Neustadt. Far from an amateur, Eisenhower was apparently an extremely shrewd politician who exercised power with a "hidden hand." See especially: Fred I. Greenstein, *The Hidden-Hand Presidency: Eisenhower as Leader* (New York: Basic Books, 1982).

12. James MacGregor Burns, *The Deadlock of Democracy: Four-Party Politics in America* (Englewood Cliffs, N.J.: Prentice-Hall, 1964), pp. 39–40.

13. Samuel P. Huntington, "Congressional Responses to the Twentieth Century," in David B. Truman, ed., *Congress and America's Future* (Englewood Cliffs, N.J.: Prentice-Hall, 1962), pp. 29–30. For a critique of Huntington's thesis, see Ronald C. Moe and Steven C. Teel, "Congress as Policy-Maker: A Necessary Reappraisal," *Political Science Quarterly* 85 (Sept., 1970): 443–70.

14. U.S. Executive Office of the President, *Papers Relating to the President's Reorganization Program* (Washington, D.C.: GPO, 1971). U.S. Congress, House, Committee on Government Operations, *Executive Reorganization: A Summary Analysis,* H. Rept. 922, 92d Cong., 2d sess. (Washington, D.C.: GPO, 1972).

15. Richard Nathan, *The Administrative Presidency* (New York: John Wiley and Sons, 1983), p. 7.

16. Reorganization Plan No. 2 of 1970 (5 U.S.C. App.).

17. Louis Fisher, "The Legislative Veto: Invalidated, It Survives," *Law and Contemporary Problems* 56 (Autumn, 1993): 273–92.

18. Ronald C. Moe, "Senate Confirmation of Executive Appointments: The Nixon Era," ed. Harvey C. Mansfield, Sr., *Proceedings* of the Academy of Political Science 32 (1975): 141–52.

19. The Volcker Commission concluded: "[T]he growth in recent years in the number of presidential appointees, whether those subject to Senate confirmation, non-career senior executives, or personal and confidential assistants, should be curtailed. Although a reduction in the total number of presidential appointees must be based on a position-by-position assessment, the Commission is confident that a substantial cut is possible, and believes a cut from the current 3,000 to no more than 2,000 is a reasonable target. . . . The mere size of the political turnover almost guarantees management gaps and discontinuities, while the best of the career professionals will leave government if they do not have challenging opportunities at the sub-cabinet level." National Commission on the Public Service, *Leadership for America: Rebuilding the Public Service* (Washington, D.C.: National Commission on the Public Service, 1989), p. 7.

20. Paul Light, *Thickening Government: Federal Hierarchy and the Diffusion of Accountability* (Washington, D.C.: The Brookings Institution, 1995), pp. 181–82.

21. Reorganization Plan No. 2 of 1970.

22. Hugh Heclo, "OMB and the Presidency," *The Public Interest* 38 (Winter, 1975): 80–98.

23. Terry M. Moe, "The Politicized Presidency," in this volume.

24. Charles A. Bowsher, Comptroller General of the United States, "The Emerging Crisis: The Disinvestment of Government," Webb Lecture, National Academy of Public Administration, Dec. 2, 1988. U.S. Comptroller General, *Managing the Government: Revised Approach Could Improve OMB's Effectiveness* (GAO Management Review) GAO/GGD-89-65. (Washington, D.C.: GAO, 1989).

25. U.S. Executive Office of the President, National Performance Review, *From Red Tape to Results: Creating Government That Works Better and Costs Less* (Washington, D.C.: GPO, 1993).

26. Gerald Riso, "The New OMB: In Search of a Management Role," *Government Executive* 21 (Apr., 1989): 59.

27. U.S. Office of Management and Budget, *Making OMB More Effective in Serving the Presidency: Changes in OMB as a Result of OMB 2000 Review.* OMB Memorandum No. 94-16. (Washington, D.C.: OMB, Mar. 1, 1994).

28. Alan Dean, Dwight Ink, and Harold Seidman, "OMB's 'M' Fading Away," *Government Executive* 25 (June, 1994): 62–64.

29. U.S. Congress, Senate, Committee on Banking, Housing and Urban Affairs, HUD/MOD Rehab Investigation Subcommittee, *Final Report and Recommendations,* Committee print 124, 101st Cong., 2d sess. (Washington, D.C.: GPO, 1990), p. 194.

30. Robert S. Gilmour and Alexis Halley, eds., *Who Makes Public Policy? The Struggle for Control Between Congress and the Executive* (Chatham, N.J.: Chatham House Publishers, 1994), p. 335.

31. Jennifer A. Utter and Phillip J. Cooper, "Executive Direct Administration: The Importance to Public Administration of Executive Orders and Proclamations," in *Handbook of Public Law and Administration* (San Francisco: Jossey-Bass, 1997). pp. 189–210.

32. 5 U.S.C. 3345–3349 (1994).

33. U.S. Library of Congress, Congressional Research Service, "Validity of Designation of Bill Lann Lee as Acting Assistant Attorney General for Civil Rights," by Morton Rosenberg, CRS Memorandum, Jan. 14, 1998.

34. Donald Kettl, "Beyond the Rhetoric of Reinvention: Driving Themes of the Clinton Administration's Management Reforms," *Governance* 7 (July, 1994): 309.

35. Ronald C. Moe and Robert S. Gilmour, "Rediscovering Principles of Public Administration: The Neglected Foundation of Public Law, *Public Administration Review* 55 (Mar./Apr., 1995): 135–46.

36. U.S. Library of Congress, Congressional Research Service, *General Management Laws: A Selective Compendium*, Ronald C. Moe, ed., CRS Report 97-613G (Washington, D.C.: CRS, 1997). U.S. Congress, Senate, Committee on Governmental Affairs, *Office of Management and Budget: Evolving Roles and Future Issues*, prepared by the Congressional Research Service, S. Print 99-134, 99th Cong., 2d sess. (Washington, D.C.: GPO, 1986).

37. Harold Seidman, "The Quasi World of the Federal Government," *The Brookings Review* 6 (Summer, 1988): 23–27.

38. National Academy of Public Administration, *Revitalizing Federal Management: Managers and Their Overburdened Systems* (Washington, D.C.: National Academy of Public Administration, 1983), pp. 11–13.

39. U.S. Congress, House, Committee on the Budget, *Management Reform: A Top Priority for the Federal Executive Branch*, Committee print, CP-4, 102d Cong., 1st sess. (Washington, D.C.: GPO, 1991). National Academy of Public Administration, *Strengthening Presidential Leadership by Establishing an Office of Federal Management* (Washington, D.C.: National Academy of Public Administration, 1988).

40. Ronald C. Moe, "The HUD Scandal and the Case for an Office of Federal Management," *Public Administration Review* 51 (July/Aug., 1991): 298–307.

41. Representative Leon Panetta, floor statement upon introducing the Office of Federal Management Act of 1991, (H.R. 2750), *Congressional Record*, daily edition, June 25, 1991, p. H5039.

   Panetta, upon his appointment as director of OMB, dramatically reversed himself by opposing the establishment of an OFM and favoring the integration of the remaining managers into the budget side of the agency. Panetta stated: "Critics of these recommendations may say the effort to 'integrate' management and budget will end in merely bigger budget divisions, whose management responsibilities will be driven out by daily fire-fighting on budget issues. . . . We believe this criticism is based on a false premise that 'management and budget' issues can be thought of separately." Quoted in "Executive Memo: OMB Management Merger," *Government Executive* 26 (Apr., 1994): 8.

42. U.S. Congress, House, Committee on Government Reform and Oversight, *Making Government Work: Fulfilling the Mandate for Change*, H. Rept. 104–435, 104th Cong., 1st sess. (Washington, D.C.: GPO, 1995), pp. 5, 8. See also: U.S. Congress, House, Subcommittee on Government Management, Information, and Technology, *Federal Budget Process Reform*, Hearings, 104th Cong., 2d sess. (Washington, D.C.: GPO, 1997), pp. 493–531.

43. Light, *Tides of Reform*, p. 228. National Academy of Public Administration, *Two Presidents: The Bureau of the Budget and Division of Administrative Management, 1939–1952*. Occasional paper by Charles F. Bingman (Washington, D.C.: NAPA, 1992).

44. U.S. Congress, Senate, Committee on Governmental Affairs, *Office of Management and Budget: Evolving Roles and Future Issues*, prepared by the Congressional Research Service, S. Print 99-134, 99th Cong., 2d sess. (Washington, D.C.: GPO, 1986), pp. 395–675.

45. The Hoover Commission, in 1949, addressed the question of assigning legal authority to subordinates within departments and agencies. "Under the President, the heads of departments must hold full responsibility for the conduct of their departments. There must be a clear line of authority reaching down through every step of the organization and no subordinate should have authority independent from that of his superior." U.S. Commission on the Organization of the Executive Branch of the Government, *Hoover Commission Report* (New York: McGraw-Hill, 1949), p. 24.

Chapter 16

Director or Facilitator?

Presidential Policy Control of Congress

GEORGE C. EDWARDS III

The notion of the dominant president who moves the country (including Congress) through strong and effective leadership has deep roots in our political culture. Those chief executives whom Americans revere, such as Washington, Jefferson, Jackson, Lincoln, Wilson, and both Roosevelts, have taken on mythic proportions as leaders.

Yet we also know that the government of the United States is not a fertile field for the exercise of presidential leadership. Nowhere is this more clear than in dealing with Congress. Every president bears scars from battles with the legislature. All presidents find that their proposals often fail to pass and that legislators champion initiatives to which presidents are opposed.

The peculiar merging of powers between the two institutions established by the Constitution prevents either from acting unilaterally on most important matters. Moreover, the differences in the constituencies, internal structures, time perspectives, and decision-making procedures of the two branches guarantees that they will often view issues and policy proposals differently.[1]

Nevertheless, the perception of presidential policy control persists. Even though we are frequently disillusioned with the performance of presidents, and even though we recognize that stalemate is common in our political system, we eagerly accept what appears to be effective presidential leadership (as in the case of Ronald Reagan) as evidence on which to renew our faith in the potential of the presidency. After all, if presidential leadership "works" some of the time, why not all of the time?

This essay examines the question of presidential domination of Congress. Because of both its proximity and of the perception of Ronald Reagan as a strong and effective leader, we focus on the Reagan administration, especially its banner year of 1981, to illustrate some of the dimensions of presidential leadership of Congress. We will dig beneath the veneer of conventional wisdom and take a careful look at why President Reagan achieved the success he enjoyed.

To guide our analysis, we can contrast two perspectives of presidential leadership by asking a series of related questions. Was the president the director of change? Through his leadership did he create opportunities to move in new directions, leading others where they otherwise would not go? Or was his role less heroic? Was he primarily a facilitator of change? Did he exploit opportunities to help others go where they wanted to go anyway, reflecting and perhaps intensifying widely held views and using his resources to achieve his constituency's aspirations?

Directors create constituencies to follow their lead, while facilitators endow their constituencies' views with shape and purpose by interpreting those views and translating them into legislation. The director restructures the contours of the political landscape to pave the way for change, while the facilitator exploits opportunities presented by a favorable configuration of political forces.

We have, then, two different conceptions of leadership. The director, who moves mountains and influences many independent actors, has the more formidable task. The director establishes the legislative agenda and persuades an otherwise reluctant Congress to support that agenda. The facilitator, in contrast, works at the margins, influencing a few critical actors and taking advantage of the opportunities for change already present in the environment. In both cases the president exercises leadership. Yet the scale of the leadership is clearly different. The range and scope of the director's influence is broad while that of the facilitator is more narrow.

The director and the facilitator types are not meant to be representations of a division in the literature of the presidency. Instead, they represent different emphases that writing on the presidency reflects, sometimes explicitly, but often implicitly. Moreover, the two perspectives are not neat categories. Our goal is neither to classify presidents nor to resolve an academic dispute. Instead, we employ these types to increase our understanding of presidential leadership by exploring its possibilities.

Party Leadership

Decentralization characterizes the American political system, creating centrifugal forces that afflict the relationship between the president and Congress. The White House requires means of countering the natural tendencies of the executive and legislative branches toward conflict. The only institution that has the potential to elicit cooperation between both ends of Pennsylvania Avenue on a systematic basis is the political party.

Thus, leading their party in Congress is inevitably one of the most important tasks of chief executives. No matter what other resources presidents may have at their disposal, they remain highly dependent on their party to move their legislative programs. Representatives and senators of the president's party almost always form the nucleus of coalitions supporting presidential proposals.

If presidents are to be directors of change, party leadership is likely to occupy a prominent place in their overall strategy, and senators and representatives must respond reliably to presidential calls for support. If party leadership is less dependable, if partisans in Congress are less amenable to presidential leadership, then the chief executive is likely to be restricted to the more modest facilitator role.

In 1981 President Reagan won several crucial votes in Congress on his taxing and spending proposals. He was immediately credited with extraordinary patty leadership, because nearly 100 percent of the Republicans in Congress supported his programs. If we examine voting on budget resolutions under Democrat Jimmy Carter, however, we find nearly the same degree of Republican Party unity in the House.[2] Thus, we should not necessarily ascribe Reagan's success to party leadership. Republican members of the House had been voting a conservative line well before Ronald Reagan came to Washington.

The most fundamental reason for the extremely high cohesion among Republicans in 1981 was that the president picked as his first priority the issue on which there was already a strong consensus among the overwhelming majority of Republicans in both Congress and the public. Reagan's choice of tax reform as his first priority in 1985, however, did not mesh with the priorities and interests of congressional Republicans. Thus, he found the going much tougher, especially in the House.

In addition, the shift in the status of Republican Party and committee leaders in the Senate in 1981 was one very likely to breed party unity. They were delighted (if not astonished) to be wielding majority power and eager to follow their party leader in the White House. This was especially true of the extraordinarily large number of junior Republican senators, but all were anxious to show that they could govern.

Power was new to Republicans in 1981, not having had a majority in either house since 1953–54. No Republican senator had ever served in a Republican Senate majority. Even before Reagan took office, the renewed party spirit of the Republicans was a source of commentary by Washington insiders. There were many freshman and sophomore members of Congress who were anxious to make their mark on policy. They were also aware that there was power in unity; many felt Reagan's policy success was the key to holding the Senate. This enthusiasm was infectious and spread to senior Republican senators.[3]

Yet sharing the burdens of governing is not a long-term adhesive. By 1983 Republican senators were terming their nearly unanimous support for President Reagan's taxing and spending proposals an "aberration," unlikely to be repeated during the remainder of his tenure in office. Senator Slade Gorton described the high levels of support as resulting from unique circumstances: a "new President with a big victory and strong views, a large number of new senators and a Republican majority for the first time since 1954." Senator Rudy Boschwitz added, "In the first two years, there was a great sense we had to govern. Now we've started to go beyond that."[4] At the end of 1984 Senate Finance Committee Chairman Robert Dole contrasted the beginning and end of Reagan's first term. At the start, "The President was fresh. The Republican Senate was fresh. We were all finally committee chairmen and subcommittee chairmen. We knew we had to stick together. Now the bloom is gone."[5]

All presidents experience substantial slippage in party cohesion in Congress. Members of the president's party often oppose him. Jimmy Carter put this dramatically when he recalled that, "I learned the hard way that there was no party loyalty or discipline when a complicated or controversial issue was at stake—none."[6]

The primary obstacle to party cohesion in support of the president is the lack of consensus among party members on policies. This diversity of views often reflects the diversity of constituencies represented by party members. Although Democratic chief executives are plagued with party divisions, Republican presidents often lack stable coalitions as well. Even though Ronald Reagan received nearly unanimous support from his party in Congress on his 1981 proposals to reduce taxes and domestic policy expenditures, when he proposed, in 1982, legislation to increase taxes, to restrict abortions and forced busing for integration, and to allow school prayer, things were different. Some Republicans were in the forefront of the opposition to these policies.

Party leadership, then, is useful for presidents. It often provides them an additional increment of support for their policies in Congress. Yet party leadership is unlikely to provide the basis for the direction of major change. It is a resource operating at the margins of coalition building. Ronald Reagan exercised effective leadership in leading his party early in his term. Yet the conditions that underlay his success were not of his making and could not be sustained or reproduced under different conditions. He was a facilitator who exercised party leadership to exploit an opportunity presented by other factors rather than a director who bent his fellow partisans to his will.

The Two Presidencies

The concept of the "two presidencies," one for foreign policy and one for domestic policy, is well established in the literature of political science. The basic argument is that presidents are much more likely to achieve their goals in the former area. Yet insofar as it applies to executive-legislative relationships, there is less to the concept of the two presidencies than meets the eye.

Although the two presidencies did flourish under President Eisenhower, the additional support for foreign policy that is supposed to characterize the two-presidencies concept has been modest since the 1960s and no longer reliably appears. Moreover, the locus of additional congressional support for foreign policy has always been the opposition party. The president's party in Congress has never provided him with an additional increment of support for his foreign policy proposals.[7]

Thus party leadership has not proven to be a reliable source of influence even in foreign affairs. Moreover, and contrary to conventional wisdom, the source of the additional support Eisenhower received from the opposition party on foreign policy was not congressional bipartisanship or deference in foreign affairs, nor was it the relative advantages of the president in foreign-policy making. Instead, the two presidencies was a natural outgrowth of a president proposing foreign policies, but not domestic policies, that appealed to a substantial segment of the opposition party. Similarly, we cannot attribute the decline of the two presidencies to the trauma of Vietnam. Simply stated, when the appeal of a president's foreign policies to the opposition diminished, so did the two presidencies. The point is that the president did not bend Congress to his will, but instead appealed to independent power holders with the substance of policies.

The Reagan administration was no exception to the general experience of recent presidents in foreign policy. His highest priority "positive" policy was a defense buildup. Although he did very well in obtaining large increases in the defense budget in his first two years in office, he suffered through his entire second term without obtaining any real increase in defense expenditures. Moreover, for most of his tenure President Reagan found Congress challenging him on all fronts, including aid to the contras in Nicaragua, development of the Strategic Defense Initiative, interpretation of the 1972 ABM treaty, compliance with the unratified Salt II treaty, deployment of the MX Missile, compliance with the War Powers Resolution, escorting reflagged tankers in the Persian Gulf, the sale of arms to Iran and the subsequent diversion of funds to the contras, negotiation of an INF treaty, development and testing of antisatellite weapons, and continuation of nuclear testing.

Leading the Public

Without question, public support is a primary resource for presidential leadership of Congress. Richard Neustadt argues, "While national party organizations fall away, while congressional party discipline relaxes, while interest groups proliferate and issue networks rise, a President who wishes to compete for leadership in framing policy and shaping coalitions has to make the most he can out of his popular connection."[8]

There are several dimensions to the popular connection, including obtaining the public's approval for the president's job performance, influencing public attitudes on policy, establishing the premises of debate on issues, and mobilizing the public to actively support the White House. In each case presidents go to extraordinary lengths to cultivate the populace, but Americans are not easily moved.

Ronald Reagan began his tenure rather low in the polls at fifty-one percent approval, lower than any modern president. His fortunes quickly changed, however. Within minutes of his taking office, the American hostages were released by their Iranian captors. Thus the new president benefited from his predecessor's negotiations and basked in the upsurge of emotion that greeted the hostages' return. Public morale received another boost from the success of the *Columbia* space shuttle. Finally, although it seems perverse to argue that an assassination attempt can be to the president's advantage, Reagan's approval ratings shot up eight percentage points after the attempt on his life on March 30, 1981.

It is true that the Reagan administration's public relations skills were impressive, but public relations skills alone could not create or sustain goodwill. Thus, the president was below fifty percent in the polls after only ten months in office and would not obtain the approval of more than half the public again until late in 1983, despite his staff's efforts at promoting a favorable image.

Public support was central to the president's success with Congress, and the support was there in 1981 when he most needed it. The fundamental conditions of public support in the president's legislatively crucial first year were established outside the White House, however, not as a result of presidential leadership.

Ronald Reagan was certainly interested in policy change and went to unprecedented lengths to influence public opinion. Nevertheless, numerous national surveys of public opinion have found that support for regulatory programs and spending on health care, welfare, urban problems, education, environmental protection, and aid to minorities has *increased*, not decreased, during Reagan's tenure.[9] On the other hand, support for increased defense expenditures was decidedly lower than when he took office.[10] In the foreign policy realm, near the end of 1986, only twenty-five percent of the public favored the president's cherished aid to the contras in Nicaragua.[11] Finally, Americans did not move their ideological preference to the right.[12]

If presidents can frame issues in ways that favor their programs, they can exert a strong influence over the terms of both the public and congressional debate on presidential proposals and thus the premises on which members of Congress cast their votes. Presidents who can structure the choices faced by Congress can influence not only those open to conversion on issues, but every member of Congress who votes on those issues.

Ronald Reagan's victory in 1981 placed a stigma on big government, and exalted the unregulated marketplace and large defense efforts. Jim Jones, the House Budget Committee chairman, and his allies drafted a Democratic budget resolution, as an alternative to Reagan's, that proposed a more modest tax cut, a smaller increase for the Pentagon, and less of a decrease in social programs. Nevertheless, the Jones plan followed the general outlines of the administration's. The president won a major victory even before the first vote.

This was a very important advantage for the new president, but it was not one of his own making. Instead, it was the result of the conditions surrounding his election. There was a widespread misperception of a mandate and a turn toward conservatism, encouraged by the surprising margin of his victory, the unexpected and sizable Republican gains in the Senate, media hyperbole regarding the significance of both these electoral outcomes, the emphasis of the Reagan campaign on policy change, the psychological impact of defeating an incumbent elected president, and the prevailing tides of opinion in the country toward trying new approaches to economic policy. Ronald Reagan did not become president and then set out to create these conditions. These conditions were present when he took office.

Although structuring choices can be a useful tool for presidents, there is no guarantee that they will succeed. Typically the environment is not accommodating. Moreover, the White House must advocate the passage of many proposals at roughly the same time, further complicating its strategic position. In addition, opponents of the president's policies are unlikely to defer to presidential attempts to structure choices on issues. Policies are very complex and typically affect many different interest groups, which inevitably evaluate programs from their diverse perspectives. Moreover, interest groups in the United States are more numerous, more politically active, and in possession of more resources than ever before. The rise of single-issue groups has only exacerbated this situation. Organized interest groups are ready and able to fight vigorously to be heard and to show how the trade-offs involved in policy choices involve far more than the dimensions of evaluation proposed by the president.

Attempts to structure decisions may actually hurt the president's cause, especially heavy-handed attempts. In 1986 Ronald Reagan was engaged in his perennial fight over his high-priority proposal to provide aid to the Contras in Nicaragua. The president equated opposition to his aid program with support for the Sandinistas. More graphically, White House Communications Director Patrick J. Buchanan wrote an editorial in the *Washington Post* and characterized the issue in stark terms: "With the contra vote, the Democratic Party will reveal whether it stands with Ronald Reagan and the resistance or [Nicaraguan President] Daniel Ortega and the communists." These overt efforts to structure the decision for Congress were not successful. Instead, they irritated members of Congress and provoked charges of White House red baiting.[13]

Sometimes merely changing public opinion is not sufficient, and the president feels that the public must communicate its views directly to Congress. Mobilization of the public may be the ultimate weapon in the president's arsenal of resources with which to influence Congress. When the people speak, especially when they speak clearly, Congress listens attentively.

Yet mobilizing the public involves overcoming formidable barriers and accepting substantial risk. It entails the double burden of obtaining both opinion support and political *action* from a generally inattentive and apathetic public. If the president tries to mobilize the public and fails, the lack of response speaks eloquently to members of Congress, who are highly attuned to public opinion.

Perhaps the most notable recent example of the president mobilizing public opinion to pressure Congress is Ronald Reagan's effort to obtain passage of his tax-cut bill in 1981. Shortly before the crucial vote in the House, the president made a televised plea for support of his tax-cut proposal and asked the people to let their representatives in Congress know how they felt. Evidently it worked, as thousands of phone calls, letters, and telegrams poured into congressional offices. How much of this represented the efforts of the White House and its corporate allies rather than individual expressions of opinion we will probably never know. But in the short run it worked. On the morning of the vote Speaker Tip O'Neill declared, "We are experiencing a telephone blitz like this nation has never seen. It's had a devastating effect."[14] With this kind of response, the president easily carried the day.

The Reagan administration's effort at mobilizing the public on behalf of the 1981 tax cut is significant not only because of the success of presidential leadership but also because it appears to be a deviant case—even for Ronald Reagan. His next major legislative battle was over the sale of AWACs planes to Saudi Arabia. The White House determined it could not mobilize the public on this issue, however, and adopted an "inside" strategy to prevent a legislative veto.[15]

In the remainder of his tenure the president went repeatedly to the people regarding a wide range of policies, including the budget, aid to the contras in Nicaragua, and defense expenditures. Despite his high approval levels for much of that time and his well-deserved sobriquet, the "Great Communicator," he was never again able to arouse the public to communicate their support of his policies to Congress. Most issues hold less appeal to the public than substantial tax cuts.

Setting Priorities

An important aspect of a president's legislative strategy, one with the specific purpose of dominating Congress, can be establishing priorities among legislative proposals. The goal of this effort is to set Congress's agenda. If presidents are not able to focus Congress's attention on priority programs, those program may get lost in the complex and overloaded legislative process.

Setting priorities is also important because presidents and their staff can lobby effectively for only a few bills at a time. Moreover, the president's political capital is inevitably limited, and it is sensible to focus it on the president's preferred issues; otherwise this precious resource might be wasted, as in 1977 when Jimmy Carter "spent his political capital to a deficit on pork barrel projects," not one of his priority items.[16]

There are fundamental obstacles to focusing congressional attention on a few top-priority items, however. In 1981 Ronald Reagan focused attention on his priorities by asking for relatively little, but in the first year of his second term the budget, tax reform, the MX missile, farm credit, sanctions against South Africa, aid to Nicaraguan rebels, and much more crowded the congressional agenda. Max Friedersdorf, the head of Reagan's legislative liaison team in both 1981 and 1985, explained, "In '81, during the whole course of the year, we only had three major votes," and they were spaced out. By May, 1985, however, "we've had five or six votes. The circuits have been overloaded."[17]

Several forces are at work here. First, the White House can put off dealing with the full spectrum of national issues for a period of months at the beginning of the term of a new president, but it cannot do so for four years. Eventually it must make decisions about them. By the second year the agenda is full and more policies are in the pipeline as the administration attempts to satisfy its constituencies and responds to unanticipated or simply overlooked problems.

Moreover, presidents' schedules will inevitably be a distraction from their own priorities. There are many demands on the president to speak, appear, and attend meetings. It becomes impossible to organize the president's schedule around focusing attention on major goals, especially a president who has been in office for long. For example, President Reagan wanted to focus attention on tax reform in 1985. Yet during a short trip to Alabama he had to react to a Senate vote on his request for aid to the rebels in Nicaragua and to the Supreme Court's decision on a school prayer case arising from the state. As one presidential aide put it, "You can't go to Alabama and not mention the school prayer decision, and if you go to Alabama and mention the school prayer decision, don't think you are going to get covered on tax reform."[18]

In 1986 the president was again pushing for aid to the contras, but his efforts were overtaken by other events. According to White House Communications Director Patrick J. Buchanan, "The Philippines intruded and dominated for two weeks, making it difficult for us to get the contra aid campaign off the ground." In addition, the president had to give a nationally televised speech on behalf of his defense budget when the *Challenger* space shuttle disaster distracted attention from the president's priorities. Thus, as one White House aide put it, "The hardest thing to do is not to get into a reactive mode and have your schedule dictated to you by events, rather than dictating events and having a schedule reflective of your priorities."[19]

Second, Congress is quite capable of setting its own agenda. The changes in Congress that we discussed earlier, changes in its aggressiveness, its institutional capabilities, and the freedom of individuals and groups to act, have not only made it more difficult for the president to persuade Congress but also to focus its attention. The public expects Congress to take the initiative,[20] and members of Congress have strong electoral incentives to respond. Thus, when President Carter sent his large legislative program to Congress, it had to compete for agenda space with congressional initiatives. As a presidential aide put it, "Congress was scheduled up before most of the items arrived."[21]

This aggressive congressional role is not unusual. *Congressional Quarterly's* list of the major legislative actions of the Ninety-ninth Congress (1985–86) includes the reauthorization of the Clean Water Act, the Safe Drinking Water Act, and the "Superfund" hazardous waste cleanup bill; sanctions against South Africa; reorganization of the Pentagon; an anti–drug abuse bill; a major revision of immigration law; the Gramm-Rudman-Hollings antideficit bill; revisions of the law on gun control; the first authorization for water projects in a decade; an extension of daylight savings time; and extended protection against age discrimination.[22] On none of this legislation did the White House take the lead. Instead, it reacted to congressional initiatives. Even the historic Tax Reform Act of 1986 was as much a product of long-term congressional momentum and committee leadership as it was of presidential agenda setting. In 1987 President Reagan found Congress already working on his two primary domestic policy initiatives for his last two years in office, catastrophic health insurance and welfare reform.

Finally, presidents may not want to set priorities and concentrate attention on a few items. Lyndon Johnson is often viewed as being careful to set priorities for Congress, but when we examine his legislative activity more closely, we find that there is less to his priority setting than we might expect. In his memoirs Johnson writes that, "One of the President's most important jobs is to help Congress concentrate on the *five or six dozen bills* [italics added] that make up his legislative program."[23] This hardly sounds like discriminating setting of priorities on a few bills and then focusing congressional and public attention on them. Instead, Johnson was more concerned about moving legislation through Congress rapidly to exploit the favorable political environment.[24]

Ronald Reagan advanced the smallest policy agenda of any modern president, and much of it was negative (i.e., reducing government activities). Asking for little lessened the burden of setting priorities, and it was easier to move rapidly in introducing legislation with a focus on cutting back or eliminating programs and with an ideological orientation that simplified the task of policy analysis.

In 1981, as the Democrats were reeling from Reagan's electoral victory and their loss of the Senate, the Reagan administration also benefited from the disarray of the opposition party and its failure to promote alternatives to the president's. Once again, Ronald Reagan's successful efforts to dominate an aspect of executive-legislative relations were assisted substantially by an accommodating environment.

Exploiting Opportunities

Presidents must largely play with the hands the public, through its electoral decisions (both presidential and congressional) and its evaluations of the chief executive's success, deals them. Presidents are rarely in a position to substantially augment their resources. They operate at the margins as facilitators rather than directors of change.

When the various streams of resources do converge, they create opportunities for leadership. Because presidents' resource bases are fragile, they must take advantage of environmental opportunities to facilitate change. The essential presidential skill in leading Congress is in recognizing and exploiting conditions for change, not in creating them.

We can best see this in the cases of those presidents most often viewed as examples of directors rather than mere facilitators of change. Those presidents who were most successful with Congress best understood their own limitations and took full advantage of their good fortune in having resources to exploit. When those resources diminished, they fell back to the more typical stalemate that usually characterized presidential-congressional relations.

When Congress first met in special session in March, 1933, following Franklin D. Roosevelt's inauguration, it rapidly passed the new president's bills to control the resumption of banking, repeal prohibition, and effect government economies. This is all FDR originally planned for Congress to do, expecting to reassemble the legislature when permanent and more constructive legislation was ready.[25] Yet the president found a situation ripe for change. As James MacGregor Burns described it,

> A dozen days after the inauguration a move of adulation for Roosevelt was sweeping the country. Over ten thousand telegrams swamped the White House in a single week. Newspaper editorials were paeans of praise. . . . A flush of hope swept the nation. Gold was flowing back to financial institutions; banks were reopening without crowds of depositors clamoring for their money; employment and production seemed to be turning upward.
>
> "I will do anything you ask," a congressman from Iowa wrote the President. "You are my leader."[26]

Thus, Roosevelt decided to exploit this favorable environment and strike again and again with the hastily drawn legislation that came to be immortalized in the "Hundred Days."

Moreover, Burns concludes that, "It is significant that the enduring New Deal emerged not out of Roosevelt's 'hundred days' of 1933, when he gave a brilliant demonstration of executive leadership, but out of the 'second hundred days' of 1935, which emerged out of decades of foment, political action, and legislative as well as executive policy-making. . . ."[27]

Lyndon Johnson also knew that his personal leadership could not sustain congressional support for his policies. He had to exploit the opportunities provided by the Kennedy assassination and the 1964 election. He told aide Jack Valenti early in his presidency, "I keep hitting hard because I know this honeymoon won't last. Every day I lose a little more political capital. That's why we have to keep at it, never letting up. One day soon . . . the critics and the snipers will move in and we will be at stalemate. We have to get all we can now, before the roof comes down."[28] Thus, in February, 1965, following his landslide victory, Johnson assembled the congressional liaison officials from the various departments and told them that his victory at the polls "might be more of a loophole than a mandate" and that since his popularity could decrease rapidly, they would have to use it to their advantage while it lasted.[29]

The Reagan administration realized from the beginning that it had an opportunity to effect major changes in public policy, but that it had to concentrate its focus and move quickly before the environment became less favorable. The president and his staff moved rapidly in 1981 to exploit the perceptions of a mandate and the dramatic elevation of Republicans to majority status in the Senate. Moreover, within a week of the president's being shot, Michael Deaver convened a meeting of other top Reagan aides at the White House to determine how best to take advantage of the new political capital the assassination attempt created.

Even those presidents who appeared to dominate Congress were actually facilitators rather than directors of change. They quite explicitly took advantage of opportunities in their environments and, working at the margins, successfully guided legislation through Congress.

They were especially attentive to the state of public opinion in determining their legislative strategies. As the most volatile leadership resource, public opinion is the factor that is most likely to determine whether an opportunity for change exists. By itself, public opinion cannot sustain presidential leadership of Congress, but it is the variable that has the most potential to turn a typical situation into one favorable for change and, being mercurial, requires expeditious action.

The facilitator is not an unskilled leader. Instead, the facilitator is one who functions in a constant state of dependence on environmental factors for creating favorable strategic positions from which to exercise leadership at the margins to turn opportunities into accomplishments. The fact that presidents are confined to the facilitator role is not necessarily cause for concern. The nature of our system is such that presidents can be little else. Although there is a certain appeal to personalizing the explanation for major change, the American political system is too complicated, power is too decentralized, and interests are too diverse for one person, no matter how extraordinary, to dominate.

It follows that we should adjust our expectations of presidential leadership accordingly. American chief executives are not, by themselves, going to bring about major changes in public policy. As Neustadt has written, "if the President envisages substantial innovations, whether conservative or liberal, then almost everything in modern history cries caution to such hopes unless accompanied by crises with potential for consensus."[30]

The Reagan administration was no exception. Despite his political skills, Ronald Reagan was not peculiarly successfully in eliciting support from members of Congress.[31] By 1987 he was winning the smallest percentage of votes in Congress of any president since *Congressional Quarterly* began keeping records.[32]

Some, especially those who desire significant changes in public policy, may find the facilitator role unsatisfactory. For those who do, our understanding of presidential leadership of Congress provides two broad and essential lessons. First, the solution is not in just identifying a great leader. To change the nature of presidential leadership requires changing the system. Second, our understanding of the context of presidential leadership of Congress forces us to recognize that providing the environment for the director role will require alterations in American political culture and a redesign of political institutions.

Such changes are highly unlikely. We are going to be living with facilitators in the White House for the foreseeable future. Now we are in a better position to evaluate the leadership of the facilitator president and focus on the true obstacles to effective leadership. The president does not dominate the American state, but is a vital centralizing force, providing direction and energy for the nation's policy making.

NOTES

This reading is based on portions of the author's *At the Margins: Presidential Leadership of Congress* (New Haven, Conn.: Yale University Press, 1989).

1. See George C. Edwards III, *Presidential Influence in Congress* (San Francisco: W. H. Freeman, 1980), pp. 35–48.
2. See Lance LeLoup, "After the Blitz: Reagan and the U.S. Congressional Budget Process," *Legislative Studies Quarterly* 7 (Aug., 1982): 321–40.
3. Allen Schick, "How the Budget was Won and Lost" in Norman J. Ornstein, ed., *President and Congress: Assessing Reagan's First Year* (Washington, D.C.: American Enterprise Institute, 1982), p. 16; Hedrick Smith, "Coping with Congress," *The New York Times Magazine,* Aug. 9, 1981, p. 20; "Numerous Factors Favoring Good Relationships Between Reagan and New Congress," *Congressional Quarterly Weekly Report,* Jan. 24, 1981, p. 172.
4. Quoted in Richard E. Cohen, "Senate Republicans' Control May Be Put to Test by Tough Issues this Fall." *National Journal,* Sept. 10, 1983, pp. 1824, 1826. See also p. 1827.
5. "Senate Republicans See Obstacles for Reagan," *New York Times,* Nov. 28, 1984, p. 11.
6. Jimmy Carter, *Keeping Faith: Memoirs of a President* (New York: Bantam Books, 1982), p. 80.
7. On the two presidencies, see George C. Edwards III, "The Two Presidencies: A Reevaluation," *American Politics Quarterly* 14 (July, 1986): 247–63.
8. Richard E. Neustadt, *Presidential Power* (New York: Wiley, 1980), p. 238.
9. William Schneider, "The Voters' Mood 1986: The Six-Year Itch," *National Journal,* Dec. 7, 1985, p. 2758; "Supporting a Greater Federal Role," *National Journal,* Apr. 18, 1987, p. 924; "Opinion Outlook," *National Journal,* Apr. 18, 1987, p. 964; Seymour Martin Lipset, "Beyond 1984: The Anomalies of American Politics," *PS: Political Science and Politics* 19 (Spring, 1986): 223; "Federal Budget Deficit," *Gallup Report,* Aug., 1987, pp. 25, 27. See also News Release, *CBS News–The New York Times Poll,* Oct. 27, 1987, tables 16, 20.

10. Lipset, "Beyond 1984"; "Supporting a Greater Federal Role," p. 924; "Defense," *Gallup Report,* May, 1987, pp. 2–3. See also "Opinion Outlook," *National Journal,* June 13, 1987, p. 1550; News Release, *CBS News–The New York Times Poll,* Oct. 27, 1987, table 15.

11. News Release, *CBS News–The New York Times Poll,* Dec. 1, 1986, table 5. See also, News Release, *CBS News–The New York Times Poll,* Oct. 27, 1987, table 17; "Americans on Contra Aid: Broad Opposition," *The New York Times,* Jan. 31, 1988, section 4, p. 1. For a broader comparison of public opinion and the Reagan administration's policies, see John E. Reilly, ed., *American Public Opinion and U.S. Foreign Policy 1987* (Chicago: Chicago Council on Foreign Relations, 1987), chapters 5–6.

12. See, for example, John A. Fleishman, "Trends in Self-Identified Ideology from 1972 to 1982: No Support for the Salience Hypothesis," *American Journal of Political Science* 30 (Aug., 1986): 517–41.

13. "Reagan Loses Ground on 'Contra' Aid Program," *Congressional Quarterly Weekly Report,* Mar. 8, 1986, pp. 535–36.

14. Quoted in "Tax Cut Passed by Solid Margin in House, Senate," *Congressional Quarterly Weekly Report,* Aug. 1, 1981, p. 1374.

15. See "Reagan's Legislative Strategy Team Keeps His Record of Victories Intact," *National Journal,* June 26, 1982, p. 1130.

16. Jack Watson, interview with George C. Edwards III, Oct. 19, 1985, West Point, N.Y.

17. Quoted in Bernard Weinraub, "Back in the Legislative Strategist's Saddle Again," *The New York Times,* May 28, 1985, p. 10.

18. Quoted in Gerald M. Boyd, "Rethinking a Tax Plan Strategy," *The New York Times,* June 12, 1985, p. 14.

19. Quoted in Dick Kirschten, "For Reagan Communication Team . . . It's Strictly One Week at a Time," *National Journal,* Mar. 8, 1986, p. 594.

20. See, for example, Adam Clymer, "Majority in Poll Expect Congress to Cut Spending," *The New York Times,* Nov. 17, 1985, section 1, p. 1.

21. Quoted in Paul C. Light, *The President's Agenda* (Baltimore: Johns Hopkins University Press, 1982), p. 54.

22. "The 99th Congress: A Mixed Record of Success," *Congressional Quarterly Weekly Report,* Oct. 25, 1986, p. 647.

23. Lyndon Baines Johnson, *The Vantage Point* (New York: Popular Library, 1971), p. 448.

24. See William E. Leuchtenburg, *In the Shadow of FDR* (Ithaca, N.Y.: Cornell University Press, 1983), p. 146.

25. James MacGregor Burns, *Roosevelt: The Lion and the Fox* (New York: Harcourt, Brace and World, 1956), pp. 166–68.

26. Ibid., p. 168.

27. James MacGregor Burns, *Leadership* (New York: Harper and Row, 1978), p. 396.

28. Quoted in Jack Valenti, *A Very Human President* (New York: Norton, 1975), p. 144.

29. Johnson, *The Vantage Point,* p. 323.

30. Neustadt, *Presidential Power,* p. 238.

31. See George C. Edwards III, *At the Margins* (New Haven, Conn.: Yale University Press, 1989), chapter 10.

32. "Reagan's Clout in Congress Falls to Record Low," *Congressional Quarterly Weekly Report,* Jan. 16, 1988, p. 91.

Chapter 17

Congress As Co-Manager of the Executive Branch

LOUIS FISHER

Congress is regularly denounced for engaging in "micromanagement" of the executive branch. It is advised to enact only broad legislative policy and stay out of details. If Congress ever complied with this advice (no chance of that), it would not escape criticism. A failure to supervise agencies, especially when there is evidence of fraud, waste, or abuse, would trigger new denunciations about a supine and irresponsible legislative branch. Congress can be assured that, whatever it does, there will be no shortage of criticism.

This essay reviews the reasons for legislative intervention in the administration of programs. Why does Congress intrude? How is that compatible with the separation of powers advocated by the framers? What tools does Congress use, both statutory and nonstatutory? What are the limits of congressional involvement?

The Framers' Intent

A good case can be made that the framers did not want Congress involved in administrative details. The inefficiencies of the Continental Congress from 1774 to 1787 unleashed a torrent of laments from George Washington, Alexander Hamilton, John Jay, and others who were responsible for prosecuting the war against England. The Continental Congress exercised all the powers of government: legislative, executive, and judicial. After completing their legislative duties the delegates had to meet in committee to handle administrative problems and cases of adjudication.

This system was so unsatisfactory that Congress struggled with makeshift arrangements to relieve delegates of some details. When committees failed to discharge managerial responsibilities, Congress tried a system of boards staffed by men recruited from outside Congress. Finally, in 1781, Congress created departments run by single executives. These officers were called a secretary for foreign affairs, a superintendent of finance, a secretary at war, a secretary of marine, and an attorney general to prosecute all suits on behalf of the United States and to advise Congress on all legal matters submitted to him. These experiments with single executives tried to fix responsibility on a single person and increase the efficiency of the war effort.

Congress also set up a Court of Appeals in Cases of Capture to handle admiralty disputes, hoping to relieve delegates of additional details and burdens. This dispersal of executive and judicial functions to bodies outside the Continental Congress reflects less of theory than of practical needs. In a striking phrase, the historian Francis Wharton said that the Constitution "did not make this distribution of power. It would be more proper to say that this distribution of power made the Constitution of the United States."[1] The Constitution owes much of its success to the continuity of executive structures from the Continental Congress to the First Congress of 1789. John Jay became secretary for foreign affairs in 1784 and served until Jefferson assumed the duties of secretary of state on March 22, 1790. General Henry Knox was elected secretary at war in 1785 and remained in that post until the final days of 1794.

The experience with the Continental Congress convinced many observers that Congress should not become involved in administrative details. Hamilton criticized the congressional committees in 1780 for keeping power "too much into their own hands and have meddled too much with details of every sort. Congress is properly a deliberative corps and it forgets itself when it attempts to play the executive."[2] Thomas Jefferson said that "Nothing is so embarrassing nor so mischievous in a great assembly as the details of execution. The smallest trifle of that kind occupies as long as the most important act of legislation, and takes place of every thing else. Let any man recollect, or look over the files of Congress, he will observe the most important propositions hanging over from week to week and month to month, till the occasions have past them, and the thing is never done."[3]

It would overstate the case to suggest that the framers believed that Congress should never intervene in departmental details. Congress regarded the secretary for foreign affairs and the secretary at war as officers involved in essentially executive duties. The superintendent of finance, however, seemed to straddle both legislative and executive powers. The first superintendent, Robert Morris, wanted full power to appoint and remove his subordinates. Congress refused. It restricted removals to cause ("incapacity, negligence, dishonesty or other misbehaviour") and required the superintendent to report to Congress his reasons for removal. Moreover, Congress appointed the comptroller rather than allow the superintendent to make that selection. The comptroller was a quasijudicial officer because he superintended the settlement of public accounts. On all appeals related to the auditing of accounts, the comptroller "shall openly and publicly hear the parties, and his decision shall be conclusive." Congress also appointed other financial officers: the treasurer, the register, and the auditors. Thus, even though Congress agreed to place responsibility in the superintendent of finance, it immediately adopted checks through the appointment and removal process.

This pattern continued in 1789, when the First Congress established the executive departments. The departments of Foreign Affairs and War were explicitly called executive departments. No such description appears for the Treasury Department. For the departments of Foreign Affairs and War, Congress identified only the secretary and a chief clerk (to be appointed by the secretary). For the Treasury Department, Congress created the office of secretary, a comptroller, an auditor, a treasurer, a register, and an assistant to the secretary. The secretary appointed only the latter.

Congressional jealousy in retaining control over the purse is evident in the debate in 1789 on the Treasury Department. Madison had argued strongly in favor of giving the president power to remove the secretaries of foreign affairs, war, and treasury. When it came to the tenure of the comptroller, however, Madison said its properties were not "purely of an executive nature." It seemed to him that "they partake of a Judiciary quality as well as Executive; perhaps the latter obtains in the greatest degree." Because of the mixed nature of the office, "there may be strong reasons why an officer of this kind should not hold his office at the pleasure of the Executive branch of the Government."[4] Only by understanding the history of the comptroller during the Continental Congress could Madison have made such remarks.

Legislation in 1795 made the comptroller's decision on certain claims "final and conclusive." This language would later appear in the Budget and Accounting Act of 1921 as part of the powers of the comptroller general, the head of the new General Accounting Office (GAO). The statute made the GAO "independent of the executive departments." All of the officers and employees of the former comptroller's office, including all books, records, documents, papers, furniture, and other property, were switched to GAO. Thus, the GAO retained its hybrid status of carrying out a multitude of powers: executive, legislative, and judicial. This unusual character has produced a number of contemporary issues for the courts, to be discussed later.

In addition to this foothold in the comptroller's office, the First Congress possessed the inherent power to investigate executive agencies. On March 27, 1792, the House of Representatives appointed a committee to inquire into the disastrous expedition of Major General St. Clair, who sustained massive losses in a battle with the Indians. The House empowered the committee "to call for such persons, papers, and records, as may be necessary to assist their inquiries." Washington's cabinet agreed on the fundamental point that the House "was an inquest" and therefore might institute inquiries and call for papers. Although the cabinet also concluded that the president should refuse to communicate any papers "the disclosure of which would injure the public," in this case it was decided that it was proper to produce all of the papers requested by the House.[5]

Tools of the Trade

Even in these early years it was evident that Congress had ample means to hold the executive agencies accountable. A careless reading of the Constitution would suggest that the president is directed to carry out the laws; however, the president "shall take Care that the Laws be faithfully executed." If a statute created an independent officer (like the comptroller) and made the officer's judgment final and conclusive, the president had no right to intervene. So long as the officer faithfully executed the duty assigned him by statute, the president was excluded.

As early as *Marbury v. Madison* (1803), the Supreme Court explained that there are two types of executive duties: ministerial and discretionary. The latter duty was to the president alone. In the case of ministerial actions, the duty was to the statute, and the head of a department acts "under the authority of law, and not by the instructions of the president. It is a ministerial act which the law enjoins on a particular officer for a particular purpose."[6] An opinion by the attorney general in 1854 stated that when laws "define what is to be done by a given head of department, and how he is to do it, there the President's discretion stops . . ."[7] Repeatedly, attorneys general instructed presidents that it was neither legally nor politically proper to interfere with certain agency decisions.

The investigative power of Congress was especially powerful in cases of corruption. President Andrew Jackson told Congress that if it could "point to any case where there is the slightest reason to suspect corruption or abuse of trust, no obstacle which I can remove shall be interposed to prevent the fullest scrutiny by all legal means. The offices of all the departments will be opened to you, and every proper facility furnished for this purpose."[8] As a prelude to impeachment, the investigative power gained even greater power. President Polk said that the power of impeachment gives to the House of Representatives "the right to investigate the conduct of all public officers under the Government. . . . the power of the House in the pursuit of this object would penetrate into the most secret recesses of the Executive Departments. It could command the attendance of any and every agent of the Government, and compel them to produce all papers, public or private, official or unofficial, and to testify on oath to all facts within their knowledge."[9]

Some early decisions by the Supreme Court defined the investigative power far too narrowly. In 1881, the Court decided that congressional investigations must relate to some legislative purpose. Investigations had to result in "valid legislation on the subject to which the inquiry referred."[10] Later, the Court adopted a more generous test, stating that a "potential" for legislation was sufficient.[11] The courts recognize that committee efforts devoted to overseeing executive agencies may take researchers up "blind alleys" and into nonproductive enterprises: "To be a valid legislative inquiry there need be no predictable end result."[12]

To reinforce the power to investigate, congressional committees may issue subpoenas to compel the production of witnesses and documents. Congress also has an inherent power to punish for contempt. This power is frequently invoked to force cooperation from reluctant executive officials, who face the prospect of jail sentences for withholding documents from a congressional investigation.

In addition to other statutory instruments, agencies and congressional committees maintain informal clearance procedures. Agencies notify committees in advance of acting in certain areas, and frequently defer to committee objections. Federal courts have found these agency-committee relationships constructive and constitutional. Committee chairmen and members of Congress "naturally develop interest and expertise in the subjects entrusted to their continuing surveillance." Executive officials have to take these committees "into account and keep them informed, respond to their inquiries, and it may be, flatter and please them when necessary." As a result, committees develop "enormous influence" over executive branch activities. Courts find "nothing unconstitutional about this: indeed, our separation of powers makes such informal cooperation much more necessary than it would be in a pure system of parliamentary government."[13]

Congress has a variety of informal, nonstatutory techniques for influencing executive agencies. A prime example is the "reprogramming" process followed by agencies and committees. Agencies want Congress to appropriate funds in large, lump-sum accounts, giving executive officials discretion to shift money within those accounts from one program to another. In return for this flexibility, Congress insists that significant reprogrammings—above a certain dollar amount or for matters of special interest—first receive the approval of congressional committees. Usually this means the approval of the appropriations sub-committees with jurisdiction over the agency, although on some occasions the authorization committees also must approve the reprogramming. This is a conventional quid pro quo. Agencies gain flexibility; committees retain control. The arrangement benefits both branches.

The process is called nonstatutory because the procedures for reprogramming are rarely included in public laws. Instead, they are spelled out in committee reports, committee hearings, and correspondence between the committees and the agencies. Executive officials place these understandings in their instructions, directives, and financial management manuals. Agency staff know the types of reprogrammings that may be done internally, with only periodic reports to Congress, and those that require prior approval from committees. Because these understandings are nonstatutory, agencies are not technically bound by law to comply with committee prior-approval requirements. However, agencies know that Congress can invoke harsh penalties for agency bad faith.

Resurrection of the Legislative Veto

Beginning in 1932, Congress relied on a "legislative veto" to control authority it delegated to the executive branch. Congress agreed to transfer significant power and discretion on the condition that it could control executive decisions without having to pass another law. These legislative vetoes, short of a public law, included one-House vetoes, two-House vetoes, and even committee vetoes. Congressional actions by a legislative veto were not presented to the president for his signature or veto.

It may appear that this procedure thrust Congress unfairly (or even unconstitutionally) into administrative decisions that should have been left to executive officials. However, the initiative for the legislative veto came from President Herbert Hoover. He asked Congress to delegate to him power to reorganize the executive branch, with the understanding that either House of Congress could disapprove his proposals. Executive officials tolerated the legislative veto for decades because they knew it encouraged Congress to delegate greater discretion and authority to the executive branch. If Congress failed to invoke the legislative veto, executive officials could, in effect, "make law" without further congressional involvement.

The experiment with the legislative veto lasted five decades before it was invalidated by the Supreme Court in *INS v. Chadha* (1983). Using a wooden formulation of the separation of powers model, the Court insisted that future congressional efforts to alter "the legal rights, duties, and relations of persons" outside the legislative branch must follow the full law-making process: passage of a bill or joint resolution by both Houses and presentment of that measure to the president for signature or veto. Anything short of the full law-making process—committee vetoes, subcommittee vetoes, one-House vetoes, or two-House vetoes—were unconstitutional.

The Court announced trite homilies about the separation of powers. Congress could no longer rely on the legislative veto as a "convenient shortcut" to control executive agencies. Legislation by Congress must be a "step-by-step, deliberate and deliberative process." According to the Court, the framers insisted that "the legislative power of the Federal Government be exercised in accord with a single, finely wrought and exhaustively considered, procedure."[14] The Court showed little understanding of the congressional process. Both Houses regularly use "shortcut" methods that pose no problem under *Chadha:* suspending the rules, asking for unanimous consent, placing legislative riders on appropriations bills, and even passing bills that have never been sent to committee.

Notwithstanding the Court's lectures on good government, the legislative veto survives. It does so not because of congressional defiance but because the Court never seemed to understand the executive-legislative accommodations that produced the legislative veto in the first place. The legislative veto was not a blatant intrusion by Congress into administrative details. It was part of a quid pro quo: a condition placed on broad authority that the executive branch wanted. That need did not disappear with the Court's ruling. From its decision on June 23, 1983, to the adjournment of the 105th Congress at the end of 1998, Congress enacted more than four hundred new legislative vetoes.

Most of these new legislative vetoes are committee vetoes. For example, here are some committee vetoes in the Treasury and General Government Appropriations Act for fiscal 1998: a new facility for the Bureau of Alcohol, Tobacco and Firearms (BATF) could not be constructed until a prospectus was approved by the House Committee on Transportation and Infrastructure and the Senate Committee on Environment and Public Works; the Internal Revenue Service was prohibited from transferring funds in excess of five percent without the advance approval of the appropriations committees; travel of Secret Service employees on protective missions could exceed statutory limitations if approval was obtained in advance from the appropriations committees; appropriations for the Federal Law Enforcement Training Center, Financial Crimes Enforcement Network, BATF, the Customs Service, and the Secret Service could be transferred between those accounts with the advance approval of the appropriations committees; and the appropriations committees had to provide advance approval for certain buildings constructed by the General Services Administration.[15]

The persistence of these committee vetoes can be understood from an early collision between Congress and President Ronald Reagan. In signing an appropriations bill in 1984, he challenged committee vetoes as a clear violation of *Chadha*. He appealed to Congress to stop adding provisions that the Court had held to be unconstitutional. Because of the Court's decision, Reagan said that the administration did not feel bound by provisions in the bill requiring agencies to seek the approval of committees before implementing certain actions.[16] In effect, he was exercising an item veto by dismissing committee vetoes and replacing them with mere requirements that agencies notify committees before doing what they wanted to do.

The response by the appropriations committees was predictable. They said they would repeal the committee vetoes and also the authority that had been delegated to the agencies. In the future, if agencies wanted to exercise some flexibility in departing from the appropriations bill, they would have to present a bill to Congress for the authority and have it pass both Houses and be presented to the president, just as the Supreme Court had directed. Clearly, this was a bigger hurdle than the committee veto. In the face of this threat, agencies renegotiated with Congress and learned to live with the committee veto.[17]

To lessen the chance of a self-inflicted wound, the Supreme Court usually abides by the prudential course not to "formulate a rule of constitutional law broader than is required by the precise facts to which it is to be applied."[18] The Court ignored that fundamental guideline in *Chadha* by issuing a decision that not only reached beyond the particular immigration statute at issue but exceeded the Court's understanding of executive-legislative relations. Through an endless variety of formal and informal agreements, congressional committees will continue to exercise control over agency actions.

The Court applied a simplistic solution to a complex issue. In doing so, it suggested that the government follow a conventional law-making process that excludes Congress from the administration of problems. That type of government does not, and cannot, exist. By misreading the history of legislative vetoes and failing to comprehend the subtleties of the legislative process, the Court directed the executive and legislative branches to adhere to procedures that would be impracticable and unworkable. Neither Congress nor the executive branch wanted the static model of government offered by the Court.

The predictable and inevitable result of *Chadha* is a system of law making that is now more convoluted, cumbersome, and covert than before. Finding the Court's doctrine incompatible with effective government, the elected branches have searched for techniques that revive the understandings in place before 1983. In many cases, the Court's decision simply drives underground a set of legislative vetoes that used to operate in plain sight. In one form or another, legislative vetoes will remain an important mechanism for reconciling legislative and executive interests. The executive branch wants to retain access to discretionary authority; Congress wants to control some of those discretionary decisions without having to pass another public law.

Why Does Congress Intrude?

Congress engages in "micromanagement" for a variety of constitutional and policy reasons. Congress has a constitutional responsibility to oversee the spending of public funds. As the Supreme Court noted in 1957, the power of Congress to conduct investigations "comprehends probes into departments of the Federal Government to expose corruption, inefficiency or waste."[19] Statutes appropriating funds are filled with conditions, restrictions, and provisos that place limits on the expenditure of funds. Agencies may question the wisdom of these conditions on appropriations, but there is no question about the constitutional authority of Congress to decide between conditional and unconditional appropriations. With few exceptions, the choice is solely one for legislative judgment. In many cases, if one will look into the history, a condition is added to penalize an agency for bad faith.

For example, during the administrations of Lyndon Johnson and Richard Nixon, Congress discovered that the Agency for International Development would take money appropriated for one purpose and apply it to another that had never been justified to Congress. The following language found its way into the appropriations bill for foreign assistance: "None of the funds made available by this Act may be obligated under an appropriation account to which they were not appropriated without the prior written approval of the Committees on Appropriations."

For a number of years, executive officials acquiesced and complied with this restriction. Then, in 1987, the Reagan administration decided to stage a confrontation with Congress. Office of Management and Budget Director James C. Miller III wrote to the appropriations committees, detailing a number of objections to the foreign aid bill. He singled out the committee-approval provision as unconstitutional because of the Supreme Court's decision in *INS v. Chadha*.

Miller's challenge was shortsighted and self-defeating. He subsequently received a bipartisan lesson from Congress. David Obey, chairman of the Foreign Operations Subcommittee of House appropriations, together with Mickey Edwards, the ranking minority member, told the OMB that it would remedy matters by repealing not only the committee veto but also the authority to obligate funds under a different account (transfer authority). Obey announced that the letter from Miller "means we don't have an accommodation any more, so the hell with it, spend the money like we appropriated it. It's just dumb on their part." Edwards noted that the OMB "has not had a history of being very thoughtful or for consulting people," and that the provision was an example of "the spirit of cooperation between the executive and legislative branches, which the administration is not very good at."[20] The OMB, conducting a hasty retreat, regretted that it had ever brought up the subject. The customary language, including the committee veto, appeared in the continuing resolution signed by President Reagan on December 22, 1987 (P.L. 100–202). After all the confrontations and constitutional challenges, what prevailed in the end was the need for reasonable accommodations between the executive and legislative branches.

This quid pro quo illustrates a larger theme. When there is a collision between formalistic doctrines and effective government, the latter will take precedence. That is so even when the agency that announces formalistic doctrines is the Supreme Court.

Congress also intervenes in agency affairs because of duties that members of Congress have to their constituents. The First Amendment provides that Congress shall make no law abridging the right of the people "to petition the Government for a redress of grievances." These petitions often go directly to members of Congress, and they act as intermediaries between citizens and the executive branch. The bureaucratic process is so complex and intimidating that legislators must assist constituents in locating the responsible agency and assuring adequate attention. Intervention by legislators often produces needed changes in administrative procedures and policies. Because of constituent complaints, members of Congress become aware of contradictory, conflicting, and arbitrary agency regulations. They also learn of defects in the law, requiring the passage of remedial legislation. Congressional intervention has value even when the agency's position is upheld. Constituents know that their complaints have been looked into thoroughly. They become more confident about their government.

Congress also intervenes when the executive branch fails to see that the laws are faithfully executed. In 1987, Vice President Bush criticized Congress for asserting "an influential role in the micro-management of foreign policy." Referring to the litigation spawned by the Iran-Contra affair, he said that the framers did not intend that "our foreign policy should be conducted and reviewed by grand juries."[21]

The reasons for this involvement by Congress and grand juries is not hard to fathom. President Reagan failed to provide adequate supervision of his subordinates. When the sale of arms to Iran was disclosed in November, 1986,

Reagan fumbled with his explanations to the public. He gave the impression either of not knowing what was happening in his own administration or knowing and not being willing to tell. In either event, he had the power and the authority to get the facts. However, instead of calling Oliver North, John Poindexter, William Casey, and the other central figures into his office and learning what happened and why, he delegated that task to other bodies: to the Tower Board, the independent counsel, and to Congress.

When the Tower Board released its report in February, 1987, it concluded that Reagan had traded arms for hostages. President Reagan responded to this finding by telling the nation: "A few months ago I told the American people I did not trade arms for hostages. My heart and my best intentions still tell me that's true, but the facts and the evidence tell me it is not."[22] It took an outside body to tell the president what he had done! Furthermore, the sending of arms to Iran violated every policy formulated and announced by the administration. It told the American people, and the world, that it was neutral in the war between Iran and Iraq; it opposed the sending of arms to either country (Operation Staunch); it opposed making concessions to terrorists or giving arms for hostages. In private, it did the opposite.

The grand jury probe of Iran-Contra results from the administration's decision to have an independent counsel appointed. After reviewing the record, Attorney General Meese recommended to President Reagan that an independent counsel should be appointed to investigate possible criminal misconduct. Reagan urged Meese to go to the special court and ask it to appoint an independent counsel.[23] The independent counsel and the grand jury carried out the task assigned to them.

With regard to the congressional investigation, President Reagan opened the door to that as well. In an address to the nation, he said: "I recognize fully the interest of Congress in this matter and the fact that in performing its important oversight and legislative role Congress will want to inquire into what occurred. We will cooperate fully with these inquiries. I have already taken the unprecedented step of permitting two of my former national security advisers to testify before a committee of Congress."[24]

The administration gave substantial assistance to the investigations by the Iran-Contra committees, furnishing more than 300,000 documents (totaling more than one million pages) from the White House, the Department of State, the Department of Defense, the Central Intelligence Agency, the Department of Justice, and other agencies. The committees deposed about 250 people, many of them current or former officials in the executive branch. At no time did President Reagan invoke executive privilege to keep documents from Congress. He even permitted extracts to be taken from his personal diary.

This congressional investigation of national security operations within the executive branch was unprecedented, both in terms of scope and depth of detail. It was brought about by President Reagan's failure to remain accountable for activities within his administration. Executive officials engaged in operations of grave harm to the presidency and to the country, but the extensive inquiries by Congress and the Tower Board could never uncover a direct line of accountability linking those operations with orders or decisions by President Reagan. The elected leaders—President Reagan and Vice President Bush—claimed to be unaware of actions taken by their subordinates. Bush offered the clumsy excuse that he was "out of the loop" partly because he had attended a football game instead of a key meeting by the National Security Council. The public naturally wondered why vice presidents do not have staff to keep them informed of meetings they cannot attend. If the president and vice president cannot exercise control of executive officials, they cannot complain when outside parties—including Congress—are asked to do their job.

Other spin-offs from Iran-Contra explain why Congress becomes more involved in agency actions. Before 1980, the Central Intelligence Agency had to report to eight different congressional committees on covert actions: the two intelligence committees, the two appropriations committees, the two armed services committees, the House Foreign Affairs Committee, and the Senate Foreign Relations Committee. Congress passed legislation in 1980 to reduce the number of committees to two: the intelligence committees. In return for this limitation on committees, the administration was expected to keep the intelligence committees fully and currently informed on covert operations. The spirit of close coordination was made clear in the legislative history:

> Out of necessity, intelligence activities are conducted primarily in secret. Because of that necessary secrecy, they are not subject to public scrutiny and debate as is the case for most foreign policy and defense issues. Therefore, the Congress, through its intelligence oversight committees, has especially important duties in overseeing these vital activities by the intelligence agencies of the United States. Section 501 is intended to authorize the process by which information concerning intelligence activities of the United States is to be shared by the two branches in order to enable them to fulfill their respective duties and obligations to govern intelligence activities within the constitutional framework. The Executive branch and the intelligence oversight committees have developed over the last four years a practical relationship based on comity and mutual understanding, without confrontation. The purpose of Section 501 is to carry this working relationship forward into statute.[25]

As enacted into law, Section 501 required the director of central intelligence and the heads of all departments, agencies, "and other entities of the United States" involved in intelligence activities to keep the intelligence committees fully and currently informed of covert actions. If the president determined "it is essential to limit prior notice to meet extraordinary circumstances affecting vital interests of the United States," he could limit notice to eight legislators: the chairman and ranking minority members of the intelligence committees, the speaker and minority leader of the House of Representatives, and the majority and minority leaders of the Senate.[26] This group came to be called the "gang of eight." The president was required to fully inform the Intelligence Committees "in a timely fashion" of covert actions.[27]

In the case of sending arms to Iran, President Reagan never notified Congress or even the "gang of eight." Congress learned about the operation ten months late—the way other Americans became informed. The story first leaked in a Lebanese newspaper. After some initial denials and obfuscation, President Reagan admitted that arms had been sent to the government that had held fifty-two Americans hostage for more than a year. The sense of "comity and mutual understanding" anticipated by the drafters of the intelligence oversight act of 1980 was violated with contempt.

Congress responded to these events by drafting new legislation to remove such general phrases as "timely fashion." Because Congress could not trust in the integrity and good faith of administration officials, it adopted the specific period of forty-eight hours as the maximum delay for notifying Congress of covert actions. Legislation was finally enacted in 1991, embodying the forty-eight-hour rule and setting forth other requirements for covert actions (P.L. 102–88).

The Limits of Intervention

Although Congress plays a vital role in scrutinizing the administration, there are limits on what members of Congress may do. Some of these restrictions are clear, spelled out either in statute or guidelines. Others are still being formed.

The bribery statute applies to any public official, including members of Congress, who seeks or accepts anything of value in exchange for an official act (18 U.S.C. 201). The conflict-of-interest statute makes it a criminal offense for congressmen to receive or seek compensation for any services relating to any proceeding, contract, claim, or other activities of the federal government (18 U.S.C. 203). A number of congressmen, in their contacts with the executive branch, have been prosecuted under these statutes.

For example, Representative Thomas Johnson (D-Md.) was accused of receiving more than $20,000 to exert influence on the Justice Department to obtain the dismissal of pending indictments of a loan company and its officers on mail fraud charges. He was found guilty of violating the conflict-of-interest statute. In 1966, the Supreme Court held that his contacts with the Justice Department were not protected by the Speech or Debate Clause of the Constitution, which states that "for any Speech or Debate in either House," Senators and Representatives "shall not be questioned in any other Place." The Court concluded that the attempt to influence the Justice Department was "in no wise related to the due functioning of the legislative process" and therefore was outside the immunity granted by the Speech or Debate Clause.[28]

The Speech or Debate Clause has been interpreted to mean not only words spoken in debate but anything done in relation to legislative business. Thus, the clause applies to remarks by members of Congress during the course of committee hearings or in committee reports. Speeches printed in the *Congressional Record* are covered, whether delivered or not. Activities by congressional staff, necessary for the legislative process, are generally protected.

What the courts have done is draw a line between legislative activities (covered) and "political" activities (uncovered). The latter include these activities by legislators and their staff: contacts with executive agencies, assistance to constituents or other individuals seeking federal contracts, and speeches delivered outside the Congress. There is no legislative immunity when disseminating documents and information outside Congress. As a result of these decisions, members of Congress who publicize agency waste or abuse by issuing press releases and newsletters to their constituents are not protected by the Speech or Debate Clause. A well-known case involved Senator William Proxmire, who regularly issued the "Golden Fleece Award" to publicize what he considered to be egregious waste. In 1975, he gave one of these awards to the National Science Foundation, the National Aeronautics and Space Administration, and the Office of Naval Research for grants made to Dr. Ronald Hutchinson for studies into animal aggression. Part of the research was devoted to such behavior patterns as the clenching of jaws when monkeys were exposed to stressful stimuli. Proxmire poked fun at the research:

> The funding of this nonsense makes me almost angry enough to scream and kick or even clench my jaw. It seems to me it is outrageous.
>
> Dr. Hutchinson's studies should make the taxpayers as well as his monkeys grind their teeth. In fact, the good doctor has made a fortune from his monkeys and in the process made a monkey out of the American taxpayer.
>
> It is time for the Federal Government to get out of this 'monkey business.' In view of the transparent worthlessness of Hutchinson's study of

jaw-grinding and biting by angry or hard-drinking monkeys, it is time we put a stop to the bite Hutchinson and the bureaucrats who fund him have been taking of the taxpayer.[29]

As it turned out, the bite was put on Proxmire. Hutchinson sued him for libel for remarks made in a press release, a newsletter, and in comments made on the Mike Douglas show. The Court held that the press release and newsletter were not protected by the Speech or Debate Clause. Proxmire could have said anything he wanted about Hutchinson in floor debate or during committee hearings, but not in publications to his constituents.

The Court's rationale has undergone substantial challenges in recent years. Do members of Congress merely legislate? Have they not also responsibilities in overseeing executive agencies and in communicating with their constituents? Two recent cases highlight the scope of legislative duties.

Representative Harold E. Ford, a congressman from Tennessee, was indicted in 1987 on tax and bank-fraud charges. A federal judge then entered a "gag order," forbidding Ford to make any comment on any aspect of the case, either to his colleagues in the House or to his constituents. The House of Representatives filed a brief with the sixth circuit court, arguing that the gag order constituted an impermissible restriction on communications within the legislative branch and between a member and his constituents. The sixth circuit court agreed that the order was overbroad and undermined a legislator's responsibility to the electorate. "A representative's legislative role is not limited to formal speech and debate in Congress but includes communication with the electorate."[30] The court also agreed with the House leadership that the doctrine of separation of powers "would be undermined if the judicial branch should attempt to control political communication between a congressman and his constituents."[31]

The second case involved Representative Don Sundquist, a congressman also from Tennessee. In 1985, he wrote to Attorney General William French Smith, pointing out that the Memphis Area Legal Services might be obstructing the administration of federal child support laws. In his letter, Sundquist identified an attorney, Wayne Chastain, as someone who was "harassing" the juvenile court and working "in concert with two convicted felons." Sundquist released the letter to the media and also expressed his objections in a letter to the Legal Services Corporation (LSC). Chastain sued Sundquist for libel.

The district court held that the letters to the attorney general and to the LSC constituted an official act of a legislator protected by the Speech or Debate Clause. However, in 1987 the D.C. circuit court reversed that decision: "We find that the communication between Congressman Sundquist and the executive branch is not protected by Speech or Debate immunity." Aside from this constitutional issue, the court also held that publicizing views in the media is not entitled to immunity for common law torts committed while acting within the scope of official duties.[32] The doctrine of official immunity, unlike the Speech or Debate Clause, is a doctrine created purely by judges. The court drew a strict line between executive and legislative duties: "Members of Congress have responsibility for making the laws, whereas executive officials must enforce the laws enacted by Congress, and do so in a manner that demands the exercise of enforcement discretion. It is this fundamental *functional* distinction between the obligations of the legislative and executive branches of government that has resulted in the extension of judicially created immunities to the letter."[33] Through this reasoning, executive officials have greater immunity under judge-made law than members of Congress have under their constitutional grant of immunity. The court acknowledged that legislators have a responsibility to oversee the executive branch, but could exercise that function only through the following actions:

> Congressman Sundquist has every right to monitor and challenge the manner in which the Legal Services Corporation operates. Within the halls of Congress, he can lobby for its overhaul, engage in oversight hearings, and, should he choose, libel with impunity the reputation and integrity of any lawyer working for the Corporation. When he ventures beyond the protection of his Chamber, he can go to the hustings and loudly proclaim the law's failure. He can use the franking privilege to seek out his constituents' views or promote his own. He can use the issue as a *cause célèbre* to raise funds from likeminded political action committees. He can stand before the press and announce his views. In short, he can attack or defend, as he sees fit, the necessity of a public legal services corporation in general or the manner in which it operates in his own district. No barrier limits his sphere of operation to the confines of the House.[34]

The author of this opinion, James L. Buckley, was formerly a U.S. Senator. Dissenting from his opinion was Abner J. Mikva, a former member of the U.S. House of Representatives. Mikva argued that the Speech or Debate Clause did not shield Sundquist from the libel action. However, Mikva said that the functions of a member of Congress "are more than legislative."[35] He denied that the role of a member of Congress was limited to what Buckley called the "responsibility for making the laws." Mikva underscored his point: "That is not the limit that the author of the opinion applied to his role as Congressman, nor that I did to my own."[36]

The House of Representatives entered the picture by passing a resolution "viewing with deep concern" the decision of the D.C. circuit court. The resolution, technically confined to urging the Supreme Court to accept the decision for review "and reach a just result," passed 413 to 0. The debate on the resolution left no doubt that the resolution was not merely a procedural action, to encourage the Court to take the case, but marked a strong repudiation of the appellate court's decision.[37] At stake in this case is the definition of what a member of Congress does under the heading of official duties. Does a member merely legislate, as a constitutional function, or do official duties also include the contacts that members have with executive agencies and constituents?

Conclusions

During the 1980s, the Supreme Court adopted a highly formalistic and rigid model for separated powers. In *Chadha,* the Court held that the legislative veto was an unconstitutional means of influencing the executive branch. As noted earlier, Congress continues to enact legislative vetoes (usually of the committee-veto variety) and agencies, for the most part, comply with these arrangements because they offer advantages to both sides.

In *Bowsher v. Synar* (1986), the Court also announced an overly strict theory of separated powers when it struck down a provision in the Gramm-Rudman Act that gave the comptroller general a role in budget cuts. The Court said that the Constitution "does not contemplate an active role for Congress in the supervision of officers charged with the execution of the laws it enacts."[38] There is some truth to that statement, but it cannot be squared with the role of Congress in investigating agencies, issuing subpoenas, or holding cabinet officers in contempt for failing to surrender documents to congressional committees. Furthermore, the Constitution does not contemplate many activities that are now accepted, such as the president's deep involvement in the legislative process or his power to make law unilaterally by issuing executive orders and proclamations. It is not even clear that the Constitution contemplates that the Supreme Court can hold a statute of Congress unconstitutional.

In *Bowsher,* the Court claimed that "once Congress makes its choice in enacting legislation, its participation ends. Congress can thereafter control the execution of its enactment only indirectly—by passing new legislation."[39] That was never the case before *Bowsher* and it will not be the case after *Bowsher.* The Court promoted a stilted and unrealistic theory of separated powers. Any observer of Congress can watch it control the execution of laws through committee hearings, committee investigations, studies by the General Accounting Office, informal contacts between members of Congress and agency officials, and nonstatutory controls. The framers never advocated a strict separation of powers. Justice Jackson captured the essential spirit that motivates executive-legislative relations: "While the Constitution diffuses power the better to secure liberty, it also contemplates that practice will integrate the dispersed powers into a workable government. It enjoins upon its branches separateness but interdependence, autonomy but reciprocity."[40] Workable government requires that Congress maintain a strong interest and involvement in the executive process.

NOTES

1. Francis Wharton, Revolutionary Diplomatic Correspondence of the United States, Vol. 1, 663 (Washington, D.C.).
2. Papers of Alexander Hamilton, Vol. 2, 404–405 (Syrett ed.).
3. Papers of Thomas Jefferson, Vol. 3, 679 (Boyd ed.).
4. *Annals of Congress,* Vol. 1, 611–12 (June 27, 1789).
5. Writings of Thomas Jefferson, Vol. 1, 303–304 (Mem. ed. 1903). See Annals of Congress, 2d sess., 1–2 sess. 493–94, 1113.
6. 5 U.S. 137, 157 (1803).
7. 6 Ops. Att'y Gen. 326, 341 (1854).
8. Cong. Debates, 24th Cong., 2d sess., Vol. 17, Pt. 2, Appendix, at 202, but see entire discussion at 188–225.
9. Messages and Papers of the Presidents, Vol. 5, 2284 (J. Richardson ed.).
10. *Kilbourn v. Thompson,* 103 U.S. 168, 194–95 (1881).
11. *McGrain v. Daugherty,* 273 U.S. 135, 177 (1927).
12. *Eastland v. United States Servicemen's Fund,* 421 U.S. 491, 509 (1975).
13. *City of Alexandria v. United States,* 737 F. 2d 1022, 1026 (C.A.F.C., 1984).
14. *INS v. Chadha,* 462 U.S. 919, 951, 958 (1983).
15. 111 Stat. 1278, 1281, 1282, 1283, 1296 (1997).
16. Public Papers of the President, 1984, II, pp. 1056–57.
17. For additional details on the survival of the legislative veto after *Chadha,* see Louis Fisher, "The Legislative Veto: Invalidated, It Survives," *Law and Contemporary Problems* 56 (Autumn, 1993): 273.
18. *Ashwander v. TVA,* 297 U.S. 288, 347 (1936), citing *Liverpool, N.Y., & Phila. Steamship Co. v. Emigration Comm'r,* 113 U.S. 33, 39 (1885).
19. *Watkins v. United States,* 354 U.S. 178, 187 (1957).
20. *Washington Post,* Aug. 13, 1987, p. A13.
21. *Washington Post,* Jan. 31, 1987, p. A16.
22. Public Papers of the President, 1987, I, p. 209.
23. Public Papers of the President, 1986, II, p. 1594.
24. Ibid., p. 1595.
25. S. Rept. No. 730, 96th Cong., 2d sess. (1980), p. 5.
26. 94 Stat. 1981, § 501 (a)(1)(1980).
27. 94 Stat. 1982, § 501 (b).
28. *United States v. Johnson,* 383 U.S. 169, 172 (1966).

29. *Hutchinson v. Proxmire,* 443 U.S. 111, 116 (1979).
30. *United States v. Ford,* 830 F. 2d 596, 601 (6th Cir., 1987).
31. Ibid.
32. *Chastain v. Sundquist,* 883 F. 2d 311, 312 (D.C. Cir., 1987).
33. Ibid., p. 322. Emphasis in original.
34. Ibid., p. 323.
35. Ibid., p. 329.
36. Ibid., p. 331.
37. 134 *Cong. Rec.* 10574–80 (1988).
38. 478 U.S. 714, 722 (1986).
39. Ibid., pp. 733–34.
40. *Youngstown Co. v. Sawyer,* 343 U.S. 579, 635 (1952).

Chapter 18

The President and the National Agenda

ROGER B. PORTER

Six days after the January 21, 1998, evening network news broadcasts began coverage of "The Presidency in Crisis" amid revelations of an alleged improper relationship between the president and a young White House intern, Bill Clinton delivered his State of the Union address. The next morning's *Washington Post* headline declared: "Clinton Pledges Activist Agenda."

David Broder described the speech as "robust yet relaxed," noting that the president had "held forth for more than an hour to a worldwide television audience." Republican Representative J. C. Watts was quoted as describing Bill Clinton's presentation as "very presidential. I think he was very smart not to say anything [about the controversy] and to stay with his agenda."[1]

The president's address, which did attract a worldwide audience, illuminates the central role the presidency has come to play in shaping the national agenda. Despite the specter of personal controversy that would persist for months, official Washington and the country remained steadfast in its expectation that the president should and would outline and pursue a wide-ranging agenda.

This essay has three principal objectives: First, to briefly describe a series of elements that have influenced expectations for presidential leadership in shaping a national agenda; second, to outline three sources or reservoirs from which presidents can draw in constructing their agendas; and third, to explore how presidents can most effectively draw from these three reservoirs in achieving their goals. This examination of the sources from which presidents draw underscores both the opportunities and the challenges presidents face in selecting which issues to elevate and which initiatives to advance.

Heightened Expectations

Much conventional wisdom regarding the three decades following the mid-1960s views the period as a succession of failed presidencies. Vietnam,

Watergate, and the unsuccessful electoral efforts of three incumbent presidents—Ford, Carter, and Bush—are cited as evidence. Moreover, a resurgent Congress, which sought to enhance its powers at the expense of the president through the War Powers Act of 1973 and the Budget and Impoundment Control Act of 1974, and the persistence of divided government have contributed to the perception of a diminished presidency.[2]

At least four factors have helped heighten expectations of the president in shaping a national agenda.

The first factor is simply the increase in the size and complexity of government. Through Woodrow Wilson's administration, executive departments and agencies sought their own legislative authorizations and appropriations with little central oversight. The process was piecemeal, often chaotic, and highly inefficient. The struggle to institute a unified budget, which began in earnest with President Taft's Commission on Economy and Efficiency, lasted nearly a decade. The result was driven in the end by sheer necessity. The government's activities had grown to a point where the need for more order and discipline was apparent. Congress responded by focusing responsibility on the president. The Budget and Accounting Act of 1921 required presidents to submit annually a unified federal budget, and created the Bureau of the Budget to assist them in preparing it.[3]

Budgets in any organization serve the useful function of defining choices and directing attention to priorities. The device of requiring a unified federal budget has had the intended effect of forcing presidents to develop comprehensive documents embodying their policy priorities. Producing a unified budget focuses attention on outlining a comprehensive and coherent account of federal spending activity. The lengthy exercise involves the consideration of policy trade-offs and priorities in a common currency—budget authority and outlays.

The growing number of governmental programs and activities has heightened another challenge—integrating policy—seeking policies that are coherent by avoiding duplication and overlap and pursuing policies that reinforce rather than diminish one another. This quest for coherence has centered largely on the White House. Legislative bodies, of necessity, undertake much work through committees and subcommittees. Congressional committees have few institutionalized ways of identifying duplication or overlap or of illuminating the interrelationships between issues. Likewise, individual executive departments and agencies have a limited capacity for identifying the implications for other programs of their activities. To the extent that policy integration occurs, it is usually the result of processes organized within the Executive Office of the President. In short, the focus is on the president to develop a comprehensive and coherent agenda.

A second factor heightening expectations flows from the evolution of presidential campaigns. The democratizing reforms that have transferred greater power to voters through primary elections have reduced even further the modest role played by formal party programs. Moreover, after securing their party's nomination, presidential candidates continue to rely principally on their own campaign organization. Their appeal to voters is based on the positions they have articulated in the long struggle to prevail in primary elections. Parties remain loosely knit organizations whose success, in a two-party system, rests on tolerating a sufficient diversity of views to put together a majority coalition.

The task of shaping an agenda falls to the president rather than a party organization. Congress has come to expect from the president not merely a unified budget but a clearly articulated and comprehensive legislative program. The task has struck many newly elected presidents as daunting and fraught with danger.

Less than two weeks after taking the oath of office, Dwight Eisenhower confided in his diary: "Today I give my first 'state of the union' talk before a joint session of the Congress. I feel it a mistake for a new administration to be talking so soon after inauguration; basic principles, expounded in an inaugural talk, are one thing, but to begin talking concretely about a great array of specific problems is quite another. Time for study, exploration, and analysis is necessary. But, the Republicans have been so long out of power they want, and probably need, a pronouncement from their president as a starting point. This I shall try to give. I hope, and pray, that it does not contain blunders that we will later regret."[4]

Today, it is inconceivable that a president would not deliver an address to the nation before a Joint Session of the Congress outlining his proposals and initiatives—his agenda—shortly after taking office. And the level of specificity expected has grown dramatically since Eisenhower's time. Congress may criticize individual proposals and ignore others, but the expectation is that the president will deliver an agenda.[5]

A third factor contributing to the growth of expectations is the skill of presidents during a quarter century of divided government in using or threatening to use their veto power. Although viewed largely as a negative weapon, the veto has given the president much leverage in negotiations as well as undercutting the aspirations of congressional leaders to advance and pursue an alternative agenda.

The potential of a veto gives the president and his representatives a place at the table. And the strength of that position is evidenced by the frustration of unified Republican majorities in late 1995 and early 1996 to enact legislation sharply curtailing the growth of government spending. The budget impasse, which shut down parts of the federal government for several days, ultimately yielded an agreement that had the effect of helping the president restore momentum for his initiatives.

Similarly, George Bush, who faced larger opposition majorities in Congress than any other elected president, used his veto power successfully to advance his agenda on issues ranging from his minimum wage proposal to most-favored-nation status for the People's Republic of China. Only one of his forty-four vetoes was overridden. Moreover, the threat of using his veto was a crucial element of his strategy on numerous issues including his most sweeping environmental initiative, the Clean Air Act Amendments of 1990.[6]

A fourth factor enhancing expectations that the president will shape a national agenda is the revolution in communications that has accentuated the role of individuals rather than institutions. The president is in a position to use the airwaves to urge his agenda more frequently and more comprehensively than the Congress or any congressional leader. He can and does draw attention to his agenda in his travels, his public appearances, and his exchanges with a press corps eager for news. Expectations rise to accord with reality.

While presidents are unable to dictate outcomes and are often frustrated by effective resistance to their most treasured initiatives, they still remain, most of the time, as the principal initiator. It is simply difficult for others to sustain a full-scale, comprehensive, competing agenda. As Hamilton urged in *Federalist* 70, "energy in the executive," has come to be viewed as "a leading character in the definition of good government."

Presidents in developing initiatives with which to shape the agenda they pursue rely heavily on three principal sources.

Electoral Issues

Modern presidential campaigns are a rich source of ideas. While campaigns generate few new or genuinely novel proposals, there is considerable pressure for candidates to develop initiatives that will distinguish them from other candidates in an often crowded field. Moreover, the increased length of modern presidential campaigns and the quest for media coverage result in aspirants for the Oval Office articulating views on a wide variety of issues. Party platforms may have diminished in importance for many voters, but this has not reduced the role of issues in campaigns.

The study of modern presidential campaigns has appropriately focused much attention on the role of the media and the extent to which campaign coverage revolves around a "horse race"—where a candidate's standing in the polls transcends a thoughtful discussion of issues.[7] Much media attention does center on public opinion polls and whether a candidate's fortunes are rising or falling. But this should not obscure the role issues play in presidential campaigns.

The evolution of the presidential nominating process has accentuated the role of individual voters and reduced the role of "party bosses." Presidential nominees are no longer selected in smoke-filled rooms by kingmakers, but at the ballot box by voters. Since the McGovern-Fraser reforms in the wake of the 1968 Democratic Party convention where Hubert Humphrey was nominated without having run in the primary of a single state, presidential nominations are now won by the candidate who emerges after successfully surviving an electoral gauntlet of state primaries. The presidential balloting at national party conventions is a mere formality drained of any drama. Indeed, neither the Republican nor Democratic Party convention has gone beyond a single ballot since 1952. In an increasingly democratic, primary-centered nomination process, appeals to voters necessitate candidates taking positions on a wide variety of issues.

Videotape captures speeches made, white papers memorialize written commitments, and campaign organizations eagerly press reams of documents on interested groups and the press to demonstrate the heft and quality of a candidate's agenda. Hundreds of speeches and thousands of pages of position papers and press releases are more thoroughly read and documented than ever before.[8]

Once a successful campaign is concluded, commitments play a powerful role. Transition staffs, which have swelled in size, eagerly compile lists of campaign promises to serve as guidance for the new administration and its political appointees. Candidate-centered organizations require and attract large campaign staffs whose members often secure appointive positions in a new administration. These "keepers of the campaign promises" play prominent roles during the early months of an administration. Candidates take their promises seriously and they expect their appointees to do so. Indeed, many of the policy discussions during the early days of an administration revolve around which campaign promises to fulfill first.

Campaign promises, as drivers and sources of the national agenda, however, are undermined by three factors. The first is the passage of time. Once in office, events intervene requiring policy responses. Campaign promises recede in importance. The art of shaping an agenda requires flexibility and seizing opportunities. The rush of events overwhelms careful planning about what issues to elevate and when.

A second factor is the difficulty of claiming an electoral mandate. Not simply are many elections closely contested (1960, 1968, 1976), but so many issues are discussed and so few are thoroughly debated or carefully defined that it is hard for presidents to assert that their victory reflects a national referendum on particular policies. Ronald Reagan in 1981 was able to persuade many reluctant House members—generally from districts where he had received over sixty percent of the vote—that a large majority of their constituents supported his economic program and that they should also. But the number of issues on which he tried and could successfully deploy this logic was extremely limited. George Bush in advancing his child care proposal benefited from having offered a detailed parental-based proposal in the 1988 campaign, in sharp contrast to the provider-based proposal supported by his opponent. Bill Clinton, who was persuaded to elevate the issue of gays in the military almost immediately after coming into office, was quickly reminded that members of Congress and the uniformed military did not consider the 1992 election a referendum on the issue.

The strength of one's claim to have an electoral mandate depends, understandably, on the number of issues that receive a high profile during the course of a campaign. It is not possible to make a successful claim that every issue discussed during an election carries with it an electoral mandate. The mandate for an initiative also rests on the extent to which a proposal represents a distinguishing approach—strengthening the claim that voters assessed the respective merits of competing approaches and voted in support of the approach advanced by the winning candidate.

Presidents use the argument of an electoral mandate both with members of their own party and with members of other political parties. A senior Clinton White House aide observed: "Bill Clinton portrayed himself as a 'New Democrat' during both the 1992 and 1996 campaigns emphasizing fiscal responsibility, ending welfare as we know it, and reinventing government. These are not traditional Democratic themes and yet he could convincingly argue to members of his party that these themes were central to his electoral victory and that they needed to support his efforts."

Third, mandates and memories fade. Even a decisive electoral victory evaporates. Harry McPherson, a senior presidential aide, reported that following his landslide victory in 1964, Lyndon Johnson told his staff: "You've got to give it all you can that first year. Doesn't matter what kind of majority you come in with. You've got just one year when they treat you right and before they start worrying about themselves. The third year, you lose votes. . . . The fourth year's all politics. You can't put anything through when half of the Congress is thinking about how to beat you. So you've got one year."[9]

References to initiatives as the fulfillment of a campaign pledge or promise diminish, not because commitments are taken less seriously, but because others consider the fact that they were once discussed in a campaign less relevant.

There are, of course, exceptions—when commitments have been made visibly and definitively—as in George Bush's "read my lips, no new taxes" pledge. Moreover, the strength of an electoral mandate is often overwhelmed by the persistent contesting of issues between elections—what Hugh Heclo and others have called the permanent campaign.

In short, with a few notable exceptions, electoral issues have a relatively short half-life. Events requiring responses, weak and imprecise mandates, and the simple passage of time all diminish the capacity of campaign promises to shape the national agenda.

Maturing Issues

Presidents must operate in an environment in which formal authority is divided and procedural arrangements are characterized by much due process. This combination has several effects. It prevents any single individual or institution from acting arbitrarily or capriciously. It forces the executive and legislative branches, factions within each branch, and those from different political parties to work together to find common ground. Procedural arrangements require legislation and regulations to clear numerous hurdles before they are enacted or adopted. Policy issues are the subject of congressional hearings, conferences, and symposia. They often benefit from much scholarly research and proposals emanating from universities, "think tanks," and policy institutes.

It is a system that, as Charles Lindblom has noted, is most frequently characterized by incremental change.[10] This incremental change is the result of much discussion among issue networks of individuals both inside and outside the government.[11] In one sense, it is appropriate to call this cluster of issues maturing issues in that change through legislation, regulation, and practice usually occurs incrementally. Policy on maturing issues is often subject to stalemate as evidenced by the repeated, unsuccessful efforts to enact comprehensive financial institution reform, health-care reform, or fundamental tax reform.

Yet maturing issues—issues which are the subject of extensive deliberation over an extended period of time—can and frequently do also experience major or comprehensive change. Policy proceeds through a series of modest incremental changes periodically punctuated with a major or comprehensive reform.

What accounts for the success of major reform efforts? Generally, two elements are crucial: skill and timing. For the president, developing policy on maturing issues requires a combination of related skills: skill in shaping a proposal within the executive branch, skill in working effectively to build a coalition in Congress, and skill in developing active support by key affected constituencies outside the government. Major change requires a united executive branch supportive not only of the aims of an initiative but of the details of its particular provisions. Building a majority coalition in Congress requires effective and timely consultation, much patience, and considerable negotiating skills. Developing support by key affected constituencies outside the government likewise requires careful organization and planning, flexibility, and trust.

Some combination of these skills is found in those responsible for the development of policy when major reforms are achieved. And yet, while such skills are necessary they are not sufficient. Presidents cannot guarantee repeating success on one maturing issue simply by deploying the same resources with the same commitment and intensity of effort, and a willingness to expend similar amounts of political capital on other maturing issues.

A second crucial ingredient is timing. One might think of these sharp or major departures from past policy as representing the culmination of a gestation period. These gestation periods—time when consensus is developed regarding the next major reform—vary enormously in length from one issue to another, and are difficult to predict with precision. Indeed, one quality of a successful president or other policy entrepreneur is the ability to sense when a gestation period is coming to an end and the time is ripe to forge agreement on a major policy initiative.

Three examples illustrate the interplay of forces. Fundamental tax reform was discussed extensively during the Ford administration,[12] and a major reform proposal was advanced by President Carter without success.[13] Against the advice of many of his advisers, Ronald Reagan included a call for fundamental tax reform in his 1984 State of the Union address, commissioning the development of a proposal that was advanced in 1985 and that became the centerpiece of his domestic legislative agenda. The enactment of the Tax Reform Act of 1986 owes much to the persistence of Ronald Reagan in relentlessly championing the idea and to the skill and flexibility of negotiators on both ends of Pennsylvania Avenue.[14] Yet, its success also reflects the extended discussion in the 1970s and early 1980s, which helped prepare the ground for the legislation that eventually received bipartisan support. The combination of skill and timing was instrumental in securing enactment of fundamental tax reform in November, 1986.

Health-care reform provides a second example. During much of the twentieth century, a succession of presidents advanced proposals for national health insurance or major revisions in the federal role in health care. The debates of the 1950s and 1960s culminated in the adoption of Medicare and Medicaid in the Social Security Act Amendments of 1965. A persistent president and the two Wilburs—Secretary of Health, Education and Welfare Wilbur Cohen and House Ways and Means Committee chairman Wilbur Mills—played pivotal roles. Again, the success was a product of skill and timing.

Presidents Nixon, Ford, Carter, Reagan, and Bush proposed a variety of modifications and changes to Medicare and Medicaid, and advanced initiatives to provide health care for the uninsured. Some proposals were major; others were modest. A variety of incremental changes were enacted, but no major reforms were embraced. President Clinton made his Health Security Act a centerpiece of his domestic legislative agenda. Accounts of the failure of health-care reform in 1994 have centered on policy development shortcomings in the initial design of the administration's proposal, on the organized resistance of affected groups, and on the lack of effective means for building bipartisan support in the Congress.[15]

Yet, it is not clear that a more skillful handling of policy development on the issue would have produced a different result. At the time the Clinton proposal was advanced the nation's health-care system was undergoing a dramatic shift to managed care.[16] Significant changes were being driven by developments beyond governmental programs or mandates. The Clinton administration plan, however packaged or promoted, was one whose time had not come. In the end, the proposal failed to secure a vote on the floor of either house of Congress.

Welfare reform represents a third example. Again, a newly elected president, Richard Nixon, made his welfare reform proposal, the Family Assistance Plan, a centerpiece of his domestic agenda in 1969. The effort failed, as did less ambitious welfare reform proposals advanced during the Carter, Reagan, and Bush administrations. Over the period, the discussion of the system and its shortcomings, the accumulation of experience with, and the evaluation of demonstration efforts in states contributed to a maturing of the issue. Ultimately, President Clinton reached agreement with bipartisan majorities in the Republican-controlled House and Senate to enact the Personal Responsibility and Work Opportunity Reconciliation Act of 1996, in the fourth year of his first term. Setting aside the specifics of particular proposals and approaches, a significant element of the enactment of welfare reform legislation and the failure of health-care reform was the matter of timing. Welfare reform had reached the end of its gestation period; health-care reform had not.

Presidential attempts to shape the national agenda on tax reform, health care, and welfare reform illuminate three characteristics of maturing issues. First, maturing issues are almost continuously under discussion. Virtually every administration seeks some changes—legislative or administrative, large or small—in almost all policy areas. Managing the development of policy on maturing issues is a central task for every White House, and skillful management of an issue is critical to its success.

Second, timing is crucial. Fundamental change faces formidable entrenched interests. Success requires not only the commitment of time, effort, and political capital. It also requires a sense for the gestation period of issues. Presidents must have ideas and convictions; they must also understand when an idea's time has come.

Third, although presidents may elevate issues on the national agenda, they can hardly control the outcome. The Tax Reform Act of 1986 bore little resemblance in its details to the proposals first advanced by Ronald Reagan in 1985. The act did, however, reflect his central objective of broadening the base and lowering rates by sharply reducing preferences and deductions while cutting marginal tax rates. In shaping the agenda, flexibility is essential. Reagan considered the final product consistent with the essence of his proposal and signed the legislation with enthusiasm.

Bill Clinton sought a prominent place for welfare reform on the national agenda, as had many of his predecessors. He discovered that one can successfully elevate an initiative, yet lose control of its content. The Personal Responsibility and Work Opportunity Reconciliation Act of 1996 differed sharply from his original proposal, prompting a spirited division within his cabinet about whether he should accept the legislation and leading to the resignation of several sub-cabinet officials over the issue when he did sign the bill.

Crisis Issues

Crisis issues constitute a third source of initiatives for presidents in shaping the national agenda. Crisis is a much-used and oft-abused term appropriated by presidents and policy entrepreneurs in the hope that it will help draw attention to an issue and stimulate the action they want.

Like most overused terms, however, officials and citizens are reluctant to concede that a genuine crisis exists in the absence of compelling evidence. A term that seems to refer to everything runs the risk of losing meaning for anything. National policy debates have therefore tended to reserve the term crisis for those issues where advocates for change are able to demonstrate convincingly that failure to act immediately will result in a significant deterioration in the underlying situation. Most issues fail to pass this litmus test.

Two examples, health care and the savings and loan industry, illustrate the point. Proponents of change sought to have both issues identified as crises for the purpose of advancing comprehensive proposals. The effort failed in the first instance and succeeded in the second.

Despite much rhetoric and repeated claims, the overwhelming majority of Americans did not view the nation's health-care system as in a state of crisis in the mid-1990s. Indeed, most Americans were satisfied with the quality of care and coverage they received through their health insurance plans. Many were concerned with the rising cost of health care, although most were partially insulated through third-party payors, but these concerns did not reach a level that led them to conclude that a crisis necessitated sweeping reform. Perhaps the overriding feature of the health reform issue for a majority of Americans was concern about quality and choice. Would a new system maintain a high quality of care and preserve their freedom of choice with respect to doctors and providers? Despite a concerted administration effort, health-care reform never successfully achieved recognition as a crisis and thus was treated as a maturing issue.

Circumstances in the savings and loan industry, however, had reached a point by January, 1989, where proponents of reform could legitimately claim that a crisis existed, that is, that failing to act now would result in a significant deterioration in the underlying situation.

Neither major presidential candidate in 1988 had viewed developments in the savings and loan industry as politically attractive and both carefully avoided raising the issue during the campaign. The deteriorating situation, however, prompted George Bush, after seventeen days in office, to propose a major rescue package, popularly referred to as the bailout of the savings and loan industry, designed to protect insured depositors.[17] He successfully made the argument that failing to act now would result in a rapid escalation in the cost of addressing the problem. The Financial Institutions Reform, Recovery, and Enforcement Act of 1989 reflected a recognition by policy makers that a genuine crisis existed requiring immediate action.

Crisis issues, especially ones dealing with domestic policy, are typically few in number despite persistent attempts to enlarge the number of issues in this category. Making the case that failing to act now will result in a substantial deterioration in the underlying situation is a high hurdle that only a few issues can clear.

Conclusions

Thinking of policy initiatives as falling into one of three buckets—electoral issues, maturing issues, and crisis issues—helps illuminate the challenges for presidential leadership.[18] The central task for the president is less one of advancing fresh, imaginative approaches to problems, and more one involving definition, timing, and the building of coalitions.

Table 1

	Electoral Issues	Maturing Issues	Crisis Issues
Ronald Reagan	Economic Recovery Program	Fundamental Tax Reform	Air Traffic Controllers Strike
George Bush	Child Care	Clean Air	Savings and Loan Financial Insolvencies
Bill Clinton	Family and Medical Leave	Health-care Reform	Domestic Terrorism

Electoral issues tend to dominate at the beginning of an administration when appeals for a mandate are strongest. The first months for a newly elected administration are also a time when the president is generally accorded greater deference by those whose cooperation he needs. Moreover, inside an administration, the "keepers of the campaign promises" are often in strategic positions to determine what is advanced, and their claims for maintaining faith with past pledges is strongest.

Electoral issues also loom large with the approach of a re-election effort. Initiatives are fashioned with particular constituencies in mind. With the lengthening of campaigns, and the advent of what some have referred to as "the permanent campaign," the number of electoral issues may be enlarging. Moreover, the cataloging of campaign promises has become more systematic and measuring their fulfillment by the media is more extensive and visible than in past decades.

Yet the passage of time and the flow of events inevitably diminishes their claims. It is difficult to assert successfully that the reason for supporting some legislative or regulatory initiative is a statement made during a campaign three years ago. Among other things, midterm elections involving all constituencies in the House of Representatives and a third of the Senate often sound the death knell to the salience of past presidential campaign issues.

Success in advancing maturing issues rests heavily on timing and definition. Ideas in this realm are abundant, the result of the broad scope accorded policy entrepreneurship in the U.S. political system. Indeed, the art of building a coalition usually requires adopting, adapting, and incorporating ideas or versions of ideas from a variety of sources. Presidents want the assurance that "experts" on the subject think well of an initiative they are advancing. Presidents need the public blessing of such "experts" for their initiatives if they are to persuade the otherwise reluctant to support the effort. Expertise that comes from long association with an issue and with active participation in an issue network can make one a valuable asset in the quest to build a coalition for change. The longer an issue has been discussed, the more refined the arguments, the greater the understanding of the consequences flowing from alternative approaches, the greater the likelihood that an issue is coming to the end of its gestation period.

Likewise, crisis issues depend heavily on timing and an ability to articulate a rationale for action. The claims that an issue is a crisis issue greatly outnumber the instances when the president can successfully make such a claim, particularly on domestic matters. This is clearly a case for not abusing a term through overuse.

Thinking of issues as electoral, maturing, or crisis issues does not mean that every issue falls neatly into one of these three categories. They do not. Many maturing issues are discussed during elections and some even gain considerable visibility. Those people heavily involved in campaigns may view the issue as an electoral one, while others may be unaware that a candidate ever took a position on the matter. The assertion that an issue is at a crisis point may be conceded by some and not by others. Intelligent and informed people may differ in their view of how best to categorize particular issues.

Nonetheless, thinking about these three types of issues can help in understanding how presidents shape the national agenda. Doing so illuminates the attraction of electoral issues at the outset of an administration but also underscores the short half-life that characterizes such issues. In capitalizing on an electoral victory, presidents are well advised to economize and to move quickly. They cannot hope successfully to claim a mandate on a large number of issues, nor can they make such claims indefinitely. They can seize the window of opportunity at the outset of a term to advance a carefully selected and coherent agenda.

Presidents must also survey the large smorgasbord of maturing issues with care. Entrepreneurs within their administrations and without will surely press presidents to place their issues high on the agenda. In selecting which issues to elevate and when, presidents should recognize that different issues have gestation periods of varying lengths. A sense of timing must accompany wise judgment and great perseverance. Shaping an agenda requires not only the skills of the analyst, but also the instincts of the visionary.

When genuine crises arise presidents can transform necessity into opportunity by pressing for reforms beyond simply addressing near-term exigencies. Delay in responding to a widely perceived crisis is often viewed as weakness. Claiming that a crisis exists, however, requires evidence, and too frequent assertions undermine one's credibility.

The modern presidency has much in the way of resources and a remarkable capacity to shape the national agenda. Yet, expectations greatly outstrip formal powers and successful presidents need all the wisdom, patience, skill, and discipline they can muster.

NOTES

1. David Broder, "Composed in the Center of the Storm," *Washington Post,* Jan. 28, 1998, p. A1.
2. During the three decades since 1969, the same political party has controlled the White House and both houses of Congress for only six years—during the Carter administration and the first two years of Bill Clinton's first term. During the seven previous decades the same political party controlled the White House and both houses of Congress for fifty-six of the seventy years.
3. An excellent brief discussion of the events leading to the adoption of the Budget and Accounting Act is found in Aaron Wildavsky, *The New Politics of the Budgetary Process,* second edition (New York: HarperCollins Publishers, Inc., 1992), pp. 56–67.
4. "February 2, 1953," in *The Eisenhower Diaries,* ed. Robert H. Ferrell. (New York: W. W. Norton & Company, 1981), p. 226.
5. Speaker of the House Newt Gingrich seemed to capture the agenda-setting role in early 1995 following the 1994 midterm elections that produced Republican majorities in both the House and Senate. His ten-point "Contract With America" initially overshadowed the Clinton administration's efforts to control the agenda. But attempts by congressional majorities to establish and maintain control of a comprehensive agenda suffer from the distribution of views within each congressional party and the difficulty of sustaining agreement on policies and priorities.
6. Other recent presidents have also posted impressive records in having their vetoes left intact. Richard Nixon had only seven of his forty-three vetoes overridden; Gerald Ford had twelve of his sixty-six vetoes overridden; Jimmy Carter had but two of his thirty-one overridden; and Ronald Reagan had nine of his seventy-eight vetoes overridden. As of 1996, Bill Clinton had only had one of his seventeen vetoes overridden. Congressional Quarterly, *Powers of the Presidency,* second edition (Washington, D.C.: Congressional Quarterly, 1997), p. 87.
7. See Thomas E. Patterson, *Out of Order* (New York: Alfred A. Knopf, 1993).
8. Jimmy Carter began the introduction to his collection of campaign speeches, *A Government As Good As Its People* with an astonishing assertion: "A member of my staff once calculated that I delivered 1,200 speeches as Governor of Georgia and another 2,100 speeches during my Presidential campaign—in all, a great many speeches by anyone's standard." Jimmy Carter, *A Government As Good As Its People* (New York: Simon and Schuster, 1977), p. 7.

   In 1992, Bill Clinton and Al Gore published *Putting People First,* a detailed outline of the agenda they proposed to pursue if elected. Governor Bill Clinton and Senator Al Gore, *Putting People First* (New York: Times Books, 1992).
9. Harry McPherson, *A Political Education* (Boston: Little, Brown, 1972), p. 268.

10. Charles E. Lindblom, "The Science of 'Muddling Through,'" *Public Administration Review* 19 (Spring, 1959).

11. See Hugh Heclo, "Issue Networks and the Executive Establishment," in Anthony King, ed., *The New American Political System* (Washington, D.C.: American Enterprise Institute, 1978), pp. 87–124.

12. A seminal document that served as the focus of much discussion and debate was *Blueprints for Fundamental Tax Reform* issued by the Department of the Treasury during the Ford administration.

13. Jimmy Carter described in his memoirs his frustration on fundamental tax reform and two other maturing issues: welfare reform and national health care. Jimmy Carter, *Keeping Faith: Memoirs of a President* (New York: Bantam Books, 1982), pp. 84–87.

14. See Jeffrey H. Birnbaum and Alan S. Murray, *Showdown at Gucci Gulch: Lawmakers, Lobbyists and the Unlikely Triumph of Tax Reform* (New York: Random House, 1988).

15. A detailed account based on interviews with a large number of participants is found in Haynes Johnson and David Broder, *The System* (Boston: Little, Brown and Company, 1996).

16. An account of this "quiet revolution" is found in Regina Herzlinger, "The Quiet Health Care Revolution," *The Public Interest* 115 (Spring, 1994): 72–90.

17. See *The Public Papers of the Presidents of the United States: George Bush 1989* Book I (Washington, D.C.: Government Printing Office, 1990), pp. 60–65.

18. Table 1 identifies examples of electoral, maturing, and crisis issues for the Reagan, Bush, and Clinton administrations.

Chapter 19

The Presidency in a Separated System

CHARLES O. JONES

The president is not the presidency. The presidency is not the government. Ours is not a presidential system.

I begin with these starkly negative themes as partial correctives to the more popular interpretations of the United States government as presidency-centered. Presidents themselves learn these refrains on the job, if they do not know them before. President Lyndon B. Johnson, who had impressive political advantages during the early years of his administration, reflected later on what was required to the realize potentialities of the office: "Every President has to establish with the various sectors of the country what I call 'the right to govern.' Just being elected to the office does not guarantee him that right. Every President has to inspire the confidence of the people. Every President has to become a leader, and to be a leader he must attract people who are willing to follow him. Every President has to develop a moral underpinning to his power, or he soon discovers that he has no power at all."[1]

To exercise influence, presidents must learn the setting within which it has bearing. President-elect Bill Clinton recognized the complexities of translating campaign promises into a legislative program during a news conference shortly after his election in 1992:

> It's all very well to say you want an investment tax credit, and quite another thing to make the 15 decisions that have to be made to shape the exact bill you want.
>
> It's all very well to say . . . that the working poor in this country . . . should be lifted out of poverty by increasing the refundable income tax credit for the working poor, and another thing to answer the five or six questions that define how you get that done.[2]

For presidents, new or experienced, to recognize the limitations of office is commendable. Convincing others to do so is a challenge. Presidents become convenient labels for marking historical time: the Johnson years, the Nixon years, the Reagan years. Media coverage naturally focuses more on the president: there is just one at a time, executive organization is oriented in pyramidal fashion toward the Oval Office, Congress is too diffuse an institution to report on as such, and the Supreme Court leads primarily by indirection. Public interest, too, is directed toward the White House as a symbol of the government. As a result, expectations of a president often far exceed the individual's personal, political, institutional, or constitutional capacities for achievement. Performance seldom matches promise. Presidents who understand how it all works resist the inflated image of power born of high-stakes elections and seek to lower expectations. Politically savvy presidents know instinctively that it is precisely at the moment of great achievement that they must prepare themselves for the setback that will surely follow.

Focusing exclusively on the presidency can lead to a seriously distorted picture of how the national government does its work. The plain fact is that the United States does not have a presidential system. It has a *separated* system.[3] It is odd that it is so commonly thought of as otherwise since schoolchildren learn about the separation of powers and checks and balances. As the author of *Federalist* 51 wrote, "Ambition must be made to counteract ambition." No one, least of all presidents, the Founders reasoned, can be entrusted with excessive authority. Human nature, being what it is, requires "auxiliary precautions" in the form of competing legitimacies.

The acceptance that this is a separated, not a presidential, system, prepares one to appraise how politics works, not to be simply reproachful and reformist. Thus, for example, divided (or split-party) government is accepted as a potential or even likely outcome of a separated system, rooted as it is in the separation of elections. Failure to acknowledge the authenticity of the split-party condition leaves one with little to study and much to reform in the post–World War II period, when the government has been divided more than sixty percent of the time.

Simply put, the role of the president in this separated system of governing varies substantially, depending on his resources, advantages, and strategic position.[4] My strong interest is in how presidents place themselves in an ongoing government and are fitted in by other participants, notably those on Capitol Hill. . . .

Pictures in Our Heads

If the presidency is to be a major source of an understanding of American politics, then it is convenient to have a set of expectations by which to test performance. Richard Rose points out that several "portraits" have been used in recent
years—some more idealistic, some more iconoclastic. "The overall effect is
confusion rather than understanding; balanced portraits are relatively rare."[5]

At least two types of expectations are frequently relied on by analysts, particularly those in the media who necessarily produce short-term commentary
and evaluations. Presidents are tested first by the broader criteria associated
with judgments about the role of the presidency in the political system. The
specifics may vary from one president to the next, but, in Walter Lippmann's
marvelous phrase, we carry "pictures in our heads" that serve as cues for evaluating behavior: "what each man does is based not on direct and certain knowledge, but on pictures made by himself or given to him."[6] Often reactions based
on these pictures are not fully or systematically articulated as models of behavior. Rather, they have to be constructed from the judgments made along the way.
Sometimes they are traceable to positive evaluations of one president: Franklin
D. Roosevelt is a frequent model. Or judgments can be traced to tests drawn
from a predecessor of the same political party: Dwight Eisenhower for Richard
Nixon, Lyndon Johnson for Jimmy Carter, Ronald Reagan for George Bush.

A second source of evaluation during an administration is a set of judgments
about how a particular president ought to behave. This test is based on who
the president is (or who everyone thinks he is), what his record has been to
that point, and what he has said in gaining office. Mark I. Rozell spotted this
second source of judgments in his study of President Carter's press relations.[7]
Journalists' conceptions of how Jimmy Carter ought to perform as president
were based on what they thought they knew about him: in a sense they were
testing him by their understanding of his criteria of performance.

If integrated, these two sources provide the basis for a balanced judgment
about presidential performance. Often, however, the two are drawn on separately and they conflict. For example, President Carter should compromise in
order to get legislation enacted because that is what a president as political leader
should do; yet a compromising Jimmy Carter is out of character and thus loses
credibility. President Ford should restore the leadership of the White House;
yet a vetoing Gerald Ford is out of character with his image for restoring harmony. President Bush should offer an extensive legislative program; yet an
activist George Bush is out of character with both the man and his limited
mandate.

There also are contrary sets of expectations associated with divided government. There are hopes for reduced partisanship for the good of the country at the same time conditions usually promote partisanship, such as when one party controls the White House and the other. Congress. These expectations apply to either a Democratic president and Republican Congress (as in 1947–48) or a Republican president and Democratic Congress. Here, for example, was editorial analysis following the 1946 elections in which the Republicans recaptured control of both houses of Congress for the first time since 1930: "The greatest danger is that a purely partisan approach to the 1948 Presidential campaign, now hardly a year and a half off, will stultify the work of this Congress. The hope must be that the President and the majority and minority leaders will realize that a narrow partisanship will hurt, not help, them in 1948."[8] As it happened, of course, the Eightieth Congress was highly partisan. Harry Truman used that fact in the 1948 campaign, he won a surprising victory, the Democrats recaptured control of Congress, and the New York Times then expressed "gratification . . . in the emergence of a unified National Government."[9]

Likewise, when the Democrats won so overwhelmingly in 1974, increasing their margins substantially in both houses, President Ford was advised "to temper partisanship in favor of collaboration with the opposition party." "A similar spirit of constructive collaboration" was expected "from the Democrats."[10]

These various impressions or expectations are not models in the systematic sense of that term. But they do serve similar functions in creating standards by which presidential performance is tested. Even when presidents exceed the expectations, there often is a subsequent return to home base, so to speak. In some cases, as with Carter, those judgments may result in less credit than is actually due the president; in other cases, as with Reagan, they may result in more. That is, Carter's penchant for hyperbole led to tests that were unrealistic; Reagan's capacity for supporting the inevitable led to praise for a positive record with Congress that was in fact questionable.

Behavior or performance that exceeds expectations is treated as just that—exceptional. Thus it is difficult to get an adjusted reading. The notion that a presidency is the composite of accommodations to changing people, politics, and policy issues is, perhaps, too demanding. Yet I will encourage it as the proper context for comparing presidents or evaluating reforms.

The Dominant Perspective

The "pictures in our heads" are impressions, not well thought-out theories of governance. The images set forth above, however, are consistent with a dominant and well-developed perspective that has been highly influential in evaluating the American political system. The perspective is that of party government, typically one led by a strong or aggressive president. Those advocating this perspective prefer a system in which political parties are stronger than they normally can be in a system of separated elections. This deficiency naturally encourages a reformist mood so as to overcome what James L. Sundquist refers to as "the constitutional dilemma."[11] Sundquist is concerned, as are many observers of the American political system, that neither conservatives nor liberals can have their way because of the potential roadblocks built into the system. "A president is expected to lead the Congress, but its two houses are independent institutions and, most of the time of late, one or both are controlled by his political opposition. And when a president fails as leader—whether because the Congress chooses not to follow or because of the many possible forms of personal inadequacy—the system has no safeguard."[12]

Sundquist quotes Douglas Dillon, secretary of the treasury in the Kennedy administration and co-chair of the Committee on the Constitutional System (a group committed to reforming the Constitution) in identifying the insufficiencies of the U.S. system: "Our governmental problems do not lie with the quality or character of our elected representatives. Rather they lie with a system which promotes divisiveness and makes it difficult, if not impossible, to develop truly national policies. . . . No one can place the blame. The President blames the Congress, the Congress blames the President, and the public remains confused and disgusted with government in Washington."[13]

In a direct challenge to Madison's thinking as expressed in *Federalist* 10, Sundquist argues: "On less partisan issues—foreign policy in particular, but also the many elements of domestic fiscal policy—a national consensus would have to arise that a government able to concert its powers and act decisively will, moat of the time, take the right action, that in positive achievements will outnumber its mistakes, that when it speaks with the authority that flows from unity it will speak mostly wisdom and not folly, and that, when it does err, a government capable of decisive action is best able to correct mistakes."[14]

Madison appeared to understand the relative advantages of a majoritarian versus a separated government. He chose the latter. Robert A. Dahl and Charles E. Lindblom described the results of this choice in this way:

> In the United States the structure of government prescribed by the Constitution, court decisions, and traditions vastly increases the amount of bargaining that must take place before policies can be made. . . . The necessity for constant bargaining is . . . built into the very structure of American government.
>
> The strategic consequence of this arrangement, as the Constitutional Convention evidently intended, has been that *no unified, cohesive, acknowl-*

edged, and legitimate representative-leaders of the "national majority" exist in the United States. Often the President claims to represent one national majority, and Congress (or a majority of both houses) another. The convention did its work so well that even when a Congressional majority is nominally of the same party as the President, ordinarily they do not speak with the same voice.[15]

The party government perspective is best summarized in the made in 1946 by the Committee on Political Parties of the American Political Science Association.

> The party system that is needed must be democratic, responsible and effective. . . .
> An effective party system requires, first, that the parties are able to bring forth programs to which they commit themselves and, second, that the parties possess sufficient internal cohesion to carry out these programs. . . .
> The fundamental requirement of such accountability is a two-party system in which the opposition party acts as the critic of the party in power, developing, defining, and presenting the policy alternatives which are necessary for a true choice in reaching public decisions.[16]

Note the language in this summary: party in power, opposition party, policy alternatives for choice, accountability, internal cohesion, programs to which parties commit themselves. As a whole, it forms a test that a separated system is bound to fail.

I know of very few contemporary advocates of the two-party responsibility model.[17] But I know many analysts who rely on its criteria when judging the political system. One sees this reliance at work when reviewing how elections are interpreted and presidents are evaluated. By this standard, the good campaign and election have the following characteristics:

- Publicly visible issues that are debated by the candidates during the campaign.
- Clear differences between the candidates on the issues, preferably deriving from ideology.
- A substantial victory for the winning candidate, thus demonstrating public support for one set of issue positions.
- A party win accompanying the victory for the president, notably an increase in the presidential party's share of congressional seats and statehouses so that the president's win can be said to have had an impact on other races (the coattail effect).

- A greater than expected win for the victorious party, preferably at both ends of Pennsylvania Avenue.
- A postelection declaration of support and unity from the congressional leaders of the president's party.

The good president, by this perspective, is one who makes government work, one who has a program and uses his resources to get it enacted. The good president is an activist: he sets the agenda, is attentive to the progress being made, and willingly accepts responsibility for what happens. He can behave in this way because he has demonstrable support.

It is not in the least surprising that the real outcomes of separated elections frustrate those who prefer responsible party government. Even a cursory reading of the Constitution suggests that these demanding tests will be met only by coincidence. Even an election that gives one party control of the White House and both houses of Congress in no way guarantees a unified or responsible party outcome. And even when a president and his congressional party leaders appear to agree on policy priorities, the situation may change dramatically following midterm elections. Understandably, advocates of party government are led to propose constitutional reform. Coincidence is not a reliable basis for ensuring their preferred outcome.

There is no standard formula under present constitutional arrangements for governing from the White House. Presidents must identify their strengths and evaluate their weaknesses in negotiating with Congress or otherwise attempting to lead. They seldom have the advantages desired by the party government advocates. Even in those cases where appearances lead one to expect "responsible party" leadership (for example, in 1932, 1936, and 1964), it is by no means certain either that the appearances are reality or that the advantages can be long sustained. The tests of performance should account for the variations in party splits and in the political and policy advantages available to the president and the Congress. . . .

An Alternative Perspective

The alternative perspective for understanding American national politics is bound to be anathema to party responsibility advocates. By the rendition promoted here, responsibility is not focused, it is diffused. Representation is not pure and unidirectional; it is mixed, diluted, and multidirectional. Further, the tracking of policy from inception to implementation discourages the most devoted advocate of responsibility theories. In a system of diffused responsibility, credit will be taken and blame will be avoided by both institutions and both parties. For the mature government (one that has achieved substantial involvement in social and economic life), much of the agenda will be self-generating, that is, resulting from programs already on the books. Thus the desire to propose new programs is often frustrated by demands to sustain existing programs, and substantial debt will constrain both.

Additionally there is the matter of who *should* be held accountable for what and when. This is not a novel issue by any means. It is a part of the common rhetoric of split-party government. Are the Democrats responsible for how Medicare has worked because it was a part of Lyndon Johnson's Great Society? Or are the Republicans responsible because their presidents accepted, administered, and revised the program? Is President Carter responsible for creating a Department of Energy or President Reagan responsible for failing to abolish it, or both? The partisan rhetoric on deficits continues to blame the Democrats for supporting spending programs and the Republicans for cutting taxes. It is noteworthy that this level of debate fails to treat more fundamental issues, such as the constitutional roadblocks to defining responsibility. In preventing the tyranny of the majority, the founders also made it difficult to specify accountability.

Diffusion of responsibility, then, is not only a likely result of a separated system but may also be a fair outcome. From what was said above, one has to doubt how reasonable it is to hold one institution or one party accountable for a program that has grown incrementally through decades of single- and split-party control. Yet reforming a government program is bound to be an occasion for holding one or the other of the branches accountable for wrongs being righted. If, however, politics allows crossing the partisan threshold to place both parties on the same side, then agreements may be reached that will permit blame avoidance, credit taking, and, potentially, significant policy change. This is not to say that both sides agree from the start about what to do, in a cabal devoted to irresponsibility (though that process is not unknown). Rather it is to suggest that diffusion of responsibility may permit policy reform that would have been much less likely if one party had to absorb all of the criticism for past performance or blame should the reforms fail when implemented.

Institutional competition is an expected outcome of the constitutional arrangements that facilitate mixed representation and variable electoral horizons. In recent decades this competition has been reinforced by Republicans settling into the White House, the Democrats comfortably occupying the House of Representatives, and, in very recent times, both parties hotly contending for majority status in the Senate. Bargains struck under these conditions have the effect of perpetuating split control by denying opposition candidates (Democratic presidential challengers, Republican congressional challengers) both the issues upon which to campaign and the means for defining accountability.

The participants in this system of mixed representation and diffused responsibility naturally accommodate their political surroundings. Put otherwise, congressional Democrats and presidential Republicans learn how to do their work. Not only does each side adjust to its political circumstances, but both may also be expected to provide themselves with the resources to participate meaningfully in policy politics.[18]

Much of the above suggests that the political and policy strategies of presidents in dealing with Congress will depend on the advantages they have available at any one time. One cannot employ a constant model of the activist president leading a party government. Conditions may encourage the president to work at the margins of president-congressional interaction (for example, where he judges that he has an advantage, as with foreign and defense issues). He may allow members of Congress to take policy initiatives, hanging back to see how the issue develops. He may certify an issue as important, propose a program to satisfy certain group demands, but fail to expend the political capital necessary to get the program enacted. The lame-duck president requires clearer explication. The last months and years of a two-term administration may be one of congressional initiative with presidential response.[19] The point is that having been relieved of testing the system for party responsibility, one can proceed to analyze how presidents perform under variable political and policy conditions. . . .

The Presidency in a Separated System

I come away from this study quite in awe of the American national government. That is not to say I believe it is faultless; angels are not available to govern, as James Madison explained long ago. It does mean that I am impressed with the capacity of a complex set of political institutions to adjust to a remarkable variation in political and policy circumstances. E. E. Schattschneider explained that "democracy is a political system for people who are not too sure that they are right."[20] His formulation draws attention to decisionmaking rather than to the decisions themselves. It is no simple matter to create, maintain, or reform a government forged to represent uncertainty and to approximate, but not necessarily achieve, policy solutions.

. . . Regardless of the topic—how presidents came to be there, how they organized their presidency, their public standing and role in agenda setting, and the patterns of partisan and institutional interactions—I found the differences among and within presidencies to be striking. It simply was not possible to generalize across all postwar presidencies. The manifold determinants of the president's strategic position assist in specifying his advantages for certifying and managing items on a continuous agenda, which may be oriented in strikingly different ways, and for participating in a law-making process that mostly takes place in another, independent branch of government.

I conclude that it is more important to make the separated system work well than to change systems. The preferred institutional interaction is that of balanced participation, with both branches actively involved in the policy process. The United States has the most intricate law-making system in the world. It will not be made better through simplification. Preponderance of one branch over the other should be a cause for concern, not celebration. Presidents are well advised to appreciate the advantages of the separated system and to define their role in it. Most do not have to be counseled on the legitimacy of Congress, but some do. Most know instinctively that their advantages are in certifying the agenda and persuading others to accept their proposals as a basis for compromise, but some have grander conceptions of presidential power. Most understand that they are temporary leaders of a convention of policy choice already in session, but some lack the skills to define the limits or realize the advantages of that status. Most realize that patience, persistence, and sharing are required for effective work in the separated system, but some are overly anxious to take immediate credit for change. And most grasp the purposes of a diffused-responsibility system of mixed representation and shared powers, but some believe that the president is the presidency, the presidency is the government, and ours is a presidential system. Those who believe these things may even have convinced themselves that they are right. They will be proven to be wrong.

NOTES

This piece was originally published in Charles O. Jones, *The Presidency in a Separated System* (Washington, D.C.: Brookings, 1994), pp. 1–6, 9–12, 17–19, 297–98 (excerpts).

1. Lyndon Baines Johnson, *The Vantage Point: Perspectives of the Presidency, 1963–1969* (New York: Holt, Rinehart and Winston, 1971), p. 18.
2. Quoted in Ruth Marcus, "In Transition Twilight Zone. Clinton's Every Word Scrutinized," *Washington Post,* Nov. 22, 1992, p. A1.
3. I should note, however, that comparative scholars typically classify the United States as a presidential system. Often, in fact, it is designated as the "model and prototype of presidential government." Classifications of democratic systems are

typically limited to parliamentary or presidential government. See, for example, the introduction and essays by Douglas V. Verney, Juan J. Linz, and G. Bingham Powell, Jr., in Arend Lijphart, ed., *Parliamentary versus Presidential Government* (New York: Oxford University Press, 1992); and by Scott Mainwaring in Gyorgy Szoboszlai, ed., *Flying Blind: Emerging Democracies in East-Central Europe* (Budapest: Hungarian Political Science Association, 1992). See also Matthew S. Shugart and John M. Carey, *Presidents and Assemblies: Constitutional Design and Electoral Awareness* (Cambridge, U.K.: Cambridge University Press, 1992). Many comparative scholars argue that the parliamentary system is superior to the presidential system (which is the label typically given to a separated system), as do many reformers in the United States. For a counterargument, see Thomas O. Sargentich, "The Limits of the Parliamentary Critique of the Separation of Powers." *William and Mary Law Review* 34 (Spring, 1993): 679–739.

4. Just as several scholars have said to expect, notably Richard E. Neustadt, *Presidential Power: The Politics of Leadership* (New York: Wiley, 1960); George C. Edwards III, *At the Margins: Presidential Leadership of Congress* (New Haven, Conn.: Yale University Press, 1989), chapters 1, 11; Paul Charles Light, *The President's Agenda: Domestic Choices from Kennedy to Carter (with Notes on Ronald Reagan)* (Baltimore: Johns Hopkins University Press, 1982), chapter 1; Erwin C. Hargrove and Michael Nelson, *Presidents, Politics, and Policy* (Baltimore: Johns Hopkins University Press, 1984), chapter 4; Mark A. Peterson, *Legislating Together: The White House and Capitol Hill Eisenhower to Reagan* (Cambridge, Mass.: Harvard University Press, 1990), chapter 3; and Bert A. Rockman, *The Leadership Question: The Presidency and the American System* (Westport, Conn.: Praeger, 1984), especially chapter 4.

5. Richard Rose, *The Postmodern President: The White House Meets the World* (Chatham, N.J.: Chatham House, 1988), p. 46.

6. Walter Lippmann, *Public Opinion* (New York: Macmillan, 1950), p. 25.

7. Mark J. Rozell, *The Press and the Carter Presidency* (Boulder, Colo.: Westview Press, 1989), p. 4.

8. "Congress and President," *New York Times,* Jan. 3, 1947, p. 26.

9. "President and Congress," *New York Times,* Nov. 6, 1948, p. 12.

10. "Tuesday's 'Mandate': For the President . . ." *Washington Post,* Nov. 7, 1974, p. A30.

11. James L. Sundquist, *Constitutional Reform and Effective Government,* rev. ed. (Washington, D.C.: Brookings, 1992), p. 1.

12. Ibid., p. 10.

13. Ibid., p. 11.

14. Ibid., p. 16.

15. Robert A. Dahl and Charles E. Lindblom, *Politics, Economics, and Welfare* (New York: Harper and Brothers, 1953), pp. 335–36 (emphasis in original).

16. American Political Science Association, *Toward a More Responsible Two-Party System: A Report of the Committee on Political Parties* (New York: Rinehart, 1950), pp. 1–2.

17. James L. Sundquist is one of the few. In an influential article, he explained his own devotion to party government, identified it to be the dominant perspective among American political scientists, and challenged political scientists to "provide a new body of theory" if it is to be abandoned. "Needed: A Political Theory for the New Era of Coalition Government in the United States," *Political Science Quarterly* 103 (Winter, 1988–89): 613–35.

18. Since the 1970s, congressional Democrats have increased staff, added analytical units (like the Office of Technology Assessment and the Congressional Budget Office), and changed scheduling and floor procedures so as to participate more actively in all phases of policy making.

19. Thus, for example, the 100th Congress, the last for the Reagan administration, was highly productive of reform legislation in the areas of trade, welfare, and health care. Few predicted that there could be such an outpouring of legislation since the president was in the last two years of his term.

20. E. E. Schattschneider, *Two Hundred Million Americans in Search of a Government* (New York: Holt, Rinehart and Winston, 1969), p. 53. Interestingly, it was Schattschneider, in his influential book, *Party Government* (New York: Holt, Rinehart and Winston, 1942), and in his leadership of the APSA Committee on Political Parties, who was a principal promoter of the party responsibility perspective. Presumably this meant that he was certain that a political party, if not the people, could be right.

Contributors

JOEL D. ABERBACH is professor of political science and director of the Center for American Politics and Public Policy at the University of California, Los Angeles. He is the author of *Keeping a Watchful Eye: The Politics of Congressional Oversight*.

PERI E. ARNOLD is professor of government and director of the Hesburg Program in Public Service at the University of Notre Dame. He is the author of *Making the Managerial Presidency* and other scholarship, particularly focusing on the development of the presidency in the early twentieth century.

GEORGE C. EDWARDS III is professor of political science and director of the Center for Presidential Studies at the Bush School of Public Service at Texas A&M University. He is the author of more than a dozen books on the presidency and U.S. Government, including *At the Margins: Presidential Leadership of Congress*.

LOUIS FISHER is senior specialist in separation of powers at the Congressional Research Service in the Library of Congress. He is the author of many books on U.S. Constitutional politics, including *The Politics of Shared Power*, and he is co-editor of *The Encyclopedia of the American Presidency*. He often testifies before Congress on issues concerning the separation of powers in the U.S. Constitution.

HUGH HECLO is Robinson professor of government and politics at George Mason University and former professor of government at Harvard. He is the author of *A Government of Strangers*, which won the Louis Brownlow award from the National Academy of Public Administration in 1978, and other books on American government and public policy.

MATTHEW HOLDEN, JR., is Henry L. and Grace M. Doherty professor of government and foreign affairs at the University of Virginia. He is former commissioner of the Federal Energy Regulatory Commission, president of the American Political Science Association, and author of a number of books on

American Government and Public Administration, including *Continuity and Disruption: Essays in Public Administration* and *Mechanisms of Power.*

PATRICIA W. INGRAHAM is professor of public administration and director of the Alan K. Campbell Institute at the Maxwell School at Syracuse University. She is the author of *The Foundation of Merit* and many other works on American public administration.

CHARLES O. JONES is former Hawkings professor of political science at the University of Wisconsin, Madison; former editor of the American Political Science Review and president of the APSA. He is the author of *The Presidency in a Separated System* and many other books on American government and politics.

STEVEN KELMAN is Weatherford professor of public management at the John F. Kennedy School of Government at Harvard University. He was administrator of the Office of Federal Procurement Policy in the U.S. Office of Management and Budget from 1993 through 1997. He is the author of *Procurement and Public Management, Making Public Policy: A Hopeful View of American Government* and other books on public management and the policy process.

SAMUEL KERNELL is professor of political science at the University of California, San Diego and author of *Going Public* and co-editor of *Chief of Staff,* a symposium of former chiefs of staff to presidents. He is author of many other books and articles on the presidency and American government.

RONALD C. MOE is specialist in American government at the Congressional Research Service of the Library of Congress. He is author of *The Hoover Commissions Revisited* and other works on the organization of the U.S. government. He testifies often before Congress on legislation concerning the organization of government.

TERRY M. MOE is professor of political science at Stanford University. He is the author of *The Organization of Interests* and numerous articles on American political institutions and organization theory.

RICHARD E. NEUSTADT is Dillon professor emeritus at Harvard University. He is the author of *Presidential Power and the Modern Presidents,* co-editor of *Thinking in Time,* and author of many other works on the U.S. presidency. He worked on the White House staff in the Truman administration and was an adviser to other presidents.

JAMES P. PFIFFNER is professor of government and public policy at George Mason University. His books on the presidency include *The Strategic Presidency: Hitting the Ground Running; The President, the Budget, and Congress: Impoundment and the 1974 Budget Act;* and *The Modern Presidency.* He has been on project staffs of the National Commission on the Public Service (the Volcker Commission), the Center for Strategic and International Studies, the National Academy of Public Administration (of which he is an elected member), and the National Academy of Sciences. He received the Distinguished Faculty Award at George Mason University in 1990, and in 1970 he was awarded the Army Commendation Medal for Valor in Vietnam and Cambodia.

ROGER B. PORTER is professor of government and director of the Center for Business and Government at the Kennedy School of Government at Harvard University. He was the top economic policy adviser for Presidents Ford, Reagan, and Bush and was one of the longest serving White House staffers in second half of the twentieth century. He is the author of *Presidential Decision Making* and other works on the presidency and public policy.

ELLIOT L. RICHARDSON has served in four administrations as secretary of Health, Education and Welfare; secretary of Defense; secretary of Commerce; attorney general; undersecretary of State; ambassador to Great Britain; and head of the U.S. Delegation to the Law of the Sea Conference. He is author of *The Creative Balance* and *Reflections of a Radical Moderate.*

BERT A. ROCKMAN is professor of political science at the University of Pittsburgh. He is the author of a number of books and articles on the presidency, including *The Leadership Question.*

**Joseph V. Hughes, Jr., and Holly O. Hughes
Series in the Presidency and Leadership Studies**

Bose, Meena. *Shaping and Signaling Presidential Policy: The National Security Decision Making of Eisenhower and Kennedy.* 1998.

Fisher, Louis. *The Politics of Shared Power: Congress and the Executive.* 4th ed. 1998.

Garrison, Jean A. *Games Advisors Play: Foreign Policy in the Nixon and Carter Administrations.* 1999.